ANTHOLOGY OF HOLOCAUST LITERATURE

ANTHOLOGY OF HOLOCAUST LITERATURE

EDITED BY JACOB GLATSTEIN

ISRAEL KNOX

SAMUEL MARGOSHES

Associate Editors:

MORDECAI BERNSTEIN

ADAH B. FOGEL

A TEMPLE BOOK

ATHENEUM NEW YORK

Published by Atheneum
Reprinted by arrangement with The Jewish Publication Society of America

Atheneum
Macmillan Publishing Company
866 Third Avenue, New York, NY 10022
Collier Macmillan Canada, Inc.

Library of Congress catalog card number 68-19609
ISBN *0-689-70343-0*

15 14 13 12 11 10

Printed in the United States of America

A generous subsidy from William Shore of Los Angeles—a modest but devoted friend of Jewish culture in both Yiddish and Hebrew—in memory of his wife and in his own name, made possible the preliminary research and the translating of material from various languages, without which the preparation of this anthology would not have been inaugurated and carried through.

Mordecai Bernstein, an associate editor, died on the 22nd of April, 1966. He was a journalist, a historian, a scholar. His knowledge of several languages, besides Yiddish and Hebrew, and his firsthand acquaintance with the literature of the Holocaust, made his role in the realization of this anthology indispensable.

Dr. Samuel Margoshes, one of the editors of this anthology—indeed, its guiding spirit—died on the 22nd of August, 1968, upon the completion of the manuscript, but prior to its publication. He was a publicist, an essayist, a figure of note in Jewish affairs, and a student of Jewish life in America.

Contents

I. INTRODUCTION xiii

II. OCCUPATION, ACTIONS, SELECTIONS

Introduction

The Death Train 3
ELIE WIESEL

Sabbath 11
MARGA MINCO

Tiengen 15
MAURICE MEIER

The Fraternal Grave of Four Jewish Settlements 25
ABRAHAM EISEN

City of Cracow 32
JULIAN GROSS

City of Cracow 33
LEON SALPETER

Our Town Is Burning 38
MORDECAI GEBIRTIG

III. LIFE IN THE GHETTOS

Introduction

from Notes from the Warsaw Ghetto 43
EMMANUEL RINGELBLUM

The Jewish Letter Carrier 57
PEREZ OPOCZINSKI

Smugglers 71
LEVI SHALIT

from The Ghetto Kingdom 78
ISAIAH SPIEGEL

With My Martyred People 81
JACOB CELEMENSKI

Vilna—Story of a Ghetto 90
ABRAHAM FOXMAN

A Cupboard in the Ghetto 102
RACHMIL BRYKS

Hell in the Streets 109
BERNARD GOLDSTEIN

IV. CHILDREN

Introduction

Meierl 115
ELIEZER JERUSCHALMI

Bodies of Children for the Animals in the Circus 117
REGINA LANDAU

Fear of Fear 118
ILSE AICHINGER

Yanosz Korczak's Last Walk 134
HANNA MORTKOWICZ-OLCZAKOWA

Prose and Poetry 138
THREE CHILDREN FROM TEREZIN

Zonderkommando in Birkenau 141
SHAYE GERTNER

From One Camp to Another 148
REUBEN ROSENBERG

Winter in the Forest 155
FEIGA KAMMER

from The Diary of David Rubinovich 158

Letters from the Ghetto 161
NUSJA AND INJA SHIFMAN

from The Diary of a Young Girl 164
ANNE FRANK

V. CONCENTRATION AND DEATH CAMPS

Introduction

A Year in Treblinka Horror Camp 178
YANKEL WIERNIK

The Story of Ten Days 186
PRIMO LEVI

The Wache 206
SALA PAWLOWICZ WITH KEVIN KLOSE

Stephen and Anne 216
ARNOST LUSTIG

The Death Brigade 225
LEON WELLS

from The Terezin Requiem 241
JOSEF BOR

Execution in Plashow 250
JAKOB STENDIG

Scoundrels' Entertainments 253
ADOLPH WOLFGANG

Maidanek 257
ESTHER GARFINKEL

The Yellow Star 259
S. B. UNSDORFER

In the Sick Hut 264
ISRAEL KAPLAN

VI. RESISTANCE

Jewish Resistance to Nazism 275
PHILIP FRIEDMAN

The Girl in Soldiers' Boots 291
SHMERKE KACZERGINSKI

Dr. Yehezkel Atlas, Partisan Commander 299
SAMUEL BORNSTEIN

from The Jewish Uprising in Warsaw 307
RACHEL AUERBACH

In Fire and Blood 309
TOVIA BOZHIKOWSKI

Hehalutz Resistance in Hungary 314
ZVI GOLDFARB

The Treblinka Revolt 319
STANISLAW KOHN

Revolt 325
SALOMEA HANNELL

Appeal of the Jewish Fighting Organization 328

The Conscience of the World 329
SAMUEL ZYGELBOJM

A Manifesto of Jewish Resistance in Vilna 332

The Last Wish of My Life Has Been Fulfilled 334
MORDECAI ANILEWICZ

Jewish Cultural Activity in the Ghettos of Poland 336
EMMANUEL RINGELBLUM

I Believe 340

On the Agenda: Death 341

Jewish Partisan Song 349
HIRSH GLICK

Captain Jaquel's Story 350

VII. THE NON-JEWS

Introduction

from At the Railroad Tracks 361
SOFIA NALKOWSKA

Polish Friends 364
"WLADKA" (FEYGL PELTL-MIEDZYRZECKI)

A Polish Woman Relates Her Story 370
CAROLA SAPETOWA

To the Polish Jews 373
WLADYSLAW BRONIEWSKI

Chambon-Sur-Lignon 375
DONALD LOWRIE

Gallows in the Balut Market 382
RIVKA KWIATKOWSKI-PINKHASIK

The Fugitives 385
BENJAMIN ELLIS

Address at the J.N.F., September 20, 1965 392
FELIKS KANABUS

GLOSSARY 397

BIOGRAPHICAL NOTES 403

ACKNOWLEDGMENTS 409

Introduction

One hesitates to use the term *anthology* for this book. An anthology is a collection of flowers, a thing of joy and beauty; it is meant to comprise the very best in a literary or artistic or intellectual genre. If these are flowers, then perhaps Baudelaire's title would be particularly apt—flowers *of evil;* not as pointing to the writers of these pieces but as reflecting the tragic content of their "tales."

Yet this too would not be wholly true. Evil there is here indeed, a darkness of evil so dense that no light could penetrate it; evil so abysmal and so depraved that no report and no portrayal can be commensurate with it. Some of this evil, or at least an intimation of it, insofar as language can depict and reveal it, is congealed in this anthology. But that is not all: there is here goodness also, nuances and modulations of goodness from the slight and barely noticeable to the heights and depths of self-sacrifice, of devotion unto death. Beyond goodness or perhaps as a component of it, there is here an epic of courage, a kind of courage that our civilization is not always willing or able to grasp.

In what sense then is this volume an anthology? Well, in the simple sense that it is a book of books, that it consists of selections from other books, carefully made with certain criteria in mind. Hundreds of books have already been written about the Holocaust, about the martyrdom of the Six Million, and many more will be written and published. Naturally these books differ in degree of merit, differ and overlap too in theme and content; some had their source and origin in the agony of the concentration camp or in the valor of the resistance, and some were done by people who had not felt the agony in their own bones and hearts directly, nor shared personally in the passion of courage. Doubtless most of these books are important and, in various ways, help to fill out the historical record or to provide the material for it.

The time may not yet be ripe for a definitive anthology, for a modern sacred book to be preserved for our children and their children and all the subsequent generations, a book commemorating forever the Six Million, as an enduring temple for their spirit. It would be presumptuous to suggest that this volume is *that* anthology. It is to be hoped, though, that it may be a precursor to that anthology of the future, and may meanwhile stimulate its initiation. To expect more than that would be not only impertinent but well-nigh irreverent.

The Book of Books, out of the depths of the Sacred Martyrdom, will not find its first and original home in English or French or Russian, but in Hebrew and Yiddish, and largely and primarily in Yiddish, the language of the vast majority, though admittedly not of all, of the Six Million. The Jewish communities that the Nazi hordes destroyed, notably those of Eastern Europe, were not merely aggregates of individuals who designated themselves, and were so designated by others, as Jewish; they were communities with a distinctive civilization of their own, with a cumulative social and ethical and religious or spiritual heritage which was embodied in a style of life uniquely and recognizably their own.

The essence of this civilization, its inner melody, its pervasive traits, achieved their crystallized expression in Yiddish. In truth, the very rise of the language, its gradual and wonderful development can be explained only as inseparable from this civilization, as growing up together with it, as the words in which the melody of this civilization could find its ineluctable rendition. The idioms of any language are untranslatable, for they incarnate the traditions of a people, a sum of experiences and values which define and characterize a people. And the idioms of Yiddish, containing as they do the experience and values of a people, non-territorial and trans-geographic, without the accoutrements of a political state, were bound to be even more subtly rooted in the social and spiritual traditions of the people and evocative of what was peculiarly its own.

2

Although much of the material in the present anthology is from the Yiddish, the anthology as such has not restricted itself with regard to language or geography. No item was included or excluded solely because of language. In this respect the anthology is, within limits, both comprehensive and representative. There are items here from Yiddish and Hebrew but also from the French and German and Russian and Polish. Although there is an intimacy in Yiddish, a cadence and a rhythm corresponding almost to the very movement of feeling and thought in the Jewish heart and mind, the sensitive and perceptive reader will discern nonetheless in these words, in English translation, the cry of anguish or the note of heroism or the strain of hope. Well, then, one of the features of this anthology is that it consists of selections from a large variety of books composed in many languages.

Geographically too the anthology is extensive. The long, hideous night of Nazism enveloped all of Europe, and the pieces in this book tell of its monstrous cruelty everywhere, in all parts of Europe, though its ultimate and ugliest deeds of evil were perpetrated in Eastern Europe. There are "tales" here of the cruelty, stark and somber, beyond the power of anyone's words, even a Dante's, to convey and to communicate; but there is also here something of the epic of the resistance with its miracle of heroism in the face of insurmountable odds; and there are here glimpses of ordinary human kindness, which, because of the enormous surrounding wickedness, take on the aspect of holiness. There is then geographically in this anthology at least a partial delineation of all the corners of the house of woe, terror, hatred—and the determined opposition to it—which was Hitler's Europe.

The diversity of authors in this anthology reaches out beyond land and language to age and sex. There are pieces here by men and women, by young and old, and by those who were very young, in some instances only children, when they were exposed as victims or witnesses or both to the utter inhumanity of Nazi atrocity. Torture, and mockery in the process of administering it, was the lot of millions at the hands of the ruthless murderers of the Third Reich, but the wanton and savage extermination of children, and the bottomless ferocity with which children were treated prior to their extermination, is unmatched in the total history of humanity. Not all the symphonies, not all the hymns, not all the sweet and easy sermons of forgiveness, can muffle the inarticulate cry of these children. Something of this cry, no matter how faint, is audible in this anthology.

Finally, all the items in this book, except for the introductions, are from the pens and hearts of men and women who were themselves victims and witnesses of Nazi wickedness and fighters against it, who had been inside the hell of a concentration camp or had endured existence in a ghetto sealed off from the civilized world by the Nazi gangsters or had pitted themselves with improvised weapons against the military engines of death of the implacable enemy.

The intent here is not to deprecate the life of the imagination, the power of authentic literature to illumine and coordinate and intensify experience, to probe beneath the surface of things and to reveal their interior quality. Yet it is true that the life of the imagination must have its source in the life of actuality, and only then can it be a clarification and a deepening of it. Literature must not be a surrogate for experience but a consummation of it. Whether the time is ready for the transmutation of the agony of Auschwitz and the heroism of the resistance into the prose and poetry of literature, it is hard to say. But this much is incontestable: the time has not yet arrived to stop gathering all the "data," the hard and solid core of what was to be, and ultimately became, to the extent of Six Million, the "final solution" in the diabolical scheme of the Nazi murderers; nor, on the other side of the historic ledger, to cease collecting and sorting out all the details of the resistance in its courage and in its martyrdom.

The transmutation of life into literature has already begun, and the transcendent "epic" of the Holocaust will most likely be a work of the imagination, like the *Book of Lamentations* in the Hebrew Scripture, but it will be a work of the imagination that will absorb and distill all the tears and all the sorrow and all the valor of the Holocaust, and then it too will be a *Book of Lamentations* for the ages, for the memory of a people for ever and ever. But as long as there are "witnesses" from the generation that knew Auschwitz and Treblinka by "acquaintance" and not by "description," that felt on their own bodies and in their own souls the torment of it all, that saw with their own eyes the ovens in the crematoriums and the faces of men and women and children as they were shoved into the gas chambers—as long as there are such witnesses, their "story" takes precedence, their "facts" must be assembled and preserved, their testimony must stand as the impregnable foundation out of which the works of imagination and intellect will rise.

3

It is difficult to peruse these pages without being shaken to the very roots of one's being. None can read these pages without mixed emotions of infinite sympathy and infinite anger. Yet there are some in our own midst who have shifted the focus of attention from the executioners and their crimes to the victims and their alleged passivity toward, and even complicity in, their own destruction.

"Do not judge your fellowman until you stand in his place" was the wise and compassionate dictum of Hillel the Sage in *Ethics of the Fathers*. Obviously this means that one is to stand in a fellowman's place *vicariously*. Yet it is hardly possible, even *vicariously*, for any of us to stand in the place of those whose awful fate it was to be hounded and beaten down by the enemy. Others too were compelled to confront this enemy, and though they possessed armies and weapons, they nonetheless collapsed before the onslaught. But the vilifiers, oblivious of Hillel's injunction, themselves untouched by the horror and bestiality of existence under the Nazis, themselves spared the sight of an inferno even beyond Dante's power of description—these vilifiers are scornful of the victims because they failed to do what none could do and what, in the calculations of these self-appointed judges, they were supposed to do. This is not the proper occasion to nullify this indictment, nor is it necessary. Yet it would not be amiss to state, without elaboration or argument, a few facts.

In less than a year after the Second World War had begun, France, with its Maginot Line and its vaunted military prowess, yielded in abasement; in just about six weeks all of Poland was conquered and lay prostrate; in the course of the war the German armies approached the threshold of Moscow and were at the gates of Stalingrad, deep within the interior of Russia. All of this is accepted without puzzlement; it is attributed to the superior might of the German armies at the start of the war. The French, the Poles, the Dutch, the Belgians, and all the others, had weapons and trained soldiers, far-flung fortifications and plans for retreat, and the Jews had none of these and were, in Eastern Europe, surrounded largely by unfriendly populations. The German armies did plenty of killing and pillaging in the occupied part of Russia. Was there any resistance there, any violent opposition? Surely the population there outnumbered manyfold the German military forces that were controlling the area. Millions of Russian soldiers were captured and transported to German prisons where their treatment was utterly brutal. There was a handful of guards for thousands of prisoners. Were there any riots, rebellions, signs of resistance?

These examples are not cited to blame and denigrate others, but only to show how difficult it is—well-nigh impossible—to fight back under a tight and relentless dictatorship with its tanks, machine guns, concentration camps, methods of physical and mental torture, deceptions, and the inculcation of fear. There were political trials in Czarist Russia, and the courage and convictions of the revolutionaries stirred the admiration of the whole world. There was none of this in the political trials under Stalin, and instead of courage there was self-degradation and moral humiliation. Surely dictatorship and totalitarianism, anchored in wickedness, can play havoc with the very spirit of man; and there are limits to human endurance of pain and terror.

And we must not forget that the hate and terror directed against the Jews was greater than against any other group (except, possibly, the Gypsies, who were also marked for genocide). The truth is that quantitative terms like *greater, more, additional* are irrelevant here; the hostility toward the Jews was different in kind and not in degree. It was abysmal, "irrational," groundless in the plain meaning of the word as having no sense, as being beyond sense, not as mere nonsense, for its consequences were dire and dismal, but as *non-sense,* as having no warrant and no ascertainable "frame-of-reference."

The slaughter of the inhabitants of Lidice could at least be accounted for, in the warped "logic" of the murderers, as vengeance for the assassination of Heydrich. In 416 B.C.E. the "glory that was Athens" attacked and devastated the island of Melos, massacred all the men, and sent into slavery the women and children. The loathsome deed haunted the conscience of Euripides, and he gave vent to his wrath in *The Trojan Women;* and the foul deed tarnished ineradicably the glory of Athens. It was a wanton and hideous "feat," but it occurred in the midst of the Peloponnesian War and Athens did not want an independent Melos, and offered it a "choice" between surrender and destruction. Had Melos agreed to an abject surrender, it would not have been harmed. In Korea and Vietnam, north and south, prisoners are often "abused," in violation of the rules and conventions governing such prisoners, but there is a "practical reason" for it, unjust as it may be—the extraction of military information, intimidation, or sheer revenge.

The animosity of the Nazis for the Jews was irrational and pathological, and the resolve to bring about their total liquidation by means of a carefully planned process of genocide was at once so shrewd and so diabolical that only such as were equally demonic could envisage it and anticipate it, least of all the Jews, who, though the victims of persecution throughout two millennia, were not practitioners of it. The Nazis were not unaware of this, and hence, on the one hand, resorted to the most "ingenious" instruments of physical and mental torture to frighten and to "depersonalize," and, on the other hand, employed the most cunning psychological tricks to shock into apathy or to lull into a state of false "security." In such circumstances, there were occasions when it required extraordinary composure not to oppose. The slightest gesture of sabotage resulted in venomous acts of reprisal, in the murder of numerous innocent hostages, in the wiping out of entire communities—men and women and children. There were scores of Lidices in the ghettos. Who could dare—by an attempt at sabotage, by an assassination—to start such a chain of reprisals, such Satanic vengeance?

4

The miracle is that there were revolts—not only in Warsaw, but in dozens of smaller places—and that the vast majority of Jews conducted themselves as they did: helping each other, sustaining themselves culturally and spiritually, clinging to their belief in human decency and in the ultimate defeat of evil. But above all it was hope that kept them together and imbued them with strength to go on till the very last moment—the hope that they would survive Hitler as their forefathers had survived the various Hamans of the ages. There was scant occasion for humor in the ghettos, but now and then this *will to be* broke through in an irrepressible "joke." It may not be out of place to mention one or two. An inmate of a concentration camp informs the guards that Hitler will die on a Jewish holiday. When asked for evidence, he replies that whenever Hitler should die, that day will be a Jewish holiday. No matter how this bit of "comedy" be explained, it illumines the continuity and complexity of Jewish history and destiny and character: the linkage of a holiday located as yet in the realm of the imagination with a holiday, Purim or Chanukah, rooted in the past; the intimation, out of the cumulative wisdom of history, that Hitler will not just die, but will die as Haman did, ignominiously and wretchedly. And here is another one, a "play on words," which circulated in the underground in the dreadful days of Hitler's sway. One Jew asks another: "What is the difference between an *Umglücksfall* (accident) and an *Umglück* (misfortune)?" And the answer is couched in the form of an example: "If Hitler should be walking in the street and a stone should fall from a building and kill him, that would be an *Umglücksfall;* but if a stone should fall and Hitler should *not* be killed, that would be an *Umglück.*" For the Jew, for the anti-Nazi, helpless before the might of Hitler and his gang, there was more than "fun" in this play on words; there was a kind of victory. Helpless before the might of Hitler and unable to get the better of him at the moment, there was the unquenchable hope, the thrilling premonition, that Hitler too would go down in defeat and so would his entire band of murderers, even as other despots and their nefarious regimes had crumbled in the past.

And this *was* their triumph—that a portion did survive, that they "disappointed" the architects of their extinction who believed that the Jews would succumb in less than a year in the vile environment that they devised for them—an environment of starvation, epidemics, filth, and incessant danger. But the will to be, to live, to outlast the contemptible enemy was indomitable, and that will was not vanquished. A spark of that flame shines and shimmers in some of the pieces in this anthology.

Much of the heroism, both spiritual and physical, remains unrecorded and unsung, because the "actors in the drama"—partisans in the forests, fighters in the smaller ghettos, captives in the concentration hells—perished without a trace, without a whisper for others to register the manner of their dying, of the courage and the wonder of it. It was no secret for the enemy, nor for non-Germans too who hindered the Jews, and, in some instances, betrayed them. But *their* reports do not disclose this; they either pass it by or falsify it. What there is of this is mainly in Yiddish and partly in Hebrew, and the accusers who would sully the memory of the Six Million, rely chiefly upon non-Jewish sources and have apparently little knowledge, if any, of Yiddish and Hebrew.

Those who were doomed to abide in Dante's inferno were informed that they must abandon all hope, but our brothers and sisters who were locked up in the ghettos, without food and medicine, pursued by a sinister foe, with their lives in perpetual jeopardy, did not forsake all hope. There are many faces to courage, and the will to hope, to maintain the simple dignity of daily existence on a human and humane level, to forge the chain of cultural and spiritual continuity from generation to generation, to cherish children by handing on to them the legacy of their people—to do all of this in the midst of peril and deprivation and omnipresent enmity, is a species of fortitude that borders on the sublime. The "critics" who charge the Jews with "passivity" are blind or forgetful of the stoutness of heart that was manifest in the ghettos, of the tenacity with which they pursued the normal cultural enterprises that prevailed in the Jewish communities prior to the Holocaust.

There is a glimpse of this in John Hersey's *The Wall,* where, despite the prospect of imminent devastation and death, and as they prepare to defy and to fight with improvised weapons, the leaders of the underground carry through a Peretz anniversary with speeches, declamations, and song. This quality of resoluteness—this holiness in valor and valor in holiness—is discernible in the Yiddish books of Vladke, Bernard Goldstein, Celemenski and others, in a volume of the *Yiddish Encyclopedia* dedicated to the Holocaust, and in a section (dealing with this theme) of this anthology. The items in this section are factual, informative, "prosaic," bolstered by statistics and tables of figures; their only eloquence is that of the solemn, quiet, granite-like firmness of men and women whose ultimate determination was never to despair. Is this, perhaps, the "secret" of Jewish existence and perseverance during the millennia? Their various conquerors and despoilers—high and haughty for a moment in history and holding much of the world in subjection—are now dust and ashes, mere footnotes to that very history which for a moment they dominated.

5

In the final analysis, words like "heroism," "courage," resistance" and their like are weak and colorless, as silhouetted against the landscape of death which swallowed up six million men and women and children, unprepared for such a deluge of destruction, unable to believe that there are other men and women so insidious as to engage systematically and relentlessly in the assassination of an entire people without rhyme or reason.

How shall we remember the Six Million? Is it fitting that we—and posterity—remember them as martyrs? There are some—unlike the slanderers—who bow their heads in respect and sorrow for the victims of the Nazis, but hesitate to call them martyrs, because the Six Million, except in solitary cases, had no way of circumventing their lot, of avoiding their destiny. The martyrs in history—so we are told—and Jewish martyrs throughout the ages, *chose* to be martyrs for the Sanctification of the Name, for their people, for their convictions.

It is true that the Nazis offered no alternatives, that one could not escape the concentration camp and crematorium by denying one's principles and embracing those of the executioner. But that is just it. It may be that this was the most vicious perfidy of all, the extreme exhibition of inhumanity, the absolute profanation of the divine image in man, the elimination of the inviolable right of man, even under despotism, to sacrifice his life in fidelity to his principles, not out of disdain for life but out of loyalty to one's deepest and highest integrity.

By advancing this argument, its advocates, in effect, are allowing Hitler and his cohorts to be the arbiters of Jewish destiny, the molders of Jewish history. They are, as it were, letting Hitler write the verdict of Jewish history upon the sacred Six Million. It was none other than Maimonides, who almost eight hundred years ago formulated the classical doctrine that all who die because they are Jews sanctify the name of Israel and Israel's God and are thereby martyrs.

The death of the combatants in the resistance, the single death, by his own hand, of Zygelbojm, as a protest against the apathy of the world; the quiet death, without tears, of mothers and fathers so as not to frighten their children; the death of a little girl who had managed to hide in a latrine but gave herself up so that others might not be killed in her stead—the death of these holy ones is the collective death of the Six Million, of the Six Million who are all martyrs. Zygielbojm's letter and testament is in this *Anthology* and none can read it without saying reverently *holy, holy, holy*—these, our brothers and sisters, were martyrs.

6

There are many who have ventured to tell the story of the Holocaust, and there are many more who will tell it again and again in the days to come. In Milton's *Paradise Lost,* Lucifer avers: "Evil, be thou my good." When evil is no longer just a deviation from the good, a heresy *within* the sphere of the good, but is itself enthroned as the good, then the moral universe has been turned upside down and the sovereignty of Satan has been established. The Holocaust Kingdom was the kingdom of Satan and those who served him. Isaiah's exhortation: "Woe unto those who call evil good, and good evil," was exchanged for Lucifer's challenge: "Evil, be thou my good"—and the logic of the Holocaust was now crystal-clear: it was the logic of a party, a country, a people that proclaimed

Lucifer, in the guise of Hitler, to be king, and decided to call evil good and to conduct themselves accordingly.

How is one to explain in natural categories the bottomless and infinite evil of Maidanek? How is one to disclose the foundations of a world in which evil was called good? Somehow the writers of the pieces in this anthology have managed to do this, at least to a degree. The result is a massive and overwhelming presentation of what life was like in the ghettos and the concentration camps during the long, hideous night of Nazism.

One can imagine what it must have cost them to tell their story, to recall the facts and details, the total and terrible drama. Yet it is a story that they could not repress and relegate to the archives of their own private memory—not for history's sake, nor for their own. For them, presumably, this literary objectification of the agony of Maidanek and the other hells was a kind of catharsis as well as the fulfillment of an obligation; for us, for posterity, it is another firsthand account, another document specifying and spelling out what the Amalek of our century did to our sisters and brothers. There are no cemeteries in Eastern Europe with graves for the Six Million; the crematoriums consumed all remorselessly. Their books —this anthology with selections from them—are a sort of cemetery too, with graves in orderly rows, and, on reading it, we are reciting *Kaddish* for those who left none to say it for them.

There is no surrogate for listening directly to their threnody, and there is no anodyne; it will break our hearts, but it cannot and should not be evaded. This anthology is a beginning, not a terminus. Others will follow, until the *Book of Lamentations* will shape up, hallowing and commemorating the catastrophe that destroyed the East European Jewish community with its distinctive milieu and civilization.

ISRAEL KNOX

OCCUPATION, ACTIONS, SELECTIONS

OCCUPATION, ACTIONS, SELECTIONS

The Nazi occupation of Poland in September 1939 was immediately followed by widespread persecution in all Jewish communities: Jews were beaten; their dwellings attacked and plundered; many were forcibly removed to labor camps. Synagogues were desecrated and demolished. The first victims in every community were always its rabbi and civic leaders. Large "contributions" by Jews were extorted.

The first step in the German master plan were the Actions—systematic mass murders of large segments of the population. In some instances this was effected locally—on the outskirts of the town; in others the victims were transported elsewhere. Supplementing the Actions were the merciless Selections in which some Jews were chosen for immediate death and others given a brief respite so the Nazis could utilize their labor.

A third method was the so-called "Resettlement," which was in reality deportation to death camps in order to make the cities and regions "Judenrein" *(free of all Jews).*

All this was a forerunner of the ghettos, in line with the Nazi plan to decimate the Jewish population by the time the ghettos were established.

ELIE WIESEL

The Death Train

TRANSLATED FROM THE YIDDISH BY MOSHE SPIEGEL

Indescribable confusion reigned.

Parents searched for their children, children for their parents, and lonely captives for their friends. The people were beset by loneliness. Everyone feared that the outcome of the journey would be tragic and would claim its toll of lives. And so one yearned to have the companionship of someone who would stand by with a word, with a loving glance.

Afterward, an ominous silence fell upon us. We squatted on the soft snow that covered the floor of the railroad car like a carpet, and tried to keep warm by drawing closer to our neighbors.

When the train started to move, no one paid any attention to it. Careworn and burdened with conflicting thoughts, each of us wondered if he was wise to continue on the journey. But in our weariness, whether one died today, tomorrow, a week or a generation later, hardly seemed to matter.

The night dragged on interminably, as though it were to go on to the end of time. When the gray dawn appeared in the east, I felt as though I had spent a night in a tomb haunted by evil spirits. Human beings, defeated and broken, sat like dusty tombstones in the dim light of early dawn. I looked about the subdued throng and tried to distinguish one from another. And, indeed, perhaps there was no distinction.

My gaze fell on one who stared blankly ahead. A wry smile seemed to play on his ice-encrusted face. Those glazed eyes, whether living or dead, seemed to ensnare my gaze. A hundred and twenty captives, shadows of human lives, extinguished flames of burned-out candles lit on the anniversaries of the deaths of their loved ones.

Wrapped in a drenched blanket, his black cap pulled down over his ears, a layer of snow on his shoulders, my father sat beside me. Could it be that he, too, was dead? The thought flashed across my mind. I tried to talk to him. I wanted to shout, but all I could do was mutter. He did not reply, he did not utter a sound. I was certain that from then on I was to be all alone, all alone. Then I was filled with a numbing sense of indifference to everyone and to myself. Well, the Lord giveth and the Lord taketh away. The struggle was over. There was nothing and no one for whom to fight now.

The train ground to an abrupt halt in a snow-covered field. Awakened by the jolt, a few curious captives struggled to their feet to look out. The scene was reminiscent of cattle staring stupidly from a livestock car.

German S.S. guards surrounded the human cargo, shouting, "All the dead are to be thrown out! All the dead are to be thrown out!"

The living were pleased; there would be more space. It would not be as crowded now.

Strong men appeared and examined each one who could not stand up, and rapped out, "Here's one! Get hold of him!"

Whereupon two men would pick the corpse by the shoulders and feet and fling it out of the car like a sack of flour.

From various parts of the car came such cries as, "Here's another—my neighbor! He doesn't move. Help me get rid of him!"

Two deportees stepped forward and tried to lift a form beside me. It was only then that I was aroused from my stupor, and realized the seriousness of the situation. And to this day I cannot understand how I summoned the strength and courage to save my father from the lurking death. I kneeled over him, tearing at his clothes, slapping his face, kissing him and screaming, "Daddy, Daddy—wake up! Get up, Daddy! Don't let them throw you out of the car. . . ."

As he failed to respond, the two men said to me, "There's no use your screaming, little fellow. He's dead! Your father is dead, do you understand?"

"No! He is not dead! He's not dead!" I wailed, repeating the words over and over indefinitely. For some reason, I seemed to fear the death of my father more than my own. I tried again and again to release him from the embrace of the angels of death, and I succeeded at last.

My father opened his glazed, ice-encrusted eyes, and regarded me in a dazed way, unable to understand what I was trying to convey to him or the commotion that was being made over him.

"See for yourselves, you murderers. He's alive, he's living!"

The two men eyed my father for a moment, then shrugged their shoulders and muttered, "Not for long," and turned to other silent forms.

There were some twenty-odd dead in our one car, and after they were stripped of their clothes, which the living snatched up, they were flung out of the car.

This task took several hours. Then the train chugged along, and as icy gusts shrieked about it, it seemed that through the accursed world about us could be heard the far-away, muffled wail of the naked bodies that had been abandoned on Polish snow-covered fields.

The journey was insufferable; and every one who lived through it later questioned the natural laws that their survival seemed to disprove.

We were deprived of even bread and water, and snow was our only source of water. Cramped for space and thoroughly chilled, we were very weak by the third day of the journey. Days were turned into nights, and the nights cast a shadow of doom over our very souls.

The train plodded along for what seemed countless days, and the snow fell, fell, fell incessantly. And the exhausted, travel-weary unfortunates lay huddled for days on end, without uttering a word, eyes closed, waiting for one thing only—the next station, where the new yield of corpses would be got rid of. That was what we looked forward to.

The journey lasted ten interminable days and nights. Each day claimed its toll of victims and each night paid its homage to the Angel of Death.

We passed through German settlements, generally in the early morning hours, only in a few instances. Sometimes men on their way to work would halt in their tracks to glare at us as though we were animals in a kind of demonic circus. Once a German hurled a chunk of bread into our car and caused pandemonium to break out as scores of famished men fought each other in an effort to pounce upon it. And the German workers eyed the spectacle with sneering amusement.

Years later, I chanced to land in the Oriental port of Aden. Some of the ship's passengers, looking for excitement and exotic thrills, tossed coins into the water to be retrieved by native boys who arrived on the scene to entertain the pleasure-seeking travelers by diving into the deep waters for the coins. At times the young divers would remain underwater for several minutes, and the passengers cheered the novel sport that could be enjoyed for a mere sixpence. . . .

I had once before witnessed such a scene. An elderly aristocratic woman from Paris, holding a handful of coins, stood on the deck amusing herself by throwing them one at a time to a dozen young dark-skinned swimmers. Each time she tossed a coin into the stream, a fierce fight ensued among the divers—a fact that seemed to delight her no end, judging by her peals of laughter. Revolted by the scene of children trying to choke each other under water for the possession of a coin, I pleaded with the woman not to throw any more coins.

"Why not?" she replied. "I love to give charity."

She loved almsgiving—and to see six- and seven-year-old children fighting each other for a worthless coin.

Then I looked back upon that morning when our train, carrying its human cargo, had halted near the German city and the worker had thrown a piece of bread into our car, perhaps in compassion, although that is hard to believe. At any rate, the morsel of food caused the death of a number of men. The scramble for bread! The fight for life! The chunk of bread brought about its own kind of war to the death. The wildest instincts of the primeval jungle had seized all of us, and we pounced upon the bread with all the savagery of enraged beasts. An atavistic throw-back?

Unfortunately, the Torah does not relate how the children of Israel received the first manna in the wilderness. Did they fight over it, and were there any casualties? And did scenes like the one in our car take place there? The German workers tarried a while, gazing at the amusing spectacle, and perhaps assuaging their conscience at the same time with the thought of their benevolence in giving bread to the hungry.

All the other German workers soon followed the example of their kindhearted townsmen. Pieces of bread were cast into all the cars. Bread and victims. And they—the good, gallant Germans—were pleased with themselves and smiled.

Strange, even while jotting down these words, the event seems incredible to me. I seem to be writing a horror novel—a novel that should not be read at night. It is hard to believe that what I set down in writing is really true, has actually happened to me.

And—only ten years ago!

I think to myself: if all that is alive in my memory, and that is seething in my heart, is really true, how am I able to sleep at night? How can I eat my food in peace?

I can still see the scenes I experienced that early morning when the bits of bread fell from heaven.

Unfortunately, the bread also fell into our car. Though I was very hungry, my exhaustion was stronger. So I didn't budge from my spot, refusing to take part in what was going on. Let bread drop down—even from heaven. I would not risk my life to get it. I lacked the strength not only to fight for the hard crusts, but even to eat them. So I squatted in my corner, watching how human beings turned into animals as they attempted to snatch the morsels of food from each others' mouths.

A piece of the heavenly bread fell in a corner of the car; the next moment another corner was emptied of its occupants. Not far from me a young lad bit the ear of someone standing in front of him, in order to get to the priceless bread first. The injured person, bent only upon reaching the bread, was oblivious to the pain. I suddenly beheld a frail, elderly Jew crawling along the floor, one hand clutching his chest. At first I thought that he had been hurt in the fight. But then I saw him take a handful of crumbs from his bosom and devour them almost with ecstasy.

A sly smile played upon his deathly pale face for a moment, and disappeared. Then someone pounced on the old man like a phantom, and the two engaged in a death struggle, clawing, biting, trampling, kicking one another. The old man managed to raise his head, a glint of joy in his bloodshot eyes.

"Little Meyer! Meyer, my son," the graybeard mumbled, "Didn't you recognize me? You have hurt me so much. . . ."

Meyer still struggled to retrieve a piece of bread from his father's bosom. Then the dying old man groaned, "Meyer, you're beating your own father . . . I brought bread for you, too. I had risked my life . . . and you're hitting, beating me—your old father. . . ."

The old man seemed on the verge of death, he no longer made any sound. Meyer had triumphed: his right hand clutched the small piece of bread, and his left wiped the blood trickling from one of his eyes. The old man held a piece of bread in his clenched fist and tried to bring it up to his mouth—to die with the taste of food in his mouth. His eyes were alert now; he was clearly aware of the situation. He was at the portals of death—a condition in which one comprehends all that goes on about him. As he brought the hand with the bread closer to his half-opened mouth, his face glowed with lust for the bread. . . . It seemed as though the old man was holding back the bread intentionally, so that the pleasure of the anticipated feast should last longer. The eyes seemed about to burst from their sockets. And as the old man was about to bite into the bread with his darkened, broken teeth, Meyer once more pounced upon him and snatched the bread from him.

The old man muttered, "What? A last will and testament?" But, except for me, neither his son nor anyone else heard him. At last he breathed his last; and his orphaned son ate the bread. He was sprawled on the floor of the car, his right hand stretched out as though protesting to God, who had transformed Meyer into a murderer.

I could not bear to look at the old man for long. The son soon found himself engaged in a new struggle. Catching sight of the bread in his hand, others then pounced upon him. He tried to defend himself, but the furious throng, thirsting for blood in their frenzy, killed him. And so the two of them, father and son, victims of the struggle for bread, were trampled upon. Both perished, starved and alone.

Suddenly, I had the feeling that someone was laughing behind me, and I wondered who it was. But I was afraid to look around for fear of learning that the laughter was not coming from behind me, but from myself. I was fifteen years old then. Do you understand—fifteen? Is it any wonder that I, along with my generation, do not believe either in God or in man; in the feelings of a son, in the love of a father. Is it any wonder that I cannot realize that I myself experienced this thing, that my childish eyes had witnessed it?

Meir Katz, a robust, energetic Jew with a thundering voice, an old friend of my father, was with us in the car. He worked as a gardener in Buna. He conducted himself gallantly, both physically and morally. He was placed in command of the human cargo in our car because of his strength. It was thanks to him that I finally arrived alive in the Buchenwald concentration camp.

It was during the third night of our journey—or was it some other?—we lost track of time. We squatted, trying to doze off, when I was suddenly awakened by someone choking me. With superhuman effort, I managed to shout one word—"Father!" That was all I managed to get out, as the unknown attacker was choking off my breath. Fortunately, my father awakened and tried to free me from the stranglehold. Unable to do so, however, he appealed to Meir Katz for help, whereupon the latter came to my rescue.

I didn't know the strangler or the reason for his violent act. After all, I had carried no bread with me. It may have been a sudden fit of insanity, or—just a case of mistaken identity.

Meir Katz also died during that journey. A few days before we reached Buchenwald, he said to my father, "Shloime, I'm on my way out. I can't stand it any longer."

"Meir, don't give up!" my father tried to hearten him. "Bear up! You've got to! Try to have courage!"

"Shloime, it's no use—I'm washed-out," Meir muttered. "I can't go on."

Then the sturdy Meir Katz broke down and sobbed, mourning his son, who was killed in the early days of the Hitler terror.

On the last day of the journey, bitter cold, accompanied by a heavy snowfall, aggravated the situation even more. The end seemed to be near. Then someone warned, "Fellow Jews, in such weather, we've got to move about; we must not sit motionless—or we'll all freeze to death!"

So we all got up—even those who seemed to be dying—and wrapped our drenched blankets about our bodies. The scene was reminiscent of a congregation wrapped in prayer shawls, swaying to and fro in prayer. The snow, the car, even the sky (heaven?)—everything and everybody seemed to be swaying, worshipping, communing with God, uttering the prayer of life, the prayer of death. The sword of the Angel of Death was suspended above. A congregation of corpses at prayer.

A shout, an outcry like that of a wounded animal, suddenly rent the air in the car. The effect was terrifying and some of the people could not endure it silently, and themselves began to scream. Their outcries seemed to come from another world. Soon the rest of us joined in the uproar; screaming and shrieking filled the air. The deafening roar rode the gusts of wind and amid the swirling snow soared to heaven, but, echoing from the closed gates there, reverberated back to earth.

Before long, twenty-five cars crowded with deportees joined us in the hysterical song of death. Everyone had reached the breaking point. The end was drawing near. The train was struggling up the hill of the Thyring forest. The divine tragi-comedy was approaching its finale. There were no longer any illusions about surviving; the thousands of deportees were aware of their doom.

"Why don't they mow us down on the spot?" Meir Katz asked through tears. "We could at least be spared further agony."

"Reb Meir, we'll soon arrive at our destination," I tried to comfort him. But the wind drowned out my words. We stood in the open car, under the falling snow, screaming hysterically.

We arrived at the Buchenwald concentration camp late at night. "Security police" of the camp came forward to unload the human cargo. The dead were left in the cars. Only those who were able to drag their feet got out. Meir Katz was left in the car; like so many others, he had frozen to death a short time before we reached our destination. The journey itself was the worst part of the ordeal. About forty of the deportees were claimed by death on that one day alone. Our car had originally started out with a hundred and twenty souls; twelve—among them my father and I—had survived the ordeal.

MARGA MINCO

Sabbath

TRANSLATED FROM THE DUTCH BY ROY EDWARDS

I looked down over my mother's book, over the finger with which she traced the lines to enable me to follow the prayers, down through the lattice-work of the screen to where I saw my father standing wearing his prayer shawl. I could not help thinking of the synagogue at Breda. There Father had had a roomy pew all to himself. It had been just like a coach without wheels. To get out of it, he had to open a little round door and descend a few steps. The door squeaked, and when I heard it squeak I would look down.

Father would go to the center of the building. I would follow with my eyes his shining top hat and his ample prayer shawl, which floated out behind him a little as he walked. He would ascend the stairs of the *almemmor,* the dais in the middle of the synagogue from which the scrolls of the Law are read, and whither he was "summoned" to distribute blessings. Suddenly I would hear our names, between the half-chanted Hebrew texts. The names sounded very beautiful in Hebrew. And they were longer, because Father's name was always added to them. Then my mother would also look down through the grille and smile at Father. The other women in the gallery would nod to my mother, to show that they had heard, and wait to see whether their husbands would give *them* a blessing, so that my mother would be able to nod to them in their turn. It was a custom in the Breda congregation.

But now I saw Father sitting somewhat toward the back, on a bench among other men. He was wearing an ordinary hat, and he remained where he was until the end of the service. It was a long service. Special prayers were said for the Jews in the camps. Some women wept. In front of me one woman was sitting who blew her nose repeatedly, huddled behind her prayer book. She had on a reddish-brown *bandeau*—the wig worn by our married women—which had sagged backward a little under her hat.

My mother had laid her prayer book beside her on the seat. She was staring fixedly into space. I put my hand on her arm.

"It's very cold in Poland now," she whispered.

"Yes, but she was able to take warm clothes with her, wasn't she?" I said softly. "She had a rucksack lying ready."

Mother nodded. The cantor raised his voice in another prayer and we all stood up. Down below, someone had taken a Scroll from the Ark. The Scroll was covered with purple velvet, and there was a silver crown on it from which little bells hung. The Scroll was carried round the building. The bells tinkled. As the Scroll went past them the men kissed the tip of the velvet.

After a while, the final hymn burst forth. It is a cheerful melody, and I never ceased to be surprised by the rather exuberant way in which the congregation plunged into it. Singing, the men folded up their prayer shawls, and the women put on their coats. I saw my father carefully stowing his shawl away in the special bag intended for the purpose.

In front of the synagogue people waited for each other. They shook hands and wished each other "Good Sabbath." Father was already there when we came out. I remembered how I had hated having to walk home with the rest after Sabbath service, when I was a child. I was always frightened of running into children from my school.

Most of the people quickly dispersed over the square. Some went in the direction of Weesperstraat; others made for Waterlooplein. An acquaintance of my father asked us whether we cared to walk part of the way home with him along Nieuwe Amstelstraat.

"I've sent my wife and children into the country," he said. "At the moment it's better for them to be there than here."

"Why haven't you gone with them?" my mother asked.

"Oh, well," he said, "that's not in my line. I'll manage all right."

"Are you on your own at home now?" Mother asked him.

"No," he answered, "I'm staying with my sister. She's not doing anything about it either, for the time being."

"What could you do, actually?" asked my father.

"Well," said his friend, "you can shut the door behind you and disappear. But then, what are you going to live on?"

"Exactly," said my father. "You've got to live. You've got to have something to live on."

We were standing on the corner near the Amstel River. An ice-cold win was blowing in our faces. My father's acquaintance shook hands all round. "I've got to go that way, to my sister's," he said. He crossed the bridge to Amstelstraat, a small, hunched figure, with the collar of his black overcoat right up round his ears and his hand on his hat.

We walked along beside the Amstel, and came to the bridge where it is joined by the Nieuwe Herengracht canal. We crossed the bridge, under the yellow board. The board bearing in black letters the German word *"Judenviertel."*

A couple of children with woollen scarves round their necks were hanging over the parapet, throwing bread to the seagulls. The birds, skimming low over the water, nimbly caught the scraps. A Black Maria drove down the other side of the canal. A woman pushed a window up and shouted something. The children dropped the rest of the bread on the ground and ran inside.

"Let's take the shortest way home," said my mother. We went along the canal.

"We'll be there in no time," said my father.

"You hear of more and more people going underground," I said.

"Yes," said Father. "We'll have to see about finding something for you too."

"No," I said. "I'm not going alone."

"If we were still in Breda it'd be easier," my mother said. "There we should have had an address in a minute. Here we know nobody."

"There we might perhaps have been able to move in with the neighbors, just like that," I said.

"Oh, we could have gone anywhere we liked," said Mother. "We had friends everywhere."

"Here it costs a lot of money," said my father, "Where am I to get it from?"

"If only we knew more people. . . ." said Mother.

"Let's wait and see," said my father. "Perhaps it won't be necessary And if it *isn't* necessary, there you sit, among strangers, and you're only a nuisance and a worry to them."

We were home once more. Father put the key in the lock. I glanced involuntarily up and down the street before I went inside.

In the living room the stove was burning and the table was set. Mother had done that before we left. Father went to wash his hands.

Then he came and stood with us at the table, took the embroidered cloth from the Sabbath bread, broke the crust off it, and divided it into three pieces while praying. He dipped the bread in salt. I muttered grace, and ate the salted crust.

"That's right," said my father, and sat down.

MAURICE MEIER

Tiengen

TRANSLATED FROM THE GERMAN BY JOHN W. KURTZ

Tiengen was the name of the town where we lived. It is a small town near the Swiss border, with the whispering pines of the Black Forest at its back, the rushing waters of the upper Rhine at its feet, and the distant panorama of the Swiss Alps before it. It was a peaceful and pleasant place in those days, a busy center of commerce by day, an idyllic rural village in the evening; a place where the sounds of trade and industry mingled with the crowing of cocks and the lowing of cattle.

Unlike most villages of its kind in Germany, Tiengen had a synagogue with a fairly large Jewish congregation. The sight of men in shiny silk top-hats walking through the streets to the synagogue on Saturday morning with their wives and children is a vivid recollection in the mind of anyone who knew Tiengen.

In general, Christians and Jews lived together in peace and harmony. The Jews honored their Christian neighbors by decorating their houses for Christmas and Easter and Whitsun, and many a Christian home was adorned with boughs of green on the Feast of Tabernacles.

As a veteran of the First World War, I had settled down in the town of Griessen in 1919 and there got my start as a farmer. In 1923 I married Martha Abraham of Rust in Baden and we established our first home in Griessen. We were the only Jews in the community, but from the very beginning we lived in happy association with our Christian neighbors. On our return from our wedding trip we found our house decorated with garlands and a banner with the greeting "Welcome and God bless you"; in the house we found our table spread with Black Forest bread and cheese; and in the evening we were serenaded, according to the Black Forest custom, by the town band, directed by the clerk of the town council.

We had many friends in the nearby town of Tiengen and in 1924 Martha founded a choir in the synagogue there. In 1926 we bought a farmstead on the outskirts of Tiengen from an acquaintance who was emigrating to the United States. I have often thought of the remark he made to me during our negotiations: "I am glad that it is you who are taking over this property—but, believe me, you would do better to emigrate to America."

Our first child, Ernst, was born while we were living in Griessen; our second, Ilse-Jeanette, arrived in 1927, after we had moved to Tiengen.

With the farm we had purchased a fine dairy business with many regular milk customers in Tiengen. By hard work we improved the farm and expanded the business so that in 1933 we had twenty-three head of cattle, including eighteen milch cows. Two farm hands, who lived with us, took care of the livestock with the help of a worker who came out from Tiengen every morning.

Our house faced the well-kept, broad highway that runs parallel with the Rhine from Constance past Schaffhausen and on to Tiengen. Just beyond our house the road forks, the left branch leading to the bridge that crosses to the Swiss side at Koblenz, the right going on past Waldshut and Basel and losing itself in the highway systems of Switzerland and Germany.

Beyond the house was Martha's flower and vegetable garden, and beyond that flat meadows and fruitful orchards gradually sloping up to the hills of the Black Forest. Our fields and pastures lay in this fertile plain. It was a prosperous domain which we had developed in the hope and expectation that it would be a home not only for us but also for our children and our children's children, too. It was a joyful home, for it was filled with Martha's gaiety and her music; filled with the joyful shouting of the children. Its doors were always open to those in need, and it was a meeting place for our many relations and guests, and for those who loved music.

The first hint that there was anything amiss in this realm of peace and contentment came unexpectedly one morning in the early spring of 1933. Felix, one of our hired men, received a telegram urging him to leave us immediately and to return to his home in the Black Forest. Two days later, on Friday, March 31, our day laborer, Thomas Maier, who had worked that day, telephoned in the evening to say that he was ill and could not come to work the next day.

It was later than usual when we went to bed that night, but we didn't sleep well because of the noise of unusually heavy traffic on the highway.

Saturday morning I was up at four to start the milking so that the milk could be delivered on time. Soon Martha came with the children to the barn. She had been frightened by what she had seen from the windows by the early light of dawn: Nazi storm troops moving into town by the road past our house on foot, on horseback, and in trucks. Even in the barn we could hear the high-pitched voices of the sergeants shouting orders.

The sun, as it rose, shone upon a new and unfamiliar scene. All street intersections in Tiengen and in the vicinity were occupied by storm troopers directing traffic. Our house, standing at the edge of town with several intersections nearby, appeared to be completely surrounded by guards. Brass bands playing military music marched up and down the streets.

Martha and the children and I went back into the house. There we found Brigitte, the maid of some friends of ours, crouching in a corner, crying and trembling with fear. She was a Christian girl who had been employed in a Jewish home for many years. This morning she had come, as usual, to fetch the daily supply of milk for the family of her employer. She was particularly frightened by the presence of the troops because on the previous Friday, when she had gone to town on an errand, she had been accosted by some of the local brown-shirts, who had told her that she must leave her Jewish employer forthwith. When she had refused they said that they would come and get her on Saturday and would publicly cut off her hair and shave her head. Now she was afraid to go to her house and begged us to hide her.

There was no time to lose, for a rolling of drums and fanfare of trumpets indicated that the "occupation" of Tiengen was about to begin. Looking down the street from an upper window, Martha and Ilse-Jeanette saw that a watch was being set in front of Jewish homes and shops and the synagogue.

Meanwhile Ernst, who was nine years old then, and the maid Brigitte and I were preparing a hiding place for her. In the loft of the barn, against a wall through whose cracks one could see the street, we made a cave of boards and bales of straw. Brigitte climbed in; we gave her a supply of food and drink, and arranged the bales in such a way that she was completely hidden but could easily remove them and leave her hiding place at will.

When we had hastily finished this depressing work it was time to deliver the milk. We loaded the cans on a hand-cart; I took the tongue, Ernst pushed behind, and we started for the street. At the gate we were stopped by the guard and told that we were not allowed to leave. We took the milk back in the barn and fed it to the calves and the cows.

The town looked as if it were under military occupation. There was a headquarters over which was hoisted the banner of the commandant and which was protected by a cordon of guards. On the meadow behind our house there was a first-aid station; the tent and the uniforms of the attendants were marked with the swastika and the red cross. A shooting range was being set up. Over the entrance gate there was a banner with the motto:

TRAIN EYE AND HAND FOR THE FATHERLAND

The targets were ugly effigies, caricatures of local citizens, labeled: JEW. Every two hours when the guard was changed, there was a pompous and noisy ceremony.

At the rear of the house rifle shots from the shooting range; on the street motorcycles roaring past at high speed with mufflers open; the strident shouting of military orders; goose-stepping platoons marching to the changing of the guard; dusty, sweating, weary troops resting along the curbs; messengers galloping past on foaming horses; all this created the oppressive atmosphere of war.

S.S. men came to the house and demanded that I hand over to them photographs and letters of Albert Leo Schlageter which they knew were in my possession. Schlageter had been in my outfit in the artillery during the first World War. He was a patriotic young idealist and a good comrade and I have only fond memories of him, despite the use which the Nazis later made of his name. For years after the war I corresponded with him, as I did with many other army buddies. Motivated by his fanatic patriotism Schlageter enlisted in the illegal army called the "Black *Reichswehr*" after the war. He once wrote me that he was not happy with his role as an illicit soldier, but that there was no way for him to return to civilian life. In the early twenties he became involved in acts of sabotage against the French occupation of the Ruhr, was convicted by a French court-martial, and executed by a firing squad. Later the Nazis chose him, along with Horst Wessel, to be one of the posthumous heroes of their movement and it was therefore important for them to eradicate any evidence that Schlageter had had association with Jews.

The S.S. men now demanded that I hand over letters from Schlageter and pictures showing him and me together. I gave them a part of what I had, but retained some, why I don't exactly know. The men were not satisfied but they left us, though not without uttering some dire threats. This incident frightened all of us, but especially Ilse-Jeanette. She was an unusually sensitive child, intelligent and mature beyond her years, and had a disposition of purest gold, but she had been born with a weak heart and such excitements frightened her, caused her severe pains, and made her lips turn blue. She objected to our calling the doctor, and it would have been useless anyhow, for no physician could have cured what ailed her.

All day Martha tried in vain to telephone her parents in Freiburg and her sister in Zürich. Every time she tried, the operator told her that the line was busy, or that the phones were reserved for official use. Even within the village it took hours to get a number, and then the connection was always cut off at the very beginning of the conversation.

In the course of the day some of our non-Jewish friends, disregarding the dangers of being photographed and marked as Jew-lovers, came to visit us, including several of Martha's women friends, and two old army friends of mine, one from Tiengen, the other from a distance of ninety miles. The latter caused the guard some embarrassment, for he had put on all his military decorations. The Nazis saluted him and couldn't quite bring themselves to keep him from entering the house. Two farmers came with their wives, and when they saw how things were with us they stayed and helped us with the evening milking. Our Christian friends visited not only us, but also other Jews on that day.

Martha told her friends where Brigitte was hidden. The women went to talk to her and agreed to come back after dark to fetch her and take her home with them.

Around noon the following incident caused a small crowd to gather in front of our house. There lived in Tiengen at that time a good-natured little old woman who subsisted on the charity of both Christians and Jews, going from house to house as the guest of a different family each day. For years she had been coming to our house for her dinner on the Sabbath. When she arrived on this day the guards stopped her at the gate and told her to go to the field kitchen for her dinner, but the little old lady drew herself up and said: "Today your field kitchen is here, but yesterday and every day before that you paid no attention to me, and tomorrow you will forget me again.

Stand aside!" She opened the door with her arthritic hands and marched past the speechless brown-shirts into the house.

With another pompous ceremony, the guards retreated in the evening. After that there was a big band concert on the square. There were frequent pauses in the concert during which lists were read of those who had joined the party or volunteered for the Storm Troops during the day, and of those who had received promotions or "battle decorations." Then there was a torchlight parade and after that merrymaking and dancing which continued at various taverns until morning.

As the sun went down an old friend, a Jewish widow whom we loved like a mother, came to call on us and we shared *Havdalah*—the blessing spoken at the close of the Sabbath—with her.

Opposite our house there was a tavern which had long been the meeting place for party members. The place had been very busy all day and now in the night it was the scene of a wild celebration. We closed the house up tight, but we couldn't shut out the sound of young men and women bawling out the party anthem, the "Horst Wessel Song":

> *When Jewish blood spurts from the knife,*
> *Then everything will be fine!*

By evening Ilse-Jeanette was quite ill and wanted to sleep in our bed with us. When she was still awake after an hour or more, her mother asked what she could do to help her go to sleep. Ilse-Jeanette asked us to bring Ernst in with us, too; so I went and carried him in and laid him beside his sister, and the four of us spent the long night arm in arm, trying to close our ears to the refrain, "When Jewish blood spurts from the knife. . . ."

In the following weeks Ilse-Jeanette recovered somewhat, but she always remained restless and full of fear whenever any of us were away from the house.

From friends we learned that scenes similar to those we had witnessed had been enacted all over Germany on that day. In the cities, where Christians and Jews lived side by side in the great apartment houses and where there were many Christian-Jewish partnerships, the demonstrations had not been as frightening for the Jews as in the small towns.

On the next Monday Ernst went to school as usual. At the end of the school day he reported to us the new rules that had been laid down: Hereafter the children were to greet their teacher not with *"Guten Morgen, Herr Lehrer,"* but with outstretched arm and *"Heil*

Hitler"; all except Ernst, that is, who as the only Jewish child in his room was required to remain seated while the others performed this ceremony of greeting.

On another day the teacher told the children: "You are fortunate to have experienced that great Saturday when our *Führer,* for whom other nations envy us, laid the foundations for our thousand-year Aryan Reich and made the cowardly Jews crawl into their holes."

Day after day Ernst was humiliated and insulted in one way or another by the teacher; but for a long time there was, strangely enough, no change in the attitude and conduct of the other children toward him. As ever, his friends came to play at our house and he went to theirs.

But in general, the atmosphere in Tiengen was different after that day, though most people tried to act as though nothing had happened.

The tavern across the street, the meeting place for the local Nazis, had previously been the scene of a party meeting only once a week. Now, since that Saturday, the membership had greatly increased and every night some organization was "on duty" there, and night after night we heard the song "When Jewish blood spurts from the knife . . ." being sung over and over again.

Toward the end of May, Ernst and his schoolmates were looking forward to and making plans for the great day of the school picnic. On the morning of the appointed day Ernst shouldered his rucksack, stuck a spray of blossoms in his hat, and went marching off to school, whistling and full of happy anticipation. About an hour later somebody came and told us that Ernst was standing alone and forlorn on the school grounds. I found him with bloody hands and face, his clothing torn, the contents of the rucksack scattered and trampled in the dust. As he walked home with me he sobbed out his story.

The teacher had read off the names of the pupils who were to go on the picnic, omitting Ernst's name. At the end of the roll call he looked at Ernst and said, "Jews are not wanted at our picnic." Ernst stepped out of the line and started to walk away, but the teacher shouted to the children, "Boys, get him and knock out of him any ideas he may have about coming to our school any more." Several rowdies thereupon attacked him, and soon the whole class was scratching, kicking, and beating him with the teacher gleefully shouting his encouragement.

The next day I called on the teacher. After I had made my complaint he launched into a tirade against the Jews. I then went to the principal of the school. He listened sympathetically and said, "I am truly sorry for you and for Ernst, but I cannot do a thing because Ernst's teacher is a party member."

"Then what can I do to save the child from such painful experiences?" I asked.

"The only advice I can give you, *Herr* Meier, is to take Ernst out of school."

This we did, and gave him his lessons at home ourselves.

In the next few days we were called upon at various times by five couples whose children had taken part in the attack on Ernst. All of them were apologetic, but most of them were also inclined to make excuses for the teacher, saying that his recent promotion to the post of Party Youth Leader in Tiengen had gone to his head and had caused him "to go too far in this particular case."

After these visits Martha and I first began to talk about emigrating. The plan which we finally developed was to sell everything gradually and unobtrusively, turning all we had into money, and to go to some foreign country. We figured it would take about a year or somewhat more. But we soon learned that we had less time than we had thought.

A few weeks after the boycott a cousin of ours wrote us that her husband had been taken away in the night and sent to Dachau, at that time the largest and most notorious of the Nazi concentration camps, to be "re-educated" because he had failed to stand at attention when a party functionary had entered his house. From then on we heard again and again of men who had been carried off to Dachau. Stories that leaked out about things that happened there made us tremble.

Once the little old lady who was our guest every Sabbath came, contrary to her custom, on a weekday. When Martha was about to take her lunch pail in order to fill it, the old lady held it back, opened it, and took out a soiled and dog-eared musical score. Beethoven's "Ode to Joy" from the Ninth Symphony with the text by Schiller:

> *Brothers, o'er the starry heavens*
> *There must dwell a loving father.*

She pressed it into Martha's hands, begging her to keep it as a remembrance. After reassuring herself that no one was near to overhear her, the old lady said: "They're talking about you all over town."

"And what are they saying?" Martha asked.

"They're saying, 'Meier is going to have to pay for the Schlageter affair.' "

"And how do you suppose they'll go about it to make us pay?"

"The plans are all made," the old lady answered, "and one of these nights they are going to get your husband."

Recently we had received an anonymous warning of a similar kind, but we had not taken it seriously. Now with this further evidence from a person whom we loved and who wished us well, we began to be deeply concerned.

That evening Martha sent our maid to buy some things in the town. She came back breathless and excited.

"They were talking about us in the store. Two women and a man. I don't know if they were talking about you or about me, but the store keeper gave them a sign and they looked around and recognized me and stopped talking."

For a long time that night Martha and I discussed what we should do. The question was, should we separate voluntarily now, or should we wait to be separated by force? We finally agreed upon the following plan: In the morning we would explain the situation to the children; then, in the afternoon, we would all go over to Koblenz in Switzerland; there we would take the children to a confectionery and treat them to whatever they chose, in order to sweeten the bitter hour of parting; from there Martha and the children would return to Tiengen and I would go on to Martha's sister's house in Zürich.

We talked for a while about the happy life we had had in Tiengen. Then, hand in hand, we made a tour of the property, experiencing again the pride that we had taken in every improvement, the satisfaction that we had felt with every new acquisition. For me it was indeed a farewell tour: after that night I never saw the place again. Returning to the house, we stood together for a long time gazing at our sleeping children.

It was late when we went to bed, but we had scarcely retired when the telephone rang; it was a friend who wished to speak to Martha. We had an extension phone, so we both listened.

The woman's voice trembled with excitement. "Have you heard about what's going on in town?"

"Not a word."

"One of our non-Jewish neighbors came to our house a while ago and said, 'There's a big mob of rowdies from Tiengen and other towns making a demonstration in front of H.'s house because he criticized the *Führer* and said there was no power on earth that was as strong as his Christian faith.' "

"Is H. in danger?" Martha asked.

"It's an open secret; the S.S. is on its way and will arrest H. and take him to Dachau in 'protective custody' in order to 'restore peace and order' in town."

"What does your husband think about it?"

"He's left the house and is hiding outside, as our neighbor advised him to do, because he's probably on the Nazi list too, just as your husband is." Then she cried, "There's no time to lose!" and abruptly hung up.

Martha and I scarcely knew what to do. We got dressed quickly, went out in the street and walked furtively in the direction of H.'s house. From a distance we could hear the hysterical mob shouting, "Lynch him. Hang him up in a tree with all his brood." Shouting mobs could be heard in other streets, too.

Terrified, we hurried back to the house. I went in to kiss the children good-bye. Martha, by this time speechless with terror, pulled me away from them, and hustled me out to the car. I drove quickly out of the yard and down the road to the bridge, and in a few minutes I was safely across the border in Switzerland. I stopped to telephone Martha that I had made it, and then drove on to Zürich.

In Zürich I went to my sister-in-law's house and the next morning I went to the city hall and applied for the right of temporary asylum in the city, which was granted without delay. A few days later Martha came with the children to join me in Zürich. She reported what had happened after I had left.

"Right after you called up from Koblenz," she said, "I turned on all the lights in the house, thinking that that would keep the mob from smashing the windows. I was with the children when somebody knocked at the door. There were several S.S. men there.

" 'We want to see the Jew Meier,' one of them said.

" 'My husband is not here; he's gone to Switzerland,' I said.

" 'Who gave you the warning?'

"As I was trying to think what to say in answer to that, one of the other men said, 'Come on, hand over everything to do with Schlageter and with the Jew Meier's army service.'

"I went and got the whole parcel of letters, photographs and clippings and gave them to the leader and they all went away."

That night two men from Tiengen were taken away to Dachau.

ABRAHAM EISEN

The Fraternal Grave of Four Jewish Settlements

TRANSLATED FROM THE YIDDISH BY MOSHE SPIEGEL

At the beginning of August a group of us left Vilna for farm work at the Zatroce camp, about a kilometer away.

It was during the *"Chapunes"* actions. Every day young men were taken from their homes, supposedly to new jobs, and were never heard from again. Almost 10,000 men were taken within a few weeks. The threat of such action, added to the unending stream of harsh decrees, led many young men to leave for work camps at Kena, Bextsan, Vaca and Bialovka. They hoped thus to wait out the fury of the Nazis. We, too, fled, and in such haste we forgot even blankets and pots.

Once we arrived we decided to send messengers to neighboring Trok to borrow such necessities. Lichtmacher, a former philharmonic musician, and I were selected. We removed our yellow Mogen Davids, for as Jews we were forbidden to leave the camp.

Before the war Trok had been the county seat and home of about 1,000 Jews. It was the fourth largest city in Poland, and its large lake and surrounding evergreens had long made it a vacation spot. Its chief curiosity was its community of exotic Karaites, who denied their Jewish heritage and claimed descent from the Cuzari (Khuzari), an ancient Mongolian people.

When I had last visited Trok, in 1938, I had spoken with their religious leader, or "cantor," who had insisted his people were Tatars, not Semites. He cited their Turkish-Tatar dialect. It is most likely their denial of Hebraic descent stemmed from fear of persecution by the Nazis. Their scheme worked well; they were left alone.

We were struck by the morbid silence that now hung over the city. It was Sabbath noon, a time when youths usually filled the streets. But now everything was ghostly quiet. Occasionally a Karaite, with his unmistakably Semitic features, showed himself and quickly vanished.

We sensed eyes upon us from the window of a house in the center of town, but we could see no faces. We sensed they were Jewish eyes, inviting us in. We went inside. There was a Jewish tablecloth on the table, flowered table covers and two brass candlesticks. Two women, apparently mother and daughter, spoke more with their eyes than lips as they asked who we were and why we were there.

We told them. In our short conversation we learned the Jewish community was not yet in any danger. The Germans had arrived six weeks before, and no atrocities had yet occurred. The decrees had come, though. Forced labor, yellow Jewish patches, an injunction against walking the streets, but nothing beyond that—yet. Many young men had escaped, and those who stayed maintained their courage. The Jews in Trok felt German rule would be short-lived. Jews from neighboring communities sought shelter there.

One of the two women we spoke with was a teacher from a women's trade school in Vilna. The spiritual strength of these two women reached us almost tangibly.

"If things are so," we asked, "why are the streets deserted?"

"It's better that way. The less they see of us the better. No sense in overdoing things."

The older woman, in her sixties, had eyes filled with hate. She glanced angrily at the ceiling, pointing. "A Lithuanian officer lives there. He told me I can't walk on the sidewalk. I said, 'I shouldn't walk on the pavement? Who made this sidewalk? Who built this house? Me! With my own hands!' And then, right in front of him, I put my hands on my hips and strutted the full length of the sidewalk. What do you think? He just pursed his lips and said nothing!"

From their home and neighbors' homes they gathered the things we needed. Soon we returned to the camp.

There were other visits to Trok that month.

Our group suffered cruelly in Zatroce. The camp was part of the German Agricultural Corporation, Ostland. Most of us were totally unsuited for heavy physical labor. There was Lubotsky, a mathematics professor; Moshe Lehrer of the Jewish Scientific Institute; Gutmal, a lawyer; a couple named Germanski, active in communal affairs at Kovno; and Lichtmacher. They were exhausted after a few weeks, hardly able to stand. And the petty officials delighted in beating the weak among us, throwing turf bricks at them often.

This prompted me to visit the Jews at Trok, to ask them to intercede with their Christian friends to stop this mistreatment. They spoke with a local priest, who delivered a sermon concerning the matter the following Sunday, and the incidents stopped.

We realized the Jews in Trok had friends among the Christians. It proved true, for after the brief period of tranquillity the Germans and Lithuanians tried to divide the Jews from their Christian neighbors. They were not allowed to buy food at market or at the farms. But peasants, risking their lives, brought them all they needed. Later, when the Jews were completely cut off from the outside world the peasants again brought food, in boats.

Such kindness strengthened the courage of the Jews in Trok. Even when they were doomed they continued to comfort us, facing their persecution with heads high. Their faith and hope was evident in their conversation. Their faith held true, but they did not live to see the German tyrants fall.

I remember the lame cobbler, Moshe. He repaired our shoes in his little workshop while his Christian customers waited. "You can wait," he told them, "but if I don't fix their shoes, who will?" Rising from his stool, his lame leg suspended stiffly in mid air, his eyes shone in his emaciated face. "He will be smashed! Though he is momentarily victorious, he is racing to his own doom!" he said scornfully.

At the table sat his father, with gray beard and calm face. Working skillfully, he remarked quietly, without raising his head, "He will be smashed because he started with the Jews. We may be a helpless, unfortunate people, but there is a Law and a Judge."

Other Jews in Trok spoke the same way. The trade-school teacher said, "We have connections, and we'll be warned if trouble threatens. They were supposed to search for arms in the synagogue, but we found out and closed it down. . . ."

The head of the community was more practical. "They need us. We are workers and artisans; they couldn't get along without us. We can't be replaced."

He said this three weeks before his community, with three other Jewish settlements, was wiped out.

In September of 1941 a ghetto was established in Vilna. With other inmates from the camp I visited there secretly. On the way back I stopped in Trok. In the Jewish homes I found groups of Christian neighbors. They had come to accept household items for safekeeping.

"What's happening?" I asked the lame shoemaker.

"Just getting ready," he replied. "They won't drive us into a ghetto unprepared. They won't find well-stocked homes here as they did in Vilna."

"Are you sure they'll make a ghetto here?" I asked the teacher.

"We're not sure yet. But it's best to be ready."

A week later we learned that the Jews in Trok had been herded into a ghetto, in a building that had housed the Polish Sea League. In spite of everything, it had happened unexpectedly. One sunny morning they were ordered from their homes with a few bundles and locked in the ramshackle structure by the lake. They were joined by deportees from Orani, Landvorov and Rodzshishki, villages outside Vilna. Altogether two thousand Jews were squeezed into that building.

On the first day of Rosh Hashana two armed soldiers appeared at the camp. They eyed us with contempt and asked, "Where are the other Jews?"

Just then the manager of the camp came over.

"How many Jews are at Zatroce?" they asked.

"Forty-five," he answered.

"Where are they?"

He told them they were in the fields, argued with them a short while and invited them in for a drink. They left an hour later, staggering. The manager walked toward us shortly afterward.

"They are members of a Lithuanian execution battalion," he said, "organized by the German occupation forces. Their mission is to kill all Jews in this region."

"What did they want here?"

"They came for the Jews at this camp. I told them I was supposed to deliver them in due time to the execution authorities at Vilna. They drank up everything in sight and left. But I don't think it's the end of it. It may be wise for you to leave; I can't guarantee your safety."

That afternoon we put a kettle of soup in the wagon and left.

We decided to hide in the forest, about a kilometer from Zatroce. Throughout the night we heard shouts from the other side of the camp, mixed with the strains of a vulgar Lithuanian soldiers' song.

Ten days they fed us horsemeat, horsemeat—
Day a pound, night a pound, horsemeat, horsemeat.
On the eleventh day we whinnied, ay, whinnied.
We trotted, ay, trotted,
We neighed like horses,
And trotted like horses.

The raw, staccato tones cut through the quiet countryside. Our embittered hearts, even the starry sky and the tall evergreens, seemed offended by the vulgar voices.

We stayed far from the camp for three days. For two days we heard steady, uninterrupted shooting from the vicinity of the lake near Trok. On the third day it was quiet. Peasants who found us told us the two thousand Jews in the Sea League building had been shot. Thy were looking for us but the danger was past. They said we could return to the camp, the execution battalion had gone.

We listened, shocked, silent. Some saw no reason for returning to Zatroce, considering it still dangerous, and returned to Vilna. The rest of us returned to the camp.

From a Pole named Vilkovski we learned the details of the slaughter.

"I live near the lake and I saw everything," he told us. "First they brought out the men. The heartrending cries of the women and children were heard in my own home. The men went quietly, for they had been promised the women and children would be spared. But once the men were dead they led out the women and children. Those who had cried so bitterly before now marched to their death with calm, stony faces. They had nothing left to live for."

Vilkovski thought a moment. "The sight of those helpless women and children—their eerie silence—so unnerved me I could not stand it. I ran away from there. I can't get over it, even now."

Eighteen Jews somehow had survived. Two were from Landvorov, one was from Rodzshishki and fifteen from Trok. Only one returned to Trok when the war was over. I want to relate what happened to the other fourteen.

One was a tailor who specialized in military uniforms. As long as the authorities had need of him they let him live. They took him to Zatroce for two days. On the third day the police took him away. We learned later he had been shot and buried near the mass grave of the others.

The others stayed in hiding for seven months. In March of 1942 police raided the surrounding villages and found them all. They were imprisoned at Trok for a month and were escorted to work every day by a tight guard. Everyone assumed they would be spared, at worst sent to the Vilna Ghetto. A truly great man soon freed us of that delusion.

He came to us at Zatroce, unexpectedly. I'll never forget his pale, refined face at the partly opened door. He shook the rain from the broad rim of his black hat. He was the wonderful man who had preached in our behalf at Trok, Stanislav Tishko. We rose quickly and invited him in.

"Pastor? What are you doing here?"

In the murky light we thought we saw a look of annoyance cross his face. "If I came, there must be a good reason."

I remembered a conversation with him the day he preached for us. A young Jew had given him some divorce papers for safekeeping. He had said, "It's only a question of whose chances for survival are greater—mine or his. . . ."

I had laughed and asked, "You're in the same fix as we are?"

"Not quite the same. The Germans dislike me; they know of my feelings about their treatment of Jews. The Lithuanians, too, resent me because I teach them religion in Polish. . . . My sins multiply!"

Now I feared he might be in trouble.

"Are you in any danger, Pastor?" I asked.

"Not I. But you are. All of you."

He told us he had learned from reliable sources that the fourteen Jews would be shot. The Lithuanian police planned to purge the entire area of Jews. The Jewish workers at Zatroce were marked for liquidation.

"It is now advisable that you return to Vilna," he said. He wrapped his cassock around him, pulled down his hat and left.

A year later, we learned afterward, he was arrested and shot.

Most of us then doubted the truth of his information, but caution was advisable in any case. We slept in our clothes and posted guards through the nights, and asked the camp manager to intervene for us with the authorities.

He succeeded and we were left alone. But in April we learned that the fourteen Jews had been shot and buried in a common grave near the lake. I went to visit the spot to learn if our information was true. The Pole Vilkovski was my guide.

We trudged a frozen path through the fields. A sharp wind cut my face with snow. We could hear the strong currents of the lake breaking through the ice.

Suddenly I stopped. Near a stand of pines among the hillocks of clay I recognized the fraternal grave. It was about fifty meters long and two meters wide, hedged with a fence of thin, freshly cut logs. Beside the large grave was a small one, probably that of the murdered tailor. A little further was another mass grave, that of the fourteen recently murdered Jews. It was covered with fresh, yellow clay.

I stood there, agonized. Here were four Jewish communities that yesterday had been bustling with life. They who had helped build the homes and streets of their villages now lay in a crowded grave between two naked hillocks, under an indifferent, leaden sky. The wind wailed over them. Why? Why?

Suddenly my body shook. Above the howling of the wind I heard the voice of the old cobbler of Trok. It rolled over the frozen lake and whistled through the pines with a roar.

Leth din v'leth dayan! There is no Law and no Judge!

JULIAN GROSS

City of Cracow

TRANSLATED FROM THE YIDDISH BY MOSHE SPIEGEL

Atrocities

On December 5, 1939, when the terrible raid on Kazmierscz took place, my uncle Maximilian Redlich happened to be on Cracowska Street, in the office of the *Judenrat,* where he was employed as a clerk. At seven o'clock in the morning, S.S. men surrounded the Jewish community and demanded that three of its officials be surrendered to them. There was sporadic shooting in the street, and the Jewish officials were afraid to go out. At last my uncle and two of his associates volunteered to go. They were taken to the synagogue on Isaacs Street and ordered to set fire to the Scrolls of the Law. When my uncle refused to comply with the command, he was promptly shot and killed. The following day, an S.S. officer visited his residence and informed his brother that Maximilian had been killed.

During my uncle's burial, we noticed an old demented Jew wandering among the graves. We learned that during the great raid of December 5, the old man was accosted on the street and taken to the gas chamber. A little Jewish boy was also taken from the street, and the old man was ordered to throw hot coals and ashes upon him. The little fellow died of the burns, and the oldster became mentally deranged. On the same day, the S.S. killed the daughter of the proprietor of a toy store, while ransacking the establishment for gold.

The S.S. continually staged and photographed all sorts of scenes in Cracow. For instance, they forced an elderly, bearded Jew to hold a revolver against an S.S. man while they photographed the scene.

LEON SALPETER

City of Cracow

TRANSLATED FROM THE YIDDISH BY MOSHE SPIEGEL

Inspections and Arrests

The month of December stands out for continual inspections and arrests, which culminated with the isolation and encirclement of the entire Jewish district by S.S. men. That took two days, during which time the inspections and pillage of Jewish homes went on. Jewelry, clothing, and other valuables were plundered. Jews in the street, in the Jewish quarters, and elsewhere were taken into restaurants or taverns, where they were inspected thoroughly.

The sex organs of the women were examined by the Gestapo and S.S. men. After the examination, the unfortunates were exposed nude to the public. This task was not accomplished without victims. The stubborn, the recalcitrant, and those who concealed valuables were shot.

During the first months of the New Year, life in the ghetto was relatively calm. It seemed as though the new order might last until the end of the war. But the optimists were due for disappointment.

The capture of Jews got under way again. Complying with orders from the Gestapo, Jewish militiamen carried out arrests of their fellow Jews at night. The following day the Gestapo would take into custody all those arrested, and the unfortunates would never be heard of again, except when, in some cases, news of their death reached surviving relatives.

Seals and Blue Lists

In June 1942, the presidium of the Jewish community was commanded to prepare the auditorium in the building of the Jewish Social

Self-Help (J.S.S.). Two assembly rooms, a typewriter, and several chairs were required for use on Saturday and Sunday. Everyone with an employment card was ordered to present himself, and a great throng appeared.

The Jewish *Ordnungsdienst* (police) maintained order. Though it was not generally known that the procedure was a prelude to death, the people were desperately afraid. Those who had no cards were fearful; identity cards of the unemployed were not stamped, nor were the cards of all the employed. It depended in great measure on the individual German official in charge. There was a score of committees, composed of representatives of the Labor Department and one Gestapo official. Of those employed in the same workshop, some had their cards stamped, while others did not. It was all a matter of chance.

Within a few days, the *Ordnungsdienst* was ordered to round up all those whose cards were not stamped. Several thousand were deported as a result of this check-up. Since the action was carried out by Jewish police, the Germans were dissatisfied with the result. Dr. Rosenzweig, president of the Jewish community, was held responsible for compliance with the order, and the German authorities also ordered that he and his family be deported. On Wednesday, at dusk, five thousand Jews were deported to an unknown destination; but it soon became apparent that they were all doomed.

On Friday of the same week, a new order was issued: all Jews holding employment or identification cards were to present themselves on Saturday and receive blue identification cards, instead of stamps.

On Saturday morning, a new registration got under way. Those who possessed no blue identification cards were restricted to the garden area of the ground, and later dispatched in groups to the Optima Square, where they were held overnight. Then a new order came through to the effect that anyone in the ghetto without a blue identification card was to be executed.

Deportation and the Decline of the Ghetto

On Sunday afternoon the German S.S. police began to deport several thousand Jews. Children were separated from their parents. There was shooting during the action and there were casualties. The inspection of documents also went on in hospitals.

With the deportation of some ten thousand Jews, the ghetto was considerably reduced. The *Staatshauptman* ordered the Jewish community to liquidate the Jewish homes that were situated on Renkowka Street, as well as parts of Wengerska, Charnieckego, and Kratusa Street, and even part of Limanowska Street. The remaining Jews of this area were supposed to move into the sparsely populated Jewish ghetto. For that purpose, the Jewish community established a Residence Bureau, whose function it was to solve the problem of living quarters in the reduced Jewish ghetto.

Second Deportation

During the night of October 27, the Jewish ghetto was surrounded by German police. The Jews were thrown into a panic, for they realized that they were confronted by a new deportation. A small group of Jews succeeded in escaping the ghetto through the canals, under cover of darkness. On the morning of the 28th, we were informed that all Jews must present themselves, according to trade categories, to the *"Arbeitsamt."* Gestapo officials then singled out some of the workers for deportation. These unfortunates were assembled on the Zgodi Square; the others returned to their work. In the main, elderly people were selected; but the deportees included also group leaders, despite the latter's skills. But in view of the fact that the number of deportees did not wholly satisfy the Germans, the Gestapo announced that the ghetto was to become *"Judenrein."* That statement was made in the afternoon. It was a ruse to lure into the open those Jews who had hidden in cellars and other places. The ruse was successful, and an additional fifteen hundred Jews were thus dispatched to the Zgodi Square, which made a total of about six thousand in all. The human cargo was loaded into freight cars at the station in Plashow and sent to Belzec. The Gestapo permitted the Jewish community to supply the deportees with bread and soup. Those who later returned from work were unaware that their brothers had been lured from the hideouts and deported. A new wail of misery. . . .

People were deported from hospitals, orphanages, children's homes and from the surrounding camps. The Germans next issued yet another decree, ordering that the ghetto, where only ten thousand Jews now remained, be still further depopulated. The leading workers of the Optima and of the Madritsch firm were to be among the deportees. Homes on Jewish streets situated on the opposite side of the Zgodi Square were to be liquidated, as well as the so-called Ukraine Dambrowska, Janowa-Volya, a part of the Lvovska (where the guard was billeted). The cruel *Sturmbanführer* Haas and the *Obergruppenführer* Scherner directed the October deportation.

Third Deportation

On Sunday, March 14, 1943, a military detachment of S.S. men, headed by Haas and Gett, marched into the ghetto. Kunde Heinrich and Neumann, the administrators of Jewish affairs, who were also present, made the rounds until they reached District "B." The Jewish residents of this district assembled on the Zgodi Square, awaiting the verdict. As lorries arrived on the scene to pick up the Jews, shots were fired on Zgodi Square. Other S.S. men made the rounds of the general hospital and the one for communicable diseases, killing all the sick, as well as the physicians and orderlies. They also did away with any Jew they encountered in District "A." During the segregating process in Zgodi Square, Gett selected a hundred and fifty to clean up the ghetto following the action. Haas, deeming this number superfluous, ordered that half of them be killed.

Twenty-five hundred Jews, young and old, were housed in District "B." The *Tagesheim* accommodated two hundred and fifty children, who were taken to Zgodi Square. Seven hundred Jews were shot there and then; approximately two thousand were sent to the gas chambers in Oswiecim. So that the victims would suffer from the knowledge that they were doomed and would harbor no illusions, they were deprived of the pitiful belongings that they had brought with them.

Zgodi Square and the surrounding courtyards were strewn with dead bodies. Those who were not killed on the spot were later beaten to death. Mothers clutching their children to their breasts fell from the barrage of bullets.

This was the last act of the tragedy of the Jews who found themselves in the ghetto of Cracow. The S.S. men issued an order on Sunday afternoon that the hospitals, the courtyards and Zgodi Square be cleared of the corpses. This task was carried out on the following day. The bodies were thrown into wagons and carted away to the cemetery at Plashow.

Retrieved From the Death Column

Nine thousand Jews perished during the June 1942 action. Since I lacked a blue identification card, I was with the throng transported to Belzec. I volunteered for deportation. At Optima I found approximately four thousand Jews who had already been lingering there some thirty-six hours under horrible conditions, without food, water or sleep in hot weather. Inspections went on apace, especially the search for money and gold. The prisoners were unaware of their destination and none of us believed that we were heading for death. Had we known the gruesome truth, many of us could have escaped the bitter end. We were lined up five abreast on Wengerska Street, under the strong police guard, and marched along Limanowska, Wielicka, and Walja-Dubacka, to the freight platform at Prokocim. There we saw the freight cars coupled to the train which carried the Jews from the surrounding towns (Jendushejev, Slomniki, Mjechow). Before we boarded the freight cars, Gestapo officers selected eight men, including me, from our group. We were then ushered into the Judenland work camp, where we were told, "You came here with a blue card. That means work—and work means life!"

Only then did it dawn on us that the human cargo on those freight cars was doomed to death.

MORDECAI GEBIRTIG

Our Town Is Burning

TRANSLATED FROM THE YIDDISH BY JOSEPH LEFTWICH

Our town is burning, brothers, burning,
Our poor little town is burning.
Angry winds are fanning higher
The leaping tongues of flame and fire,
The evil winds are roaring!
Our whole town burns!

And you stand looking on with folded arms,
And shake your heads.
You stand looking on, with folded arms
While the fire spreads!

Our town is burning, brothers, burning,
Our poor little town is burning.
Tongues of flame are leaping,
The fire through our town goes sweeping,
Through roofs and windows pouring.
All around us burns.

And you stand looking on with folded arms,
And shake your heads.
You stand looking on with folded arms
While the fire spreads!

Our town is burning, brothers, burning.
Any moment the fire may
Sweep the whole of our town away,
And leave only ashes, black and gray,

Like after a battle, where dead walls stand,
Broken and ruined in a desolate land.

And you stand looking on with folded arms,
And shake your heads.
You stand looking on with folded arms
While the fire spreads!

Our town is burning, brothers, burning.
All now depends on you.
Our only help is what you do.
You can still put out the fire
With your blood, if you desire.

Don't look on with folded arms,
And shake your heads.
Don't look on with folded arms
While the fire spreads!

LIFE IN THE GHETTOS

LIFE IN THE GHETTOS

After the occupation of Poland the first Nazi orders were to concentrate and isolate the Jews in ghettos.

The German High Command accompanied the instructions with a suggestion that the isolation be motivated as follows: "As a reason for the formation of the ghettos, it should be stated that masses of Jews participated in the partisan movement and in plunder. . . ."

German local officials made no secret of the real purpose of the ghettos. In a circular dated December 10, 1939, concerning the establishment of the Lodz Ghetto, the last paragraph contains a statement by Uebelhör, chief of the Kalisch region: "The ghetto is evidently only a temporary measure. I have yet to decide by which methods and under which terms the ghetto and the entire city of Lodz is to be cleansed of Jews. The ultimate aim is to burn out this abscess. . . ."

Although the official order for creating ghettos was issued in the General Government on September 13, 1940, the Germans, as we have seen, had already made their preparations.

The ghettos were located in the poorest, most unsanitary sections of the city. Jews were driven out of their former homes without being allowed to take any possessions, and squeezed into cramped, narrow quarters. Smaller surrounding cities were made Judenrein *by herding their occupants into the ghettos of the larger cities.*

The ghettos were hermetically sealed off from the outside world. Some were surrounded by thick walls; other by wooden fences or barbed wire. Leaving the ghetto was punishable by death.

The ghettos were another coldly calculated step in the Nazi plan of extermination. From the ghettos the road led inevitably to death in the various murder factories and death camps.

EMMANUEL RINGELBLUM

Notes from the Warsaw Ghetto

TRANSLATED FROM THE YIDDISH BY JACOB SLOAN

JULY–DECEMBER 1942

They Escaped From the Wagons!

Those who had experience.
Young men.
One [young man] escaped two times—organized eight "springers" —people who escaped extermination in Oswiecim by springing out of the railroad wagons taking them there.

Resistance

The Jew from the Small Ghetto—who grabbed a German by the throat. The other was shot—went berserk and shot thirteen Jews in the courtyard (Panska or Twarda Street).—The Jew from Nalevskes Street who tore a rifle out of a Ukrainian guard's hand, and fled.

The role the youth played—the only ones who remained on the battlefield [were the] romantic phantasiasts—Samuel—couldn't survive the tragedy of the ghetto—the decisions by the [various] factions involved in the resistance—the attempt at [setting the ghetto on] fire —the [resisters'] appeals of the 6th of September for the populace to resist deportation regarded [in the ghetto] as [Nazi] provocation. Attempt to assassinate Szerynski*

* Head of the Jewish police in the ghetto.

The group of porters who had lost their families and dreamed of revenge—[the people who] offered money to avoid deportation—the idea of using coal gas in defense against the Jewish police—partisans —diversionary acts.

Why? *October 15*

Why didn't we resist when they began to resettle 300,000 Jews from Warsaw? Why did we allow ourselves to be led like sheep to the slaughter? Why did everything come so easy to the enemy? Why didn't the hangmen suffer a single casualty? Why could 50 S.S. men (some people say even fewer), with help of a division of some 200 Ukrainian guards and an equal number of Letts, carry the operation out so smoothly?

The shops as traps: they took the best specialists away—"a couple of porters" laughed—they were taken away—the professionals were taken away. They looked at their hands, *clean palms*. Office employees taken away . . . only wearing work clothes—wearing slippers. Accompanied on the way [to the *Umschlagplatz*] by Ukrainians—they kept shooting.

Selection for deportation in the street among whole blocks—at first, on the basis of working papers, later on the basis of appearance (people dyed their gray hair).

They shaved off all the beards—tore off all the frock coats, earlocks. The street dead all day, except for after the barricade† and from five in the morning to seven—the movement from one street to another, where there had already been a barricade. But the others kept barricading the same neighborhood day after day. The Jewish agents informed the others about the populace's mood, about the hideout methods.

The role the shop owners played in the barricades—their cooperation with the S.S.—how they fooled people, for example, [the shop owner] Toebbens at 65 Niska Street. He said he wanted to avoid a barricade, so he took away all the workers' laundry.

Jewish [work] directors helped catch the illegals,* for example, at Hallman's shop.

† Streets were barricaded to prevent any Jew from escaping the selection for deportation.

* Those who had no work permits.

The Umschlagplatz—*What it Looked Like*

The heroic nurses—the only ones who saved people from deportation without [asking for] money. Szmerling†—the hangman with the whip.

The scenes when the wagons were loaded—the industriousness of the Jewish police—the tearing of parents from their children, wives from their husbands, Rabbi Kanal, Lubliner.

The shooting on the spot of those who tried to escape through holes in the wall at night—the exemption of people who pretended to be doctors. Nurses' headkerchiefs saved hundreds of professionals, employees of the Jewish council.

The Great Pursuit—Szmerling currying the others' favor.

More than once he tore the badges off policemen who had saved Jews from the *Umschlag*.

Faithful executor of their orders—introduced a check of the nurses because they allowed people to escape without paying money.

Great grafter—took more than 100 zlotys per head. Most of those who were exempted—bought off the watch at the gate.—The police made enormous sums.

["The Thirteen"] Special Service made a lot of money exempting people too; com.[munity] institutions set up a fund to save the professionals.

The tragedy of those seized two, three, and five times—the mother who wouldn't go without her child—the husband who wouldn't go without his wife, etc.—and afterward they all went in the same wagon—hundreds of families went to the *Umschlag* together because of the children.

Because the quota wasn't met, the Germans seized people on the street, drove them directly into the wagons, not to the *Umschlag* but straight into the wagons—12,000 killed during the resettlement.

The Pot on Niska Street

The 6th of September—the cruelty. In the middle of the night Lejkin was instructed to have all the Jews in the quadrangle bounded on one side by Gesia, on another by Smocza, on a third by Niska,

† Commanding the Jewish police at the *Umschlagplatz*.

and on the fourth by Zamenhofa to select [deportees] and round up illegals.—Massacre of 25,000 people, perhaps even more. Of the barracks that were emptied out (everyone ordered out of the barracks) two or three houses set aside for each shop, most of them in the country—some shops' [workers] got back into their apartments that day—others not till the next day, or the day after.

"Ah, but we had a fine pot!" said Witasek, who directed the resettlement operation.

The tens of thousands who remained on Niska Street—the continual slaughtering—seventy people killed in one apartment on Wolynska Street—in two days, 1,000 people killed, taken to the graveyard—hundreds killed in the street during the selections, all forced to kneel on the pavement [to be killed].

Hundreds and thousands of people lay in their hiding places all week, without water (a water main burst), without food.

Hoffman's shop consists of two industries. One is reworking old things collected in Germany. The things are washed, mended, and then sent back.

"Illegals." Illegals are those people who do not have [work card] numbers, people who, according to the law, should have been on the *Umschlagplatz,* and yet are still alive. How many there are of this kind nobody knows. There are various estimates. Many people place the number of illegals at 7,000, others estimate 10,000 and even 15,000. The fact is, they *are!*

Who are they? A large number are members of the family of "legal persons"—mostly the police, Jewish Council officials, etc.

The illegals also consist of officials of the council, or of the Y.Y.G.A., [Jewish Self-Aid Society], who were let go, but did not go to the *Umschlagplatz;* instead they went into hiding, and now they huddle close to their former colleagues for protection.

And then there is a third category—"everyday Jews," who simply hid out and are still in hiding. They pay off the Work Guard and live at home. Many of the illegals are people who worked in shops that were given up, who managed to save themselves from the *Umschlagplatz.* Shops of this kind were Hans Miller's, where many Jewish artists, actors, and others perished. There are houses, such as 35, 37, 41, etc., Nalewki Street, which are entirely occupied by hundreds of illegals.

The problem of offering relief to the illegals is becoming daily more pressing. The ex-officials among them receive a ration of soup and bread.

Yom Kippur, September 22

The day there was a selection in the shops.—The slaughter of women, children, illegals.

The practice of torturing Jews in the cities on Yom Kippur.

The barricade of the German and Jewish householders—selection supposedly on the basis of craft,* actually on the basis of graft—the "good Germans" turned bad, e.g., Toebbens.

How the Selection Took Place

In the Jewish council, around 3,000 employees,† elsewhere [in other community institutions] entire departments were sent to the *Umschlag.*—At Hallman's [shop] 700 were numbered off and [exempted] on the spot; the remaining thirty carpenters with their wives and children were taken away.—At the brush factory, 1,200 were numbered off [and exempted], the rest sent away, mechanically, including the shop where the *halutzim* worked, valuable human material, the young.

Thousands of people who had managed to save their lives all the time by staying in their hiding places went to the Niska [quadrangle], because they believed they would be leaving the ghetto for good.

The goal [of the Niska Pot]: to get the secret Jews—the ones in hiding—to come out. [It] succeeded. Tens of thousands taken in the Niska Pot.

Prehistory of the Resettlement

Letter from Lublin [warning about]—Szamek Grayer‡—about 60,000 Jews [to be left] in Warsaw, about a work ghetto [to be set up in Warsaw]—letter from Wlodawa about the [sacrificial] "altar" being set up in the Warsaw neighborhood—the rumor about Pelcowizne—Kohn and Heller's warnings—the S.S. threat to stifle bloodily those who spread these rumors. . . .

The arrival of [Oscar] Lotisz*—the readying of special wagons to Treblinka.

* Handicraftsmen were supposed to be exempt from deportation.

† At one time, the Jewish Council had as many as 5,000 employees.

‡ Jewish Gestapo agent from Lublin sent to Warsaw to help in the extermination.

* The Lett collaborator, to help in the extermination.

How the Blocks Were Set Up

The slaughter at Schultz's [shop]—Nowolipie Street [the site of] the first German barricade—They took thousands of people—gave them half a day to move—the same true at Toebbens'. The activities of the "Jew boys," who proposed such plans, Hallman's humane behavior—negotiated with the House Committees for the gradual yielding of apartments.

The Blocks as Special Ghettos

[With their] own bakeries, drug stores, grocery stores, shoe stores, barbers, even synagogues—separate towns, even to the point of local patriotism—when it came to fund raising.

The hyenas of the shops—workers had to pay money to get into a shop—money for every registration [of the shop's workers].

The work the shops were supposed to do during the barricades—[shops] sprang up quickly, had no orders, had no raw material, [workers] left the factories, except when the Germans came—the same true of the brush factories.

The shops as a means of looking after the workers' families—at first the families were taken to the shops to spend the night there [and avoid being picked up for deportation at home]—hence the idea of blocks—self-contained living and working areas—the slaughter on Nowolipie Street.

Shameful document cited by the Jewish council about the rumors that there would be a resettlement [of Jews from the Warsaw Ghetto] to the east.

[At the same time] the council's work office knew the resettlement meant death.

The suicide of Czerniakow*—too late, a sign of weakness—should have called for resistance—a weak man.

Work Regulations in the Shops

Work period in the summer from seven to seven—O.B.W. [East German Woodworks]. The Jewish inclination to sabotage at Schultz's

* The head of the Jewish council committed suicide on July 24, 1942, after a visit from two S.S. officers, who demanded that the daily quota of those resettled be raised from 5,000 to 7,000 and eventually to 10,000.

two shops—hard work, little food.—The only way to help yourself is to *shabrir*—i.e., to sell the possessions formerly belonging to people who have been resettled—thefts continuing to this day—commerce [in stolen goods].

Confiscation of [the workers'] possessions in the area of [?] the shops—[on the basis of a] new theory: Everything in the shop belongs to the firm—unwritten constitution.

Passes [required] for anyone living outside the shop limits to take anything out of the shop limits.

Language: everything changed to German—all signs—the correspondence at Hallman's conducted in German.

Werkschutz (*Werkschmutz*)†—former policemen—smugglers—underworld characters, etc. Their chief earnings [came from blackmailing] illegals, smuggling, illegal bakeries—Gestapo agent Konrad Toebbens, fictitious shop, took money [from pretended workers] and then sent them to the *Umschlag*—took away the machines that Jews had set up.

1. Earnings from live merchandise—from doing business with [work permit] numbers.

The continuous extortion of the shop workers by the German entrepreneurs, in return for the right to live—for example, Hoffman taxes all the well-to-do [workers in his shop]—the same in other shops, [the pretext for the extortion being] so that the German [entrepreneur] would be interested in protecting "his Jews."

2. Earnings from production—recently have—it seems—dwindled—therefore. . . .

3. Earnings from food supply. Means of subsistence allocated to the workers by the Food Supply Office are sold on the free market.

Health Situation in the Shops

The ambulatory first-aid stations at the brush factories closed—almost all the apothecaries removed, even from the shops.

Apartment Hiding Places

The horrible crowding at Schultz's, Toebbens'—better at Hallman's—the managements' favoring of their relatives—at Toebbens' eight to ten workers in a room—many apartments at Schultz's with-

† A pun. The *Werkschutz,* meaning "work guard" were called *Werkschmutz*—*schmutz* means "filth" in Yiddish.

out light and gas, because the former owners of the apartments didn't pay their electricity bills. Apartments without women—consequently filthy, neglected.

The Distance Between the Residence Block and the Place of Work

There are a number of shops where the distance is great. It is necessary to get up at 5:30 A.M. to go to work. Walk a long distance, and then at night, about six, walk home again without having had anything warm to eat all day. Turns people into real slaves.

Working for Nothing

Everyone has to work for nothing: the workers in the shop, the tailor, the shoemaker, the barber, the doctor, etc.—People live by informing or *"shabriring."*—Since the resettlement, [they] have stopped paying the workers, who used to get starvation wages. The Master Dallmann [?] at Hallman's, who used to earn 100 zlotys a day, nowadays pays 30 zlotys a day for food. Jews may not receive any wages, nor can officials from the Jewish council and other public institutions.

The managers of some of the work shops, inasmuch as they have saved their workers' lives, claim the right to have them work for nothing and insist on the workers' obligation to find their own food. In general, the shop managers regard themselves as philanthropists, who can do whatever they wish, and their workers daren't raise their voices.—They are living a far better life [than they did] before the war, at the expense of the working men, who are robbed in almost every shop. In Hallman's shop, the flour distributed to the shop for feeding the workers is used to bake rolls and doughnuts for the managers and their relatives—and, at the same time, the workers are given bad bread which makes them sick. The managers don't care.

Insecurity, Unclarity of the Situation

Deadline. The Damocles sword of extermination hangs constantly over the heads of the Warsaw Jews. Their fate is tied to that of the shops. So long as the shops have orders, the Jews have the right to live. But it so happens that not all of the shops have long-term orders. Not long ago (mid-October), Schultz's received orders and raw material [sufficient to last] until April—there was universal rejoicing. People drank toasts, threw parties, and the like. But an early deadline hangs over some of the shops. Included in this category is a shop that is one of the most valuable, socially speaking, the O.B.W. shop, whose deadline ended the 20th of October. Eventually, the deadline was extended another thirty days. Put yourself through an effort of the imagination in the minds of those people whose fate is linked with that of the shops. If the shops go out of existence, they lose the right to live. They become people without [work card] numbers, without homes, without food-supply cards.

The Signs of Modern Slaves

1. Numbered and stamped.
2. Live in barracks—without their wives.
3. Wives and children removed, because slaves don't require families.
4. Walk in crowds, not individually.
5. Beaten and terrorized at work.
6. Inhuman exploitation (agreement at Schultz's [?]) like coolies.
7. Ban on organization of any kind.
8. Ban on any form of protest or sign of dissatisfaction.
9. Every slave dependent for his life on his master and the [master's] Jewish assistant. At any moment a man can be sent to the *Umschlagplatz*.
10. The murderous discipline, and the sending of workers to forced [labor] camps because of lateness as happened at Schultz's.
11. Compulsion to work, even [when worker is sick] with temperature.
12. Worse off than slaves, because they must look after their own food.
13. Confiscation of property from a dead worker's family, because the right of inheritance has been abolished.
14. Locked inside the residential block.
15. Ban on leaving your apartment and walking in the street after work hours.
16. Limitation of personal freedom, of movement.
17. Worse than slaves, because the latter knew they would remain alive, had some hope to be set free. The Jews are *morituri*—sentenced to death—whose death sentence [has been] postponed indefinitely, or has been passed.

18. The sick and the weak are not needed, so ambulatory clinics, hospitals, and the like have been liquidated.

Communication

Every shop is a unit in itself; by the decree of [the 29th of] October, one may not leave the shop's bounds. This is true of the ghetto, too. Persons caught in the street without a pass are sent to the *Umschlagplatz.* After work hours (seven in the morning until six or five in the evening in some shops), one can move about somewhat more freely—by attaching oneself to a group that is going from work to its residence block, or to an outside work detail on its way home—but such a group is usually under close supervision, particularly if it is a small one. Individual Jews may not move about the streets.

A second way of being out in the street during the workday hours is to ride in a carriage. They are not bothered, and this is held to be a safe method of passage.

Treblinka—The news about the gravediggers (Rabinowicz, Jacob),* the Jews from Stok who escaped from the wagons . . . loaded with gold and foreign currency—the unanimous description of the "bath," the Jewish gravediggers with yellow patches on their knees. —The method of killing: gas, steam, electricity.

The news about Treblinka brought back by the investigators sent out by the families of those deported there.*—The story about the tractors: According to one version, tractors plow under the ashes of the burned Jews. According to another version, the tractors plow the earth and bury the corpses there [by covering them over].

Treblinka as the Jewish populace sees it—they become aware of the recent extermination.

The Jews from Western Europe have no idea what Treblinka is. They believe it to be a work colony, and on the train ask how far it is to the "industrial factory" of Treblinka. If they knew that they were going to their death, they would certainly put up some resistance. They arrive carrying brand-new valises.

Women, children: shops without women—the breaking up of families—children, whole families annihilated—[parents who] refused

* An escapee from Treblinka, who was the informant.

* In July 1942, Zygmunt (Frydryck) had been delegated to verify the news about Treblinka. He reached Malkinia, where he met Esrael Wallach, an escaped prisoner from Treblinka, who confirmed the worst reports.

to leave their children; husbands who refused [to leave] their wives —the father who wraps his child in a coat to conceal his presence and takes him along to the resettlement. The little criminals who must hide in a room for months on end—the face of a child grimacing with fear at a blockade.

The tragedy of families: thousands of men without wives, men who have remained alive and don't know what they are living for— in general, the tragedy of persons who have lost some thirty members of their family—left all alone in the world—without a purpose in life.

Unhappy the women who had [work card] numbers—depended on them [to be exempted from deportation], and stood in line— those without numbers remained [behind, but] hurried to register their children as errand boys, handwagon pullers—they were all taken away—men protected their wives and children.

The heroism of Dr. Korczak, Koninski, Janowski, refused to leave the children from their home. Korczak built up the attitude that everyone [including directors of the home] should go to the *Umschlag* together. There were directors of homes who knew what awaited them at the *Umschlagplatz,* but held that at a difficult time such as this they could not let the children go alone and must go to their death with them.

The tragedy of parents—the problem of old people—some people poisoned [their elderly] parents—others went to the *Umschlagplatz* with parents; the home for the aged liquidated—[its inmates] carried in rickshas to the *Umschlag* with their valises—children sacrificed themselves to save their parents, most of the older generation done away with—many saved in hiding places—children who didn't [?] protect their parents—in the Y.Y.G.A.—there were scores of eighty-year-old cleaning women.

Most of the old people were lost at the Niska [Street Pot]—[or when their children were] moving into the new residential blocks— or are lying in hiding to this day.

Polish organizations combatted and did away with blackmail. Guard the streetcars.—Pol.[ish] professionals frightened, refuse to accept any Jew.[ish] friends [for protection] outside of the Jewish elements [belonging to their own profession].

As of the end of October, 150 Jews have been seized [who escaped to] the other side. Polish streetcar people's attitude to the Jews very good. Police assigned to work at the streetcar platforms allowed them [Jews] to work without permits, received Jews cordially, good relations. The same true of other outside work details where Jews happened to work alongside Poles.

[Polish] professional colleagues took care of their Jewish associates: Prof. Hirszfeld, Bruno Winawer, etc. [taken care of].

Commerce—Economy. The resettlement produced a great revolution in the economy both of the ghetto and of the Aryan side of Warsaw. Certain items became cheap. Clothing, and particularly linen, was sold at four or five times less than before the resettlement. . . . Bedding was valueless. Pillow cases were removed, and the red [comforter] covers and feather stuffing let out. Bedding lies around in every street, in every courtyard. In some courtyards they set fire to it. Nor have dishes any value—they're thrown into garbage cans. This is true of glass and porcelain dishes, as well as tin ones. Beds, and furniture in general, are worthless. They chop up furniture to heat apartments with the wood. Linen has value only if it is brand new. Second-hand or mended linen is worthless and cannot be sold. A man's suit can be sold for some 300–400 zlotys, i.e., the cost of 2 kilos of ham or butter (1 kilo of butter costs more than 200 zlotys).

The graveyard is an important business center, Christian smugglers coming there. Prices are a little higher there, too. The chief middlemen between the ghetto and the Aryan side of Warsaw are the workers in the outside details, who take things with them to [sell on] the other side. But commerce with the other side has become more difficult lately, because every single work detail is checked, and they are not permitted to take either money or things with them. There was the case of a gendarme shooting a man in a work detail because he was wearing two pairs of pants—one of which he was going to sell on the other side.

Street selling is vigorously combatted by the Germans and their assistants—the Jewish police and the Work Guard. Until a short time ago, the remaining 10 per cent of Warsaw Jews were selling what they had left on Smocza and other streets; now all the selling is going on in the blocks, in homes, and the like. People are busy selling [their last possessions] after work hours.

The Polish police are the most active buyers of Jewish things. The police stations are really commercial agencies where business is transacted all day long. They also purchase gold (35 zlotys a gram as of the end of October), diamonds, foreign currency (a paper dollar is worth 40 zlotys, a gold one 200 zlotys).

Why Were 10 Per Cent of the Jews of Warsaw Allowed to Remain?

Many people have attempted to answer this question, because the answer to a series of fundamental questions hangs on it. How long shall we remain in the ghetto? How long shall we live? How long shall we survive? When shall we be done away with? The opinion of a large group of perceptive persons is that the motive behind their allowing 10 per cent of the Jews to remain in Warsaw is not economic but political. It matters little to them that the Jews are producing, even for the *Wehrmacht*. Germany, which dominates all Europe, can easily make up the [economic] loss sustained by a deportation of Jews. If they took the economic factor into account at all, they would not so casually have sent thousands of first-class craftsmen to the *Umschlagplatz* (incidentally, the S.S. are literally searching high and low for Jewish craftsmen now—carpenters, apprentices, and [offering] good work conditions). The same was true in the provinces, where complete cities were cleaned out of Jews, although the entire Jewish population was engaged in working for the *Wehrmacht*—as for example in Zamoszcz.

The fact remains that, insofar as Jews are concerned, economic criteria do not apply—only political criteria, propaganda. This being so, the question poses itself even more strongly: Why, then, has a "saving remnant" been allowed to remain in Warsaw? The answer is political. If all the Jews were to be cleared out of Warsaw and out of the Government General [of Poland] as a whole, they would lose the Jewish argument. It would be hard for them then to attribute all their difficulties and failures to the Jews. The Jews have to remain, in keeping with the proverb: "God grant that all your teeth fall out, except one to give you a toothache!"

There is another factor that influences the Germans to allow a handful of Jews to remain in Warsaw for a while. It is world public opinion. They have not publicly acknowledged the massacre of millions of Jews. When 40,000 Lublin Jews were liquidated,* the Warsaw newspaper published a news item describing how well off the

* In March and April 1942.

Jews were in Majdan,† how wonderfully they have turned smugglers and fences into "productive elements," living respectable lives in Majdan.

The same is true of Warsaw. They don't want to admit to the world that they have murdered all the Jews of Warsaw, so they leave a handful behind, to be liquidated when the hour strikes twelve—not just for the toothache, but also for the world to see. Hitler will use every means in his power to "free" Europe of all the Jews. Only a miracle can save us from complete extermination; only a speedy and sudden downfall can bring us salvation.

Hence the bitter pessimism dominating the Jewish populace. *Morituri,* that is the best description of our mood. Most of the populace is set on resistance. It seems to me that people will no longer go to the slaughter like lambs. They want the enemy to pay dearly for their lives. They'll fling themselves at them with knives, staves, coal gas. They'll permit no more blockades. They'll not allow themselves to be seized in the street, for they know that work camp means death these days. And they want to die at home, not in a strange place. Naturally, there will only be a resistance if it is organized, and if the enemy does not move like lightning, as [they did] in Cracow, where, at the end of October, 5,500 Jews were packed into wagons in seven hours one night. We have seen the confirmation of the psychological law that the slave who is completely repressed cannot resist. The Jews appear to have recovered somewhat from the heavy blows they have received; they have shaken off the effects of their experiences to some extent, and they calculate now that going to the slaughter peaceably has not diminished the misfortune, but increased it. Whomever you talk to, you hear the same cry: The resettlement should never have been permitted. We should have run out into the street, have set fire to everything in sight, have torn down the walls, and escaped to the other side. The Germans would have taken their revenge. It would have cost tens of thousands of lives, but not 300,000. Now we are ashamed of ourselves, disgraced in our own eyes, and in the eyes of the world, where our docility earned us nothing. This must not be repeated now. We must put up a resistance, defend ourselves against the enemy, man and child.

† The camp at Maidanek, where the Jews from Lublin province were sent for extermination.

PEREZ OPOCZINSKI

The Jewish Letter Carrier

TRANSLATED FROM THE YIDDISH BY E. CHASE

A Jewish postman? Eh, you should be well! Tell me, please, whom do you want? whom are you looking for? We know everyone, you won't have to search long. Do you see, people, luck is with us—we already have a Jewish postman, just like in Palestine.

With these or similar words many a Jew greeted the Jewish letter carrier on the first day of his rounds in the ghetto, and there was something pathetic in the childishly smiling face of the greeter. He looked and he wondered—really? a Jew—a government clerk? One lived through many years in a minority, deprived of rights, so one became bewildered and for a moment forgot the adversities of the ghetto, of the most rightless rightlessness that he was experiencing and wanted rashly to pretend the arrival of a new era, of Jewish autonomy, at least to say. . . .

"Will you wear a postman's cap, too? Ribbons? Numbers?"

"And a leather sack with a strap, too?" inquired another who thought the best part was that the Jewish letter carrier would wear a sword or some other weapon that represents the majesty of the "might." And if not this, at least a cap with a shining visor, a number, a sign, an inscription.

In every Jewish home the letter carrier was met with happy exclamations, amazed kindly eyes, and the friendly welcomes raised him in his own esteem. He drew a feeling of importance from his position, though not often from his social tasks, and the Jewish postman started off on the right foot.

The job aroused among Jews such envy that thousands of men and women looked upon the Jewish letter carrier as upon a select fortunate person at whom lady-luck smiled. No one knows for sure if this was because the letter carrier's post has something romantic about it, that he brings with him a whiff of distant lands, of seas and deserts, or ships and trains; or because he brings happy tidings from sons to old mothers, from bridegrooms to brides, tidings about business successes, weddings and circumcision rites; or simply because Jews reflected on the generous "payoffs" they made, before the war, to the gentile postman, though tips were officially prohibited, and they believed that the Jewish letter carrier, too, would make a nice living at a time when the vast majority of Jews in the ghetto had no means to earn a penny and drew sustenance by selling one by one the household goods. Those were enough reasons for looking with great envy upon the Jewish letter carrier; and this envy was the first drop of poison in his cup of joy. Whenever he entered a house with a letter, the recipient would put it down so indifferently as if it had not mattered, as if something else were of greater importance, and soon quietly, quietly began in cautious words to inquire how he obtained his post—with whose help—through what "pull?"

Another one is eager to accompany the postman downstairs to put it in a businesslike fashion. He speaks in Yiddish and says frankly: "Listen, Mister, you'll get from me two 'centuries' if I get the job. . . ."

In some homes, where no such propositions are made, the inhabitants cannot refrain from remarking seemingly apropos of nothing: "Well, you're all right, you've got a government job."

And people really thought so. They recalled the recent past, when a Polish letter carrier received from the government treasury a monthly salary plus free lighting, heating, shoes, clothing and other allowances, and they naively believed that the Jewish postman, too, must be receiving the same. Particularly when the community gets such high rates for letter deliveries, in addition to the stamps. Others simply imagined that the delivery charge for the letters goes directly to the letter carrier. Which of them could have thought that the "Jewish Post Office" was by the Germans a "storehouse for mail," that the real post office was located on Napoleon Street, outside the limits of the ghetto, and that the community did not receive from the Germans a groshen in support of the "Jewish Post Office?"

When the letter carrier had to listen, in every home, to the complaints against the community, watch the angry looks, see the wry faces, the froth upon the lips with which they fell upon him, as if he truly were the living incarnation of the hated council, he became disgusted with life. Going up the stairs, down the stairs, in each apartment the letter carrier faced the constant nagging harassment, as a man from the State, a council employee, so that he was always irritated, unnerved and found it hard to remain polite and proper.

The attitude toward the Jewish letter carrier could be classified according to population groups. He was best received by the simple folk, worst by the intellectuals and the Hasidim. The simple folk not only paid the service charge but also gave the letter carrier a few groshen as a tip. They did it naturally, without compulsion, in the understanding that each of us wants to live. . . .

Whenever the letter carrier dropped into the basement apartment of the poor shoemaker to deliver a domestic postal card, he would get fifty groshen, and in reply to the admonition that the charge is only twenty groshen, the shoemaker would say in earnest: "The rest is for you, the council does not pay enough to over-eat. . . ."

On the other hand, the demeanor of the bourgeois intellectuals, particularly the doctors, vis-à-vis the letter carrier bordered on hostility. . . . In this case, they, the doctors, stood near to the powers that be. Many of them even worked in the city or government institutions, so, naturally, for them the letter carrier ranked lower in importance as a government employee. They never gave a tip. They were intellectuals and read in the Polish-Jewish sheet, the *Jewish Gazette* (in that sheet which had stated, after the Cracow Edict, that the Government carried out the deportation of 40,000 Jews in a humane manner) the council's appeal to the Jewish population not to pay for mail delivery more than the requisite twenty or thirty groshen. . . . Only a simpleton would give more than the requisite twenty or thirty groshen . . . but they, the intellectuals, knew the "law." They had read it, black on white. . . .

The Hasidim, though, were mainly tradespeople, and if they were not merchants, as such, they had learned the laws of buying and selling, and none of them would offer one grosh above the established price. If the Hasid did differ from the intellectual it was by the demand that the letter carrier speak Yiddish, but even this, it seems, was more politics than genuine impulse, more appearance than Yiddishness. . . .

The benign feeling toward the Jewish letter carrier gradually began to cool off, not due to any fault of his, but to the job itself, the manner of work, due to the community, due to the demoralization brought about by corrupt individuals who wormed their way into the public institutions and by their misdeeds undermined the prestige and prospect of community work in general. This affected the psychology of the masses to such an extent that each community job holder was regarded by them as a representative or agent of a clique. And consequently, the letter carrier's appearances at the homes of the war survivors so excited their already shattered nerves that they often let go at the carrier a torrent of invectives.

That the mail should arrive without delay was of tremendous importance to all; not only to the merchants or the tradespeople, but also the people-at-large. For the little piece of paper, written in a mixture of half Jewish and half corrupted German, often contained the last means of rescue from misfortune—bread and help from relatives in the provinces.

With particularly great hope were awaited the letters from Russia. Many thousands of Jews, after running away to Russia and making a new life there, began sending food packages to their relatives in Warsaw. Husbands sent packages to their wives and children, sons and daughters to their parents, and others to their relatives and friends. The packages from Russia arrived not only well wrapped in linen and sealed with seven seals to prevent pilferage, but they contained food which was here highly prized. The relatives from Russia sent rice, tea, coffee, chocolate and, at the beginning, even whisky and tobacco, too. They sent smoked meats, salami, bacon, cheese and butter and even caviar. When a Warsaw Jew received such a package, he could sell a part of it, as, for example, tea, coffee, tobacco, and whisky, for good money which was enough to live on for several weeks, and use the rest for himself. At the homes where the packages arrived regularly they experienced no want. The packages from Russia had their influence on the market prices and also brought in articles which the Germans would not allow to be imported or which would be very expensive.

Before the arrival of such a package, the sender, of course, would inform about it in a letter, which ordinarily would be received in advance of the package. Therefore, a letter from Russia was regarded not as a piece of paper with writing on it, but as a living messenger of help to come. Old mothers pressed tenderly to the heart with trembling fingers their sons' letters, containing an announcement of a sent-out package, which they imagined would contain goose fat, giblets and delicacies, with which they had regaled their guests at happy family occasions in the past. And wives discerned, with women's intuition, in the enumeration of the things in the letter if the husbands remained faithful. . . .

"You see, Rivkeh," a woman boasted to a neighbor, "my Sholem still remembers that I hanker for a nice piece of goose salami, so he actually sends salami each time, we should all have such a good year!"

And then suddenly they established the Jewish post office. I hope it burns to the ground, and you get no mail and you receive no packages. Whole days you sit at home and wait for the arrival of the letter carrier, but he does not come, and if he does—the letter is —for who do you think?—for the subtenant, for the one who doesn't have there a real relative, but some kind of an acquaintance and he sends him packages. Well, can't one become disheartened? One must have luck in all things. . . .

The town talked; the Jews, terribly incensed, cursed and reviled the Jewish post office, its administration and the whole wretched establishment, but in spite of that the functioning of the post office did not improve at all. . . . The anger of the Jewish population toward the post office was directed against the letter carrier. Whenever he showed himself in a yard, he was surrounded on all sides, pulled by the sleeve, yelled at in his ears, questioned a dozen times the same thing: "No?—there's really no mail for Greenberg? and for Rosenthal? for Morgenstern?" "Mr. Postman" cries a man from his fourth floor apartment, "You have a letter for Tsemach, no? A letter from Russia, have you? No? Take another look. . . ."

Others rush up to the postman, pull the mail out of his hands under the pretext of being helpful, to ease his burden, show the way or spare him stair climbing, and when convinced that he really has no letter for them, they say without mincing words that the fault is the Jewish post office's—before they used to get mail regularly!

The higher the cost of living, the tighter the noose around the neck for the Jews in the ghetto, the more insistent became the inquiry after mail. Tens of thousands of Jews walked around, hands in pockets and one single thought in their minds: Oh, if they but get a letter, be it from Russia, be it from America or if not from there, then even from Konske-Volye, Prashnitz, or Kotsk, where they have relatives—they should remind themselves of our existence and send a package. Some people do get packages from the small towns in Poland, why not we—why should we be miserably unlucky?

This waiting for a package made people deranged. Women would surround the letter carrier and pour such a deluge of questions that he would become physically weary from answering them.

"Mister—you have no letter for me?"

"What is your name?"

"Goldstein."

"Your house number?"

"70."

"No."

"Maybe you have one for number 76? And maybe for number 30?"

"You live in all three apartments?"

"No."

She asks because she is just curious if her neighbor, that slovenly woman who eats non-kosher, had not received perhaps a letter, and she *must* know.

It happens that the letter carrier by chance passes through a neighborhood where he has never delivered mail and where the people on the street don't know him, but they do know that the Jewish post office does not assign a steady carrier to a district, the carriers are changed almost daily—yet, he is stopped by strangers who inquire: "Listen, Mister, have you a letter for me? No? Not perhaps from Russia?"

A letter from Russia, a letter from Russia—that was the pleasantest dream for most people, their sweetest hope, their last comforting thought. Even the children, whose hearts beat in unison with their parents' suspenseful expectancy, never permitted the carrier to make an unmolested step on the street. They would besiege him, and with their young screeching voices deafen him. And if fortune smiled and the letter carrier *had* a letter for the parents, the child rushed helter-skelter up the stairs, yelling at the top of his voice and bursting into the house announced breathlessly: "Daddy dear, Mamma dear, a letter from Srulik, from Isirel, Yohebed. I saw with my own eyes the letter with a Russian stamp. . . ." "Oh, children, a letter from Srulik, no ill come to me"—the woman would clutch her heart—"run children quickly, bring the letter. Here, take this money, Oh, Father dear in heaven. . . ."

The woman's head reeled. The letter assumes the guise of a big head of cheese, a long salami, a sizeable slice of creamery butter. She sees nothing else, she hears nothing, she reaches out with her hands as if to grasp the fat delicious foods to put them into the pot.

The letter carrier feels weary and worn. The people, nervous and hungry, pull him by the sleeve and want an answer to a thousand questions a day, not alone about letters, but about new post office regulations, about sending money, registered mail, air mail, police, taxes and what have you. Isn't he a government personage, a man close to the "might?"

The carrier's lot is an unhappy one. He rises at five in the morning and works till nine, ten in the evening and, in spite of that, he receives no weekly wage, but gets paid by the piece—six groshen per letter, and after subtracting all taxes and contributions to "social insurance," from which he, as a Jew, cannot benefit according to the canons of the occupation authorities, but for which he enjoys the privilege of paying, there hardly remains five groshen net. The delivery of one hundred, even one hundred and fifty letters a day nets him a ridiculous sum, when a loaf of black bread costs between 22 and 24 gilden. . . . The few tips he gets do not change the situation much. The conditions under which he works are so unbearable that they affect his health. The "energetic" director who wants to carry on like a drill master and disciplinarian often calls the employees to a conference, and demands of them sternly to come to work not later than eight o'clock in the morning, otherwise he will take strict measures, he will be swayed by nothing, you may believe him, he does not like just to throw around words in the air, and, he concludes pathetically, if he wants to, he can fine and even discharge one from the service, because there must be order!

And the order was such that carriers came to work in winter, in freezing weather and snow, not at eight, but rather six in the morning, because first come first served. The sorting machine worked from morning till night, yet it did not produce enough bundles of mail for carriers to distribute. A number of carriers always were forced to go home empty handed after waiting all day, hungry and freezing, in the cold corridors with cement floors. Who was lucky to get a bundle of mail in the first place? Only those who came at five or six o'clock in the morning and of them mainly the people belonging to the "battalion," which really meant the director's people, with whom he worked under the Germans.

The battalion people are a special chapter in the life of the Jewish post office. They were Polish speaking, the heirs to the "shmendriks." It was they who brought with them the military order of the German work gangs, where they formerly were section leaders. They boasted of being privileged, of having received decorations and awards for merit. It was rumored that some of them served the Germans in a confidential capacity and were informers. These people were employed in all institutions of the community, and were feared even by those in higher positions. They were known as "Gestapo Men." The battalion people absolutely refused to utter a single word in Yiddish.

They had their set of morals. Being approximately sixty of a total number of one hundred letter carriers, the power resided in their hands. They posted their men at the door where packages of mail were issued. The distributor of the packages, too, was of their men, and naturally favored the battalion men by giving them packages for the richest streets, houses with easy stairs to climb, clean apartments and good tips, while the others received packages for distribution in the poorest streets and alleys with houses having stairs in poor repair, dark cellars, damp attics impregnated with typhus germs.

In the beginning the more favored packages were given out surreptitiously, later on openly and shamelessly. The argument was that the battalion people earned the preference for the "services" rendered to the Jewish community, and those who had the effrontery to disagree were treated harshly.

Their people with their peculiar social concepts were responsible, it seems, for the suspicion that the carriers were guilty of theft. There were cases when women came to the post office and swore that when the carrier left the house, a golden watch left it too, or that letter carrier stole a pair of galoshes. . . .

But why talk about house theft, when the theft of arrived packages was enough to put the entire Jewish post office under suspicion.

True, the post office for mail delivery and the package unloading station were located on two different streets, and the letter carriers and package carriers had no contact with each other, although both wore the identical arm bands with identical inscriptions, but the ordinary garden variety of Jews did not know about the fine points of difference, and when a letter was delivered to a home, the recipient would fall upon the letter carrier in a disgraceful manner, because the last package delivered was tampered with and half of the contents stolen.

Often enough, instead of sugar the recipient would find salt (to make up the weight), instead of cocoa from Portugal, wormy peas, or sometimes the package would just be deficient in weight, and the package carrier, in addition, would charge double for delivery and pocket the overcharge.

Of course, it was difficult to ascertain how the thefts were done, since the packages first came to the real post office on Napoleon Street and only then were sent to the ghetto post office. One may assume that the employees of the Polish post office pilfered heavily, knowing well, that the onus would, in the end, fall on the last deliverer, the Jewish post office. Yet it was certain that there were large thefts in the Jewish post office, too. This could be noted in the fact that the employees were in cahoots when a theft complaint was lodged. . . . Jews who had relatives in the small Polish towns that were "united" with the German Reich often received letters in which would be enclosed five paper marks (legally it was not allowed!), and the letters just as often arrived minus the money. Who did it, remains a mystery. . . .

It is true, that when the letter carrier received his bundle of mail not at nine in the morning, as the custom was before the war, but at four or five in the afternoon, the difficulties of satisfying the demands of his conscience greatly increased. For the distribution of mail in the evening in the Jewish neighborhood, where the house numbers were twisted and turned and could not be read, became an almost impossible task, particularly in wintertime, when climbing the slippery stairs, often broken down or still ruined since the bombardment, presented a threat to life and limb. In addition the Jewish house watchmen, the guards of the house, were "new faces."* When asked where this or that tenant lived, they could not answer, or often insisted that no such person lived in the house, when it was known that he lived right under the watchman's nose.

And then again, the knocking at the door late in the evening was a frightful experience! Jews, because of tortures and searches, trembled when they heard a knock on the door even in daytime, and for that reason the residents of large apartment houses, which had additional entrances through the kitchens, put up heavy locks outside on the front doors to give the impression that no one was home. . . . Imagine their feelings, when in a snowy or rainy dark winter evening, while the apartment was dim, cheerless and quiet, and the least noise sounded to them, because of their shattered nerves, like the rumbling of the wheels on a bridge; imagine then their feeling when at this time someone banged on the door and, receiving no immediate response, banged again and again, for the mail must not tarry, and it was late. Blood congealed in the veins,

* After separating the ghetto from the city and removing the Polish population from Jewish streets, the jobs of house watchmen in Jewish neighborhoods were filled, naturally, exclusively by Jews.

and the more insistent the banging, the more the panic rose. When finally, gambling with their lives, they inquired, "Who's there?" and received back the answer, "The post," their hearts nearly succumbed. And when they at last opened the door to admit the unexpected guest, they were not overjoyed at his coming, even had he brought a registered letter from Russia. For the enmity against the Jewish post, against the hated council, could not be stifled, and the postman got all they could give.

In the Homes on Krochmalnia and Ostrowska Streets

The endless claims and arguments against the letter carrier can be summed up as follows: he knocked too loudly on the door, the mail delivery was needlessly delayed, the packages were being pilfered, and finally—the most important—the payment for delivery. These words poisoned the carrier's life, made him weary in body and mind, because the argument about payment was really justified. In some streets, as many as 80 per cent of the recipients could not redeem their letters and had to rush to borrow from their neighbors. On many occasions a recipient of a letter knocked at the doors of all neighbors on his floor, on the floor above, on the floor below, from the top to the ground floor until he could finally borrow the necessary twenty or thirty groshen, for hardly anyone had a grosh in the house. For if they got a few gilden from the sale of some household thing, they ran forthwith to the storekeeper to buy a quarter kilo, at best, a half kilo of bread.

Ordinarily, the recipient would appeal to the carrier to lend them payment money—"It is only twenty groshen," was the pathetic plea. "Have a heart, it's such a small sum; when you pass by another time, I'll pay back."

When the carrier would explain that most of the houses had no money and he would be forced to lose out of his own pocket several gilden daily instead of earning any—he was not believed. "You're worse than the goyim," was the angered reply. "The goy carrier always trusted me, but the Jewish post, the council with its 'clerks,' are such as to deserve eternal perdition, like Cain."

But all this pain and trouble was nothing against the desolate pictures of helplessness and need the letter carrier must have encountered in his going from house to house in the valley of tears of Krochmalnia, Ostrowska, Smocza and Niska.

In these streets the doors of the houses remained locked till late in the day. People lay in bed until two or three in the afternoon. Others never got up. There was no reason to get up. On winter days one could find in the homes of the larger families ten to twelve people, oftentimes young adult men or women, lying in bed, with pale faces and feverish eyes, and swallowing their saliva. Mothers lay in bed together with two or three children; they lay in red rashes because of the lack of the few groshen needed to buy soap for washing the bedsheets. In the house the things were scattered about in frightful disorder, which proved the truth of the saying: "Their dress bespeaks their state." The people had but one single insane thought —where to get a piece of bread? Mothers were no housekeepers and fathers no repairmen. Doors did not fit, stoves did not work, chairs and tables were unclean, floors unscrubbed. What for? Who cares? . . .

From lying constantly in bed, people became weaker and weaker, and many already could not take a step, others had bodies swollen to the waist and higher. The eyes of some could hardly be seen, they disappeared behind the swollen lumps around the eye sockets. This gave them the appearance of dark Mongols, of hungry Eskimos.

On entering the homes of such hunger-tortured people, the letter carrier had two alternatives: take the letter back to the post office with a notation that the recipient was unable to redeem it because he had no money, or to remember that the delivered letter might contain help to save the wretched man, and often this was the case. The letter carrier himself, therefore, had to egg on the neighbors to redeem the letter, himself assume the social responsibility of doing something. For it was no feat at all to return to the post office and say that this one or that one could not pay. The letter with the explanatory notation would calmly be taken back by a clerk. The loquacious director, who never ceased talking glibly about social responsibility, did not himself possess enough social responsibility to convince the council that, for instance, the refugees, the extremely poor, the sick and even the insane, should have their mail delivered free. The director was "smart" enough to keep the budget balanced, to see to it that the post office has no deficit. As to the rest, let the letter carrier break his head—and he really did.

When the letter carrier returned home at night to his wife and children and a cold house, with his meager earnings of the day, he was in a state of irritation from the endless arguments. He was haunted by the scenes of poverty and misery which he witnessed throughout the day. All this depressed his spirit and gave him no peace. It did not take long for the letter carriers themselves to become swollen from hunger and hard work, and acquire weak hearts from continually climbing up and down the stairs. But the community remained the community. It cared as little about the welfare of the carriers, whom it refused to provide even with shoe repairs, as it did about the refugees, the newcomers or the homeless children roaming the streets. Is it a wonder that carriers often fell sick and that their rate of mortality increased tremendously?

As if this were not enough, false accusations were heaped upon the Jewish letter carrier. A Jew loves to demand his due. Many Jews boast of their ability to reach the high and the mighty. It's not enough to talk to an ordinary clerk, they want the head. As a result they ran every Monday and Thursday to the post office for all sorts of nonsense. They would not rest till they got to the boss himself, to the director, that is; and he, the "boss," sticking out his chest and turning his head to one side, as it was his wont, half-closed his eyes, became very serious, like an angry Hebrew teacher, and called out the carrier against whom a complaint was lodged. First, the boss ordered in a loud voice that the accused be temporarily relieved of his duties of distributing mail until his case was decided. And the inquiry began. The director opened the investigation with wise remarks, attempts to trap the accused wth his own words, with needling him, so that the one who brought the accusation derived tremendous satisfaction and pleasure. What a smart fellow (knock wood!) the director is, thought the accuser. And the director himself was pleased, no doubt, with his conduct of the inquiry and, in his heart, admired his own wisdom and power. Thus, the inquiry went on and on, and such inquiries on many occasions delayed the distribution of mail for two or three hours. Well, only a Jewish post office director can permit himself the enjoyment of such things.

It was usual for the director, after such a triumphant inquiry, to come out to the people in the cold corridor with the concrete floor—he was dressed in those cold winter days in his wife's plush jacket, which reached just over his knees, to show, to prove that there is a war on and that he is the man who knows how to save and how to spare the community the necessity of heating the post office—to announce triumphantly that soon, in the near future, benches would be provided in order that people wouldn't have to stand on their feet from five in the morning until four or five in the afternoon.

He said this very definitely in a voice trembling with pathos and preoccupied with human injustice until his anger passed, and he said this again on a similar occasion two weeks later. Thus, in the end, five months after the establishment of the post office, the benches became a reality. . . .

However, the letter carrier with a truly social approach to his duties experienced also minutes of joy and happiness that partly outweighed the heartrending griefs of the day. This occurred when he succeeded in delivering a letter to an unknown recipient.

Letters used to arrive, mainly from across the seas, to people at their addresses of 15 or 20 years before. People had relatives in America or Argentina, Uruguay or South Africa from whom they had never received any letters. But now such relatives in the far away places learned from the newspapers about the hellish sufferings of the Polish Jews and their hearts melted. Immediately they dispatched letters, probably ready to send help upon the receipt of an answer.

And it was impossible to find the addressee. It was useless to go to the watchmen for information, because, as mentioned before, the new watchman did not have the least idea. What was left to do? Go from house to house and inquire. This required patience, social responsibility, and the will to do the right thing.

But if the reader had witnessed the scene when the letter carrier, after a long search, finds an old mother to whom a daughter writes from Paris, after four years of silence, and inquires if she, her mother, needs anything, maybe a package of food, how this old mother claps her hands, tears streaming from her eyes, and clutches at her heart crying out: "O, my Broche dear, my good child, you did not forget your old mother!" If the reader had witnessed this, he would have confessed that the letter carrier had some compensation for his troubles, not so much in money, as in the warm glances of a mother's eyes, which is worth much more than money. . . .

In another house, the letter carrier delivers a letter from a son to his parents. The son writes from overseas that he learned his family is alive, saved miraculously during the terrible bombardment of Warsaw. The sister, a bride-to-be, is holding her brother's letter in her hand in a delirium of joy. The mother is speechless from astonishment, and an old grandfather, his hair snow white, stands in the middle of the room with face pale from excitement and hands upraised, as in a priestly benediction, and looks with deep gratitude on the letter carrier.

Someone of the household goes to the letter carrier and hands him a tip of a few groshen, and the letter carrier stands, as if implanted, and eagerly swallows with his eyes this remarkable picture. Of what value are the few groshen compared to the expressions of human solidarity and loving kindness?

The Jewish letter carrier is only an ordinary man, one among the many against whom the extermination machine is directed. He has a heart, and in every house, where he brings unexpected letters to the mothers awaiting them for years, he quietly shares in their joys.

And suddenly—b-o-o-m!

War with Russia!

The thousands and thousands of homes, which regularly receive packages from Russia, are aflutter and atremble. Firstly, what will one do now, how will one live? Secondly, the children in Russia, in the newly occupied places, in Bialystok or Baranowich, in the first line of fire. . . .

He goes from house to house, from parents with one son, who is located near the front, to parents with two or three sons—all of them in Russia. And everywhere they ask him, the man from the government, to tell them, for he probably knows: What threatens them, what awaits them? Will they live to see their children?

The first returnees already appeared on the Smocza. Lads, straight as trees, they didn't think long and quickly ran back to Warsaw. Parents wait and hope that their children, too, shall decide to do the same—and there is pandemonium at the post office. The letters become fewer day by day. Thousands of letters sent out to Russia in the last few days are coming back with a stamped German notation "Post Office Closed." It is thought that in a few days all mail from Russia will come to a full stop, and with this, also, a great part of the income of the Jewish post office. The director half closes his right eye and says, like the wiseacre that he is: "And maybe . . . who knows, maybe the post office will be closed for good," and this way, he thinks, he answers all questions of the letter carriers about insufficient food, hard work, worn-out shoes and impaired health.

The nightmare in Jewish Warsaw becomes thicker, the hopes—slimmer. There are no more letters from Russia, no more packages from Russia. There are only brick tenements, red, monotonous, cold ghetto-tenements, like disheartening prisons. Who cares about the Jewish post office, who worries about the Jewish letter carrier's swollen feet?

LEVI SHALIT

Smugglers

TRANSLATED FROM THE YIDDISH BY ADAH FOGEL

If you wanted to survive in the ghetto you had to risk your life—unless you were among the handful who had hidden away huge amounts of cash, gold and diamonds, and could afford to live on the chances taken by others. For a large sum of money you could get anything—even during the starvation days when the Lithuanian police and the S.S. guarded every hiding place in the ghetto day and night. But the Jews outsmarted them, and bought off the sentries with gold and diamonds.

These "traders" took great risks. They walked right into the lion's jaw, and many times paid with their lives.

Why did they do it?

Were they compelled by nothing more than a primitive lust for riches even here, on the threshold of death? Or did their behavior manifest a form of resistance, a bold determination to survive while keeping others from starving to death?

At any rate, the dealers supplied and supported the ghetto, providing its hapless inhabitants with potatoes, bread, and sometimes even a piece for meat—for nothing.

Did they intend only to appease the hunger-maddened populace and protect themselves against informers? What were the motivations of these defiant dealers and life-givers who moved about the ghetto in tight-lipped silence, their faces stiff with obstinacy and fear?

Their subsequent struggle in the concentration camps in defense of Jewish honor and human rights suggests that only intense nationalism could have awakened them in the dark nights, thrust them through the barbed wires of the ghetto, and driven them, without their yellow patches, through hostile villages to keep the ghetto from starving.

For some it was like an exciting game of chance, a gamble. Strong and impetuous, they could not tolerate confinement behind the dense wires so long as there was the merest crevice through which to escape. And the narrower the opening, the more enticing the game. The triumph of surmounting hazards was stronger than fear.

Only a handful became traders for the sole purpose of amassing wealth by taking advantage of the market situation.

It is the first winter in the ghetto. Like gray-black hair fringing bald pates, the grimy snow lies in the gutters along both sides of the bare streets.

Everyone travels by wagon, but Artzik Krupnik has a sled. Although Artzik pushes with his burly shoulders twice as hard as his horse, the poor beast is bathed in sweat, because it can barely budge the sled over the cobblestones. Artzik has calculated the risk involved. His sled, like his cart, has a hidden double deck, but because it is so low-slung, the police at the ghetto gates never take the trouble to lie down and search below, as they do with the cart.

Like the other two drivers in the ghetto, Artzik was allowed to keep his horse in order to bring supplies to the cooperative. He does not spare his animal. Quietly he talks things over with the horse: "Come on, Max, you won't drop dead if you drag another two hundred pounds of potatoes hidden in the bottom of the sled, in addition to the two hundred pounds on top, among the chunks of wood. The Jews are hungry. I promised to bring them potatoes today." The horse hauls potatoes, flour and meat—everything that is loaded on to his skinny back, and Artzik, with his last ounce of strength, helps push the sled.

With words and with the whip, Artzik makes it clear to Max that they must hurry and get to the ghetto gates right now, because the policeman on guard is a friend of his, or the workers are marching back into the ghetto. At the calculated moment Artzik drives his wagon headlong into the cluster of Jews waiting for roll call at the ghetto gates. In the ensuing confusion, the Jews sneak into the ghetto. Artzik tears off his coat, and with great bravado tells the sentry that he is prepared to overturn the wagonload of wood or flour which he is delivering to the ghetto bakery. Let it be inspected! But by this time the harassed policeman takes Artzik's word for it—he believes that Artzik is carrying only what can be seen in the wagon.

But sometimes the policeman turns out to be a dolt who is not impressed by Artzik's valor, and orders him to unload for inspection. In such a predicament, a thousand marks is not too much, and if the sentry is unusually obstinate, the ghetto can produce a gold watch—if only to save Artzik from death.

When the wagon enters the dark courtyard of the ghetto, it is surrounded by a swarm of women and children. They plead, shout, pull at Artzik's coattails. Artzik remains calm. He wipes the sweat from his brow and begins the distribution. Yentl and Feiga each get twenty pounds of potatoes gratis, as he had promised, because their children are sick. But the lawyer's wife pays twenty marks for a hundred pounds—to compensate for those who can't pay. Artzik quickly empties the wagon, in which the potatoes had been camouflaged under pieces of wood. Then he drags out the half-side of beef from the sled's belly and distributes that, selling it in large pieces. He has no scale. He cuts the meat as best he can.

Nattes and Yaches live in the same house, share one barn and one business: a butcher shop.

At night, while the ghetto sleeps its deep sleep, they are awake. They have made a pact with the night: she serves them best when she is starless—the darker, the better.

Their house stands close to the barbed-wire fence. When the electric light in their house is switched off and on one time, the peasant waiting with the cow on the other side of the fence knows the road is clear, that the sentry has either been bought off or is asleep. Behind the hill the peasant with the cow starts toward the ghetto. If the cow is black, good. If not, she is wrapped in a coat. The peasant leads her just up to the fence. Yanke-Mende, the butchers' apprentice, pulls apart the wires at a spot where he had cut them, creating an opening. The cow's hoofs are wrapped in rags to blot out her footprints in the snow, and they hold her mouth closed with their hands. The butcher is waiting in the barn, and by sunrise the meat is waiting in the baskets left the night before. Each one comes for his basket, pays 30 marks per kilo, and takes his share.

The Jewish police are annoyed with the Nattes-Yaches enterprise. It is too risky. Every day a cow, and so "openly." They confiscate the meat, but Yaches takes payments on loan. The next day he brings another cow and this time he has to watch out for the Jewish police, too.

For half a year the ghetto thus enjoys kosher meat, and Yaches maintains: "For a kilo of meat you get arrested, but for a whole cow—never. If you post sentries by the wire fence, I'll drop the cow into the ghetto by parachute."

Finally the Security Police find out about the meat business in the ghetto. Although they don't catch anyone red-handed, they force the community council to disclose the culprits. Yaches and Nattes are sentenced to prison, but not before the dealer Glizenstein is forcibly surrendered for execution. Those who are most active in appeasing the ghetto's hunger are hidden.

In a dilapidated shack by the wall of the ghetto cemetery, seven young men took up residence. They called themselves the Revisionist Kibbutz—a remnant of a Revisionist Kibbutz in Lutsk, Poland; comrades of Solomon ben Joseph. They had fled to Lithuania, and later landed in this ghetto. They lived together, shared every morsel of bread. They persuaded the Jewish leader of the Labor Brigade to allow the youngest of their group to keep house for them. He washed all their clothes, cooked, and tidied the little room while the other six worked in the *Kommandos* (work detail). The seven looked like brothers: strapping, broad-shouldered, with secretive eyes behind which lurked an eternal, unspoken conspiracy.

When two of them were assigned to hard labor in the peat bogs outside the ghetto, all six took turns; the burdensome and the easy tasks were divided among them.

It was the second winter in the ghetto and the situation was critical. People were starving. The group decided to activate its strength and daring. After work, two of the comrades in the railway detail detached themselves from the group and remained in hiding until it got dark. Then they bought fifty or more loaves of bread from someone, crammed them into a sack and returned to the ghetto, waiting outside the cemetery fence for a signal. Inside their comrades watched for the moment when the sentries gathered at the gate, or were patrolling inside the ghetto. Then the signaler, who was posted on the roof of their shack with a flashlight, was alerted. At his signal, the boys on the other side raced toward the cemetery wall with the sack of bread; those inside ran across the cemetery to meet them and helped them climb over the wall.

They worked all winter. One night a shower of bullets burst over their heads. Hillel Katchuba, the oldest and strongest of the seven, tossed his comrade together with the sack of bread over the fence—and he himself was caught by the police.

Several days later Kellier, chief of the Security Police, told the Jewish representatives: "I've never seen such a Jew. I practically beat him to death, but he refused to tell me where he got the bread and who his accomplices are."

Three months later, when the Germans needed Jews for labor in the peat bogs, they released from prison all the Jews who were still alive—about seventy in all. Katchuba was among them. He was replaced in the peat bogs by the comrade whom he had rescued.

Long months afterward, Katchuba's body still showed the raw places from which chunks of flesh had been torn out.

His comrades found a better occupation—helping to plan the resistance movement in the ghetto. Some of them went into the forest.*

More than once Baylke has come face to face with death. More than once bullets have grazed her as she leaps over the barbed wire fence. But now that she has the task of transporting excrement out of the city, there is much less risk.

Actually her husband was assigned to the job, but Baylke, who is more capable and more daring, seizes the reins in her chunky hands and drives the horse herself. The cart filled with feces trundles on two huge wheels through all the remote streets of the town to the public toilets, which the city council had ordered to be cleaned. After they are emptied, the waste is deposited outside the city.

Baylke is everywhere, constantly in touch with her Christian neighbors in the surrounding villages; she sells them everything the ghetto gives her in exchange for produce. Her hiding-place is safe—inside the sealed tin box in the cart of excrement.

Twice a day, at noon and in the evening, she rides into the ghetto, takes the hidden box from the wagon, and removes from it bread, butter, fat and meat.

Everyone in the ghetto knows where Baylke takes the merchan-

* A week after the liberation of Dachau in May 1945, one of the seven—Yehuda Turiski—put a loaf of bread under his arm and, dressed in the uniform of the concentration camp, set out to make his way to Palestine. Another one, Buzik, was one of the leaders of the exodus from Europe. Katchuba and Eliyahu are in Palestine. Itzik died fighting the Germans.

dise, but nobody objects. On the contrary—they plead with her to take something to sell or exchange. They know their things won't get lost or confiscated. Not from Baylke's hiding place.

Edelman was born to be a poet, but the struggle for subsistence forced him to become a fisherman. He rode out over rivers and lakes, caught fish and sold them. Every woman who bought his fish received a gift of several rhymes. Those who didn't buy were serenaded with couplets . . . until they yielded. Even Edelman's advertisements about his fish business were in rhyme.

Although Edelman was already in his forties, he still wanted very much to be a poet. From time to time one of his light, satirical verses would appear in a newspaper, and in this way Edelman appeased his frustration over the fish business. The one good part of it is that he had to spend a great deal of time on the broad, shining waters, under open skies.

In the ghetto there are no rivers, except rivers of blood and tears. Edelman sings about all the events in the ghetto, and his admirers listen and weep, listen and laugh.

You can't survive on poetry in the ghetto, so Edelman became a fish dealer, too. He gets his supplies from friendly gentile fishermen, smuggles them into the ghetto, and the Jews are able to enjoy a piece of fish on the Sabbath—to spite all their enemies!

Although Edelman is in the fish business, sometimes it can't hurt to throw in a piece of meat. . . .

A friendly policeman was on guard at the ghetto gate, and Edelman made a pact with him. He disappeared for just a few minutes, and returned with a sled full of meat—right into the clutches of the police. His friend had betrayed him.

When the Gentile woman, Adamowicz, who had sold the meat to Edelman, learned that he was in prison, she ran to the Lithuanian police, knowing full well that she, too, was in danger. Adamowicz was constantly helping the Jews. Those whom she knew she gave things to for nothing; with others she did big business. She bought Jewish merchandise and paid for it with food and basic needs. If Edelman were forced to reveal her name, the police would find in her possession a vast store of Jewish goods which had been smuggled to her at night. Adamowicz finally made a deal with the Lithuanian police: the next day, when Edelman was turned over to the Security Police, they found only one of the four sacks of meat—full of bones.

The Jews waited for Edelman in the ghetto, anxious to know how severely he was beaten and how he had escaped death. But Edelman, bruised as he was, rushed for pen and paper. "Later, I'll tell you everything later." The description was complete in his head, down to the last rhyme.

At night he emerged from seclusion, feverish from his wounds and his creative fire. Edelman read his biting parody, and the Jews roared with laughter. The poem did not tell about the beatings, but about Elijah the Prophet, who opened the sacks, cut off the meat, and left only the bones. It told about German stupidity and Lithuanian simplicity:

As many teeth from our foes
As there was meat
On the bones. . . .

ISAIAH SPIEGEL

The Ghetto Kingdom

TRANSLATED FROM THE YIDDISH BY MOSHE SPIEGEL

A pale streak of light cuts through the dark, heavy clouds of night, as if it were a sword smiting the sky. Soon the east is streaked with soft red light, and the dark clouds withdraw and fade into the blushing dawn. The morning breeze carries a pale gray mist over them and, all at once, the sky is white and transparent. The edge of a sad, red, rayless sun appears over the city while the whisps of clouds vanish.

It is still night over the ghetto, as if daylight were ashamed to rest on the silent wooden thresholds and old walls of Balut. It comes timidly, moving jerkily and strangely through the streets.

As the sickly sunlight descends upon the ghetto, thin, tired figures emerge from semi-darkness under stairwells, from dank cellars and tiny huts. These were once rich, proud people who now hurry haggardly through the ghetto streets with small sacks held close to their chests. They move in small armies, like companies of mice, attracted by the rotting, gray offal and sticky muck in the garbage pails on the ghetto streets. The pails hold no discarded food, for who would throw away anything that could somehow be made edible? There are not even potato peelings in these pails, for it has been found that if rubbed carefully under well water, washed and ground into flat cakes, potato peelings taste as sweet as cake, even though they are black and sticky and gritty in the mouth. They still can stir bright dreams of wheat bread from far away kitchens in a far away life.

At noon a tired, wan sun gives faint light over the narrow alleys. The scavenger armies retrace their steps, their eyes flickering with an unhealthy green sparkle. Their sacks are filled with the offal they could find, and when they reach home their children fall upon the garbage eagerly. Mother buries her emaciated fingers into the muck, searching, finally raising a hand holding something dark and slippery. Her cheeks, green and hollow, seem to shine.

Ghetto dwellings seem to float into some strange land on another planet, under a different sky, no longer sickly and pale. Good tidings warm the children's hungry hearts, for in their little hands they hold the newly found food, still hot, sizzling, black and sinister.

In the marketplace, once overflowing with greenery and delicacies, strange people stand selling sticky, dark food stained a false green. At a table women in dark head scarfs with golden Mogen Davids sell sliced, quartered pieces of bread soft and moldy with age. This is the bread that can be obtained on ration. The women selling it look at the bread with half closed eyes, looking as if bewitched by the food. They wail funereally, their emaciated bodies and fallen breasts caught up in sorrow.

One man is walking back and forth, three potatoes in his hands. Two are smooth and large, the third, rotten. The buyer must take all three. A knot of people gathers to stare at the treasure. None can buy, but it is good to see a real potato again.

Mothers hold their children, trying to drag them home, remembering the years when the marketplace was filled with good food.

Suddenly peasant wagons, carts and tents filled the market. Peasants sit among the open sacks filled with vegetables, potatoes and red beets. Young men hold cracking whips to chase the petty crooks who slip behind the wheels into the carts. Women sit on the sides of the carts, sacks of cabbages and radishes between their knees. The smells of the country fill the air. A woman walking near the carts siezes her throat, as if suffocating, and falls to the ground in a faint.

Behind the marketplace is the red gate of the Holy Mary Church, silent, deserted, imprisoned within the Jewish ghetto. The winds of past generations blow through its cracks, and the low fence encircling the church seems to have shrunk even smaller. The huge iron doors are rusted and always hang open. Jewish women in head kerchiefs and men covered with white feathers run through its long, cold, empty corridors. This is the place where bedding used by Jews is stuffed—with white down and soft feathers brought from nearby villages and stained with Jewish blood and tears. High in the cupola, the clock has stopped, and only the wind moves around the bells. On the narrow window panes round-faced saints watch the busy Jews with sorrowful eyes. From their golden halos comes a shaft of yellow light, carried by the wind high up to the bells, which tinkle occasionally in the breeze.

The Jews, stuffing their big gray sacks with down, look up suddenly at a shaft of light. A soft sound comes from the muted bells. The bells, as if bewitched, begin to sway gently, their music growing stronger and reaching out over the nearby fields. The Jews are afraid to raise their heads now, and while the corridors fill with sound they huddle together in a corner, their heads bent in terrible fear of church shadows. One of them sobs a prayer. "Oh, Lord of the Universe! Have mercy on Thy people Israel! Take pity on Thy poor people!"

Above, the wind whistles from the empty lofts.

It is evening, and the marketplace and the church are veiled in the blue haze of twilight. Tall chestnut trees rustle in the night wind beside the church. Curfew has come for the Jews.

In a small street not far from the church stands a shrine housing an eternal light. Within stands a marble figure of the crucified one. As the darkness deepens the red, constant light behind the statue grows sharper. The holy flame lights the face of the last Jew hurrying home before curfew is enforced. Across the barbed wire of the ghetto entrance jackboots pound the earth. The Germans are entering the ghetto. The shrine in the heart of the ghetto is aflame. His emaciated, tortured, Jewish body is shrouded in a warm crimson cloak of blood.

JACOB CELEMENSKI

With My Martyred People

TRANSLATED FROM THE YIDDISH BY MIRRA GINSBURG

For over five years during World War II, I lived under the Nazi reign of terror in Poland. I endured all the suffering and faced all the dangers and ordeals that destiny had meted out to the Jews. Again and again, I was on the brink of destruction, but each time something helped me to return to life. Whenever I seemed to walk the final road, a narrow pathway would appear that led me back into the struggle.

Fate had allotted me a special mission. I was able to assume the identity of an "Aryan," and as such I visited great numbers of Jewish cities and towns in Nazi-occupied Poland. As a courier of the underground Bund (the Jewish Socialist Workers' Union), I carried aid and the forbidden Jewish printed word to Jews confined in ghettos and camps, and later also to those who had found hiding places on the Aryan side, in cities, villages and forests. Before my eyes passed the whole tragic story of my people's martyrdom.

My travels began when the great Jewish communities of Poland still existed, and continued throughout the period when they were bled to death. I also visited small towns where the last Jews struggled through the days before they, too, were taken to their ultimate destruction. I traveled by railway as a "Pole," trying to bring help to the few surviving remnants of Polish Jewry in their pitiful hiding places, where death loomed over them from every side. My eyes were witness to the picture of my people in its last agony. Finally, in September 1944, I also fell into the net of the Nazi hangmen and remained in it until the end of the war.

Today I am one of the survivors. For twenty years I have constantly heard within my mind the very cry of the murdered: Tell it to the world! I knew it was my duty to fulfill this last bequest of those who were driven away to destruction. Yet, I have always asked myself: Can it be told? Will the story truly reflect the suffering of our martyred people? Doubts bound my will. . . .

But time is leaving those terrible days further and further behind. And I began to fear that the pictures engraved in my memory and in my heart might, after all, start fading. I have therefore decided to tell what I have lived through and what I have seen of the great Jewish catastrophe.

I remembered the town of Menzerzyce from prewar days. I had often visited it as a representative of the Jewish Labor Bund and of various trade unions. I was familiar with its marketplace and its charming streets lined with small wooden or brick houses. Menzerzyce had a large population of Jewish workers, chiefly brushmakers. Brushmaking was an exclusively Jewish trade, handed down from father to son. Jewish workers in Menzerzyce also engaged in other occupations, particularly tailoring. I knew a number of people in the town. One of them was Mordekai Cuker, a cab driver, nicknamed Honey by the townsfolk. Tall, powerful and always cheerful, Mordekai Honey was a simple man who knew little about politics, but his two daughters were active and dedicated members of the Bund from their earliest youth.

Now I was once again going to Menzerzyce—this time not as a Bundist worker, Jacob Celemenski, but as the Pole, Czeslaw. In the train, on my way to Menzerzyce, I was filled with anxiety. I knew that the railway station was a good distance from the town proper. How was I to get to town? Evening was drawing near, and it was dangerous to be about in the dark. It might also arouse suspicion if I were seen at a late hour entering the district to which the Jews were now confined.

I was deep in these troubled thoughts when suddenly I heard one of the passengers exclaim to another: "What are you doing here? How is it you were allowed to travel by train?"

Every head turned to the man addressed. I saw that he was a Jew, small, narrow-shouldered, with an armband bearing the Star of David. The Polish passengers showed no hostility toward him. Every man in the car was absorbed in his own concerns. The Jew replied to the Pole, who was evidently an acquaintance: "I represent the Jewish community of Menzerzyce. I was given special permission for this trip on community business."

I was heartened to see him. When the train reached Menzerzyce, it was already dark. Together with several Polish passengers, the Jew climbed into a horse-drawn cart. I sat down next to him. The Polish driver whipped the horse and the cart rumbled off in the direction of the town. I asked the Jew quietly in Polish, "Excuse me, I wonder if you can help me."

He turned a startled face to me, but I said: "I am a relative of the cab driver Mordekai Honey. I want to see the family."

This seemed to put him at ease. Mordekai Honey was well known in town. He asked me: "Do you want to visit him at such a late hour?"

"No. But perhaps you can advise me where to go for the night."

"You are right," the Jew agreed. "You are not registered here and you might get into trouble. In a few minutes we shall pass a Jewish bakery. Get off, and you'll be able to spend the night there. You may not sleep, but you will at least be warm."

Soon after that he told me, "It's here."

I paid the driver and got out. I opened the door of the bakery and was greeted by a gust of delightfully warm air, filled with the smell of baking bread. At the fiery oven, I saw the baker in a white apron and with a flour-whitened beard, and his apprentice, a young boy with rolled-up sleeves. They were surrounded by troughs of dough. Loaves of freshly baked bread were laid out on the stone floor. The baker, a Jew past middle age, looked up at me, surprised and startled, but I quickly reassured him, "I am a Jew. The cab driver Mordekai Honey is a relative of mine. I have to see him, but I'd rather not go there until morning."

The baker smiled and said:

"I doubt whether you'll be able to sleep here, but you will certainly keep warm."

He told me of another guest he had put up several months earlier. It was a woman, a representative of the American Joint Distribution Committee in Poland, who had promised to secure several sacks of flour for him. I understood that he was referring to my fellow Bund member, Itke Lazar-Melman, who was a courier for the Joint and also did errands for the Bund.

I did not sleep that night. I dozed off several times, only to wake abruptly after a few minutes. A succession of thoughts and images passed in confusion through my mind. I spent the night sitting on the floor, leaning against the sacks of flour, until the first bluish rays of dawn. The baker treated me to a glass of hot tea and a slice of excellent bread. I bid him a warm goodbye and left. I knew where the cab driver lived, in a small, poor house on the narrow Brisk Street. I began to meet more Jews, shabbily dressed and all of them with yellow armbands. The day was cold and dismal. The faces of the Jews I met were heavy with gloom and dejection. I sought out the house of the cab driver and knocked. The master himself opened the door. He looked at me, puzzled, without recognition. I said:

"Good morning. You don't remember me?"

Hearing me speak in Yiddish seemed to allay his anxiety. He peered at me, and his face suddenly brightened: "Of course I know you. I drove you to the train a number of times."

He opened the door wide and I entered. His whole house consisted of one room and a small kitchen. Everything here spoke of joyless poverty. Only the man himself stood smiling, pleased at my visit. He was a widower, and his younger daughter lived with him. His older daughter, Golda, was married and lived separately.

He made me sit down at the table, and before I had time to say anything, he ran to the kitchen, where a few logs were burning in a stove. He put up a kettle of water. I said, "Please don't trouble. I cannot stay long, and every minute counts. I would like to see your daughter Golda.'

"Oh, Golda!" He suddenly recalled that his daughter and son-in-law used to meet me during my previous visits. She would be happy at my coming, he said excitedly. If I waited a few moments, he would bring her over.

He hurriedly put on a short coat and went out. I remained alone, and for the first time I became aware of my fatigue, of lack of sleep and of the cold. My eyes were closing with drowsiness, but before long the door was flung open, admitting Golda Cuker, her husband, Abraham Zdanovicz, and finally old Mordekai Honey.

Golda was a tall, black-haired woman. Everything about her spoke of will, energy and firm resolution. She was one of the most active members of the Bundist organization in Menzerzyce. Before the war she had made occasional visits to Warsaw on party business. She had visited Warsaw under the German occupation as well. Her husband, Zdanovicz, a brushmaker by trade, was the complete opposite of his wife: quiet, mild, unhurried in speech and movement. They greeted me with warm joy.

The father, Mordekai, served us tea in cups and stayed away at a distance. He understood the purpose of my coming, and pretended that he neither saw nor heard anything.

Golda Cuker had been a Bundist virtually since childhood. She had been brought up in the SKIF, the Bund's organization for children, and later went on to the Bundist youth movement, *Zukunft.* In Menzerzyce, the home town of militant revolutionary brushmakers, the Bund had once had a strong organization, with active trade unions, a large youth movement, a sports club, numerous schools and many cultural activities. Now all of this was shattered. I asked about a number of our comrades. After almost every name, Golda answered with sorrow, "Gone, gone." Some were in prison, some in labor camps, others in Russia, still others, lost without a trace. I asked her to call a meeting of the remaining committee members.

She left with her husband, and I remained. Old Mordekai Honey wanted to cheer me up a little. He had always been a man ready with puns and proverbs, and now too he tried to drive away my gloom, but this time without success. Finally he sat down across the table from me and said: "You've come at a bad time. Something terrible happened here yesterday."

He told me that the Gestapo had shot the rabbi in the street the day before. The rabbi, a small, hunchbacked man, was famed for his learning and kindness. The Germans had wanted to deport him, but he refused to deliver himself into their hands and went into hiding. The Gestapo then took twenty-five of the town's Jews as hostages and announced that they would all be shot if "the Jews" failed to surrender. As soon as he learned of this, the rabbi went to the Gestapo. He was tortured, and later taken out into the street and shot. The whole town was crushed and heartsick over it.

It did not take long before Golda and her husband returned, bringing several people: Moyshe Ezra Edelstein, the chairman of the local Bund organization; Hershel Borowsky, an active member of the Bund since Czarist times; Alter Sztokman, a former city councilman and a warden of the Jewish community, and Moyshe Grinbaum, of the youth organization.

The meeting opened in a depressed mood. The chairman, Moyshe Ezra Edelstein, reported in a few short words on Jewish life in Menzerzyce. A ghetto had not yet been established, but there was a segregated district, and conditions there were unendurable. The Nazis had emptied all the surrounding towns of their Jewish populations and transferred them to Menzerzyce. The Jews of Menzerzyce itself were racked with hunger and fear. There was no bread for the newcomers, and no corner where they might lay their heads. All the work done in the town was solely for the benefit of the Germans. Before the war, there had been two Bundist representatives in the community organization. Both had refused to continue their work in the organization. The reason was the same as in many other towns—the demoralization and corruption that had become prevalent in the Jewish councils, the *Judenrat.* Not far from Menzerzyce, some nine kilometers from the city, the Germans had established a labor camp, where they interned several hundred men. Golda Cuker, who looked like a Pole, was the liaison between the city and the camp. Together with her sister, she made the rounds of neighboring villages to buy food for the comrades in the camp. She also bought butter, eggs and milk for Jewish children in Menzerzyce.

The members of the committee also told me what had become of the brushmakers' cooperative. The cooperative owned a considerable stock of hogs' bristles. Most of it had been hidden. From time to time some of the stock was sold, and the money was used to help members of the brushmakers' union and women and children who had been left without their providers.

As in all other towns and cities, the Germans were constantly carrying out manhunts. They could easily obtain the needed numbers of laborers through the *Judenrat,* but they preferred the manhunts, which transformed every town into a jungle where Jews lived in constant terror of capture. Despite that, the Jews conducted themselves with great courage and dignity. The last May Day had been celebrated by the workers in a touching manner. They walked through the streets in small, silent groups. Not a word was spoken, and not a song was sung, but the whole town was impressed by the extraordinary demonstration. The Bund, my friends told me, was active again. The movement was divided into small units, and there were also youth groups. Everyone read with great interest the bulletins and other publications sent here from Warsaw. The clandestine literature helped at this dark and bitter time to raise the spirit of the comrades.

At the end of the meeting I reported on our work in Warsaw and in other cities and towns. I told the group that the central committee of the Bund was planning to call a nationwide conference and asked them to select a delegate from Menzerzyce. If they preferred not to do it in my presence, it could be done later. I also told them about the financial status of the party organization and the leading committees in Warsaw, which had to provide funds to other cities as well. The committee decided to contribute the large sum of 25,000 zlotys to the work. The chairman then turned to the youngest man in the room, Moyshe Grinbaum, who was sitting a little apart, and said to him: "You are the youngest among us, you have the best chance of surviving. Let this money be handed over by you." (He has indeed survived and is now living in the United States.)

I was deeply moved to accept the gift for the party from the trembling hands of the young man.

Before the meeting was closed, the old Bundist, Hershel Borowsky, took a bottle with some whisky from his pocket. "This is all I have left from better times. We have always welcomed guests with banquets. Let us take a drink this time as well."

There was only enough for a small sip for everyone. After that I gave my friends a bundle of newspapers, which I had brought for them and they left one by one, in a somewhat better mood.

In the evening, when it became sufficiently dark, I went to the home of the comrades Zdanovicz, where I spent the night. The couple had two little daughters, and their mother, Golda, constantly fondled them and kept them close to herself. Her work—making the rounds of the neighboring villages in search of food for the inmates of the labor camps—exposed her to daily danger. And she seemed perpetually to be saying goodbye to her children, as though she were seeing them for the last time.

Early in the morning Golda awakened and began to prepare for her long walk to the camp. She invited me to accompany her. My visit, she said, would raise the morale of our imprisoned comrades.

We came out into the cold gray street. The camp was nine kilometers from town, but before going there we would have to turn off to several villages to buy food. The time to come to the camp was five o'clock in the evening, when the inmates were brought from various places of work back to the compound, which was surrounded by barbed wire. Golda, who had become an expert in trading with the peasants, bought everything she needed, and we returned over the narrow country roads winding between the villages to the highway which led directly to the camp. Sparse woods stretched on either side of the road. Golda gave me a sign and I looked ahead.

The camp was now in sight. I saw the fence made of widely spaced wooden posts bound by thick rows of barbed wire. Within the compound were wooden barracks, now without a sign of life. The only man we could see was an armed S.S. guard patrolling the entrance. Golda glanced at her wristwatch. "They should be coming soon. Let us wait for them somewhere nearby, on a side road. We cannot risk attracting attention. We'll come out when we see them coming." We were not the only ones there. Several Poles, who had come to sell things to the Jewish prisoners, were also waiting for their arrival.

For five or ten minutes we waited on a narrow pathway off the main road. Suddenly we heard the sound of hundreds of feet. We separated and quickly came out upon the road. I saw a dense, marching crowd escorted on either side by two or three S.S. men and several Jewish "overseers." The marching Jews were so exhausted they were barely able to drag their feet. They immediately caught sight of Golda who walked up without hesitation to one of the crowd and gave him the packages of food. Neither the S.S. men nor the Jewish *Kapos* interfered, although they saw her. A moment later the crowd was swallowed up by the camp and the gates closed behind it.

I was already turning to leave when I heard a desperate scream from behind the barbed wire. I quickly turned and saw an S.S. man just inside the fence savagely beating a Jew with a wooden club. The Jew was middleaged, with a short beard covered with blood. A young man broke away from a group standing huddled nearby and rushed with outspread arms to shield the older man, but soon his face was also running with blood. The S.S. man ordered the Jews who witnessed the beating to lift the bleeding man on their shoulders and dance through the camp grounds. I glanced at Golda. Like myself, she stood there numbed with shock. But a moment later she signaled to me to follow her, and we started on our homeward trek.

For a long time we were both silent. Afterward she told me who the beaten man was. The young man who had tried to shield him was his son.

We returned to Golda's home in a depressed mood. When we entered, Golda's husband told us a comrade from the town of Ostrolenko, a former Bundist town councilman, and his sister were at one of the collection centers where Jews were driven together from the surrounding towns. We went there. The "Hotel" was a dark, dreary building. Every available inch of space was taken up by Jewish families—men, women and children, sitting and lying on the floor, surrounded by bundles, bags and other remnants of their poor belongings.

When we found our comrade from Ostrolenko, we halted before him in stunned silence. Stolarcik sat huddled on a bundle. Near him, on the floor, lay his sister, covered with a shawl. She was dead. Golda called him by name, and he slowly raised his head, but lowered it again at once, staring with seemingly unseeing eyes at his dead sister. He sat motionless, as though he himself were dead. After a while he raised his head again and said in a low voice: "She died two hours ago. She just lay down and died. She is better off than I am."

I had no courage to approach him with condolence or consolation. My throat was constricted. The hall was cold and filthy. The air was dense with stench.

We left silently. At the door I told my companions that we must get him out of there as quickly as possible. Golda said the local comrades would do something immediately to get the dead woman buried and to find lodging for her brother. At home we found several people waiting for us, but I had no strength or energy left to speak to anyone.

I was exhausted after the long day and the sleepless nights that had preceded it, but I could not fall asleep and spent the night turning restlessly in bed. In the morning I said good-bye to my hosts and their two children and set out to continue my journey on to Lublin.

The premonitions that haunted Golda every time she left her children to go out on her mission were realized soon enough. As I learned later, Golda had left the ghetto one day to look for homes for twenty-five Jewish children with the peasants of nearby villages. That was her last journey. She never saw her husband or her children again.

Her younger sister suffered a similar fate. She went out to buy food from the villagers and never returned. Golda and Chancia, two daughters of the cab driver Mordekai Honey—heroic children of their people and selfless Bundists—went of their own will to their deaths in the service of their suffering people.

ABRAHAM FOXMAN

Vilna—Story of a Ghetto

Social and Cultural Life in the Ghetto

The *Judenrat* established a Cultural Department in the ghetto. The Cultural Department supervised and coordinated the activities of the school section, theater section, the orchestra, the Yiddish and Hebrew choirs, the library, reading room, archives, statistics bureau, book store, museum, sports section, music school and the publication of *Geto Yediot* (Ghetto News).

SCHOOLS

A few days after the creation of the ghetto in September 1941, a group of teachers formed a *"farein,"* which later organized the educational system of the ghetto. In the initial registration for school, 3,000 children signed up.

In the beginning, school attendance was voluntary. In April 1943, school attendance became compulsory:

The directive No. 3, issued by the Ghetto Representative on April 28, 1943, makes attendance in the ghetto schools compulsory. All children from five to thirteen years of age must attend the ghetto schools which are tuition free. . . . The block commander will be responsible that all school age children attend school.

During the first year of the ghetto more than twenty educational units were established, which encompassed more than 80 per cent of the children of school age in the ghetto. Schools were also opened in *Keilis* and *H.K.P.*, labor establishments (treated below).

In 1942, the schools provided a summer program. Gens received permission from the Germans to fence off an area in the forest outside the ghetto. The teachers went out four times a week with groups of 100–150 children to the forest. Due to an epidemic of Scarlet Fever, the schools opened late in 1942. In October, when they reopened. 1500–1800 children attended. There were approximately sixty teachers who worked 42 hours a week. They spent 24 hours teaching, and the remaining 18 hours were devoted to work in the kitchen, visiting students and parents at home, repairing books and notebooks, and holding various meetings.

The principles set down for education in the ghetto were the cultivation of love and respect for the Jewish heritage and history (with special emphasis on the national independence movements in Jewish history, such as those of Bar Kochba and the Maccabees), the recognition of the unity of the Jewish people, the hope of a rejuvenated nation, the universal struggle for right and justice, and identity with the Land of Israel.

When the schools were first established there was no specific curriculum. Teachers would meet with the students and discuss various topics. Later a special committee worked out a curriculum which consisted of Yiddish, Hebrew, Mathematics, Science, Geography, Jewish, and General History, Latin, German, and Religious Studies.

In addition to the regular studies, special courses were provided in Music and Song. There were also trades courses for graduates of the schools.

RELIGIOUS ACTIVITIES

The Germans were determined to destroy the spiritual life of the Jews in Vilna. Before the ghetto was created on July 12, 1941, they arrested all the rabbis they could find. Most of the rabbis of Vilna were arrested and killed.

Any religious activities that existed in the ghetto had to be unofficial and therefore do not appear in any of the ghetto reports or documents.

The rabbis that remained alive carried out various religious activities in the ghetto. They gave sermons about the laws of Sabbath, *kashruth,* and justice. They provided *matzoh* for Passover and established a kosher kitchen.

The rabbis forbade weddings in the ghetto. They declared that it was permissible to work on the Sabbath, Yom Kippur, and other Jewish holidays, since not working endangered life. For a few months there was obligatory rest in the ghetto on the Sabbath for all those that did not work for the Germans (no business or public smoking).

There were three "synagogues" in the ghetto. Groups of Jews also assembled daily, after work, to study Talmud and other holy writings.

Two *yeshivoth* (religious schools) were established in the ghetto, with an attendance of approximately two hundred pupils.

There were from sixty to seventy Torah Scrolls hidden in the ghetto. The religious Jews tried to observe the Jewish holidays and customs as much as possible under the circumstances

The Resistance Movement in Vilna

RESISTANCE

The word resistance usually signifies an organized, armed collective action prepared and carried out according to the rules and regulations of military strategy. This, however, is not the only means of resistance. Resistance does not necessarily have to be armed, organized, collective or active.

The Jewish resistance was a varied one. It was armed and unarmed, organized and unorganized, planned and spontaneous, collective and individual, passive and active, offensive and defensive, moral, spiritual and psychological. Each one of these types of resistance involved the risk of life.

The greater part of resistance was of a passive nature. Attempting to stay alive was passive resistance. Escaping, hiding, or giving birth to a child in the ghetto was resistance. Praying in a congregation, singing, or studying the Bible was resistance.

One of the most brilliant aspects of the life of the Jews in the Vilna Ghetto was in the area of spiritual resistance. The Jewish Community of Vilna, which had been for generations a cultural center of Jewish life in Europe, and which had been called "Jerusalem of Lithuania," became the "Jerusalem of the Ghettos" and a symbol of spiritual resistance against German authority. In spite of the danger of death, pain, suffering and hunger, the cultural dedication of the Jews of Vilna remained creative in all its aspects.

The first resistance acts in the ghetto were passive, without arms. At the liquidation of ghetto Number Two, in 1941, hundreds of Jews refused to go to Ponar and lay down on the ground. During the "Actions" of the "Yellow Certificate" many Jews refused to leave the ghetto and were shot on the spot.

Before any organized resistance movement came into existence the Jews, out of a desire for revenge, sought ways and means of causing damage to the German war effort. They performed various acts of sabotage while working in German installations. Workers would remove vital parts of machines, destroy documents, and produce defective products.

UNDERGROUND ACTIVITIES

At the outbreak of the war in 1939, a Joint Coordinating Committee of the *chalutzim* (Pioneer) Zionist Movements was formed under the leadership of Mordecai Tenenbaum. This committee formed the nucleus of the resistance in Vilna during the early days of the occupation. With the creation of the ghetto this committee served as the center of the organized underground activities in the Vilna Ghetto. It conducted various activities during the first few weeks of the ghetto. Correspondence and *shlichim* (messengers) were dispatched to the ghettos of Warsaw, Bialystok, and other Jewish centers. The job of the *shlichim* was to find out what was happening in other ghettos and to inform the Jews of the other Jewish communities of the true meaning of "transports" and "work camps." They also attempted to call the Jews to action and revolt.

On January 1, 1942, the Zionist organizations held a memorial meeting in memory of those Jews killed in Ponar. It was at that meetings that the first call to resistance was made:

Let us not be led like sheep to the slaughterhouse! Jewish youth, do not believe those that are trying to deceive you. Out of 80,000 Jews of Vilna, only 12,000 are left. Before our own eyes, our parents, our brothers and sisters were taken away. Where are they, those hundreds of men abducted and taken to forced labor by the Lithuanians? Where are the naked men, women, and children who were taken out in that night of terror of the "provocation?" Where are the Jews of the Day of Atonement? Where are our own brethren from the other ghettos? Those who are taken out through the gate of the ghetto will never return. All the Gestapo's roads lead to Ponar and Ponar means death. You, the people who have within you seeds of despair, do not be deluded. Your children, your husbands, your wives are no longer. Ponar is not a labor camp. All there were shot. Hitler plotted to destroy all the Jews of Europe. It was the fate of the Lithuanian Jews to be the first ones. Let us not be led like sheep to the slaughter. True, we are weak and helpless, but the only response to the murdered is self-defense. Brethren, it is better to die fighting, like free fighting men, than to live at the mercy of the murderers: To defend oneself to the last breath. Take courage!

After the January 1 memorial meeting, the various political organizations held meetings to discuss the creation of an armed resistance in the ghetto, and on January 23, 1942, laid the groundwork for the formation of a unified fighting organization, called in Yiddish by its initials, F.P.O.

F.P.O.—UNITED PARTISAN ORGANIZATION

The F.P.O. was formed by all the political groups in the ghetto with the exception of the Bund. Its first meeting chose a staff of operations. The commanding staff was composed of three people: Yitzhak Vittenberg (Communist), under the code name "Leon" served as chief; Abba Kovner (*Hashomer Hatzair*), known as "Uri," and Joseph Glazman (Revisionist), who took the pseudonym "Abram," were the other two members.

From the beginning the F.P.O. was faced with a dilemma which agitated other ghettos. The problem was whether to fight in the ghetto or join the partisans in the forests. Some members were of the opinion that they should lead the fight in the ghetto itself in order to show the world and posterity that the Jews revolted against their German oppressors and died an honorable death. The proponents of this view were well aware that they could not count on the support of the non-Jewish population. In no country was the Jewish underground treated on an equal footing with the recognized national independence organizations. Jewish requests for weapons were refused outright in Vilna. They were in full recognition of the fact that it would be a struggle for honor and history, and not life.

The opposing opinion argued that the purpose of the resistance movement was to combine and participate in the general struggle against the German enemy. The proponents of this view felt that it was necessary to smuggle out to the forests as many fighters as possible so that they might join in the over-all struggle against the Germans.

Those who were for the struggle in the ghetto argued:

The FPO is a national organization whose aim is struggle and defense of the lives and honor of the Jews. The departure to the forest is only a search for personal security and life.

Those in favor of partisan action in the forests argued:

The struggle inside the ghetto is destined to failure, because the surrounding population will send us no aid. The struggle within the ghetto walls will not inflict damage or losses upon the Germans and will not save Jewish lives. On the contrary, the fight of the partisans in the forests, in Jewish National Units, will be the real struggle for Jewish honor. Only by going to the forests can we save the lives of hundreds and thousands of Jews. The groups of Jewish partisans will be able to help the ghetto in time of need.

In the end Vittenberg's refusal to desert the ghetto prevailed. His plan was to await the decisive hour when there would be sufficient ammunition to arm the masses, then to blow up the ghetto and the Nazi ammunition dumps and lead the Jews into the forests to join the partisans.

The goals of the F.P.O. were three: (1) To prepare for an armed revolt in the ghetto and to defend the lives and honor of the ghetto Jews. (2) To carry out acts of sabotage in the German installations and institutions. (3) To make contact with the partisan movement in the forests.

The organization was structured upon military principles. The smallest fighting unit consisted of five members. Special units for sabotage, mine layers and intelligence were added to the organization.

The signal for mobilization was *"Iize Ruft"* (Liza Calls). Liza Magen was a member of the F.P.O. She was caught by the Germans when she tried to communicate with another ghetto and was tortured to death without betraying the resistance movement.

The first revolver was smuggled into the ghetto in January 1942. By the middle of 1943 the Vilna Ghetto possessed an arsenal of all kinds of weapons: 50 machineguns, 50 grenades, 30 revolvers, a few rifles and a few thousand bullets.

At one of the meetings of the F.P.O. command, Yitzhak Kowalski suggested that a secret press be organized, and that this press publish a newspaper for the non-Jewish population of Vilna. The suggestion was accepted, but in order to minimize the danger to the ghetto, it was decided to set up the press outside the ghetto walls. Kowalski secured a job at the German Press *Austra* and managed to steal type. The newspaper, published in Polish and called *Standart Wolnoszi* (Freedom Flag), was the propaganda organ of the underground. It continuously attacked the German regime and publicized news that the German controlled newspapers did not print.

An important job of the underground press was the printing of forged documents. In order to raise money for the F.P.O. the secret press printed forged food cards and sold them.

FIGHTING GROUP JECHIEL

Besides the F.P.O. group, another organization arose under the leadership of Jechiel Sheinboim. This resistance group consisted of several partisan groups united in the desire to leave the ghetto and fight in the forests. The organization was made up of several smaller groups: Borka Friedman's Group, Antek Ring's Group, Gordonia Group, Akiva Group, and the Group of the "field cities."

The Jechiel Fighting Group joined forces with the F.P.O. and the ghetto resistance movement became unified. The problem of whether to fight in the ghetto or in the forests was resolved by the tragic events that shaped a synthesis of both objectives. The F.P.O. changed its original stand:

> We will go to the forests after the struggle. After we fulfill our obligations we will take with us many, and as a part of the partisan army, we will continue our fight with the murderers.

After a great deal of negotiations and meetings the Bund also joined the F.P.O. With the inclusion of the Bund, the F.P.O. was a representative resistance organization of all the political views in the ghetto.

THE GLAZMAN AFFAIR

Joseph Glazman, a member of the ghetto administration, served as chief of the Housing Department and as a member of the Command Staff of the resistance organization F.P.O. When the Vilna Ghetto police was sent to set up various small ghettos, Jacob Gens wanted Glazman to go to Shventziony and make "housing arrangements" there. Glazman refused to go and at a meeting of the Jewish police he chastised the police and the authorities for collaborating and not joining in the plans for revolt. Gens arrested Glazman after his speech and refused to obey orders. The F.P.O. command sent a delegation headed by its commander Vittenberg and requested Glazman's release. Gens refused to bow to the request, and Glazman was chained and led to the gate to be taken to a work camp, Sorok-Tatar, 15 kilometers outside of Vilna. A group of F.P.O. fighters freed Glazman at the gate. The Jewish ghetto authorities requested that Glazman leave the ghetto of his own free will so that the prestige of the ghetto administration should not suffer. It was agreed by the command that Glazman go to the work camp Reshe.

Glazman was brought back a few weeks later and interrogated by the Jewish police about the underground movement, and released. Thus the first attempt by the ghetto administration and police to weaken and disrupt the organization of the underground movement failed.

THE VITTENBERG DAY

On July 9, 1943, the leaders of the Communist city committee of Vilna were arrested by the Germans. They were tortured, and it is believed that one of them revealed to the Gestapo their contact with Vittenberg and the underground in the ghetto.

The details of the Vittenberg Day vary with the sources. One version is that Kittel of the Gestapo asked for Vittenberg and was told that he was dead. Another version is that Gens ordered Vittenberg to surrender and when he refused he was arrested by the Jewish police and handed over to the Lithuanians. A third version is that Vittenberg was asked to come to a meeting of the *Judenrat,* and when the two Gestapo officers walked in on the meeting, Sala Wessler pointed to Vittenberg, saying, "This is the commander of the underground, arrest him!

While Vittenberg was being led out of the ghetto the fighters of the underground attacked the guard and freed him. The leaders of the resistance knew that there would be a price to pay for this act of defiance and ordered mobilization of all the fighting units. It was clear that the critical moment had arrived.

The ghetto administration headed by Gens assembled the populace and told them that Vittenberg was endangering the life of the ghetto. Gens said that he had been given this ultimatum by the Germans:

> If by 6 A.M. the next morning the ghetto does not hand over Vittenberg to the Germans, they will come with tanks and airplanes and wipe out the ghetto.

Gens organized the brigadiers, police and four hundred members of the underground to look for Vittenberg. Panic overtook the ghetto and the population demanded that Vittenberg surrender. There was no mistaking the temper of the ghetto; it was Vittenberg or bloodshed.

The F.P.O. held an emergency meeting. The first decision was that if it was necessary to fight the Germans the F.P.O. would fight. But the F.P.O. would not fight Jews. The Communist members of the F.P.O. decided that Vittenberg surrender, but the latter refused to accept the decision:

> It has never yet happened that an organization should by its own will surrender its commander. An organization that does that is doomed to failure.

After further discussion and a second decision, that Vittenberg surrender, Vittenberg decided to commit suicide. He was persuaded not to commit suicide, since there was always the possibility that he might return alive. He was also promised poison, to use in case he was tortured.

On July 16, 1943, Dessler, the ghetto police chief, handed over Vittenberg to the Gestapo. The next day Vittenberg was found murdered, in the Gestapo corridors.

As a result of the events that occurred during July 15 and 16, 1943, the F.P.O. became disorganized. The ghetto population was opposed to its existence and activities, due to fear of extermination.

The F.P.O. Command decided to change its tactics:

As a result of the events of July 16, we are forced to evacuate and transfer our activities to the forest.

The first detail of partisans left the ghetto on July 25, 1943, headed by Joseph Glazman. On the road they were joined by others from surrounding work camps who were seeking an opportunity to fight as partisans. They were successful in reaching the forest, but there they were ambushed and most of them perished. Only fourteen of the group reached the forests of Narocz, where they formed the nucleus of the Jewish partisan unit, "The Vengeance," whose contingent grew to four hundred fighters.

On the 26th of July, Neugebauer, of the Gestapo, came to the ghetto and demanded the surrender of the families of all those who had been shot in the forest. He also wanted the 32 brigadiers of the work groups to which the partisans had belonged. Eighty Jews were taken to Ponar and shot. The work camp, New Vilaika, was completely destroyed in reprisal for the flight of the partisans there.

On August 1, 1943, the following article appeared in the *Geto Yediot* No. 50:

According to the order of the German Security Police and S.S., a number of Jews, and among them brigadiers, were arrested.
We want to remind the ghetto of the words and warning of the Ghetto Representative, that as of the latest order received from the German authorities, all Jews are collectively responsible.
It is your duty to yourself and to the ghetto to inform on any activity which might endanger the existence of the ghetto.

The remaining ghetto fighters were again faced with a dilemma. If they left the ghetto to go to the forests they endangered the lives of their families. The Germans also introduced the wearing of metal "dog tags" to facilitate identification. They now were able to bring back identification tags of the murdered partisans for public exhibition.

THE BEGINNING OF THE FIELD

On August 1, 1943, the Jews left the ghetto for their work installations as usual. The workers were surrounded by units of Gestapo, S.S., Lithuanians and Estonian soldiers and were ordered to enter prepared boxcars for a journey to an unknown destination. They were sent to a *K. Z.* [concentration camp] in Estonia. The first shipment of 2,000 Jews was the beginning of the liquidation.

The next day the Germans issued an order that all relatives of those Jews that were sent to Estonia must "volunteer" to join them. If they did not, all the inhabitants of the apartment would be taken. On August 22, 1943, another transport of Jews was sent to Estonia. This time the Jews resisted and some were killed on the spot.

Liquidation and Resistance

On September 1, 1943, the ghetto was sealed off. The Germans, with Lithuanian and Estonian troops to help them, surrounded the ghetto. Neugebauer issued the following order: "As of today, no one is permitted to leave the ghetto."

The F.P.O. was immediately mobilized. Some wanted to fight immediately, but Abba Kovner, the new commander, ordered them to wait till the situation became clear. In the morning the Germans, Lithuanians and Estonians entered the ghetto, and the first chance for effective action was missed.

The F.P.O. fighters took up their positions. They set up barricades in two places, one at No. 6 Spitalna Street and the second at No. 12 Strashun Street. The first position at No. 6 Spitalna Street was surrounded by the enemy, and because of a lack of ammunition most of the fighters were captured. Those that escaped went to Strashun Street No. 12. The Germans proceeded to surround the second position. As they approached the barricade, Jechiel Sheinboim, who was in command, began to fire. The Germans opened with a barrage and blew up the house. Sheinboim and several other fighters lost their lives defending their positions.

Gens and Dessler petitioned that the Germans, Estonians, and Lithuanians leave the ghetto. They feared that a battle between the enemy and the fighters would bring immediate destruction to the ghetto. The Germans accepted the petition and withdrew from the ghetto. It was then that the F.P.O. decided to evacuate, and during the days of September 8–11, two hundred fighters left to join the partisans in the forest.

The "action" of assembling Jews for deportation to Estonia lasted four days, from September 1–4. During those four days, 8,000 Jews were deported to Estonia. After this evacuation, Neugebauer and Kittel came to the ghetto and announced that the deportations would stop and that the remaining Jews would be given work in the ghetto.

On September 14, 1943, Geno was summoned to Gestapo headquarters. He was accused of having helped the partisans and was shot on the spot by Neugebauer. Sala Dessler was appointed Ghetto Representative in his place.

On the 15th of September, the ghetto was again surrounded by soldiers, and seven trucks of soldiers entered the ghetto. The remaining F.P.O. fighters were again mobilized. The Germans had come with the intention of taking the rest of the Jews for deportation, but when they learned that the ghetto fighters were mobilized to fight, they withdrew from the ghetto.

On September 23, 1943, Kittel arrived and ordered the Jews to be ready for evacuation by 12 A.M. The ghetto was then officially to be closed and all the Jews sent to Estonia.

The Gestapo officer, Franz Miller, when he was captured by the Russians, gave the following version of the ghetto liquidation:

> The liquidation of the ghetto was postponed for a few weeks in order to hunt for the partisans in the forests. But Kittel wanted to be promoted, so he asked for two hundred Ukrainian soldiers to aid him in liquidating the ghetto. He received permission, and on September 23, 1943, he began the liquidation.

On that day the F.P.O. evacuated the last of its fighters through the underground canals. Some were captured while escaping and resisted with arms. They were later publicly hanged. On the following day, the Ukrainians and Germans entered the ghetto and carried off the last remaining Jews.

KEILIS AND H.K.P.

After the liquidation of the ghetto, the Germans left two Jewish work installations outside the walls of the ghetto: *Keilis* and H.K.P. These installations contained approximately 3,000 Jews. *Keilis* was a fur factory. (*Keilis* is the Lithuanian word for fur.) The Jews worked there making winter clothing for the German Army. H.K.P.

was the *Heers Kraftfahr Park* (Army Vehicles Park). The Jews in this installation were also employed in the army hospital and at various chores at Gestapo Headquarters.

On March 27, 1944, the Jews of *Keilis* and H.K.P. were ordered to bring their children to the hospital to receive injections against typhus. Two hundred children who were brought by their parents were taken by the Germans to a hospital in Cracow. The skin and blood of these children were used to heal German soldiers. Mothers who refused to give up their children were immediately shot.

On July 2 and 3, 1944, both H.K.P. and *Keilis* were surrounded by the Germans and Lithuanians, and all the inhabitants were taken to Ponar to be shot.

RACHMIL BRYKS

A Cupboard in the Ghetto

TRANSLATED FROM THE YIDDISH BY S. MORRIS ENGEL

Hershel Zeif was an emaciated man with a pale, peaked face and lusterless eyes. A native of Kalisz, he had been married in Lodz just before the war. He and his wife, luckily, were able to bring with them into the ghetto their entire wedding outfit, all their clothes, as well as twin beds, a table, several chairs and a clothes cupboard.

For a long time Hershel Zeif ran to the Civil Administration every day looking for work. After a while he became exasperated with the false promises of the officials and decided that if you had no "shoulders" (protection) you couldn't get anything. Now he and his wife spent most of the day in bed—he in one of the twin beds, she in the other—writhing from hunger and cold, like all their neighbors.

Mrs. Zeif was small and thin, with hollow cheeks and big black eyes. She was a quiet woman who never raised her voice. Silently, within herself, she endured the grief and agony of hunger and cold. Both she and her husband were positive that the war would end any day.

When the sun rose higher and lavished its rays, also brightening their window, Hershel and his wife hung their wedding clothes out to air. There was Zeif's black winter coat with a velvet collar; a blue capote with a vent in back; trousers with a crease and cuffs; a pair of boots and a pair of shoes; a half-dozen white shirts; undershirts; a pair of soft leather bedroom slippers and a hard black hat, round as a coin, with a crescent brim like a new moon.

Mrs. Zeif had a black winter coat; a light summer coat; a suit; several dresses; a plush hat and a hand-knitted hat; underclothes; linens and four pairs of shoes.

All these things were brand new, they had never been worn. They were coated with green mildew. After several days in the sun the mildew whitened and then vanished. But after a few days in the house the green mildew appeared again. They decided to air their wedding clothes every day, sunny or not, just as long as it didn't rain. They made a pact: one day he hung his clothes outside the sunny window for several hours—the next day she hung hers. The sun never reached the other window, because it was in a corner opposite a high wall.

When Zeif saw that the mildew was gone a smile of pleasure lit up his haggard face: "Yes, the war might end any minute. God can do anything, and we'll go home in our new clothes. Yes, yes, my dear Henye." His wife nodded in agreement: "That's right."

Hershel Zeif invited his neighbor Bluestein into his house. "Guess how my wife cooked supper today," he said in his weak voice, looking into Bluestein's eyes with a mischievous smile, like a schoolboy trying to confuse a friend with a difficult riddle.

Bluestein looked around, in all the corners, and saw that all was as before: the mouldings of the door and windows and floor had long ago been swallowed up by the tiny kitchen stove. The floor itself could not be ripped up, because it was the second story and they would fall through. Besides, one of "Emperor" Rumkowski's men came by every few days to inspect the floor. Bluestein also saw that the beds, the clothes cupboard, the table and chairs were all there. The beds, by the way, were new and modern. The Zeifs had gotten them in exchange for their old oak beds, and were even paid for the difference in weight.

Bluestein wracked his brain. He wanted to guess the answer, he didn't want to be fooled.

"Come on, guess! You can't guess, can you?" Zeif teased him.

"I know!" Bluestein cried confidently. "With the board you got from the tinsmith."

"Ha-ha! A likely story! Why don't you say with last year's snow? That board was used up long ago—even the ashes are gone," Zeif shouted triumphantly.

This was what had happened. It had rained in, and Zeif had to put pans on the beds. After much pleading, the administrator of the buildings in the neighborhood sent him a tinsmith to fix the roof. The tinsmith climbed into the attic, and immediately Zeif heard boards being pried loose over his head. Soon the tinsmith climbed down calmly, with a pile of boards under his arm. Zeif started to shout: "You're a robber! You've ruined me! I almost died until you finally got here! Instead of fixing the roof so it shouldn't rain in on me, you destroyed it and are taking home the wood!? You've made it worse! Don't you have any feelings?"

"Oh, come on now," the tinsmith replied calmly, "why should you eat your heart out over such a little thing? The house isn't even yours. Until it rains again the war might end. Look how hot it is. You know it rains very seldom in the summer, and when it does, it's hardly more than a drizzle. The roof doesn't even get wet. Anyway, we are having a dry summer, and by the fall we'll all have forgotten that there was ever a war, with a ghetto, with an 'Emperor' Rumkowski."

"God forbid that the war should last until the fall," Zeif interrupted him. "It's lasted almost two years already."

"Of course. Now take a board for yourself for fuel and it'll bring you luck—you'll see the end of the war," and he thrust a board under Zeif's arms.

Zeif thought: "As I live and breathe, the man is right." Aloud, he said: "What can I do with you? Shall I report you to the 'Emperor's' police? How can I?" He seized the board with both hands and pointed to Bluestein: "But *he's* the one you have to watch out for. He sees that nobody steals any wood."

The tinsmith grew a little frightened, but Bluestein looked at him pityingly and he felt better. Zeif added: "Don't be afraid. I should live so long what a nice man he is, huh, Mr. Bluestein? I swear he would never hurt anyone."

The tinsmith left quickly with his bundle and Zeif went into the house with the board and broke it into small pieces for several days' fuel.

"Mr. Bluestein, can you guess what my wife used for fuel when she cooked supper tonight? You can't guess, can you?"

"No", said Bluestein firmly.

Zeif opened the clothes cupboard with the expression of an inventor demonstrating his work. Bluestein saw that everything was ship-shape. The glassware, the china; even the paper shelving lay flat and smooth, and the linens were arranged in neat piles. Bluestein wondered: "What is he trying to show me?"

Zeif could no longer refrain from boasting. Quickly he lifted up the paper shelving and pointed: "See? Why do I need whole boards on the shelves? The wooden strips are enough." He cut an arc through the air with his thumb, chanting in talmudic fashion: "So I removed the boards. I chopped up three boards, split two of them into strips, put four strips on each level, laid out the shelving paper with the clothes and all the rest of the things and there are my shelves. Can you tell the difference? Now my wife will be able to cook and cook for a long time." He pointed to the bunches of wood which he had divided into four tiny strips each. "More than that isn't necessary. I'm like 'Emperor' Rumkowski with his rations. I dole out rations to my wife. And, thank God, we have what to cook." He showed Bluestein a big heap of cabbage roots.

Not far from Zeif's house there was a large field which the Agriculture Division had rented to one of Rumkowski's officials—formerly a rich man. After the cabbage was picked, Zeif dug out the roots, which were hard and bitter, and also took home the wild cabbage leaves that grew near the roots.

Two weeks later Zeif called Bluestein again and said: "Well, be smart and guess with what my wife cooked her cabbage stew today."

The same game was reenacted. Bluestein pondered, searched, examined every corner of the house and couldn't find any clues to the riddle. Finally Zeif solved it for him. He flung open the door of the cupboard. "Why does a cupboard need a back wall when it stands against a wall? I removed the rest of the wall and now I'll have fuel for a long time."

From the roots and wild leaves Mrs. Zeif prepared appetizers, fish, meat, soups, tsimmes. She let the cabbage cook a while and then put in a lot of bicarbonate of soda, because soda boils up in hot water. She thought: "It is cooking and at the same time the soda draws out the poisons." (The cabbage roots don't get soft even over the biggest fire.)

From the poison Zeif made "marinated herring" (his own invention). He removed the bulbs from the roots, salted them heavily and let them stand. Then he mixed a little vinegar and water, added some paprika ersatz and saccharin. Into this mixture Zeif dipped his scrap of ersatz bread and sighed with pleasure: "Ah—ah—delicious," smacking his lips as in the good old days over a savory roast. He hummed a hasidic tune, drumming his fingers on the table in rhythm. "Oh, a delicious marinated herring! Henye, our enemies should never enjoy it!" And his wife nodded in agreement as they ate with relish.

Two weeks later Zeif called in Bluestein again and asked: "Well, guess how my wife cooked today? This time you must guess!" and he pointed to the cupboard that was covered with a blanket. "See?

Today I got still smarter! Why does a cupboard need a door? What's bad about this? Anything wrong? With the door my wife will be able to cook for a long time, and the cupboard is still a cupboard!"

Bluestein touched the cupboard with one finger and it began to sway back and forth.

Zeif defended the dignity of the cupboard: "That's nothing! Who's going to fight with it? A cupboard doesn't have to be strong, man!"

Bluestein's heart ached because of Zeif's decency—and he agreed that Zeif was a smart, practical man, a real inventer. Zeif tried to smile, but a grimace distorted his face.

The next day Mrs. Zeif, sobbing with terror, called in Bluestein: "Mr. Bluestein, look what's happened to my husband!"

Zeif lay in bed, unable to move. Overnight he had grown so swollen and his head and face so huge, that it covered the entire pillow. The bed was too narrow for his body.

Zeif said in a weak voice: "Look what happened to me! And all because I have no 'shoulders!' "

Bluestein tried to console him: "Don't worry, Mr. Zeif, the war will end any day now, and we'll go home together."

"Yes, Mr. Bluestein, my wife and I haven't even used up our wedding outfit."

"Listen to me, Mr. Zeif, sell some of your wedding clothes and buy yourself some bread and a bit of meat. When you go back to the city you'll get new clothes, maybe even better ones."

"We'll never sell anything from our wedding outfit. I just told you, we didn't even replace any of it. To spite the Germans we'll go home in those clothes!"

Bluestein didn't urge him, because he didn't want Zeif to doubt that the war would end any day. He said lightly:

"Don't worry about the swelling, it's nothing," but he was sure that Zeif would soon lose the battle with his hunger. At the door he said: "Mr. Zeif, in the middle of the night I'll come running in to tell you that the war is over!" and he left the house. He recalled that he had read in the forbidden *Deutsche Zeitung* the speech which Hans Greizer, may his name be blotted out, delivered to the Hitler youth on May 1, 1940, the day when the ghetto was sealed off with barbed wire:

"The Jews are finished," Greizer said. "Hunger will turn them into mad dogs. They will bite chunks of flesh from each other. They will devour themselves!"

"It's true, we are dying out because of hunger," Bluestein thought, "but we have not become wild beasts. Not only are we not biting chunks of flesh from each other, but we don't even want to exchange a single garment from our wedding outfits for a piece of bread and meat. We don't steal and we don't kill. No, he will not turn us into mad dogs! On the outside we look like corpses, but inside we have preserved the image of God."

Early next morning Bluestein went to see how Hershel Zeif was feeling. He was afraid that Zeif had not lasted the night, or that he had taken his own life because of his suffering and despair.

But Bluestein was surprised! Overnight Zeif had grown as thin as a rail, and his skin was like that of a corpse. He couldn't get off the bed. Again Bluestein consoled him: "See, the swelling is gone! That's a good sign. You're getting better, you'll soon be well. Be patient, Mr. Zeif, we'll go home together."

"Oh, I haven't lost faith yet! What's this nonsense about my getting well soon? I'm not sick! I was never sick in my life! I'm just a little weak from hunger. I have pain—but that's nothing. The hell with 'them!' Do you remember what Greizer, may his name be blotted out, said in those days? You should remember. He said: 'The Jews are finished.' Believe me, Mr. Bluestein, 'They are finished!' Last night I had a wonderful dream. I saw my father, of blessed memory, and—the war was over and I was beating up the Germans and 'Emperor' Rumkowski and his henchmen. How I took revenge! How I cooled my heart! I should be as sure of meeting my family again as I am sure that 'they' will die an unnatural death!" Zeif ranted in his weak voice.

"It's good, Mr. Zeif, good that you haven't lost faith! I admire you. You'll see, we'll go home together!"

Bluestein walked down the stairs with an aching heart, thinking: "Who knows what will happen to him? Hunger has already turned him into an obituary. The Angel of Death has placed his mark on him."

A little later Bluestein received the new ration which contained two kilos of potatoes. He brought one kilo to the Zeifs: "Mrs. Zeif, I'm lending you a kilo of potatoes. When you get your ration you'll give it back. Cook the potatoes right away. They'll be a good medicine for Zeif."

Husband and wife didn't know how to thank Bluestein. They showered blessings on him. With several slivers of wood Mr. Zeif boiled the potatoes half-raw in their skins. When they were eating, Henye tried to give the larger portion to Zeif and he tried to give the larger portion to her. After eating a few potatoes Zeif felt better: "See, Henye, all we need is faith. With God's help we'll survive the war. Do you have any wood left for cooking?"

"Yes, for a few more times," she replied with satisfaction.

"See, Henye, the cupboard is still a cupboard," he smiled.

And they dipped the unpeeled potatoes in salt and ate. Because the ghetto Jews said: "The peel is healthy. In the peel there is iron and under it there is sugar, and that's why cattle are so healthy and strong—because they eat the peel."

BERNARD GOLDSTEIN

Hell in the Streets

TRANSLATED FROM THE YIDDISH BY MIRIAM HOFFMAN

No artist can adequately portray the ghetto streets. My pen fails me. I strain my dimmed memory to recapture scenes, experiences. And yet, I cannot term them "experiences." An experience is something fleeting. Actually, it was a continuous miasma of five years' duration, uninterrupted, unfaltering—a constant nightmare.

The year is 1941. Typhus rages in the ghetto, taking a monthly toll of six to seven thousand. It is dawn. A courtyard on Mila Street. The cobblestones are strewn with naked corpses that are covered with dirty paper. There is no money for burial, so a cardinal sin—desecration of the dead—is committed against those most dearly loved—parents, brothers, sisters, children. The few leftover rags of the deceased must be used for the survivors. The dead, who had been so cherished in their lifetime, are tossed out during the night with dirty paper covering their faces.

These nameless corpses, with no one to chant the Prayer for the Dead for them, are gathered in heaps on the cemetery and thrown into collective graves. There are thousands upon thousands of such nameless corpses. It's impossible to abide by the holy laws and dig individual graves. And, furthermore, why? For whom?

Half-dead, half-naked swollen human beings, with lacerated, parchment-yellow bodies are scattered alongside the wall of the Catholic church on Leszno Street. Sickly infants with pussy eyes breathe heavily, emitting gurgling sounds. The older ones, pale and emaciated, beg with their last bit of strength: "A pi...ece of bread!" The street is already crowded. Everyone tries to make his way carefully for fear of touching someone infected with typhus. A bedraggled, filthy

Jew, bare-footed and frothing at the mouth, is dragging a small wagonload of children who wail: "Bread, bread. . . ."

Suddenly, there is a commotion and someone shrieks: "Nab him!" A barfooted urchin, munching greedily on a hunk of bread, sloshes through the mud with his filthy feet. He stumbles on a corpse and falls with the bread in his hands. The fellow whose bread it was grapples with him, trying to retrieve the loaf that had been so difficult to get, and which is now chewed up and soiled with the spittle of the "grabber," a fellow who might even be infected with typhus. These "grabbers" were a peculiar sort. Though panic-stricken and hungry, they still had a bit of strength and gumption left to break the sacred law of "property rights" for—a piece of bread. They were beaten mercilessly both by those whom they robbed and by the police, but it was as impossible to eliminate them as it was to obliterate the hunger.

There is a tumult again—shouting, screaming, a screeching of sirens. A truckload of German police whizzes by. It is about noon time. The prison guard is changing. The truck drives right into the midst of the Jewish throng, and the Germans start beating the "dirty" Jews, those "sore-infested typhus spreaders," with their whips and bayonets, yelling: "Filthy Jews, get out!"

On the corner of Chlodne and Zielazne Streets, where the ghetto is divided in two by Chlodne, there is a bridge that Jews must cross on. Beneath it, on "holy" Aryan ground, the gentiles tread. Here, as well as the ghetto boundaries on the corner of Leszno and Zielazne, many hellish incidents occur. The German guards constantly nab Jews and "drill" them. One sees several emaciated, lamentable-looking Jews, arms loaded with bricks and stones, hardly able to stand up under the weight of the mass they are carrying. Their tormentors beat and harass them, and jeer at them as they force them to pick up and drop their burden repeatedly. This is how the "master race" teaches gymnastics!

A cacophony of wailing, of crying, of moaning and of shrieking fills the air. And, in the midst of all this, one suddenly hears the sound of music, of singing, of symphonic music and of jazz. The music emanates from a courtyard at the end of the street. A group consisting of former actors, singers, musicians, choristers, members of the Philharmonic of days gone by, is trying to eke out a bleak livelihood, a bit of bread, by singing in the streets and in the courtyards. People drop a few coins into outstretched caps and plates. The performers thank them sullenly, and move on, singing:

Poverty leaps,
Poverty dances,
Poverty sings a little song.

Shortly before the Warsaw Ghetto Uprising, we managed to bring some of our friends who had been in hiding in the woods and forests to Warsaw; among them were Chanele Krystal and Jan Bilak. Chanele's husband, Gabriel Frishdorf, a ghetto fighter, had been killed in the Wishkover woods. We hid our friends in a bunker. During the uprising, Chanele was arrested, together with Bilak and Miss Papierna from Novidor. They were brought to Gestapo headquarters on Shucha Street where Bilak was shot immediately. The scoundrels then forced Chanele and several other women to clear the streets of German corpses, something they themselves were afraid to do because of the shooting coming from the insurgents on the other side of the street. After a while, Chanele and Papierna managed to escape, beneath a hail of bullets to the side of the fighters.

Chanele was then in her ninth month of pregnancy, waiting to give birth momentarily. At first, we got her into an institution for aged women, but we had to take her out of there and put her into an underground maternity clinic. The battle was in full force. I scurried about in search of the bare necessities for the expectant mother as well as for the child who was about to enter this "beautiful" world—an old shirt from which to make diapers, a sheet, some underwear, cereal, a little boiled water. Just imagine: a dark cellar housing a dear comrade, a ghetto fighter, herself but a young child, suffused with pain, starved and thirsty, awaiting the birth of a baby that would be named for its own father, who had lost his life in battle. Where could one scrounge for even the bare essentials for these two? And all this at the peak of the fighting, in the hell of fire and destruction!

Six days after the birth of the child, the uprising was quelled, and three days later everyone had to flee to Prushkow. Chanele was extremely weak; her infant could hardly breathe. Their greatest hazard, however, was the fact that Chanele had a "Jewish face." The Germans would surely kill them. I made my decision: I would throttle the baby and take Chanele to a bunker. These were the thoughts that plagued me all night. In the morning, I went down to the cellar. It was dark and damp there. It was with difficulty that I made my way to the spot where she lay on a pile of rags, together with her infant. Chanele lit a bit of candle, which illuminated her deathly-pale face. I held the week-old child in my arms. What does one do! There was tumult all about us; people running about, crying: "Only a few days' time!" I looked at the child—a "nuisance" in these horrible times. At that very moment, the noose of death hovered over him and his mother. For a fleeting moment, I was obsessed with the appalling thought: One squeeze and we'll be rid of him. However, I didn't have the strenght to do it; I hesitated; my fingers faltered. . . . It was as if Gabriel Frishdorf, the infant's heroic father, had emerged from his unknown grave, his tortured soul pervading his namesake in my arms. And, he seemed to live again in his child.

I remained in the ruins of Warsaw. As for Chanele, I gave her some money and, together with her child, she joined the masses swarming toward Prushkow. Among them there were several Jews whom I had helped when they had been in hiding; now I asked them to look after her. Afterward, Chanele managed to place the child with a farmer near Czestochowa. She returned to Warsaw, where I met her again in April 1945. Her money had petered out and she had to seek out friends to help her. Later, we brought Chanele and Gabriel back to Warsaw. After the liberation, they lived in Lodz, where I visited them. I held the boy in my arms; I kissed him and wept. Only then did I tell his mother how I had weighed Gabriel's fate at birth. It was a secret that had been locked within me all that time.

CHILDREN

CHILDREN

Most tragic of all was the plight of the Jewish children. Their existence became totally chaotic. The tearing away of their parents in the "Actions" left a vast army of homeless, disordered youngsters.

The primary goal in the Nazi plan for total annihilation of the Jews was the cutting off of its progeny. Thus the children were the first victims in the Actions, Selections and Resettlements. There were also special "Children's Actions" during which they were seized and taken out of the ghetto to be slain.

While some adults were temporarily spared by the Nazis because of their labor potential, the children were immediately removed to the gas chambers and crematoriums.

At least one and one half million Jewish children were murdered by the Nazis during the Hitler occupation.

ELIEZER JERUSCHALMI

Meierl

TRANSLATED FROM THE GERMAN BY ADAH FOGEL

The life of this child was short—only 3 years, 5 months and 5 days. But this brief span was filled with suffering and agony.

When he was a year and a half his father, together with hundreds of other Jews, was thrown into prison, and never came home again. In the ghetto his mother left him by himself, because every morning, before sunrise, she had to hurry to work in the factory. He remained alone in the house, watched over by a bedridden neighbor who could not give him any help. From the first day, he had to stand on his own feet and learn to take care of himself. He adapted himself very easily to this existence. He quickly learned to wash and dress himself and keep his scanty possessions in order. He knew how to take the few morsels his mother left for him, and learned how to get food when she had nothing to leave him.

He knew the exact hour of the neighbors' mealtimes, and when hunger tormented him, he appeared at their tables and stood watching. He did not ask for food, he said very little; he did not stretch out his skinny arms for bread—but his huge, hungry eyes gazed at their plates, and followed every spoonful they raised to their mouths. Naturally, the people took pity on him and shared with him their meager rations.

He performed tricks with knives and forks. He knew that everyone at the table smiled when they watched him, and used this to get another morsel. He did his tricks with a serious face, and did not allow the laughter of his hosts to alter his expression.

When he wanted fresh vegetables, he simply went into the vegetable garden and took a radish from here, a carrot from there, or broke off a piece of cauliflower and ate it raw. But when the sun began to sink in the West and the hour approached when the Forced Labor Brigade returned to the ghetto, he went with the grownups to the ghetto gate to wait for his mother. She was a small, thin woman, and next to her Meierl felt masculine and protective. Proudly he put his small arm in hers and led her home. His entire being, and all his actions, radiated serenity. He talked very little. Many people in the ghetto had never even heard his voice, in fact there were some who thought he was a mute. Only his closest neighbors sometimes heard him speak and admired the clear, short, but logical sentences with which he came to an understanding with his environment.

On the day of the "Children's Action" he hid himself even more carefully than usual. He climbed into his sick neighbor's bed and kept quiet as a mouse, without moving a muscle. He did not even lose his control when the Ukrainians, assisting the S.S., made a house search.

The Ukrainians found him, but the sick old woman ransomed him with a gold watch. As soon as the hoodlums were outside, they sent in a second group, who knew about Meierl. But she did not have another watch, so the boy was seized and taken to the children's collection point.

I saw him during these final moments. He skipped between the two soldiers, trying to keep up with their stride. From time to time he raised his large, questioning eyes to them, as though asking: "Why all this?" Although the soldiers were drunk, those innocent child's eyes sobered them and slowed their steps. In one of them a human emotion flickered and he said to his companion: "He's a Jew, but still he's a child." He looked at Meierl sympathetically, took his hand and lifted him into the wagon among the desperately sobbing sacrifices. Meierl seemed calm. He stood quietly among the crying children and looked around with his large, naive eyes, until the cart started to move.

REGINA LANDAU

Bodies of Children for the Animals in the Circus

TRANSLATED FROM THE YIDDISH BY MOSHE SPIEGEL

In September of 1939 the Germans ordered us to leave Lanzut across the San, under threat of death. We were to gather in the square at 6 A.M. and to leave the city by 1 P.M.

Some went toward the San, but others went to nearby villages to wait for the danger to pass, as I did. When I returned to Lanzut I found my home had been plundered.

The Gestapo came from Jaroslav to "capture" Jews on the streets. Some twenty-four men and women were seized. They were imprisoned for several months, then taken to the cemetery and shot. After the execution a man and a woman, both wounded, feigned death and managed to escape. The man was able to elude the Gestapo, but the woman was caught in a Szezchow hospital and shot.

I managed to leave Lanzut before the massacre. I hid in cornfields and potato patches during the day, or with a friendly peasant. I also was able to hide my sister's two children, a girl of seven and a boy of nine, in the stable of their former home. They were half-starved, so I stole vegetables for them from the fields. But in a few days someone denounced them to the Gestapo. They were seized and interrogated, in hopes they would reveal hideouts of other Jews. But the children endured their tormenting and betrayed no one.

As the children were led to the cemetery they were urged not to cry, for they would "go to heaven, and meet their mother, father and aunts." After the children had been shot the Gestapo took their bodies to the circus performing in Lanzut, to be eaten by the beasts.

ILSE AICHINGER

Fear of Fear

TRANSLATED FROM THE GERMAN BY CORNELIA SCHAEFFER

The mirror was like a big, dark escutcheon. In the middle was the star. Ellen laughed happily. She stood on her toes and crossed her arms behind her head. That wonderful star, that star in the middle.

The star was darker than the sun and paler than the moon. The star had big, sharp points. In the twilight its radius was undefined, like the palm of a stranger's hand. Ellen had taken it secretly out of the sewing box and pinned it to her dress.

"Never in the world!" her grandmother had said. "Be happy you're spared that. You don't have to wear it, like the others." But Ellen knew better. Allowed, that was the word: allowed. She sighed deeply and felt relieved. When she moved, the star in the mirror moved too. When she jumped, the star jumped and gave her a wish. When she stepped backward, the star went with her. She put her hands to her cheeks for the happiness of it all, and closed her eyes. The star remained. For a long time it had been the most secret idea of the secret police. Ellen reached for the hem of her skirt and whirled in a circle, dancing.

Damp darkness rose out of the cracks between the boards. Her grandmother had gone away. She had turned the corner, like a rolling ship. As long as she could still be seen, her umbrella drove like a black sail against the wet wind. Indecisive rumors blew frostily down the alleys of the island. Her grandmother had gone away to discover more information.

Information?

Ellen smiled thoughtfully at the star in the mirror. Her grandmother wanted certainty. Between two mirrors. How uncertain all certainty. Only uncertainty was certain, and had become more and more certain since the creation of the world.

On the floor above, Aunt Sonya was giving piano lessons. Secretly. In the room to the left, two boys were fighting. Their clear, angry voices were very audible. In the room to the right, the deaf old man shouted to his bulldog: "Do you have any idea what's happening, Peggy? They don't tell me anything. No one tells me anything!"

Ellen got two saucepan lids out of the cupboard and clanged them angrily. The janitress was shouting in the courtyard. It sounded like: *pack—pack—*.

Ellen stared for a moment at the empty gray walls that rose out of the mirror behind her and the star. She was at home alone. Strangers lived in the rooms to the right and the left. She was alone in this room. And this room was home. She took her coat from the hook on the door. Her grandmother might be back soon; she had to hurry. The mirror was like a big, dark escutcheon.

She tore the star from her dress with trembling hands. One had to light the way when it was as dark as this, and how better to light it than with a star? She would not have this forbidden her, not by her grandmother nor the secret police. Quickly, with big, uneven stitches she sewed the star to the left side of her coat. Then she put it on, slammed the door behind her, and ran down the stairs.

She stood beneath the house portal for a moment, breathing deeply. Fog hung in the air. Then she flung herself into the late autumn. She loved it, without knowing it, because it enfolded everything in something deep and dark; and out of this all things rose like something marvelous; it returned to them a notion of the intangible, lending mystery to bareness. It wasn't open and dazzlingly showy like spring—see, I'm coming—it was withdrawn, like someone who knows more—come to me.

Ellen ran. She ran through the foggy old streets, past things unconcerned and smooth, and threw herself into autumn's concealed arms. The star on her coat gave her wings. Her shoe soles slapped noisily on the hard pavement. She ran down the streets of the island.

The cake in the half-lit bakery-shop window brought her to a stop. The cake was white and shiny, and written on it in pink sugar was "Happy Birthday." The cake was for George; it was like peace itself. Folded red curtains surrounded it on all sides, like translucent hands. How often they had stood here and stared. Once it had been a yellow cake and once a green one. But today's was the best of all.

Ellen pushed open the glass door. She entered the bakery like a foreign conqueror, walking up to the counter in long strides.

"Good evening," said the saleswoman absently. Then she lifted her eyes from her fingernails and was silent.

"Happy birthday," said Ellen. "That's the cake I'd like."

Her hair was long and wet on the collar of her old coat. The coat was much too short, and her plaid skirt showed two hands' breadths beneath it. But that wasn't it. It was the star that was responsible for the turn of events. Bright and calm, it was resplendent on the thin dark-blue cloth, as though convinced it was in the heavens.

Ellen laid the money on the counter; she had saved for weeks. She knew the price.

All the clients stopped doing what they were doing. The saleswoman leaned her thick red arms on the silver cash register. Her glance soaked up the star. She saw nothing but the star. Behind Ellen somebody got up. A chair was pushed against the wall.

"Please, the cake," said Ellen again, pushing the money nearer the cash register with two fingers. She didn't understand this hesitation. "If it costs more," she mumbled unsurely, "if maybe it costs more now, I'll fetch the rest. I still have some at home. And I can hurry. . . ."

She lifted her head and saw the saleswoman's face.

What she saw was hatred.

"If you're still open that long—" stammered Ellen.

"Get out of here!"

"Please," Ellen said anxiously, "you're making a mistake. I know you're making a mistake. I don't want you to give me the cake; I want to buy it! And if it costs more, I'll pay, I mean I'm ready to—"

"Nobody's asking you," explained the saleswoman icily. "Get out! Go! Now! Or I'll have you arrested!"

She removed her arms from the cash register and started walking slowly around the counter.

Ellen stood very still, looking at the woman's face. She wasn't sure she was really awake. She ran her hand over her eyes.

The saleswoman stood close before her. "Go! Can't you hear me? Be happy I'm going to let you go!" She was screaming.

None of the customers budged. Ellen turned toward them, looking for help. It was then they all saw the star on her coat. Some began to laugh jeeringly. Others produced pitying smiles. No one helped her.

"It costs more," said one of the customers.

Ellen looked down. Suddenly she knew the price of the cake. She had forgotten it. She had forgotten that people wearing the star weren't allowed in the stores and still less in a bakery that served coffee and cakes at tables. The price of the cake was the star.

"No," said Ellen, "no, thank you."

The saleswoman reached for her collar. Somebody pushed open the glass door. In the dimly lit display case was the cake. Like peace.

The star was searing. It burned through the blue sailor coat and drove Ellen's blood to her cheeks. So one had to choose. One had to choose between one's star and all other things.

Ellen had envied the children with the star—Herbert, Kurt and Leon, all her friends, but she hadn't understood their fear. Now the saleswoman's grip brushed the back of her neck like a shudder. Since the edict she had fought to have the star, but now it burned like flaming metal through her coat and dress to her skin.

And what was she going to tell George?

Today was George's birthday. Panels had been laid into the tabletop so it would be as large as possible, and it was covered with a big bright cloth the color of apple blossoms. The lady who lived in the room beside the kitchen had lent it to George for his birthday.

George thought it strange to be lent something for his birthday. Lent. The thought wouldn't leave him. He sat, stiff and alone, at the place of honor and waited for his guests; he froze. His bed and his father's had been pushed to the wall in order to make room. Still, they would not be able to dance, as Bibi wanted. George wrinkled his brow and laid his hands on the table before him. He was sad that he wouldn't be able to offer his guests everything they wanted. The big black cake stood helplessly among cups, as though it had been enthroned against its better judgment. It was all a mistake; it wasn't chocolate, it was just black.

George sat very still. He had waited so long, unreasonably happy, for this day. He was as happy as his parents had been fifteen years earlier when they carried him out of the lighted hospital, down the street into the falling dusk. George was glad to have been born. But his gladness had never been as enormous as this last year.

For weeks they had talked about his birthday party; for weeks they had planned and talked it all over with one another. To make it more of a celebration, his father had lent him a dark-gray suit. A narrow leather strap held his trousers up. The jacket was broad and double-breasted, and from George's shoulders it hung down, quite calm and unconcerned. If only the star hadn't been there, the big yellow star on the handsome jacket!

It spoiled all George's joy.

The star was the color of the sun. It had unmasked the sun, that beloved, beaming constellation of childhood. If you scrunched up your eyes, it grew a black rim that expanded and contracted. In the middle it said "Jew."

Despairingly George laid his hand over it, then let it fall. Veils floated out of the still courtyard, through the dull window panes, and tried to muffle the star. The secret police had forbidden hiding the star. So the dusk became punishable, like the moon, as often as its mocking light was thrown over the blacked-out city.

George sighed. His guests rang the bell. He jumped up and ran around the table.

"Are you all here?"

"Ellen's missing."

"Maybe she isn't coming any more."

"Maybe she doesn't want to come."

"Maybe it's not a good thing to be with us."

"I don't believe that," said George thoughtfully. The veils still drifted through the panes. And the cake still stood, black and unhappy, in the middle of the table.

"Ellen's bringing another cake," said George urgently. "A real one. Ellen doesn't have to wear the star. She just pushes open the door, puts the money down on the counter, and says, 'The cake, please,' and she gets it. That's possible. You can have anything if you don't wear a star."

Bibi laughed, but it didn't sound as though she was really laughing. The others sat in a circle and tried vainly to make conversation with quiet and noncommittal voices like grownups; as though they couldn't hear the crying in the room next door, and as though they weren't afraid.

George stood up, pulled in his belt, and laid his hands flatly and unsurely on the tablecloth. He coughed and drank a swallow of water. He wanted to make a speech and he wanted to do it ceremoniously. He wanted to say: I thank you most sincerely for coming; it makes me very happy. I want to thank Bibi and Hannah and Ruth for the three silk handkerchiefs which I really need. I want to thank Kurt and Leon for the leather tobacco pouch; I'd been wishing for one for a long time. When the war's over, I'll pull it out of my pocket suddenly and we'll all smoke a peace pipe. I want to thank Herbert for the red water ball; it belongs to us all now. Next summer we'll play dodge ball again.

George wanted to say all that. That's why he stood up and laid both hands on the tablecloth. That's why he kept tapping his fingers on the edge of the table. He was rapping for silence.

The children had been silent for quite some time, but not the young man next door. His crying drowned George's words in his mouth, as a wind will blow out one match after another.

George wanted to make a great speech. He wanted to say everything, but now he only said, "Somebody's crying," and sat back down again.

"Somebody's crying," repeated Kurt sullenly.

A spoon fell on the floor. Bibi slipped under the table and picked it up.

"Isn't it silly," said Herbert, "to cry like that? Because of nothing and nothing."

"Nothing and nothing," said Leon despairingly, "that's it. That's it, I tell you."

"Have some cake!" called George. It was supposed to cheer them up but it sounded rather frightening. They all took some cake. George watched them anxiously. They ate quickly, forcing themselves; the cake was too dry. They gagged. "Ellen will be here soon with the other cake," said George. "It's always good to have the best last—"

"Ellen isn't coming," interrupted Kurt. "She doesn't want to be seen with us any more."

"Because of the star."

"She's forgotten us."

Ruth got up and went around pouring tea, quietly and quickly without spilling any. The children's lost eyes met over the white cups. Herbert pretended something had gone down the wrong way and began to cough.

George went slowly from one to the other, slapping them on the shoulder as he went by and saying "Old man" or something like it, and laughing. The others laughed with him. As soon as they stopped even for a second they could hear the crying next door very clearly. Kurt wanted to tell a funny story, and turned over a cup by mistake.

"It doesn't matter," said George. "It doesn't matter at all."

Bibi jumped up and laid her napkin under the wet spot.

The veils coming in through the windows changed from gray to black.

Bibi whispered something to Kurt.

"No secrets on my birthday!" muttered George irritably.

"Just be glad you don't know," Bibi called across the table in her clear, somewhat loud voice. "Be glad, George, it's nothing for your birthday." Bibi was happy when she could have a secret. She thought no further than that—about what it contained. If it was a secret, she was pleased.

The crying next door went on and on. Suddenly Hannah jumped up. "I'm going to ask him," she called excitedly. "I'm going to ask him. Right now."

George blocked the door. He spread his arms and pressed his head against the wood, a living barricade against the crying which is always next door if you can hear it. Hannah grabbed his shoulders and tried to push him away.

"I've got to know, you hear me?"

"It's none of our business. It's bad enough that we have to live door to door with strangers. Why they laugh or cry is none of our business."

"It is our business," Hannah shouted, beside herself. "It always has been our business, only we thought we were being tactful. But now it's become urgent." She turned to the others. "Help me. You've got to help me! We've got to make certain!"

"You can't ask for certainty," George said softly. "That's what grownups do, almost all of them, and that's why one dies. Because one demands certainty. However much you ask, it will always remain uncertain. Always, you understand? For as long as you live." His fingers were cramped on the door jamb. After a while his arms grew limp and threatened to drop.

"You're sick," said Hannah. "You're sick, George."

The others stood around in a silent circle.

Herbert pushed to the front.

"Do you want to know what Bibi said just now? I know! I heard it. Shall I tell you? Shall I?"

"Tell!"

"Don't tell!"

"Herbert, if you do—"

"Bibi said—she said—"

"I don't want to know!" screamed George. "Today's my birthday and I don't want to know!" His arms finally dropped. "Today's my birthday," he repeated exhaustedly, "and you've all wished me happiness. All of you."

"He's right," said Leon. "Today's his birthday and that's all. Let's play something."

"Yes," said George, "please." His eyes began to shine again. "I've gotten out the cards for Old Maid."

"What'll we play for?"

"For honor."

"For honor?" Kurt jeered. "Whose honor? In that case you might as well play for the star."

"You're beginning all over again," said George stiffly.

"So now I'll tell you," Herbert stammered. "Now I'll tell you what Bibi told me. She said"—and before she managed to put her hand over his mouth he went on—"Bibi said: the star means death."

"That's not true!" said Ruth.

"I'm scared," said Hannah. "I still want to have seven children and a house on the Swedish coast. But sometimes, lately, my father runs his hand over my hair, and then, before I can turn around, he starts whistling—"

"The grownups," Herbert said excitedly, "the grownups in our houses speak to each other in foreign languages."

"They always do that," said Leon. "They always have." Then his voice changed. "It's all becoming clearer."

"Unclearer," said Ruth.

"It's clouding over," explained Leon. It seemed to him as though he was telling a secret he would have done better to keep. Give yourself over to uncertainty so that you may find something sure.

The others turned away. "May we, George? It's getting stuffy in here." They threw open the window and leaned out. It was as dark and deep as the sea. The courtyard was unrecognizable.

"If we were to jump now?" Kurt said hoarsely. "One right after the other. It would take just a moment, and then we wouldn't be afraid any more. Not afraid. Just think of it!"

The children closed their eyes and saw themselves clearly, jumping one after the other. Black, quick and straight, as though there were water below.

"Isn't that good?" said Kurt. "They'll find us all soft and motionless. Some people say the dead laugh. Then we'll be laughing at them."

"No!" screamed Herbert. "No, you can't do that!"

"Mama won't let you!" jeered Kurt.

"It's something everyone has to know for himself," Ruth said quietly, out of the dark room. "You don't throw away what you get as a birthday present."

"And today's my birthday," announced George. "You're all very impolite." He tried with all his strength to lure the others away from the window. "Who knows whether we'll be together next year? Maybe this is our last party."

"Next year!" Kurt said bitterly.

Despair again fell over the children.

"Please have some cake!" screamed George, frantically. If only Ellen were here. Ellen might have helped him. Ellen would have persuaded them to come away from the window. But she wasn't here.

"Suppose we did it," Kurt pressed on. "Suppose we did it now! We've nothing to lose."

"Nothing but the star."

Ellen was terrified.

The veil of fog tore open, and the sky became a high, arched mirror. It no longer reflected a figure—no outline and no definition; no question and no fear. Now it reflected only the star. Glimmering, calm and relentless.

The star led Ellen through damp, dark streets, away from George, away from her friends, away from all her desires, in a direction that was the opposite of all other directions, where all became one.

Giddily she reeled along, her arms spread, stumbling after the star. She leaped and reached, but nothing was within her reach. The star hung on no wires.

Had her grandmother's warnings been right?

"Don't you dare take out that star—be glad it doesn't apply to you! No one knows what the star means. And no one knows where it leads."

No, and you weren't supposed to know. You weren't allowed to know. You had only to follow it, and this decree applied to them all.

Therefore why should one be afraid? What was the use of a prophet as long as there was the star? Wasn't it within the star's power to dissolve time and break through fear? Ellen suddenly stopped. She seemed to have arrived. Slowly her glance left the star and wandered down the sky until it met the rooftops. And from the roofs it wasn't a long way to numbers and names. It was all the same; they hid themselves from the star.

Ellen stood in front of Julia's house. Julia, whom no one mentioned, whom they had shut out after she had shut herself out. She didn't want to belong to them; fear was written in their faces. They were bound to misfortune. Even long ago, on the quay, Julia hadn't wanted to play with them. She should have worn the star, but she didn't. Since the law about the star had been enforced Julia no longer went out into the street.

She no longer counted herself among the children with the star. "I'm going to leave my house only to go to America!"

"You won't get a visa. I didn't get one."

"Not you, Ellen, but I'll get one. I'm going to leave with the last train, with the very last train."

Since then Ellen hadn't seen Julia any more. Julia was the name of everlasting success, while Ellen was the name of incomprehensible, everlasting failure. Besides, the children considered a visit to her as betrayal. But her grandmother had said, not so long ago: "I think Julia's going to America. You should say good-bye to her."

"Say good-bye? To her? Maybe you want me to be cheerful and wish her a happy trip?"

Ellen groaned and pulled up her coat collar.

A few seconds later she was folded into a pair of arms and told, among many quick, tender kisses, that Julia had been granted a visa for America only a few hours ago.

Julia was sixteen years old and wore long silk underpants; she occupied herself sorting handkerchiefs according to color.

Ellen sat on a light-green stool, all pale and stiff, trying to keep down her tears. She pulled her legs in under her so she wouldn't dirty the scattered clothes.

A big truck stood in front of the window.

"I used to play at packing," said Ellen heavily.

"Play!" exclaimed Julia.

"I haven't done it for a long time," said Ellen.

"Why are you crying?" asked the older girl, in amazement.

Ellen didn't answer. "Green with white rims!" she said instead, picking up a pair of sunglasses with admiration. "Are you going to take along a prayer book?"

"A prayer book? That's a strange idea, Ellen! That's a product, I believe, of your development."

"Most ideas come from your development," muttered Ellen.

"What would I need a prayer book for?"

"Maybe . . ." said Ellen, "I thought, in case the ship sinks. In that case it would be a good idea to have. . . ."

Julia dropped her handkerchiefs and stared at Ellen in fright.

"Why should the ship sink?"

"Aren't you scared?"

"No!" screamed the older child angrily. "No, I'm not scared. Why should I be scared?"

"It's possible," Ellen persisted calmly. "It's possible, you know. Ships do sink."

"Maybe that's what you want to have happen to me?"

Both of them were breathing heavily. And before either of them came to their senses they had pulled each other down to the floor.

"Take it back!" They rolled under the piano. "You're envious of me. I'm going off on a huge adventure!"

Pain lent Ellen strength. While Julia pinned her arms to her sides, she butted her head against Julia's chin. But since the older girl was bigger and much more agile, it was quite easy for her to defend herself. So she held on and whispered cruelly: "The ocean is blue-green. They're waiting for me on the pier. And in the west there are palm trees."

"Stop it!" gasped Ellen, and she tried to gag Julia with her hand.

But Julia burbled on about college and golf, straight through Ellen's fingers, and when she let go for a moment Julia said clearly: "Three people have vouched for me."

"Yes," screamed Ellen bitterly. "And nobody will vouch for me."

"Nobody could vouch for you."

"Thank heaven not," said Ellen.

Exhausted, they both fell silent.

"You envy me," said Julia. "You've always envied me."

"Yes," replied Ellen. "That's true. I've always envied you. Even way back when you could walk and I couldn't, when you had a bicycle and I didn't. And now? Now you're going to sail across the sea and I'm not. Now you're going to see the Statue of Liberty, and I'm not—"

"Now I'm going off on a huge adventure. A bigger adventure than you'll ever have," said Julia triumphantly.

"No," said Ellen quietly, and she let go. "I think the bigger adventure is not to have all those things."

Julia reached again for Ellen, pressed her shoulders to the wall and looked at her with fear. "Do you want my ship to sink? Yes or no?"

"No!" Ellen shouted impatiently. "No, no, no! Then you'd have the bigger adventure, and besides—"

"Besides?"

"Then you couldn't give my mother my love." She stopped, terrified, and the end of the battle took place in silence.

Anna opened the door and stood outlined against the dark. She was wearing a pale scarf, and laughing. "Like drunken sailors!" she said calmly. She lived in the same house and sometimes came upstairs. She was older than Julia.

Ellen jumped up, bumped her head against the edge of the piano, and called: "I can see your star gleaming!"

"I washed it yesterday," replied Anna. "If I've got to wear it, it might as well gleam." She leaned her head against the doorjamb. "Really, everybody should wear stars!"

"Not me," said Ellen bitterly. "I'm not allowed to wear one! I've got two wrong grandparents too few. And so they say I don't belong."

"Oh, you know," said Anna and she laughed again. "Maybe it's all the same whether you wear it on your coat or in your face."

Julia picked herself up slowly and painfully. "In any case, you wear it twice—on your coat and in your face. Do you always have a reason for being so cheerful?"

"Yes," replied Anna. "Don't you?"

"No," said Julia hesitatingly. "Even though I'm going to America next week. But Ellen envies me."

"Why?" asked Anna.

"It's clear as anything," murmured Ellen.

"Perfectly clear," said Anna. "America. I just wanted to know specifically."

"The ocean," stammered Ellen in confusion. "And freedom."

"That's less specific," replied Anna quietly.

"How do you do it?" Ellen said. "I mean, do you have a special reason?"

"What do you mean?"

"What I said a minute ago—you gleam."

"I've no special reason," said Anna slowly.

"Yes, you do!" insisted Julia. "Why did you come?"

"I came to say good-bye to you."

"But I only got the visa today, and you couldn't have known—"

"No," Anna said heavily. "I didn't know. Still, I came to say good-bye."

"I don't understand you."

"I'm going away too."

"Where?"

Anna didn't answer.

Ellen jumped up. "Where are you going?"

Julia was pink with pleasure. "We'll go together!"

"Where are you going?" repeated Ellen.

Anna gazed quietly at her very pale, tormented face.

"Do you envy me, Ellen?"

Ellen turned away her head, yet she felt obliged to look.

"Yes or no?"

"Yes," said Ellen softly, and it seemed to her as though in her despair her words remained hanging in the room. "Yes, I envy you."

"Be careful!" called Julia jokingly. "Now she'll start a fight with you."

"Leave her alone," said Anna.

"She's right," murmured Ellen tiredly. "But my mother's over there. And freedom."

"Freedom, Ellen, is where your star is."

She pulled Ellen to her. "Is it really true? Do you envy me?"

Ellen tried to pull herself away, biting her lips, but she couldn't. Again she turned away and again she felt obliged to look at this face. There she saw for a moment a break in the shine. In Anna's face she saw fear, deathly fear, and a tortured mouth.

"No," stammered Ellen in terror. "No, I don't envy you. Where are you going?"

"What's the matter with you both?" said Julia impatiently.

Anna stood up and pushed Ellen away. "I came to say good-bye."

"Can we travel together?"

"No," said Anna. "Our directions are different." She leaned against the wall and tried to find words.

"I've been—I've been ordered to Poland."

This was what they didn't dare mention: her grandmother, Aunt Sonya, all of them, all of them. This was what they trembled before. For the first time, Ellen heard it aloud. All the fear in the world was locked in it.

"What are you going to do?" asked Julia, rooted.

"Go," said Anna.

"No, I don't mean that. I mean—what are you going to hope for?"

"Everything," said Anna. And the shine of an enormous hope flooded over the fear in her face.

"Everything?" Ellen asked softly. "Did you say—everything?"

"Everything," repeated Anna quietly. "I've always hoped for everything. Why should I stop now?"

"That's . . ." stammered Ellen, "that's what I meant. That's what the star means—everything!"

Julia looked from one to the other in confusion.

"Wait!" said Ellen. "I won't be long. I'm just going to get the others."

And before someone could stop her she had slammed the door behind her.

Startled, they moved away from the window.

"Come with me!"

"Where to?"

"If you want to know what the star means. . . ."

They were weakened by fear and asked no more questions, so glad they were to be pulled away from the sucking void.

They ran behind Ellen silently. They no longer saw the small heavily laden vans at the edge of the railroad in the dark, nor the tearful faces nor the smiles of the uncaring guards. Like Ellen, they saw only the star. They stopped short in front of Julia's house.

"Not to Julia!"

"No," said Ellen, and she opened the door.

Julia had put away the scattered handkerchiefs. When she greeted the children, she never mentioned her visa and she didn't look them in the face.

"We'd never have come to see you," said Bibi in her high voice. "It's Ellen's doing."

"Never!" repeated the others.

"We'd have found this easy to do without," said Kurt.

Their heavy shoes left tracks on the clean floor.

"Anna's here," said Ellen.

Anna: it was like a breath; like taking and giving at the same time.

Anna was sitting on the trunk and she smiled a greeting. They lost their constraint. "Don't you want to sit down?"

They sat down in a circle on the floor. Steerage passengers. It suddenly seemed as if they'd been traveling a long time.

"What do you want to know?"

"We want to know what the star means."

Anna looked quietly from one to another. "Why do you want to know that?"

"Because we're scared." Their faces flickered.

"And what are you afraid of?" asked Anna.

"Of the secret police!" They all said it together.

Anna lifted her head and looked at them all. "Why, of all things, are you afraid of the secret police?"

The children were silent in confusion.

"They forbid us to breathe," said Kurt, and he grew red with anger. "They spit at us and chase us."

"Very strange," said Anna. "Why do they do that?"

"They hate us."

"Have you done something to them?"

"Nothing," said Herbert.

"You're in the minority. You're relatively smaller and weaker than they are. You're unarmed. And still they can't seem to stop."

"We all want to know what the star means!" shouted Kurt. "What's going to happen to us?"

"When it gets dark," said Anna, "when it gets very dark, what happens then?"

"You're afraid."

"And what do you do?"

"You defend yourself."

"You lash out at things, do you?" said Anna. She paused. "And then you notice that it's no use. It gets darker still. Then what do you do?"

"You look for a light," shouted Ellen.

"A star," said Anna. "It's very dark around the secret police."

"You think—you really think that's true?"

Restlessness spread among the children. Wildly, whitely, their faces gleamed.

"I know!" George jumped up. "I know now. I know!"

"What do you know?"

"The secret police is afraid!"

"Of course," said Anna. "The secret police *is* fear. Living fear, nothing else." The shine on her face deepened.

"The secret police is afraid!"

"And we're afraid of them!"

"Fear of fear—they cancel out."

"Fear of fear, fear of fear!" said Bibi and laughed.

They started jumping around the big trunk.

"The secret police has lost its star."

"The secret police follows a strange star."

"The one they've lost and the one we wear is the same!"

"Suppose we're wrong to be glad," said Bibi, stopping suddenly. "Suppose it's still true, what I've heard?"

"What have you heard?"

"That the star means death."

"How do you know that, Bibi?"

"Because my parents thought I was asleep."

"Maybe you understood wrong," murmured Ellen. "Maybe they meant that death means a star?"

"Don't let yourselves be led astray," said Anna softly. "That's all I can tell you. Follow the star. Don't ask grownups; they won't tell you the truth, not the deep truth. Ask yourselves. Ask your angel."

"The star!" said Ellen, with glowing cheeks. "The Wise Men's star—I knew it all the time!"

"Be sorry for the secret police," said Anna. "They're afraid of the King of the Jews again."

Julia stood up and said as she drew the curtains, "How dark it's gotten!"

"So much the better," said Anna.

HANNA MORTKOWICZ-OLCZAKOWA

Yanosz Korczak's Last Walk*

The day was Wednesday, 5th August, 1942, in the morning.

The gendarmes close off the streets. The Ukrainian police surround the house. The Jewish policemen enter the courtyard.

Horrible screams: "All Jews—out!" (in German); and then in Yiddish: "Quickly! Quickly!" The efficient organization for which the orphanage—thanks to Steffa Wilczenska—is well known can now be seen in operation. The children who, surprised in the middle of their breakfast, have their normal day's routine upset at a moment's notice, descend quietly and line up in fives below.

Miss Steffa and the doctor go down with the children without forgetting to take the green flag with them—the flag of the orphanage.

We return to the legend. It is long and many-sided. There are many versions, all very descriptive, of the last trip which was taken by the children educated by Yanosz Korczak.

Is it not a fact that many of the people who were in the ghetto at the time say that they saw Korczak walking at the head of his children on the way to the assembly place? The implication is that in those days there was as yet no fear, no panic, nor terror of kidnapping or death, and spectators could just stand along the footpaths watching the festive procession of the condemned.

According to eye-witnesses, the children were dressed in their holiday clothes, as though they were going for a trip or for a holiday in the country. Some say they wore their ordinary clothes, while

* Janosz Korczak was a famous Jewish educator in Poland who died a heroic death at the hands of the Nazis.

others say they had blue knapsacks with them. Another version says that their arms were folded on their breasts. However, those who have personally seen a deportation day or who have personally made their fearful way to a Nazi assembly place, assure us that those times were not particularly suited to special sartorial effects. Perhaps the common sense of Steffa—who did not follow the good doctor in his illusions—caused her to make sure that the children were wearing the best clothes possible when they set out on their long way. Somehow or other, Korczak's children were always distinguished from the general poverty around them. Even on ordinary days their clothing was clean and neat. That was why the impression made by the small, quiet and well-behaved group, which was following the doctor with complete confidence, was so pleasant and aesthetic.

Yanosz Korczak walked at their head. We know that at the time he was weak and that he had been ill. His feet were swollen and his heart was giving him trouble. I doubt whether he had the strength to carry two of his charges in his arms—even the tiniest ones—as the legend alleges.

They were pulled, stopped, crowded together and pulled along again in the burning heat of August, accompanied by cruel cries and rifle-blows. If Korczak really took some child with painful feet into his arms, it was probably the five-year-old Romacia Stockman, daughter of two of his pupils, Rosa and Yosef, who had returned to work with him in the orphanage. It is possible that Korczak held the feverish, tired, sweating hands of two children, as they drummed with their little feet to his right and his left. . . .

Did Korczak tell them they were going for a picnic, to the country? We cannot know . . . but the terror, the fear of death and of deportation, must have affected all of them, and it is very doubtful whether it was possible to delude them—at least the older children—with a fiction of this sort. It is, however, almost certain that to the very last moment he assured the children of something which he himself no longer believed—that they were going to work in agriculture, in the forest, felling trees.

Did they sing? Possibly, yes. For years before that, the little Jewish boys used to march in pairs, with young Korczak in the lead, singing in Polish.

> We are going, going to bathe.
> We shall return clean and merry. . . .

Was it really this song, so full of joy and confidence which accompanied Korczak's children to the threshold of the devilish "bathhouse," which turned out to be a gas chamber?

At the assembly place near the waiting carriages, Dr. Korczak was called aside. In that world of bestial cruelty, tempered with a few European conventions, a physician's position and person still commanded some respect, because he was needed. Korczak was well known and respected in the ghetto. He could be of some use in the future. He could serve as a disguise and a decoy.

We may therefore have full confidence in the story of the offer to release him at the last moment. We do not know whether the matter took a long time or not, nor in what manner they wanted to pardon Korczak.

Neither do we know Korczak's words: but we know their content. He refused, without any hesitation. Can it be considered as bravery? Undoubtedly. Many people, motivated by their animal instincts, often forgot all moral obligations in the face of death—and saved their own lives at the expense of loved ones or parents. On the other hand, there is a very old rule, which says that a captain goes to the bottom of the sea together with the passengers on his boat.

As though in a dream of the past, thirty years earlier, the children's procession marches forth with song and flag. The tired old man, in the officer's uniform, whose heart is breaking from unbearable pain, slowly leads it. The nightmarish ghetto street is dusty, parched and burning—so that it reminds us of that first Via Dolorosa in Jerusalem. The children are suffering and sweating. They want to drink. They are overcome by heat and terror. Now and again they raise their voices and we can hear the weak, childish choir. Then they lose the tune and the choir ceases. The doctor moves his legs with great difficulty, bending beneath his load and his troubles—but then straightens himself in a mighty effort to hold out to the end. Above him flutters the green flag of the orphanage.

Steffa, who is accompanying the older children, is at the end of the procession. She is so large, with her broad shoulders. She is so good hearted—a shield against trouble in bad times. This time, though, her aid is ineffectual.

They continue walking. They cross the border between life and death, cross the bridge between now and eternity. They shall never return.

Of all the deeds and creations of Yanosz Korczak, the artist and reformer; of all Steffa Wilczenska's efforts; of all the games, smiles and hopes of two hundred boys and girls—this one last walk will be remembered forever: because, with one daring leap (naturally, accidentally, unintentionally), it overcame murderous brutality.

This small group, under the leadership of Yanosz Korczak, has received eternal glory. It is a small group, the members of which are known by name, among the tens of thousands whose names a malevolent fate caused to be forgotten forever in the chaos of the general extermination.

Our eyes still see them walking slowly and quietly—the doctor's companions in spirit, his traveling companions in their fateful ghetto journey: Stephana Wilczenska, Mr. Henryk Osterblum, the veteran bookkeeper of the Home, Felix and Balbina Gzieb, Natzia Boz, Rosa Stockman, Sabina Leiserowicz, Dorka Solnicka, the four Moniushes, little Hanka with the lung trouble, Yolek who was ill, Abrasha of the burning eyes, who only a short time ago so successfully played a child about to die.

And you, the others, brave and courageous as those whom I have just mentioned, in your work for children, together with them in the ghetto and in death! The teaching and medical staff in Dzielna, Dzagliona, Tvarda, Dzicka, Milna—thousands of children, hundreds of pedagogues and doctors, all of them anonymous and forgotten—your name and your symbol is the legend of Yanosz Korczak.

To the accompaniment of the green waving flag they will go on to eternity in all time and in all countries of the world. From the scaffold of the ghetto and from the smoking crematoria of Treblinka—they travel on their way to eternity.

Prose and Poetry by Three Children from Terezin

FROM THE PROSE OF 15 YEAR OLD PETR FISCHL (BORN SEPTEMBER 9, 1929), WHO PERISHED IN OSWIECIM IN 1944.

We got used to standing in line at 7 o'clock in the morning, at 12 noon and again at 7 o'clock in the evening. We stood in a long queue with plates in our hands, into which they ladled a little warmed-up water with a salty or a coffee flavor. Or else they gave us a few potatoes. We got used to sleeping without beds, to saluting every uniform, not to walk on the sidewalks and then again to walk on the sidewalks. We got used to undeserved slaps, blows and executions. We got accustomed to seeing people die in their own excrement, to seeing piled-up coffins full of corpses, to seeing the sick amidst dirt and filth and to seeing the helpless doctors. We got used to it that from time to time, one thousand unhappy souls would come here and that, from time to time, another thousand unhappy souls would go away. . . .

HOMESICK

I've lived in the ghetto here more than a year,
In Terezin, in the black town now,
And when I remember my old home so dear,
I can love it more than I did, somehow.

Ah, home, home,
Why did they tear me away?
Here the weak die easy as a feather
And when they die, they die forever.

I'd like to go back home again,
It makes me think of sweet spring flowers.
Before, when I used to live at home,
It never seemed so dear and fair.

I remember now those golden days . . .
But maybe I'll be going there soon again.

People walk along the street,
You see at once on each you meet
That there's a ghetto here,
A place of evil and of fear.
There's little to eat and much to want,
Where bit by bit, it's horror to live.
But no one must give up!
The world turns and times change.

Yet we all hope the time will come
When we'll go home again.
Now I know how dear it is
And often I remember it.

Anonymous
1943

TEREZIN

The heaviest wheel rolls across our foreheads
To bury itself deep somewhere inside our memories.

We've suffered here more than enough,
Here in this clot of grief and shame,
Wanting a badge of blindness
To be a proof for their own children.

A fourth year of waiting, like standing above a swamp
From which any moment might gush forth a spring.

Meanwhile, the rivers flow another way,
Another way,
Not letting you die, not letting you live.

And the cannons don't scream and the guns don't bark
And you don't see blood here.

Nothing, only silent hunger.
Children steal the bread here and ask and ask
and ask
And all would wish to sleep, keep silent and
just to go to sleep again. . . .

The heaviest wheel rolls across our foreheads
To bury itself deep somewhere inside our memories.

Mif
1944

SHAYE GERTNER

Zonderkommando in Birkenau

TRANSLATED FROM THE YIDDISH BY MOSHE SPIEGEL

At first we were evacuated from Lodz to Konske. It was very bad there. Though I was not quite fourteen, I was very independent, and I was permitted to travel to my uncle in Skorzhisk. I spent five weeks there, but I became rather restless when I received no news from my parents, two sisters and a brother. I returned to Konske, and at that time Jews were also coming back to Lodz, because the "evacuation" order had been revoked; others smuggled themselves back. It was more agreeable to be in one's own town than be wretched far away from home. A *Judenrat* came into being in Lodz, headed by Rumkowski. He drove through the city like a count, always accompanied by militiamen. One of the public kitchens of the "Approvization Sczenshlivi" still functioned. All those connected with it regarded themselves as big shots and assumed the Germans would leave them alone.

Autumn 1940—a time when they began to fence in the ghetto with barbed wire. Jews were being kidnapped in the streets, and I was one of them. Seven hundred men were rounded up and sent to Czarnecki Prison. After being jailed only two days, I was transferred to Posen, where I worked with Poles in the local workcamp. Things were not too bad, but being only fourteen, how could I carry on among total strangers without my parents? I brooded and continually racked my brains to plan a way to return home.

Once, marching with my work detail early on a dark autumn morning, I managed to slip down into a ravine. I lay there quietly until everyone had passed on, then shuffled off toward Lodz.

There I found the ghetto already closed, its entrance guarded by Jewish militia. Quickly, I noticed a trolley car passing along Znierska Street in the ghetto. I rode to and fro on the trolley, to become familiar with the situation. All I had to do was jump off as the car passed Popzhechna Street, where the ghetto gate was, then wait until a wagon entered or left the ghetto, and jump through the gate

I kept on riding for a long time, waiting for an opportunity. But a Jewish militiaman, a real blockhead, seized me and took me to a German. I ended up in Gestapo headquarters on Anstaat Street.

I told my interrogator everything, for I still believed the Germans would be compassionate toward a youngster. I said I could not be without my mother. "You wish to join your mother? Very well, you will go to her!" my interrogator told me. And soon I was on my way to the S.K. [Punitive Commando] in Dachau. I never saw my parents again; and most likely they did not know I was so anxious to be reunited with them.

I traveled with a transport of 120 Jews and Poles, mostly picked up for various "crimes," just like myself. In the S.K. I was the youngest, and no one harmed me, not even the S.S. men. We worked in pairs, carrying limestone to a ditch where it was burned, fifteen hours a day. Toilers fell from exhaustion and hunger. S.K. prisoners were starving. When someone collapsed the S.S. men threw him into the lime pit, where he was consumed in the flames. At least two or three men died that way every day.

I suffered many privations for four months, hoping things would get better. But the only prospect seemed to be landing in the lime pit. Then I teamed up with four other Jews, and we began to "organize" food.

There was a food storehouse not far from our barracks. At night I would crawl through a casement window and hand out bread, sugar, marmalade and sausage. For a long time no one suspected anything, until I stepped one night into a keg of marmalade that was near a window, and left tracks all over the camp. A search was initiated. A Czech who had seen me eat my fill denounced me. Adults would have been punished by hanging; all I got was twenty-five lashes.

Later, whenever possible, I "organized" again. I was whipped every once in a while, so that my buttocks became tough as leather, and I didn't mind the beatings so much. Word reached the block foreman that I seemed to make light of my punishment, and I was warned that my next offense would be punished by hanging. I was well aware the threat would be carried out, and since I could not go on in the S.K., I decided to escape again.

Barbed wire arrived at the station, and we were ordered to unload it. I watched for my chance, slipped under a lorry and got to Posen. I was prepared for a journey; I carried 14,000 marks. It was fairly easy to obtain money in the camp; some inmates had considerable sums and didn't know what to do with their money. I knew no one in Posen. Although I had had some experience in Dachau, I was still childishly foolish. I stayed the night with a Pole, who turned out to be a *Volks-Deutsche*. He took my money while I slept and turned me over to the Gestapo in the morning.

After being interrogated by the S.S. I was taken to Birkenau, and assigned to the *Zonderkommando* Field D, Barracks 32. There were 400 men, mostly Jews, some Poles, and a few Germans. Some wore red emblems [political prisoners]; others the usual green [criminals].

During the first few days I didn't go to the ovens, but did housekeeping chores. But then the squad leader Müller appeared and said, "Such a sturdy lad ought to be assigned to a shift." And I started to work on the ovens. The first days were very hard, and I began to wonder how to extricate myself. Our *Kommando* had just plunged into the task. Everyone knew that within three months all of us would be dispensed with and replaced by others.

Our unit consisted of 400 men, working in two shifts. One oven belonged to us. We were accompanied by orchestral music on our way to work. The S.S. leader, Dr. Mengele, was our supervisor. He delivered the inmates to the gas chambers. He was followed in rank by Müller, then the Jewish *Kapos,* Poles and Germans. We were generally guarded by five S.S. men. When new transports of human cargo arrived, people were unaware of just what was in store for them. Before entering the building carrying the sign "Baths" the people had to disrobe completely, and received a number for their belongings, presumably to be reclaimed later. They got soap and towels for their shower. Then the *Kapos* would dash in to beat the unfortunates, to create confusion. During the ensuing commotion, when people trampled over one another, the door of the gas chamber would be thrown open, the prisoners pushed in, and then the door would bang shut after a cylinder of poison gas was flung into the mass.

I worked ten weeks in the *Zonderkommando*. I never entered

the gas chamber itself; only *Kapos* were admitted there. After the gassing a door in the other side of the chamber would open; there the *Kapos* would enter to throw out the corpses. All of us wore rubber gloves and wads of cotton in our mouths. The corpses exuded a pungent odor that could asphyxiate one. Small cars, loaded with forty corpses apiece, would ride along rails that extended from the gas chamber to the oven. The cars disgorged their cargo into the oven, where the bodies were reduced to ashes by electric current in ten minutes. A weak current left the bones intact; a strong current left small heaps. There was an apparatus, known as an exhauster, that blew the ashes into an adjoining pit, where they were piled into barrels by workers, then hoisted by an elevator and ultimately dumped into the Sala River.

The corpses I loaded onto the carts were yellow from the gas. Some of the cadavers had open, glazed eyes, hands holding their mouths, or clutching stomachs. None of us in this work could tolerate it. We often spoke of escape. The "S" camp bordered on ours, and we occasionally exchanged words with friends, whom we urged to make an attempt to avoid our lot—or even to be gassed.

What could they do? Many resorted to the only alternative: get near the electrically charged wires and die quickly. I felt this death was preferable to being gassed. On my way to work in the early morning, I would occasionally catch sight of the suicides clinging in an upright position to the wires, instead of lying prostrate. They looked as though alive.

I had it fairly good then. Each day I got a loaf of bread, a piece of butter, two eggs, a pint of milk and a special soup. But how could anyone enjoy food under those circumstances? Many inmates destined for the gas chamber carried considerable provisions, frequently fine clothes, especially in the case of foreign transports; and anyone could help himself to these things. We were also allowed to wear civilian clothes. Twice a week we got extra bread rations. But who cared for all that?

From the intimate daily conversation there evolved an organization. We began to assemble weapons obtained from fellow inmates engaged in the warehouse of plundered belongings. Later, in January, a group of Poles arrived, presumably from an uprising, and we got hand grenades from them. We hid these weapons in crates and buckets and straw sacks. A Polish officer, whose name I don't recall, was our leader. He taught us, with permission, calisthenics. He instructed us in all the motions an escape would require, crawling, dropping to the ground, and so on. The Germans watched us and asked, a bit baffled, "Do you intend to make soldiers out of them?" He replied that, as an officer, he could not proceed in any other way. We discussed our plans in the barracks at night. The *Kapos* had also been drawn into the conspiracy, for they too could not stand the work and wanted to escape.

The escape occurred in January 1944—perhaps the 18th day. The day before we learned a great human cargo was due to be gassed, and all 400 of us would be called to work simultaneously. This seemed a good time for an escape. Dr. Mengele appeared; he singled out 73 "Mussulmen," i.e., the frail and sick, and told them to remain in the barracks. The remaining 327 men proceeded to the work detail.

During the preceding night the leaders of our group dug a subterranean passage beneath the electrically charged barbed wire, leading beyond the crematorium to the open fields and woods. To avoid the shock of strong electric current, an open barrel was placed under the wires, and we crawled through it without mishap. The Polish officer taught us to go in single file, and hold on to one another.

When we got to work that morning, we changed into civilian clothes because some of us wore the camp uniform. We told the German squad leader our uniforms were getting soiled and we wished to change. He consented. The second leader of our group we nicknamed Franz von Mannheim, a German from the city of Mannheim.

Everything was in order. It was resolved to shoot anyone disobeying the commands. At a signal from the Polish officer, we killed one S.S. man, and threw the German squad leader into the lime pit. Then we began to throw grenades into the oven. Those on the other side of the gas chamber with the other three S.S. men, who guarded the new arrivals, shouted that it was an air attack alarm. Hearing the explosions, the S.S. men believed it and ran for cover. The inmates, standing in front of the gas chamber, were at a loss for what to do. Meanwhile we left individually at the command. When the last one had left, the Polish officer signaled us to run for our lives.

An hour and a half went by before the Germans really got their bearings. Then they opened fire in all directions and began to reconnoiter the surrounding area. I learned later from witnesses that about 200 men were killed in the wake of that event. The rest escaped; it is hard to determine the number killed among the latter.

I was trudging together with a group of 27 men in the direction of Germany. We were led by a Jew from Berlin familiar with the land. We had plenty of money, so we bought shovels and marched along, singing German songs in the manner of German workers. We had already penetrated deep into Germany, when we were taken by the German authorities in some town. We declard that we had escaped from a transport in Dachau; they believed us and sent us to Dachau.

I was back in Dachau in March 1944. I said my name was Casiemierz Dudzinski (though they knew I was Jewish).

At that time there was a munitions factory 100 meters underground Dachau, producing the weapon, "*Fau* 1." There were huge chambers, linked by electric trolley cars. We not only produced bombs, but manufactured the entire apparatus, including five bombs and a bombing vessel. The Germans boasted before us that this weapon would wipe England off the face of the earth. They would point to newspaper reports telling of the daily devastation by those bombs in England. We were aware of their lies and did not believe everything told us. But it was no comfort to realize we contributed to the production of such deadly weapons.

Former Soviet officers working with us taught us the art of sabotage. They told us to drop a few straws into receptacles filled with gasoline. When the mechanism would be heated the straws would ignite and create havoc. We also mixed sand with the powder. The sabotage was not carried out carefully, and one day all the apparatus was destroyed in the same manner. A military commission investigating the explosion found sand and straw. A roll call of those employed in the tunnel followed, separating the Jews, the Poles and the Russians. Every tenth man was condemned to death—160 deaths all told. Thereafter the supervisor was most rigorous. At the least suspicion 30 to 50 workers would be hanged. Later we resumed the sabotage, so that two or three parts of the apparatus would be defective.

We lacked proper food. Though the bread ration was increased, the soup was rotten, as usual. I learned locksmithing on this project. On May 15 we were loaded into railroad cars, but in the absence of a locomotive we soon were sent back to camp.

The S.S. armed the German *Kapos,* so they could guard us properly. It was an unforgettable moment when those *Kapos* started target practice, and an American tank appeared in the distance. The *Kapos* turned away and discarded their rifles.

The next day the Americans came to our camp. The first American soldier I met was a Jew from Lemberg. We spent four weeks with the Americans. Of the 28,000 inmates, 4,000 were Jewish. There was not enough bread, but plenty of chocolate.

I returned to Lodz, but found not a single survivor of my family. I am all alone, and there is no reason for my staying here. In the environs of Lodz, bandits shot at my companion and robbed us. I wish to leave this place.

REUBEN ROSENBERG

From One Camp to Another

TRANSLATED FROM THE YIDDISH BY MOSHE SPIEGEL

When the Germans occupied Adamow and the region around Lublin in 1939, they expelled everyone from the village and planned to burn it. But pleas from German nationals prevented this. Everything in the surrounding area was burned, hamlets like Volia Boczetska and others. They raided in search of arms and Polish soldiers.

Adamow was inhabited by 2,000 people, 250 of whom were Jews. Germans lived on the Aukzhea estate. Everyone was taxed 10,000 zlotys, and furniture and household goods were confiscated in absence of payment. There was no school for children. The *Judenrat,* or Jewish council, was composed of 12 people. A contingent of S.S. men arrived in Adamow in 1940, and two years later Jews began buying arms and fleeing to the forests. During the evacuation on October 20, 1942, all fled to the forests to fight the Germans, even the Jewish militia. Only 30 people remained.

On the first day Germans and Ukrainians surrounded the city, drove the people into the street and shot them summarily. Poles also turned in Jews and helped fight them in the forests. This liquidating "action" resulted after an accidental fire caused by a Polish woman, a fire which enveloped Adamow. Poles suspected Jewish partisans had started the blaze.

During this action I escaped to Demblin. I was not accepted for work there and had to bribe the leader, a German national. I worked at the aviation depot for the Werman firm, later owned by Schultz. The work was difficult, canalization, concrete and other tasks. Sometimes youngsters deliberately wounded their feet on the rails to be freed of the labor for a few days. The work was unbearable.

Two boys were killed for stealing potatoes. They were dragged to the cellar of the gendarmerie, where dogs bit them to death. The worst of the gendarmes was called Petersen.

In the spring of 1943, ten Jews, of whom two were militiamen, took ammunition from the airplanes and fled to the forest. Attempts to find them failed, but they succeeded in killing Petersen and his dog outside the city limits. They took weapons from two other gendarmes and permitted them to return, naked, to the city. Of the ten, five were older men. The young left the old, and robbed the Poles for revenge. The A.K. [Polish Partisans] surrounded and killed them, but the older ones still live. Their commander was Liebman, of the town of Riki.

When the [Soviet] offensive began and the Lublin S.S. men were taken prisoner in July of 1944, the colonel of the aviation depot wanted to leave us behind. But the Jewish camp leader, Wagonhardt, had a personal enemy and wanted to flee to the Germans. His enemy was Meyer Haldisch; S.S. men from Czestochowa had demanded 200 workers, and Wagonhardt sent thieves and Haldisch. But Haldisch escaped and was determined to avenge himself.

Wagonhardt arranged with the chief of the railroad depot for 80,000 zlotys to provide us with railroad cars and provisions for escape. We used to get food for two months in one shipment. Besides provisions from the S.S. we also got something from the *Wehrmacht*. We became known as good workers, and private firms, pressured by the colonel, supplied us with provisions. A General Florer was there, and he was satisfied with our work. He used to treat us to cigarettes.

Toward the end we worked with the Junaks, who beat us when we worked. They were a company of 800, and the colonel would penalize them for throwing stones and knives at us. For a time the Uzbeks also worked beside us. They were friendly. They later joined the army, swore allegiance to the Germans and got good food and uniforms.

Before the evacuation 60 boys escaped. We had had a drunkard staff sergeant, whom we called "whisky sergeant," and we got away from him. The Poles caught some boys and killed them with axes. Wagonhardt saw them escaping and alerted the evacuation force.

In Czestochowa there was a dour work security leader and the Jewish militia. They took everything from us, but when we were in Buchenwald we got even with some of them.

There were two work places here, the iron foundry, Rakov,

and Felzer, an ammunition factory. The food was bad, the labor hard, and we were almost naked. They divided up those from Demblin. There were 700 of us. The three barracks were surrounded by barbed wire. Two people slept on one straw sack; there were 250 men, infested with vermin, sleeping in each barrack. Fifteen women and two children under twelve were kept for cleaning and laundry.

We worked in the iron foundry in two shifts, three shifts in transportation. One foreman, a German Jew known as Heinrich of Berlin, often informed on Jews to the security guard. Heinrich was killed in Buchenwald, on a sentence carried out by Gustav of Lemberg, of the Gestapo. Gustav had been a spy for the communists, and was sent to Buchenwald as a political prisoner. He had a free hand as block foreman, and if he heard a complaint about a militiaman treating Jews badly he would mete out punishment. The Germans never interfered with this.

At Rakov, the work—loading iron, tar, coal and coke—was very hard. Heinrich would even augment the rules of security guard leaders. In Buchenwald Gustav told Heinrich to hang himself within two days. Heinrich would not, so Gustav beat him and others finished him.

When the workers saw that people were being sent to Auschwitz from Krashnik and other places they tried to escape. The Poles would catch them, return them to the workshops or put them in jail. They no longer shot them, and many saved themselves in Czestochowa by being thrown into prison.

There were some terrible accidents at the workshops. Men fell asleep from hunger or fatigue at their machines, and their hands or feet would be torn away. There were three Jews hiding on the factory grounds, and one worker brought them food. One of the men had a wife, on whom the Germans found a letter from her husband. She was tortured and finally revealed the name of the man who fed them. All four were arrested. The evacuation of Czestochowa was horrible; they dynamited homes where people were hiding.

In Czestochowa the workshop leader was called "Getsel." In Demblin the men who drove army troops to Czestochowa were Jews. On the way they were stopped by the S.S., and they had no papers, only their badges marked "Construction Headquarters." They had to confess they were Jews, and the S.S. murdered them.

Everybody from Rakov was taken to Buchenwald, but those who worked at Warte and Felzer remained at their jobs. We rode for three days in locked wagons, well guarded by factory guards. We did not know that three days later the Soviets occupied Czestochowa.

Buchenwald was a camp for political prisoners. Because of the offensive new convoys arrived all the time. Eighty thousand persons were sent there.

Buchenwald had brick bunkers and small gardens in the forest. There was a school for S.S. men and one for dogs. The camp was clean; twice a week there was a check and a disinfection. On the athletic field the older people from the big blocks played football. Because there was not enough space, tents were set up.

It was impossible to escape. The camp was surrounded by triple barbed wire, towers, and a canal. Reflectors illuminated every arriving train. S.S. men took count during roll call to see if anyone was missing.

We were first quarantined for three weeks, during which eight persons slept on every two sacks. The factory there was bombed so badly by the Americans and English that it was shut down.

After quarantine we were dispersed to barracks and other camps. Everyone was awakened at six A.M. Some rose at five, to get to the coffee sooner. Breakfast of bread and coffee was at seven, lunch at ten and coffee at two. Bedtime was nine o'clock.

We were separated into small groups, and got six injections against disease. Prisoners were in the office, and S.S. men supervised but did not interfere while English, Yugoslavs and others received parcels from the Red Cross. The Jews got nothing.

For work we had to rise at four A.M., walk two kilometers to the station and detour ten kilometers to Weimar. We worked from nine to four, with frequent roll calls. There was one loaf of bread and some soup for five people. Twice a week there was sausage. Our work was to clean up the debris after a bombing; there were air attacks every day. We dragged German corpses from the cellars. We lived together with foreigners and German political prisoners. They were treated like the Jews. Relations were friendly among camp inmates. We called each other "colleague" or "comrade." The word *"Herr"* disappeared from our speech. There was a movie in the camp, and a casino. We paid with special marks issued by the office, not money. Beer was also for sale.

The Jewish "power" apparatus included the block elder, ten members of the camp advisory council and the camp elder. Twice a day we listened to the radio. Gustav called for solidarity and collectivism. We were permitted to take food from wrecked homes, but not household articles—stealing these was punishable by death. Gustav said the food should be shared. He gathered children from ten to sixteen and cared for them. There were several young boys, about eighteen, who carried out his commands. Gustav was a prominent figure. There were only Jews in his block. He wore a Polish military uniform.

A transport of prisoners from Auschwitz was once brought in, in an open coal railroad car. There were 1,100 frozen and half-frozen cripples. There were no gas chambers in Buchenwald, only an oven to burn the corpses.

As the front narrowed, people were brought in from all camps. We were later sent to Flussburg, thirty kilometers from Leipzig. There were 1,100 people already there; we were 400 Poles, French and Russians. The K.L. of the S.S. was a real hell-raiser. At this camp there was a factory that made bazookas. There was one S.S. man for every four prisoners. Every day 15 men died, aside from those who died "from natural causes." We ran to work. Work intended for 20 people was done by ten. We worked from six A.M. to seven P.M. We collapsed. Many people committed suicide. In two weeks 500 died. Filth, no water, two days without heat, no bath, and no underwear. There was 25 lashes for stealing potato peelings. They called us the race gang, communists, cadets, soap-bags, criminals and bolsheviks.

The Poles, who worked in the open air, would bring us beets to trade for bread. The one-handed top group leader, whom we called "Lapka," said he would kill everybody.

Because things were bad at the front they hurried us and always beat us at the factory. The factory was to open on February 1, but it was bombed. They took it out on us. We were to repair all damage in one day, which was impossible. They beat us mercilessly.

As the Americans approached an order came not to kill, but the S.S. men took little notice of it. The S.S. kitchen always short-rationed us, too. At last the factory was ready.

To load the bazookas we had to use picric acid and trotil. We worked without gas masks, and after a few weeks the lungs and feet would cave in. The young were chosen for this task. S.S. men would kill them while they worked, so there was always a shortage of workers. People would be missing during call-ups, too. We would stand in the rain for hours during call-ups. In the last week, the

S.S. men left and civilian experts took over operation of the camp Things got a little better. The German block elders among the prisoners did not have to be present during the call-up. During the call-up they would steal from the kitchen. They would even kill to earn the favor of the top squad leader. We worked on the railroads, highways and quarries without rest or definite work hours. The last five days we were without supervision or work. There were constant air attacks. We decided to provide ourselves with some food and got the key to the beet storehouse. The Ukrainian camp guard caught a boy with two pails of beets. He said an Italian gave him the beets, but he was sentenced to hang. Because of the ban on killing, though, he was given 300 lashes.

The next morning they put us in railroad cars and moved us aimlessly, without food or drink. We suffocated from the trotil in the cars. We rode for seventeen days. The first three days we had nothing to eat; later there was one hundred grams of bread every other day. We were heading for Chemnitz, where a women's convoy was attached. People died constantly. The S.S. men "comforted" us, saying we were going to a "heavenly command." Every second day they opened the cars slightly, so we would not suffocate altogether. Of 1,500 people, 500 arrived at Mathausen. The S.S. would shoot into the cars. We were always thirty kilometers from the front. The S.S. men did not want to go to the front, and said that we had to be guarded.

They led us gradually to martyrdom. They brought us to the Sudeten in Czechoslovakia. The Czechs stood at the station and brought us food. The S.S. did not allow this, and took the food for themselves. One day, when we had about 80 corpses in the car, they made the Jews dig graves. A Czech came and said he would not permit innocent people to be buried in his field. The S.S. relented but forced him to harness his horse and wagon and take the dead to a cemetery. They could not bury them, though, because the front was getting nearer.

We were taken toward Austria without food. Healthy men fled but usually were caught and shot. When we got to Mathausen, fifty of us who could not walk out of the cars were shot. The camp was three kilometers away, and 320 finally reached it. We were going toward the crematorium. We were told we were on our way to the baths, but we knew we were on our way to—death. A transport of 1,500 people had preceded us the same day. We had to wait three days. For the time, we were billeted in a block. From the baths we were driven, men and women together, naked, a kilometer to the block. Numbers were tattooed on our breasts.

We waited to be gassed. Our hair was cut. Five of us slept on a single bed. A "liter" of soup and eight "deca" of bread. That was called a hospital. We lay on bare boards without straw pallets. We ate the hides of horses and the raw flesh of the corpses.

The next day the S.S. men vanished; the *Folkssturm* took charge. The Jews were treated worst of all, but we were not sent to the gas chamber. We were in a separate block—a ghetto.

Three days before the capitulation, the gas jets were destroyed. When the block elders became aware of this, they began to repair the damage to avoid panic.

When the Americans arrived, they found two thousand dead. The rest of us were moribund, in a dying state.

FEIGA KAMMER

Winter in the Forest

TRANSLATED FROM THE YIDDISH BY MOSHE SPIEGEL

We were about to entrust the children* to peasants, but the children would not leave their mother. It was January, 1943, freezing cold, and the snow half-a-meter high. At midnight we decided to escape, and we set out without a crumb of bread, for the village of Zaluzhe, five kilometers from our town of Lyubatchow,** where a Pole we knew made his home. We hid in his loft without his knowledge. Here we parted. I remained there with the children, and my husband set out for the forest.

On the third day they swooped down on the Jews from Lyubatchow who had sought shelter here. The local peasants betrayed them. All those Jews were rounded up in the *Geminah,* and from there the S.S. troopers took them to a field where animal carcasses were usually buried, shot them and buried them. I remember the names of some of the Ukrainians: Stephan Holub, the *Woyt* [village elder] Mosa. . . .

After three days the proprietor turned me out from the house. With small children, I set out in freezing weather for a village where my little girl, aged ten, served a peasant family as a shepherdess. We trudged along frozen rivers and forests, and on reaching our destination the peasant woman refused to admit us, for fear of her neighbors. That night we walked nine kilometers to the village of Dachnow. There, too, no one would admit us. The children were chilled to the bone and hungry, and their cries seemed

* Three children, ages 5, 10 and 11.

** Forty kilometers from Rowa Ruska, not far from the Belsen death camp.

to touch no one's heart. Then we went to the small forest four kilometers from Lyubatchow, and there I saw the bloody "Action" against the Lyubatchow Jews. Four Ukrainians and Germans shot at the Jews, who were lined up in rows. Since only one bullet was allotted per person many [wounded] Jews lay in the graves for hours, or moved about in the field until they froze to death.

Then peasants came with axes and chopped off feet which wore high boots, or fingers with gold rings on them. The executions went on for ten weeks. Day after day the neighboring Ukrainians and Poles would search out bunkers, from which Jews would be dragged. We remained three days in the woods.

At night I ventured out to buy bread for the children. Later, we would hide in stables, granaries, haystacks and so on, without the knowledge of their proprietors. But this could not go on, and we returned to the forest. We were seen by the Germans and Ukrainians who happened to be hunting rabbits. They started to shout, *"Jude! Jude!"*—but the Germans were more anxious to catch rabbits just then.

It was twelve days after the "Action." My ten-year-old daughter said to me, "Mother, why do you suffer so much on our account? Just leave us here, and try to save yourself." She had heard the peasants remark occasionally that they would hide me alone, but feared to hide the children.

"Mother," my little girl would say, "pray to God that we may have an easy death, and let us go by ourselves."

At last, one woman took pity on us and let us stay for the night. Early in the morning she told us to leave. In the courtyard we sought shelter in a chicken coop, from which we had been removed because of the severe cold. As we lay there, huddled, my daughter insisted on visiting a friendly peasant woman, merely to ask her for an easy death. The peasant gave her food and let her warm up. A Ukrainian boy, who happened to be in the house, followed her out and tried to make her disclose our hideout. She would not, and he let her go. She proceeded along a devious, circuitous route, unaware that he trailed her at a distance. She got to the hideout. I had left a few minutes earlier in search of food, and I was admitted to a peasant home. While there, I saw through a window the Ukrainian boy beating my child, choking her, torturing her, and dragging her to headquarters for interrogation of my whereabouts.

Later on, the Ukrainian guards reiterated her words: "Four lives must not perish on account of one. My life is lost anyhow." She pleaded for mercy, since she had not harmed anyone. She was taken to the small forest (I observed it from a distance). I knew she was about to be executed. She pleaded with the Ukrainians, "My blood will not let you rest." But in vain. She had to wait for a transport of 200 Jews from Lyubatchow. She then asked to be shot, and her request was granted.

I am a simple Jewish woman and cannot describe what I endured while my innocent child was being killed.

From January 13 until February 11, my little son and I wandered through the villages, sleeping in stables without the peasants' permission. Our feet were frostbitten. When I would ask my child, "Are you hungry, Yankele?" he would answer, "Why do you ask, Mother? Are you going to help me?" I was desperate. The children could not endure any more, and pleaded for death.

On a pitch-black night, I walked nine kilometers to a peasant, to whom I had entrusted my pitiful belongings. He chased me out. (He was eventually killed by the Germans.)

When I was about to surrender to the Germans, a kindly peasant woman let us stay in her granary, under the hay. She fed us soup. We did not remove our shoes for four weeks. My elder son was troubled by a frostbitten, swollen leg, and his high boot had to be cut down. In the process I cut off the heel of his foot. He did not cry, and I was too benumbed. I had neither medication nor bandages, so I used my only undershirt. There was considerable bleeding, but luckily no serious infection. Later, I wrapped his ailing foot with straw and hay, and carrying the little one, we trudged from one village to another.

The youngest, a child of five years, was suffering from bruised, frostbitten toes that were wrapped in rags. After considerable pleading I found a peasant woman who agreed to take the child, for the few gold coins I had cached underground. The child was kept hidden in the granary.

The Diary of David Rubinovcih

TRANSLATED FROM THE YIDDISH BY ADAH FOGEL

May 5

There are rumors flying about that tonight there will be a police raid on the Jews. Papa hasn't been home since yesterday—and what if he returns today right in the middle of the raid? We wrote him a letter that he and my cousin shouldn't come today, and gave it to the boy from Kraino who just happened to be here.

May 6

A terrible day. At about 3 A.M. I was awakened by banging. It was the police, starting the raid. I wasn't frightened—Papa and my cousin are in Kraino and they know that the other cousins are in hiding. A few minutes later there was knocking at the door, and my uncle quickly opened. Two policemen came in—one Polish and one Jewish—and immediately began to search the house. One of them told me to get dressed, but the other one asked me how old I was shaking. When the police left I fell asleep. Very early my cousin woke me up, because Papa had arrived in a wagon. I was, and when I told him, "Fourteen," he left me alone. They snooped around a bit, but they didn't find anyone, just the two men from Plotzk, whom they took with them. Although I didn't feel afraid, I dressed quickly and went outside, but he had already left—he couldn't wait because of the raid.

The stuff on the wagon had already been unloaded. Just then I saw a policeman turning into our yard. I started to run, but he began to yell: "Where are the potatoes? Bring the rest!" and other things which I couldn't make out. "Now it is really the end," I thought. When they had finished loading everything he went back to police HQ.

Papa isn't here. What were we going to do? Mama and my aunt went to the police. I was awfully upset. They had taken everything we owned, now we would die for a piece of bread. Soon Anshl came and told us that Papa and my cousin had been arrested. I started to cry. They had taken Papa away from us, they had taken all our possessions. Suddenly I felt a deep yearning for Papa. Who cared about the things? Mama ran to the *Judenrat* to ask them to release Papa because he's sick and can't live without his medicine, and if they should assign him to hard labor in a concentration camp it would be a disaster.

At the *Judenrat* they told her Papa would be released after they examined him, and we began to hope he might be set free. I didn't go into the street because I might be caught, too, but my brother and Anshl took food to the prisoners. When Anshl came home he told us that his brother-in-law was also in prison. The panic was horrible. Everyone hid wherever he could find a corner, and the relatives and wives of the prisoners were sobbing hysterically? How could you not?

The Bielin police were helping to conduct the raid. When things calmed down a bit, two automobiles drove up. One of them had a platform in the back. When I saw them the thought struck me that Papa might be sent away, and I began to weep uncontrollably. Papa had told my brother to bring him food, several pairs of underwear, and a small pan. When I saw my brother packing the things I burst into tears again.

All this time Mama was at the *Judenrat* asking them to intervene, and they kept telling her Papa would be released. My brother came to get a warm hat, but he was too late—the automobile was already on the next block. I began to scream when they approached: "Papa, where are you, let me see you just once more!" Then I saw him, in the last car, and he was crying. I watched the car until it disappeared at the crossroads. I burst into tears and felt a deep love for Papa, and his love for me, and realized that when I had written on May 1 that he didn't love me it was a lie, totally false, and, who knows, maybe I would have to pay for suspecting him of something that wasn't true. God willing, when he comes home, I will behave differently toward him. I cried for a long time, and when I remembered Papa's tear-stained face I cried even harder. Papa was the most precious of all, and he had been taken away from us, and he was sick, too.

When we quieted down Mama went to the police because it was getting close to 2 o'clock. I stayed in the house and thought about the fate which awaited Papa and the bad luck which had already struck us. My sister arrived and said:

"Go to the police, but take someone with you, because they have given everything away." Anshl and I started out, and on the way we met Mama. Anshl took the bundle she was carrying, and I went along with her. We had to make several trips before we brought all the things back to the house. You can't imagine what a joy it was, but our happiness was really superficial, because our hearts were heavy with an indescribable sadness. Mama had pleaded with the entire *Judenrat* to help her salvage the merchandise, and nobody wanted to help, but God saw to it that we got it back without them. When we came home we were visited by a policeman, who wanted to know if all our possessions had been returned to us. He was a friendly German, and if not for him we wouldn't have gotten a stick. Mama was as exhausted from this one day as if it had stretched for four weeks.

When I got into bed I thought of Papa. Here I was in a comfortable bed and Papa was in a barrack, and maybe without even a handful of straw on which to rest his head. My heart constricted with pain and I started to cry, and cried myself to sleep.

NUSJA AND INJA SHIFMAN

Letters from the Ghetto

TRANSLATED FROM THE YIDDISH BY MAX ROSENFELD

Dear, Beloved Daddy: *November 4, 1942*

Your birthday is approaching, our last autumn family holiday. I only hope that this letter reaches you in time to bring you the heartfelt wishes of your little girls; that it brings you strength and energy and sustains you in this difficult moment of our lives. Most important: that you stay well, and, like us, never lose courage and faith in a better tomorrow. First of all, you must be strong, you, our best and dearest protector. We gain much strength from the certainty that we still have you, that with your fatherly hand you will help us and take care of us every moment of our lives.

Daddy dearest, more than ever before, I now think constantly of my parents; I understand the power of your love, and I see what kind of human beings, in the fullest sense of the word, you were. I see it most clearly now, when life has forced me to make my own decisions about Inja and myself. I see that only thanks to the fact that I was brought up in such a wholesome home can I manage to maintain my spiritual equilibrium and somehow make the right decisions. Being so far away from you both, I love my parents more each day, because with every passing day I understand and know them better. "Great love is the daughter of great recognition." Loluszec, celebrate your birthday as happily as we shall here. Let us think about how happy we were when we celebrated it together. And how happy we shall be when we again all celebrate it together. I truly believe it.

I hug and kiss you, Daddy,

Your Nu

I kiss you warmly; I am brave and full of hope.

Inja

* * *

My Dear, Dear Daddy: *November 16, 1942*

It is late, I am very sleepy, but still I must write you a few words. We receive your letters in regular order. We have already written to you several times, but have received no reply as yet. Today we received from you 200 zlotys; they will be very useful to us. Today we had a sweet day—we were given marmalade and candy.

Lolusz! Your birthday is approaching. This is already the fourth time that we shall celebrate it separately, but full of hope and faith that next year God will grant that we all be together. Our own dear Daddy—you must be strong and steadfast and believe, as we do, that the moment of our meeting is close and we will all be together and happy.

My eyes are closing. I can't write anymore. Good night, Loluszec! Don't worry. I hug and kiss you—I'm full of hope. My heart and soul are with you—

Inja

Dear Lolek!

We're all well and wait impatiently for your reply. Many thanks for the greetings from Stera. We don't know about the rest of them. You be well and strong and in good hope—

I kiss you,

—Nusja

* * *

Dear Daddy: *February 4, 1943*

You must be very anxious about us. We sent you the last letter two weeks ago. The mail delivery is very bad here, so we don't get any letters from you at all. (For some time there was no mail at all.) It's just lucky that I had three sheets of letter-paper. It it continues to be so bad with the mail, I will send you the next letter in about two weeks. Here not long ago we moved to another room. It is bigger and more comfortable than the previous one. It is warm and pleasant. My work is easy and not tiring. Inja is busy with a little girl; she plays with her and takes her for walks. Grandma mends and cooks for us. We are well prepared for winter. We have three sweaters, woolen stockings, socks, good shoes, two dresses and coats for each of us. We eat well. Our hygienic conditions are excellent. (A bathroom).

How are things going with you, Loluszec? How is your work—how do they treat you? Are you still living with your friend Glassman? Write us about everything, Daddy. I do so want to know clearly about everything that has to do with you.

I hug you, dear daddy—

We miss you,

Nu

Regards from Inja

ANNE FRANK

The Diary of a Young Girl

TRANSLATED FROM THE DUTCH BY B. M. MOOYAART

Dear Kitty, *Friday, 30 June, 1944*

Bad weather, or *bad weather at a stretch to the thirtieth of June.** Isn't that well said! Oh yes, I have a smattering of English already; just to show that I can, I'm reading *An Ideal Husband* with the aid of a dictionary. War going wonderfully! Bobroisk, Mogilef, and Orsa have fallen, lots of prisoners.

Everything's all right here and tempers are improving. The super-optimists are triumphing. Elli has changed her hair style, Miep has the week off. That's the latest news.

Yours, Anne

Dear Kitty, *Thursday, 6 July, 1944*

It strikes fear to my heart when Peter talks of later being a criminal, or of gambling; although it's meant as a joke, of course, it gives me the feeling that he's afraid of his own weakness. Again and again I hear from both Margot and Peter: "Yes, if I was as strong and plucky as you are, if I always stuck to what I wanted, if I had such persistent energy, yes then . . . !"

I wonder if it's really a good quality not to let myself be influenced. Is it really good to follow almost entirely my own conscience?

Quite honestly, I can't imagine how anyone can say: "I'm weak," and then remain so. After all, if you know it, why not fight against it, why not try to train your character? The answer was: "Because it's

* In English in the original.

so much easier not to!" This reply rather discouraged me. Easy? Does that mean that a lazy, deceitful life is an easy life? Oh no, that can't be true, it mustn't be true, people can so easily be tempted by slackness . . . and by money.

I thought for a long time about the best answer to give Peter, how to get him to believe in himself and, above all, to try and improve himself; I don't know whether my line of thought is right though, or not.

I've so often thought how lovely it would be to have someone's complete confidence, but now, now that I'm that far, I realize how difficult it is to think what the other person is thinking and then to find the *right* answer. More especially because the very ideas of "easy" and "money" are something entirely foreign and new to me. Peter's beginning to lean on me a bit and that mustn't happen under any circumstances. A type like Peter finds it difficult to stand on his own feet, but it's even harder to stand on your own feet as a conscious, living being. Because if you do, then it's twice as difficult to steer a right path through the sea of problems and still remain constant through it all. I'm just drifting around, have been searching for days, searching for a good argument against that terrible word "easy," something to settle it once and for all.

How can I make it clear to him that what appears easy and attractive will drag him down into the depths, depths where there is no comfort to be found, no friends and no beauty, depths from which it is almost impossible to raise oneself?

We all live, but we don't know the why or the wherefore. We all live with the object of being happy; our lives are all different and yet the same. We three have been brought up in good circles, we have the chance to learn, the possibility of attaining something, we have all reason to hope for much happiness, but . . . we must earn it for ourselves. And that is never easy. You must work and do good, not be lazy and gamble, if you wish to earn happiness. Laziness may *appear* attractive, but work *gives* satisfaction.

I can't understand people who don't like work, yet that isn't the case with Peter; he just hasn't got a fixed goal to aim at, and he thinks he's too stupid and too inferior to achieve anything. Poor boy, he's never known what it feels like to make other people happy, and I can't teach him that either. He has no religion, scoffs at Jesus Christ, and swears, using the name of God; although I'm not orthodox either, it hurts me every time I see how deserted, how scornful, and how poor he really is.

People who have a religion should be glad, for not everyone has the gift of believing in heavenly things. You don't necessarily even have to be afraid of punishment after death; pugatory, hell, and heaven are things that a lot of people can't accept, but still a religion, it doesn't matter which, keeps a person on the right path. It isn't the fear of God but the upholding of one's own honor and conscience. How noble and good everyone could be if, every evening before falling asleep, they were to recall to their minds the events of the whole day and consider exactly what has been good and bad. Then, without realizing it, you try to improve yourself at the start of each new day; of course, you achieve quite a lot in the course of time. Anyone can do this, it costs nothing and is certainly very helpful. Whoever doesn't know it must learn and find by experience that: "A quiet conscience makes one strong!"

Yours, Anne

Dear Kitty, *Saturday, 8 July, 1944*

The chief representative of the business, Mr. B., has been in Beverwijk and managed, just like that, to get strawberries at the auction sale.* They arrived here dusty, covered with sand, but in large quantities. No less than twenty-four trays for the office people and us. That very same evening we bottled six jars and made eight pots of jam. The next morning Miep wanted to make jam for the office people.

At half past twelve, no strangers in the house, front door bolted, trays fetched, Peter, Daddy, Van Daan clattering on the stairs: Anne, get hot water; Margot, bring a bucket; all hands on deck! I went into the kitchen, which was chockfull, with a queer feeling in my tummy, Miep, Elli, Koophuis, Henk, Daddy, Peter: the families in hiding and their supply column, all mingling together, and in the middle of the day too!

People can't see in from outside because of the net curtains, but, even so, the loud voices and banging doors positively gave me the jitters. Are we really supposed to be in hiding? That's what flashed through my mind, and it gives one a very queer feeling to be able to appear in the world again. The pan was full, and I dashed upstairs again. The rest of the family was seated round our table in the kitchen busy stalk-picking—at least that's what they were sup-

* It is compulsory in Holland for all growers to sell their produce at public auction.

posed to be doing; more went into mouths than into buckets. Another bucket would soon be required. Peter went to the downstairs kitchen again—the bell rang twice; the bucket stayed where it was, Peter tore upstairs, locked the cupboard door! We were kicking our heels impatiently, couldn't turn on a tap, even though the strawberries were only half washed; the rule is: "If anyone in the house, use no water, because of the noise," was strictly maintained.

At one o'clock Henk came and told us that it was the postman. Peter hurried downstairs again. Ting-a-ling . . . the bell, right about turn. I go and listen to see if I can hear anyone coming, first at our cupboard door and then creep to the top of the stairs. Finally Peter and I both lean over the banisters like a couple of thieves, listening to the din downstairs. No strange voices, Peter sneaks down, stops halfway, and calls out: "Elli!" No answer, one more: "Elli!" Peter's voice is drowned by the din in the kitchen. He goes right down and into the kitchen. I stand looking down tensely. "Get upstairs at once, Peter, the accountant is here, clear out!" It was Koophuis speaking. Peter comes upstairs sighing, the cupboard door closes. Finally Kraler arrives at half past one. "Oh, dearie me, I see nothing but strawberries, strawberries at breakfast, strawberries stewed by Miep, I smell strawberries, must have a rest from them and go upstairs—what is being washed up here . . . strawberries."

The remainder are being bottled. In the evening: two jars unsealed. Daddy quickly makes them into jam. The next morning: two more unsealed and four in the afternoon. Van Daan hadn't brought them to the right temperature for sterilizing. Now Daddy makes jam every evening.

We eat strawberries with our porridge, skimmed milk with strawberries, bread and butter with strawberries, strawberries for dessert, strawberries with sugar, strawberries with sand. For two whole days strawberries and nothing but strawberries, then the supply was finished or in bottles and under lock and key.

"I say, Anne," Margot calls out, "the greengrocer on the corner has let us have some green peas, nineteen pounds." "That's nice of him," I replied. And it certainly is, but oh, the work . . . ugh!

"You've all got to help shelling peas on Saturday morning," Mummy announced when we were at table. And, sure enough, the big enamel pan duly appeared this morning, filled to the brim. Shelling peas is a boring job, but you ought to try "skinning" the pods. I don't think many people realize how soft and tasty the pod is when the skin on the inside has been removed. However, an even greater advantage is that the quantity which can be eaten is about triple the amount of when one only eats the peas. It's an exceptionally precise, finicky job, pulling out this skin; perhaps it's all right for pedantic dentists or precise office workers, but for an impatient teen-ager like me, it's frightful. We began at half past nine, I got up at half past ten, at half past eleven I sat down again. This refrain hummed in my ears: bend the top, pull the skin, remove the string, throw out the pod, etc., etc., they dance before my eyes, green, green, green maggots, strings, rotten pods, green, green, green. Just for the sake of doing something, I chatter the whole morning, any nonsense that comes into my head, make everyone laugh, and bore them stiff. But every string that I pull makes me feel more certain that I never, never want to be just a housewife only!

We finally have breakfast at twelve o'clock, but from half past twelve until quarter past one we've got to go skinning pods again. I'm just about seasick when I stop, the others a bit too. I go and sleep till four o'clock, but I'm still upset by those wretched peas.

Yours, Anne

Dear Kitty, *Saturday, 15 July, 1944*

We have had a book from the library with the challenging title of: *What Do You Think of the Modern Young Girl?* I want to talk about this subject today.

The author of this book criticizes "the youth of today" from top to toe, without, however, condemning the whole of the young brigade as "incapable of anything good." On the contrary, she is rather of the opinion that if young people wished, they have it in their hands to make a bigger, more beautiful and better world, but that they occupy themselves with superficial things, without giving a thought to real beauty.

In some passages the writer gave me very much the feeling she was directing her criticisms at me, and that's why I want to lay myself completely bare to you for once and defend myself against this attack.

I have one outstanding trait in my character, which must strike anyone who knows me for any length of time, and that is my knowledge of myself. I can watch myself and my actions, just like an outsider. The Anne of every day I can face entirely without prejudice, without making excuses for her, and watch what's good and what's bad about her. This "self-consciousness" haunts me, and every time I open my mouth I know as soon as I've spoken whether "that ought to have been different" or "that was right as it was."

There are so many things about myself that I condemn; I couldn't begin to name them all. I understand more and more how true Daddy's words were when he said: "All children must look after their own upbringing." Parents can only give good advice or put them on the right paths, but the final forming of a person's character lies in their own hands.

In addition to this, I have lots of courage, I always feel so strong and as if I can bear a great deal, I feel so free and so young! I was glad when I first realized it, because I don't think I shall easily bow down before the blows that inevitably come to everyone.

But I've talked about these things so often before. Now I want to come to the chapter of "Daddy and Mummy don't understand me." Daddy and Mummy have always thoroughly spoiled me, were sweet to me, defended me, and have done all that parents could do. And yet I've felt so terribly lonely for a long time, so left out, neglected, and misunderstood. Daddy tried all he could to check my rebellious spirit, but it was no use, I have cured myself, by seeing for myself what was wrong in my behavior and keeping it before my eyes.

How is it that Daddy was never any support to me in my struggle, why did he completely miss the mark when he wanted to offer me a helping hand? Daddy tried the wrong methods, he always talked to me as a child who was going through difficult phases. It sounds crazy, because Daddy's the only one who has always taken me into his confidence, and no one but Daddy has given me the feeling that I'm sensible. But there's one thing he's omitted: you see, he hasn't realized that for me the fight to get on top was more important than all else. I didn't want to hear about "symptoms of your age," or "other girls," or "it wears off by itself"; I didn't want to be treated as a girl-like-all-others, but as Anne-on-her-own-merits. Pim didn't understand that. For that matter, I can't confide in anyone, unless they tell me a lot about themselves, and as I know very little about Pim, I don't feel that I can tread upon more intimate ground with him. Pim always takes up the older, fatherly attitude, tells me that he too has had similar passing tendencies. But still he's not able to feel with me like a friend, however hard he tries. These things have made me never mention my views on life nor my well-considered theories to anyone but my diary and, occasionally, to Margot. I concealed from Daddy everything that perturbed me; I never shared my ideals with him. I was aware of the fact that I was pushing him away from me.

I couldn't do anything else. I have acted entirely according to my feelings, but I have acted in the way that was best for my peace of mind. Because I should completely lose my repose and self-confidence, which I have built up so shakily, if, at this stage, I were to accept criticisms of my half-completed task. And I can't do that even from Pim, although it sounds very hard, for not only have I not shared my secret thoughts with Pim but I have often pushed him even further from me, by my irritability.

This is a point that I think a lot about: why is it that Pim annoys me? So much so that I can hardly bear him teaching me, that his affectionate ways strike me as being put on, that I want to be left in peace and would really prefer it if he dropped me a bit, until I felt more certain in my attitude towards him? Because I still have a gnawing feeling of guilt over that horrible letter that I dared to write him when I was so wound up. Oh, how hard it is to be really strong and brave in every way!

Yet this was not my greatest disappointment; no, I ponder far more over Peter than Daddy. I know very well that I conquered him instead of he conquering me. I created an image of him in my mind, pictured him as a quiet, sensitive, lovable boy, who needed affection and friendship. I needed a living person to whom I could pour out my heart; I wanted a friend who'd help to put me on the right road. I achieved what I wanted, and, slowly but surely, I drew him towards me. Finally, when I had made him feel friendly, it automatically developed into an intimacy which, on second thought, I don't think I ought to have allowed.

We talked about the most private things, and yet up till now we have never touched on those things that filled, and still fill, my heart and soul. I still don't know quite what to make of Peter, is he superficial, or does he still feel shy, even of me? But dropping that, I committed one error in my desire to make a real friendship: I switched over and tried to get at him by developing it into a more intimate relation, whereas I should have explored all other possibilities. He longs to be loved and I can see that he's beginning to be more and more in love with me. He gets satisfaction out of our meetings, whereas they just have the effect of making me want to try it out with him again. And yet I don't seem able to touch on the subjects that I'm so longing to bring out into the daylight. I drew Peter toward me, far more than he realizes. Now he clings to me, and for the time being, I don't see any way of shaking him off and putting him on his own feet. When I realized that he could not be a friend for my understanding, I thought I would at least try to lift him up out of his narrow-mindedness and make him do something with his youth.

"For in its innermost depths youth is lonelier than old age." I read this saying in some book and I've always remembered it, and found it to be true. Is it true then that grownups have a more difficult time here than we do? No. I know it isn't. Older people have formed their opinions about everything, and don't waver before they act. It's twice as hard for us young ones to hold our ground, and maintain our opinions, in a time when all ideals are being shattered and destroyed, when people are showing their worst side, and do not know whether to believe in truth and right and God.

Anyone who claims that the older ones have a more difficult time here certainly doesn't realize to what extent our problems weigh down on us, problems for which we are probably much too young, but which thrust themselves upon us continually, until, after a long time, we think we've found a solution, but the solution doesn't seem able to resist the facts which reduce it to nothing again. That's the difficulty in these times: ideals, dreams, and cherished hopes rise within us, only to meet the horrible truth and be shattered.

It's really a wonder that I haven't dropped all my ideals, because they seem so absurd and impossible to carry out. Yet I keep them, because in spite of everything I still believe that people are really good at heart. I simply can't build up my hopes on a foundation consisting of confusion, misery, and death. I see the world gradually being turned into a wilderness, I hear the ever approaching thunder, which will destroy us too, I can feel the sufferings of millions and yet, if I look up into the heavens, I think that it will all come right, that this cruelty too will end, and that peace and tranquillity will return again.

In the meantime, I must uphold my ideals, for perhaps the time will come when I shall be able to carry them out.

Yours, Anne

Dear Kitty, *Friday, 21 July, 1944*

Now I am getting really hopeful, now things are going well at last. Yes, really, they're going well! Super news! An attempt has been made on Hitler's life and not even by Jewish communists or English capitalists this time, but by a proud German general, and what's more, he's a count, and still quite young. The *Führer*'s life was saved by Divine Providence and, unfortunately, he managed to get off with just a few scratches and burns. A few officers and generals who were with him have been killed and wounded. The chief culprit was shot.

Anyway, it certainly shows that there are lots of officers and generals who are sick of the war and would like to see Hitler descend into a bottomless pit. When they've disposed of Hitler, their aim is to establish a military dictator, who will make peace with the Allies, then they intend to rearm and start another war in about twenty years' time. Perhaps the Divine Power tarried on purpose in getting him out of the way, because it would be much easier and more advantageous to the Allies if the impeccable Germans kill each other off; it'll make less work for the Russians and the English and they'll be able to begin rebuilding their own towns all the sooner.

But still, we're not that far yet, and I don't want to anticipate the glorious events too soon. Still, you must have noticed, this is all sober reality and that I'm in quite a matter-of-fact mood today; for once, I'm not jabbering about high ideals. And what's more, Hitler has even been so kind as to announce to his faithful, devoted people that from now on everyone in the armed forces must obey the Gestapo, and that any soldier who knows that one of his superiors was involved in this low, cowardly attempt upon his life may shoot the same on the spot, without court-martial.

What a perfect shambles it's going to be. Little Johnnie's feet begin hurting him during a long march, he's snapped at by his boss, the officer, Johnnie grabs his rifle and cries out: "You wanted to murder the *Führer,* so there's your reward." One bang and the proud chief who dared to tick off little Johnnie has passed into eternal life (or is it eternal death?). In the end, whenever an officer finds himself up against a soldier, or having to take the lead, he'll be wetting his pants from anxiety, because the soldiers will dare to say more than they do. Do you gather a bit what I mean, or have I been skipping too much from one subject to another? I can't help it; the prospect that I may be sitting on school benches next October makes me feel far too cheerful to be logical! Oh, dearie me, hadn't I just told you that I didn't want to be too hopeful? Forgive me, they haven't given me the name "little bundle of contradictions" all for nothing!

Yours, Anne

Dear Kitty, *Tuesday, 1 August, 1944*

"Little bundle of contradictions." That's how I ended my last letter and that's how I'm going to begin this one. "A little bundle of contradictions," can you tell me exactly what it is? What does contradiction mean? Like so many words, it can mean two things, contradiction from without and contradiction from within.

The first is the ordinary "not giving in easily, always knowing best, getting in the last word," *enfin,* all the unpleasant qualities for which I'm renowned. The second nobody knows about, that's my own secret.

I've already told you before that I have, as it were, a dual personality. One half embodies my exuberant cheerfulness, making fun of everything, my high-spiritedness, and above all, the way I take everything lightly. This includes not taking offense at a flirtation, a kiss, an embrace, a dirty joke. This side is usually lying in wait and pushes away the other, which is much better, deeper and purer. You must realize that no one knows Anne's better side and that's why most people find me so insufferable.

Certainly I'm a giddy clown for one afternoon, but then everyone's had enough of me for another month. Really, it's just the same as a love film is for deep-thinking people, simply a diversion, amusing just for once, something which is soon forgotten, not bad, but certainly not good. I loathe having to tell you this, but why shouldn't I, if I know it's true anyway? My lighter superficial side will always be too quick for the deeper side of me and that's why it will always win. You can't imagine how often I've already tried to push this Anne away, to cripple her, to hide her, because after all, she's only half of what's called Anne: but it doesn't work and I know, too, why it doesn't work.

I'm awfully scared that everyone who knows me as I always am will discover that I have another side, a finer and better side. I'm afraid they'll laugh at me, think I'm ridiculous and sentimental, not take me seriously. I'm used to not being taken seriously but it's only the "lighthearted" Anne that's used to it and can bear it; the "deeper" Anne is too frail for it. Sometimes, if I really compel the good Anne to take the stage for a quarter of an hour, she simply shrivels up as soon as she has to speak, and lets Anne number one take over, and before I realize it, she has disappeared.

Therefore, the nice Anne is never present in company, has not appeared one single time so far, but almost always predominates when we're alone. I know exactly how I'd like to be, how I am too . . . inside. But, alas, I'm only like that for myself. And perhaps that's why, no, I'm sure it's the reason why I say I've got a happy nature within and why other people think I've got a happy nature without. I am guided by the pure Anne within, but outside I'm nothing but a frolicsome little goat who's broken loose.

As I've already said, I never utter my real feelings about anything and that's how I've acquired the name of chaser-after-boys, flirt, know-all, reader of love stories. The cheerful Anne laughs about it, gives cheeky answers, shrugs her shoulders indifferently, behaves as if she doesn't care, but, oh dearie me, the quiet Anne's reactions are just the opposite. If I'm to be quite honest, then I must admit that it does hurt me, that I try terribly hard to change myself, but that I'm always fighting against a more powerful enemy.

A voice sobs within me: "There you are, that's what's become of you: you're uncharitable, you look supercilious and peevish, people dislike you and all because you won't listen to the advice given you by your own better half." Oh, I would like to listen, but it doesn't work; if I'm quiet and serious, everyone thinks it's a new comedy and then I have to get out of it by turning it into a joke, not to mention my own family, who are sure to think I'm ill, make me swallow pills for headaches and nerves, feel my neck and my head to see whether I'm running a temperature, ask if I'm constipated and criticize me for being in a bad mood. I can't keep that up: if I'm watched to that extent, I start by getting snappy, then unhappy, and finally I twist my heart round again, so that the bad is on the outside and the good is on the inside and keep on trying to find a way of becoming what I would so like to be, and what I could be, if . . . there weren't any other people living in the world.

Yours, Anne

EPILOGUE

Anne's diary ends here. On August 4, 1944, the Grüne Polizei *made a raid on the "Secret Annexe." All the occupants, together with Kraler and Koophuis, were arrested and sent to German and Dutch concentration camps.*

The "Secret Annexe" was plundered by the Gestapo. Among a pile of old books, magazines, and newspapers which were left lying on the floor, Miep and Elli found Anne's diary. Apart from a very few passages, which are of little interest to the reader, the original text has been printed.

Of all the occupants of the "Secret Annexe," Anne's father alone returned. Kraler and Koophuis, who withstood the hardships of the Dutch camp, were able to go home to their families.

In March 1945, two months before the liberation of Holland, Anne died in the concentration camp at Bergen-Belsen.

CONCENTRATION AND DEATH CAMPS

CONCENTRATION
AND
DEATH CAMPS

The principal and most effective sites for total annihilation of the Jews were the varied camps which the Nazis built in Germany and in the occupied countries.

There were literally thousands of camps of various categories: transit camps, prison camps, labor camps, concentration camps, etc. For some nationalities the penal camps were also labor camps; but for the Jews they were only death camps. Jews were kept temporarily in the labor camps, only until their maximum work capacity was utilized and then—exhausted, starved and ill—were sent to the place originally intended for them: the death camp.

The death factories were the final stations in the German plan of extirpation.

In Poland the Germans erected six death camps, not only for Polish Jews but for Jews from all of Europe. Millions perished there. Below is a table based on information gathered by the Committee to Investigate Nazi Crimes:

ANNIHILATION CAMPS

CHELMNO	December 8, 1941–January 18, 1945	360,000 Jews; 5,000 gypsies from the Lodz Ghetto
AUSCHWITZ	January 1942–November 1944	2.5 to 4 million Jews
BELZEC	March 1942–December 1942	600,000 Jews
MAIDANEK	April 1942–July 22, 1944	500,000 Jews

SOBIBOR	May 1942–November 1943	250,000 Jews
TREBLINKA	July 23, 1942–November 1943	700,000 Jews; of these, 300,000 were from Warsaw

To this list must be added PONAR outside of Vilna; and two labor camps which served as transit to the death camps: PLASHOW in Cracow; JANOW in Lemberg.

YANKEL WIERNIK

A Year in Treblinka Horror Camp

TRANSLATED FROM THE YIDDISH BY MOSHE SPIEGEL

The Treblinka camp was divided into two sections. In Camp One there was a railroad spur and a debarkation platform for unloading human cargo. Next was a large area where the belongings of the newcomers would be laid out. The foreign Jews brought the most luggage. Nearby was an infirmary (measuring 30 x 1 x 2 meters). Two men worked there, wearing white smocks and Red-Cross brassards, and passing as physicians. From the arrivals they chose the aged and ill, and seated them on a long bench facing a trench. Behind them stood Germans and Ukrainians. They killed the victims by shooting them in the back, so the bodies fell at once into the mass grave. When they had assembled a large number of cadavers, they gathered them together and set them on fire. They were consumed by the bright flames.

Nearby stood barracks occupied by Germans and Ukrainians. There was an office building, barracks for Jewish workers, workshops, stables, pigsties, food depots and ammunition magazines. Trucks were parked in the courtyard. To the unsuspecting observer the place looked like a genuine labor camp.

Camp Two was altogether different. The workers' barracks was 30 x 10 meters. Here was a laundry, a small laboratory, a special domicile for seventeen women, a sentry house and a well. There were also thirteen chambers in which the victims were asphyxiated by gas. The buildings were surrounded by barbed wire. Both wire barricades were three meters high. Between the fences there were tangles of steel wire. Ukrainian sentries stood all around. The entire camp was fenced with barbed wire four meters high. The fence was adorned with small shrubs. There were four observation towers, each four stories high, and six one-story towers, fifty meters high. Beyond the last barrier anti-tank guns were stationed.

When I arrived at the camp, three gas chambers were functioning. The remaining ten were added during my stay. Each chamber measured about twenty-five square meters and was two meters high. The roof opening was hermetically sealed, and the terra-cotta floor sloped toward the debarkation platform.

The brick building was separated from Camp One by a wooden wall. Both walls, of wood and of masonry, formed a corridor rising eighty centimeters above the roof. The gas chambers were connected with the corridor. Hermetically closed steel doors provided entry into each chamber. A platform, raised above the ground, connected the three chambers. The doors of every room on the side of Camp Two opened only from the outside, swinging upward and out with the help of iron supports, and were shut by bolts fixed in sash frames. The victims were ushered through the doors from the corridor, and their bodies were dragged through the doors facing Camp Two. Along the gas chambers stood an electric station, about as large as the chambers but somewhat higher. This station provided light for both camps. A motor from a Soviet tank pumped in the gas, which reached the chambers through influx valves. The speediness of the execution depended upon the quantity of the gas intake.

Two Ukrainians operated the death machines. One was called Ivan, a tall man with pleasant eyes, nevertheless a sadist. He found much enjoyment in the tortures and agonies of the victims. More than once he ran to us and nailed our ears to the walls, or ordered us to lie down and beat us savagely. In his sadistic frenzy he joked and laughed uproariously. He murdered his victims in various ways, according to his whims. The other, Nicholai, was shorter, pale and looked as if spiritually possessed.

The day I first saw men, women and children being led to their doom I nearly went mad. I tore my hair and wept unrestrainedly. I suffered most when I looked at the little ones walking beside their mothers, or at the others walking alone, who had no thought of the quick and cruel death impending. Their eyes were wide with fear and wonder. "What is all this? What is it for?" seemed to be congealed on their lips. When they saw the stony faces of their parents, however, they kept silent and prepared for whatever might come. They remained stock still or nestled against one another or cuddled up to their parents, awaiting the ghastly end. Suddenly the entrance doors would swing open. Ivan would appear with a thick gas pipe, a meter long. Nicholai was with him, swinging a sword. At a signal the victims would be driven in, clubbed and lashed without mercy. To this day the fearful screams of the women and the crying of the children ring in my ears. There was despair and agony in the screams, a plea for mercy, a cry to God for vengeance. I shall never forget the horrible sights there.

Into the chamber of twenty-five square meters 450 to 500 people were jammed. The congestion was unbelievable. The victims carried in the children, somehow hoping thus to save them from death. On their way to die they were beaten and driven by truncheons and gas pipes. Dogs were set upon them; barking, they threw themselves upon the victims. Everyone, eager to escape the blows and the dogs, rushed screaming into the lethal chamber. The stronger pushed the weaker. But the tumult did not long endure. The doors closed with a clang on the packed chamber. The motor was connected with the inflow apparatus and switched on. In twenty-five minutes, at the most, all lay dead. But they did not really lie, for they had no room to fall. They died standing, their legs and arms entangled. There were no more screams. Mothers and children were clasped in death's embrace. There was no friend or foe, no envy. No one was more beautiful or ugly—all were suffocated, yellowed by gas. No rich, no poor—all were alike before the Lord.

Why all this? I found it most difficult to stay alive, but I had to live, to give the world the story of this depravity, this bestial depravity.

Their fiendish operation over, Ivan and Nicholai looked around to see that all was in order. They went around to the other side, where the doors faced the loading station. They opened the doors and tossed out the bodies. The task of carrying the corpses to the mass grave devolved on us, though we were very weary after a day's labor at building. But protest would merely bring us beatings, and the same death, or an even more terrible one. So we did as we were told. A *Hauptmann,* of medium stature and with pince-nez, whose name I did not know, stood over us. All he did was yell and beat us. I turned a pleading glance toward him; he halted for a moment. "If you weren't a carpenter you'd be killed!" said he. I looked about me. The other laborers were getting the same treatment. A whole pack of dogs was attacking us, helping the Germans and Ukrainians who were lashing us. One quarter of the workers were felled. We hurled the newly dead into the mass grave indiscriminately. Our numbers had been reduced when we returned. Luck was with me, for after the *Hauptmann* had gone the *Unterscharführer* had let me off further work.

Every day 10,000 to 12,000 people were asphyxiated. We built a narrow-gauge railway, and transported the bodies directly to the graves on a flatcar. After a day of hard work we were conducted not to Camp One but Two. There we saw an entirely different sight. My blood congealed at it. Going by the loading platform I saw thousands of corpses, sprawled all over the camp grounds. They were fresh victims. The Ukrainians and Germans were shouting commands. They screamed wildly, inhumanly beating with truncheons and cudgels the workers with bloody faces and gouged-out eyes and clothes torn by the dogs. They put their heads between the lower rungs of ladders to the two one-story observation towers at the camp entrance. The victims could not move in this position while the group leader expended his murderous savagery against these poor wretches without mercy. The least punishment consisted of twenty-five lashes. I saw this for the first time that night, while the moon and the floodlights illumined the practically massacred, half-dead sufferers, and the dead lying near them. The groans of the smitten men mingled with the sharp crack of the whips swinging down upon their backs.

When I arrived Camp Two had but one barrack, the other structures still being incomplete, and the field kitchen stood in the court. I met many of my old Warsaw acquaintances. They had changed almost beyond recognition. They looked desolate, bloated, and battered. But I spent little time in joyous reunion. New faces, new acquaintances, without end. Always new—always death. I learned to look upon every living person as one soon destined for oblivion. I scrutinized the potential victim, pondering his weight and the person likely to bear him to the grave and to be beaten himself in the bargain. Can one believe that in such circumstances one can occasionally raise a smile and jest? A man can accustom himself to anything.

The German governmental system is among the most thorough—a complete bureaucracy, swarming with all manner of functionaries, departments and sub-departments. More significantly, every man is in his proper and appointed place. Where unyielding determination is required, or annihilation of "evil and subversive elements," patriots are always to be found to carry out the edicts. It is remarkable how in these offices there is no lack of men to destroy and kill those near to them, employing the most rigorous forms of repression. I never noticed any commiseration or remorse in their makeup. They never bemoaned the lot of the innocent. They were automatons, who on the slightest provocation would rush headlong to execute any assignment, no matter how heinous. Such jackals enjoy the best opportunities in time of revolution or war. The road to evil is the readiest and the pleasantest. A resolute, just system can, however, overcome inherent evil through education, example, and proper order.

Shady types conceal themselves in their dens, and carry on their reprehensible activities from there. All that is moral and equitable has now become superfluous. The more vile and base one is, the higher the position one is given. It all depends upon the extent of one's destructiveness and murderousness. The hands, dripping with the blood of defenseless people, are something to bow down before. Do not wash them off. Hold them high, that they may be hosanna'd. The filthier the hands and conscience, the greater the praise accorded.

The next and most remarkable characteristic of the Germans is the readiness with which they can recruit perverted assistants from among other peoples, who display their own lack of morality. The Jewish camps were also in need of Jewish hangmen, spies and stool pigeons. They found them. These reprehensible souls included Moshka of Lower Sochotshev; Itzik Kobila of Warsaw; Chaskel, the Thief of Warsaw; and Kuba, a brigand and a pimp, another Warsaw character.

The sound structure on which I worked, located between Camp One and Two, was erected in great haste. It consisted of ten gas chambers, all larger than the previous ones, measuring about 50 square meters. After they were completed, 1,000 to 1,200 persons could be packed into each chamber. They were built along a corridor, five on each side. Each had two doors. The first, on the corridor, admitted the victims, and from the other the corpses were taken into the court. The general construction was like the other chambers. The new structure, seen from Camp One, revealed five terraces, on both sides of which hedges and flowers were prettily set out. The corridor was very long. On the roof, on the camp side, was a Shield of David. The structure resembled an old-fashioned temple. When it was completed the *Hauptsturmführer* remarked to his underlings, "At last, the Jew-town is ready!"

The work on the chambers lasted five weeks. For us it was an eternity. We labored from dawn to dusk, under lashings and beatings. One of the overseers, Woronkoff, beat and tortured us without mercy. Each day he murdered several of the laborers. Our physical sufferings transcended the most fantastic imaginings. But we suffered still more greatly in morale. Every day new parties arrived. The people were immediately ordered to disrobe and taken to the three old chambers, to be asphyxiated. The way to the chambers passed through the area where we worked. More than one worker recognized his children, his wife, his kin in the stream of victims. Whenever one could restrain himself no longer and ran to his kin, he was murdered forthwith. Under such conditions we built the death rooms for ourselves and our brethren. After the five weeks' labor, I was recalled to Camp One, where I set up a barbering establishment. Before execution they cut off the women's hair, which was carefully preserved, though I do not know for what purpose.

Now I was living in Camp Two, whence I was taken each day to Camp One, due to a shortage of skilled workers. *Unterscharführer* Hermann would come to see us. He was about fifty, tall and amiable. He understood and sympathized with us. When he first crossed Camp Two and saw the heaps of corpses he turned pale and showed fright and compassion. He hurried me along with him, so that I need not look further. He treated the workers well. Often he smuggled food to us from the German kitchens. His glance was so kindly that one felt like pouring our his troubles to him. He actually feared his colleagues. He never spoke with them, but every act of his bespoke his good heart.

While working in Camp One I saw our brethren being conducted into gas chambers, and the fearful agonies they were forced to suffer. New trainloads arrived. As soon as the train departed, the women and children were driven into the barracks. The men were left in the court. Then the women and children were ordered to disrobe. The more naive women took out towels and soap, thinking they were about to bathe. The murderers came to demand order and quiet. They began their beatings and tortures. The children cried. Grown-ups sobbed and shrieked. But nothing availed. The lashing became more powerful. It weakened many, gave strength to others. Then the girls and women entered the barber's room for haircutting. Now they felt sure they were going to the baths. Through the other exit they were conducted to Camp Two, where they stood naked, awaiting their turn, in the bitterest frost. Tiny tots stood barefoot and naked in the open. For a long period they awaited their turn in the gas chambers. The children's feet froze to the earth. They wept and shuddered. The Germans and Ukrainians paced up and down the ranks beating them. Ivan's favorite victims were the little ones. When he assailed women who begged him to desist because they held children in their arms, he would tear the child from the woman's grasp, tear it in two, or, holding it by feet or hand, smash its head against a wall. These were not rare instances—they were repeated at every few steps.

The men suffered a hundredfold more terribly. They undressed in the court, and were compelled to carry their clothes and place them in an orderly fashion among other heaps of garments; then they were sent into the women's barracks and bidden to carry the clothes from there to the same piles. When they again resumed their places in the rows, the guard picked out the strong, healthy and well-built men and started torturing them. They were beaten into a bloody pulp, in the most savage ways. Then, massed together, women and men, old people and children, they started off at a signal. They were to go from Camp One to Camp Two, to the gas chambers. When they came to a certain small building, an official seated therein ordered them to surrender all articles of value. Some, still under the illusion that they would be permitted to live, took the trouble to conceal everything possible. But the hangmen found everything—if not before death, then after. Everyone passing through this building had to raise his or her hands. Thus, with arms upraised, the entire sorry procession went to the chambers of death. There a Jew, chosen by the Germans, was stationed as a so-called "bath master." He ordered everyone to enter the room at once, since the water was becoming cold; and thus they were forced in, amid shrieks and blows. As already related, the space was very narrow. Men suffocated in the close quarters. Since the motor for the new chambers was functioning poorly, the unfortunates there, unable to move, suffered interminably. Not even Satan could have thought of more fearful torment. When the chambers were reopened, some few might be found half alive, and they were dispatched by rifle butt, a bullet, or vigorous kick. Sometimes the vicitms were left in the chambers all night, without using the motor. The close confinement and pressure were able to kill most of them, but many remained alive, particularly the children, who had greater endurance and were removed still breathing. A German revolver, however, soon remedied this. Perhaps the worst part was the standing stark naked in the frost, awaiting the horrible death. But the chambers themselves were no less horrible.

The hangmen greeted each new contingent with wild joy. To allay suspicion of their ultimate disposition, the deportees had been sent in passenger coaches and permitted to take along everything they considered needful. They arrived well clad, bearing much food and clothing. Some had large amounts of fats, coffee, tea and various foods in their luggage. But upon arrival they were dragged from the cars and realized the horrible truth quickly enough. On the second day, after laborious hours of burying them, there was not a sign left of them save their clothes and food.

The number of trainloads grew from day to day—now there were thirteen gas chambers operating. There were days when 20,000 were asphyxiated. The screams and sobs and groans never left our ears. The corpse-removal crew, still kept alive, fasted and wept on the days when the trains came in. The more weak and emotional ones broke down and committed suicide. These were generally the more intelligent. When they returned to the barracks after their ghastly work, still hearing the screams of the doomed, they would hang themselves during the night. Fifteen or twenty each night. They could not longer endure the torture of the German officers, or the suffering of the doomed.

PRIMO LEVI

The Story of Ten Days

TRANSLATED FROM THE ITALIAN BY STUART WOOLF

Already for some months now the distant booming of the Russian guns had been heard at intervals when, on January 11, 1945, I fell ill of scarlet fever and was once more sent into Ka-Be. *"Infektions-abteilung"*: it meant a small room, really quite clean, with ten bunks on two levels, a wardrobe, three stools, and a closet seat with the pail for corporal needs. All in a space of three yards by five.

It was difficult to climb to the upper bunks as there was no ladder; so, when a patient got worse he was transferred to the lower bunks.

When I was admitted I was the thirteenth in the room. Four of the others—two French political prisoners and two young Hungarian Jews—had scarlet fever; there were three with diphtheria, two with typhus, while one suffered from a repellent facial erysipelas. The other two had more than one illness and were incredibly wasted away.

I had a high fever. I was lucky enough to have a bunk entirely to myself: I lay down with relief knowing that I had the right to forty days' isolation and therefore of rest, while I felt myself still sufficiently strong to fear neither the consequences of scarlet fever nor the selections.

Thanks to my by-now long experience of camp life I managed to bring with me all my personal belongings: a belt of interlaced electric wire, the knife-spoon, a needle with three needlefuls, five buttons, and last of all eighteen flints which I had stolen from the Laboratory. From each of these, shaping them patiently with a knife, it was possible to make three smaller flints, just the right gauge for a normal cigarette lighter. They were valued at six or seven rations of bread.

I enjoyed four peaceful days. Outside it was snowing and very cold, but the room was heated. I was given strong doses of sulpha drugs, I suffered from an intense feeling of sickness and was hardly able to eat; I did not want to talk.

The two Frenchmen with scarlet fever were quite pleasant. They were provincials from the Vosges who had entered the camp only a few days before with a large convoy of civilians swept up by the Germans in their retreat from Lorraine. The elder one was named Arthur, a peasant, small and thin. The other, his bed-companion, was Charles, a school teacher, thirty-two years old; instead of a shirt he had been given a summer vest, ridiculously short.

On the fifth day the barber came. He was a Greek from Salonica: he spoke only the beautiful Spanish of his people, but understood some words of all the languages spoken in the camp. He was called Askenazi and had been in the camp for almost three years. I do not know how he managed to get the post of *Frisör* of Ka-Be: he spoke neither German nor Polish, nor was he in fact excessively brutal. Before he entered, I heard him speaking excitedly for a long time in the corridor with one of the doctors, a compatriot of his. He seemed to have an unusual look on his face, but as the expressions of the Levantines are different from ours, I could not tell whether he was afraid or happy or merely upset. He knew me, or at least knew that I was Italian.

When it was my turn I climbed down laboriously from the bunk. I asked him in Italian if there was anything new: he stopped shaving me, winked in a serious and allusive manner, pointed to the window with his chin, and then made a sweeping gesture with his hand toward the west.

"Morgen, alle Kamarad weg."

He looked at me for a moment with his eyes wide-open, as if waiting for a reaction, and then he added: *"todos, todos"* and returned to his work. He knew about my flints and shaved me with a certain gentleness.

The news excited no direct emotion in me. Already for many months I had no longer felt any pain, joy or fear, except in that detached and distant manner characteristic of the *Lager,* which might be described as conditional: if I still had my former sensitivity, I thought, this would be an extremely moving moment.

My ideas were perfectly clear; for a long time now Alberto and I had foreseen the dangers which would accompany the evacuation of the camp and the liberation. As for the rest, Askenazi's news was merely a confirmation of rumors which had been circulating for some days: that the Russians were at Czestochowa, sixty miles to the north; that they were at Zakopaxe, sixty miles to the south; that at Buna the Germans were already preparing the sabotage mines.

I looked at the faces of my comrades one by one: it was clearly useless to discuss it with any of them. They would have replied: "Well?" and it would all have finished there. The French were different, they were still fresh.

"Did you hear?" I said to them. "Tomorrow they are going to evacuate the camp."

They overwhelmed me with questions. "Where to? On foot? . . . The ill ones as well? Those who cannot walk?" They knew that I was an old prisoner and that I understood German, and deduced that I knew much more about the matter than I wanted to admit.

I did not know anything more: I told them so but they continued to ask questions. How stupid of them! But of course, they had only been in the *Lager* for a week and had not yet learned that one did not ask questions.

In the afternoon the Greek doctor came. He said that all patients able to walk would be given shoes and clothes and would leave the following day with the healthy ones on a twelve mile march. The others would remain in Ka-Be with assistants to be chosen from the patients least ill.

The doctor was unusually cheerful, he seemed drunk. I knew him: he was a cultured, intelligent man, egoistic and calculating. He added that everyone, without distinction, would receive a triple ration of bread, at which the patients visibly cheered up. We asked him what would happen to us. He replied that probably the Germans would leave us to our fate: no, he did not think that they would kill us. He made no effort to hide the fact that he thought otherwise. His very cheerfulness boded ill.

He was already equipped for the march. He had hardly gone out when the two Hungarian boys began to speak excitedly to each other. They were in an advanced state of convalescence but extremely wasted away. It was obvious that they were afraid to stay with the patients and were deciding to go with the healthy ones. It was not a question of reasoning: I would probably also have followed the instinct of the flock if I had not felt so weak; fear is supremely contagious, and its immediate reaction is to make one try to run away.

Outside the hut, the camp sounded unusually excited. One of the two Hungarians got up, went out and returned half an hour later laden with filthy rags. He must have taken them from the storehouse of clothes still to be disinfected. He and his comrade dressed feverishly, putting on rag after rag. One could see that they were in a hurry to have the matter over with before the fear itself made them hesitate. It was crazy of them to think of walking even for one hour, weak as they were, especially in the snow with those broken-down shoes found at the last moment. I tried to explain, but they looked at me without replying. Their eyes were like those of terrified cattle.

Just for a moment it flashed through my mind that they might even be right. They climbed awkwardly out of the window; I saw them, shapeless bundles, lurching into the night. They did not return, I learned much later that, unable to continue, they had been killed by the S.S. a few hours after the beginning of the march.

It was obvious that I, too, needed a pair of shoes. But it took me an hour to overcome the feeling of sickness, fever and inertia. I found a pair in the corridor. (The healthy prisoners had ransacked the deposit of the patients' shoes and had taken the best ones; those remaining, with split soles and unpaired, lay all over the place.) Just then I met Kosman, the Alsatian. As a civilian he had been a Reuter correspondent at Clermont Ferrand; he also was excited and euphoric. He said: "If you return before me, write to the mayor of Metz that I am about to come back."

Kosman was notorious for his acquaintances among the prominents, so his optimism seemed a good sign and I used it to justify my inertia to myself; I hid the shoes and returned to bed.

Late that night the Greek doctor returned with a rucksack on his shoulders and a woollen hood. He threw a French novel on my bed. "Keep it, read it, Italian. You can give it back to me when we meet again." Even today I hate him for those words. He knew that we were doomed.

And then finally Alberto came, defying the prohibition, to say goodbye to me from the window. We were inseparable: we were "the two Italians" and foreigners even mistook our names. For six months we had shared a bunk and every scrap of food "organized" in excess of the ration; but he had had scarlet fever as a child and

I was unable to infect him. So he left and I remained. We said goodbye, not many words were needed, we had already discussed our affairs countless times. We did not think we would be separated for very long. He had found a sturdy pair of leather shoes in a reasonable condition: he was one of those fellows who immediately find everything they need.

He also was cheerful and confident, as were all those who were leaving. It was understandable: something great and new was about to happen; we could finally feel a force around us which was not of Germany; we could concretely feel the impending collapse of that hated world of ours. At any rate, the healthy ones who, despite all their tiredness and hunger, were still able to move, could feel this. But it is obvious that whoever is too weak, or naked or barefoot, thinks and feels in a different way, and what dominated our thoughts was the paralyzing sensation of being totally helpless in the hands of fate.

All the healthy prisoners (except a few prudent ones who at the last moment undressed and hid themselves in the hospital beds) left during the night of January 18, 1945. They must have been about twenty thousand coming from different camps. Almost in their entirety they vanished during the evacuation march: Alberto was among them. Perhaps someone will write their story one day.

So we remained in our bunks, alone with our illnesses, and with our inertia stronger than fear.

In the whole Ka-Be we numbered perhaps eight hundred. In our room there were eleven of us, each in his own bunk, except for Charles and Arthur who slept together. The rhythm of the great machine of the *Lager* was extinguished. For us began the ten days outside both world and time.

January 18. During the night of the evacuation, the camp kitchens continued to function, and on the following morning the last distribution of soup took place in the hospital. The central-heating plant had been abandoned; in the huts a little heat still lingered on, but hour by hour the temperature dropped and it was evident that we would soon suffer from the cold. Outside it must have been at least 50° F. below zero; most of the patients had only a shirt and some of them not even that.

Nobody knew what our fate would be. Some S.S. men had remained, some of the guard towers were still occupied.

About midday an S.S. officer made a tour of the huts. He appointed a chief in each of them, selecting from among the remaining non-Jews, and ordered a list of the patients to be made at once, divided into Jews and non-Jews. The matter seemed clear. No one was surprised that the Germans preserved their national love of classifications until the very end, nor did any Jew seriously expect to live until the following day.

The two Frenchmen had not understood and were frightened. I translated the speech of the S.S. man. I was annoyed that they should be afraid: they had not even experienced a month of the *Lager,* they hardly suffered from hunger yet, they were not even Jews, but they were afraid.

There was one more distribution of bread. I spent the afternoon reading the book left by the doctor: it was interesting and I can remember it with curious accuracy. I also made a visit to the neighboring ward in search of blankets; many patients had been sent out from there and their blankets were free. I brought back some quite heavy ones.

When Arthur heard that they came from the dysentery ward, he looked disgusted: *"Y avait point besoin de le dire";* in fact, they were polluted. But I thought that in any case, knowing what awaited us, we might as well sleep comfortably.

It was soon night but the electric light remained on. We saw with tranquil fear that an armed S.S. man stood at the corner of the hut. I had no desire to talk and was not afraid except in that external and conditional manner I have described. I continued reading until late.

There were no clocks, but it must have been about 11 P.M. when all the lights went out, even those of the reflectors on the guard-towers. One could see the searchlight beams in the distance. A cluster of intense lights burst out in the sky, remaining immobile, crudely illuminating the earth. One could hear the roar of the airplanes.

Then the bombardment began. It was nothing new: I climbed down to the ground, put my bare feet into my shoes, and waited.

It seemed far away, perhaps over Auschwitz.

But then there was a near explosion, and before one could think, a second and a third one, loud enough to burst one's eardrums. Windows were breaking, the hut shook, the spoon I had fixed in the wall fell down.

Then it seemed all over. Cagnolati, a young peasant also from the Vosges, had apparently never experienced a raid. He had jumped out naked from his bed and was concealed in a corner, screaming. After a few minutes it was obvious that the camp had been struck. Two huts were burning fiercely, another two had been pulverized, but they were all empty. Dozens of patients arrived, naked and wretched, from a hut threatened by fire: they asked for shelter. It was impossible to take them in. They insisted, begging and threatening in many languages. We had to barricade the door. They dragged themselves elsewhere, lit up by the flames, barefoot in the melting snow. Many trailed streaming bandages behind them. There seemed no danger to our hut, so long as the wind did not change.

The Germans were no longer there. The towers were empty.

Today I think that if for no other reason than that an Auschwitz existed, no one in our age should speak of Providence. But without doubt in that hour the memory of biblical salvations in times of extreme adversity passed like a wind through all our minds.

It was impossible to sleep; a window was broken and it was very cold. I was thinking that we would have to find a stove to set up and get some coal, wood and food. I knew that it was all essential, but without some help I would never have had the energy to carry it out. I spoke about it to the two Frenchmen.

January 19. The Frenchmen agreed. We got up at dawn, we three. I felt ill and helpless, I was cold and afraid.

The other patients looked at us with respectful curiosity: did we not know that patients were not allowed to leave Ka-Be? And if the Germans had not all left? But they said nothing, they were glad that someone was prepared to make the test.

The Frenchmen had no idea of the topography of the *Lager,* but Charles was courageous and robust, while Arthur was shrewd, with the practical common sense of the peasant. We went out into the wind of a freezing day of fog, poorly wrapped up in blankets.

What we saw resembled nothing that I had ever seen or heard described.

The *Lager,* hardly dead, had already begun to decompose. No more water, or electricity, broken windows and doors slamming to and fro in the wind, loose iron-sheets from the roofs screeching, ashes from the fire drifting high, afar. The work of the bombs had been completed by the work of man: ragged, decrepit, skeleton-like patients barely able to move dragged themselves everywhere on the frozen soil, like an invasion of worms. They had ransacked all the empty spread its heat, something seemed to relax in everyone, and at that moment Towarowski (a Franco-Pole of twenty-three, typhus) proposed to the others that each of them offer a slice of bread to us three who had been working. And so it was agreed.

Only a day before a similar event would have been inconceivable. The law of the *Lager* said: "Eat your own bread, and if you can, that of your neighbor," and left no room for gratitude. It really meant that the *Lager* was dead.

It was the first human gesture that occurred among us. I believe that that moment can be dated as the beginning of the change by which we who had not died slowly changed from *Häftlinge* to men again.

Arthur recovered quite well, but from then on always avoided exposing himself to the cold; he undertook the upkeep of the stove, the cooking of the potatoes, the cleaning of the room and the helping of the patients. Charles and I shared the various tasks outside. There was still an hour of light: an expedition yielded us a pint of spirits and a tin of yeast, thrown in the snow by someone; we made a distribution of potatoes and one spoonful of yeast per person. I thought vaguely that it might help against lack of vitamins.

Darkness fell; in the whole camp ours was the only room with a stove, of which we were very proud. Many invalids from other wards crowded around the door, but Charles's imposing stature held them back. Nobody, neither us nor they, thought that the inevitable promiscuity with our patients made it extremely dangerous to stay in our room, and that to fall ill of diphtheria in those conditions was more surely fatal than jumping off a fourth floor.

I myself was aware of it, but I did not dwell long on the idea: for too long I had been accustomed to think of death by illness as a possible event, and in that case unavoidable, and anyhow beyond any possible intervention on our part. And it did not even pass through my mind that I could have gone to another room in another hut with less danger of infection. The stove, our creation, was here, and spread a wonderful warmth; I had my bed here; and by now a tie united us, the eleven patients of the *Infektionsabteilung.*

Very occasionally we heard the thundering of artillery, both near and far, and at intervals the crackling of automatic rifles. In the darkness, lighted only by the glow of the embers, Arthur and I sat smoking cigarettes made of herbs found in the kitchen, and spoke of many things, both past and future. In the middle of this endless plain, frozen and full of war, we felt at peace with ourselves and

huts in search of food and wood; they had violated with sensel
fury the grotesquely adorned rooms of the hated *Blockälteste,* f
bidden to the ordinary *Häftlinge* until the previous day; no lon
in control of their own bowels, they had fouled everywhere, poll
ing the precious snow, the only source of water remaining in t
whole camp.

Around the smoking ruins of the burnt huts, groups of patien
lay stretched out on the ground, soaking up its last warmth. Othe
had found potatoes somewhere and were roasting them on th
embers of the fire, glaring around with fierce eyes. A few had had th
strength to light a real fire, and were melting snow in it in an
handy receptacle.

We hurried to the kitchens as fast as we could; but the potatoes were already almost finished. We filled two sacks and left them in Arthur's keeping. Among the ruins of the *Prominenzblock* Charles and I finally found what we were searching for: a heavy cast-iron stove, with the flue still usable. Charles hurried over with a wheelbarrow and we loaded it on; he then left me with the task of carrying it to the hut and ran back to the sacks. There he found Arthur unconscious from the cold. Charles picked up both sacks and carried them to safety, then he took care of his friend.

Meanwhile, staggering with difficulty, I was trying to maneuver the heavy wheelbarrow as best as possible. There was the roar of an engine and an S.S. man entered the camp on a motorcycle. As always when I saw their hard faces I froze from terror and hatred. It was too late to disappear and I did not want to abandon the stove. The rules of the *Lager* stated that one must stand at attention with head uncovered. I had no hat and was encumbered by the blanket. I moved a few steps away from the wheelbarrow and made a sort of awkward bow. The German moved on without seeing me, turned behind a hut and left. Only later did I realize the danger I had run.

I finally reached the entrance of the hut and unloaded the stove into Charles's hands. I was completely breathless from the effort, large black spots danced before my eyes.

It was essential to get it working. We all three had our hands paralyzed while the icy metal stuck to the skin of our fingers, but it was vitally urgent to set it up to warm ourselves and to boil the potatoes. We had found wood and coal as well as embers from the burnt huts.

When the broken window was repaired and the stove began to

with the world. We were broken by tiredness, but we seemed to have finally accomplished something useful—perhaps like God after the first day of creation.

January 20. The dawn came and it was my turn to light the stove. Besides a general feeling of weakness, the aching of my joints reminded me all the time that my scarlet fever was far from over. The thought of having to plunge into the freezing air to find a light in the other huts made me shudder with disgust. I remembered my flints: I sprinkled a piece of paper with spirits, and patiently scraped a small pile of black dust on top of it and then scraped the flint more vigorously with my knife. And finally, after a few sparks, the small pile caught fire and the small bluish flame of alcohol rose from the paper.

Arthur climbed down enthusiastically from his bed and heated three potatoes per person from those boiled the day before; after which, Charles and I, starved and shivering violently, left again to explore the decaying camp.

We had enough food (that is, potatoes) for two days only; as for water, we were forced to melt the snow, an awkward operation in the absence of large pots, which yielded a blackish, muddy liquid which had to be filtered.

The camp was silent. Other starving spectres like ourselves wandered around searching, unshaven with hollow eyes, grayish skeleton bones in rags. Shaky on their legs, they entered and left the empty huts carrying the most varied of objects: axes, buckets, ladles, nails; anything might be of use, and those looking furthest ahead were already thinking of profitable commerce with the Poles of the surrounding countryside.

In the kitchen we found two of them squabbling over the last handfuls of putrid potatoes. They had seized each other by their rags, and were fighting with curiously slow and uncertain movements, cursing in Yiddish between their frozen lips.

In the courtyard of the storehouse there were two large piles of cabbages and turnips (those large, insipid turnips, the basis of our diet). They were so frozen that they could only be separated with a pickaxe. Charles and I took turns, using all our energy at each stroke, and we carried out about 100 pounds. There was still more: Charles discovered a packet of salt and (*"Une fameuse trouvaille!"*) a can of water of perhaps twelve gallons, frozen in a block.

We loaded everything on to a small cart (formerly used to distribute the rations for the huts; there were a great number of them abandoned everywhere), and we turned back, toiling over the snow.

We contented ourselves that day with boiled potatoes again and slices of turnips roasted on the stove, but Arthur promised important innovations for the following day.

In the afternoon I went to the ex-surgery, searching for anything that might prove of use. I had been preceded: everything had been upset by inexpert looters. Not a bottle intact, the floor covered by a layer of rags, excrement and medicaments. A naked, contorted corpse. But there was something that had escaped my predecessors: a battery from a lorry. I touched the poles with a knife—a small spark. It was charged.

That evening we had light in our room.

Sitting in bed. I could see a large stretch of the road through the window. For the past three days the Wehrmacht in flight passed by in waves. Armored cars, tiger tanks camouflaged in white, Germans on horseback, Germans on bicycle, Germans on foot, armed and unarmed. During the night, long before the tanks came into sight, one could hear the grinding of their tracks.

Charles asked: *"Ça roule encore?"*

"Ça roule toujours."

It seemed as if it would never end.

January 21. Instead it ended. On the dawn of the 21st we saw the plain deserted and lifeless, white as far as the eye could see, lying under the flight of the crows, deathly sad. I would almost have preferred to see something moving again. The Polish civilians had also disappeared, hiding who knows where. Even the wind seemed to have stopped. I wanted only one thing: to stay in bed under my blankets and abandon myself to a complete exhaustion of muscles, nerve and willpower; waiting as indifferently as a dead man for it to end or not to end.

But Charles had already lighted the stove, Charles, our active, trusting, alive friend, and he called me to work:

"Vas-y, Primo, descends-toi de là-haut; il y a Jules à attraper par les oreilles. . . ."

"Jules" was the lavatory bucket, which every morning had to be taken by its handles, carried outside and emptied into the cesspool; this was the first task of the day, and if one remembers that it was impossible to wash one's hands and that three of us were ill with typhus, it can be understood that it was not a pleasant job.

We had to inaugurate the cabbages and turnips. While I went

to search for wood and Charles collected the snow for water, Arthur mobilized the patients who could sit up to help with the peeling. Towarowski, Sertelet, Alcalai and Schenck answered the call.

Sertelet was also a peasant from the Vosges, twenty years old; he seemed in good shape, but day by day his voice assumed an ever more sinister nasal timbre, reminding us that diphtheria seldom relaxes its hold.

Alcalai was a Jewish glazier from Toulouse; he was quiet and discreet, and suffered from erysipelas on the face.

Schenck was a Slovak businessman, Jewish; a typhus patient, he had a formidable appetite. Likewise Towarowski, a Franco-Polish Jew, stupid and talkative, but useful to our community through his communicative optimism.

So while the patients scraped with their knives, each one seated on his bunk, Charles and I devoted ourselves to finding a suitable site for the kitchen operations. An indescribable filth had invaded every part of the camp. All the latrines were overflowing, as naturally nobody cared any more about their upkeep, and those suffering from dysentery (more than a hundred) had fouled every corner of Ka-Be, filling all the buckets, all the bowls formerly used for the rations, all the pots. One could not move an inch without watching one's step; in the dark it was impossible to move around. Although suffering from the cold, which remained acute, we thought with horror of what would happen if it thawed: the diseases would spread irreparably, the stench would be suffocating, and even more, with the snow melted we would remain definitively without water.

After a long search we finally found a small area of floor not excessively soiled in a spot formerly used for the laundry. We lit a live fire to save time and complications and disinfected our hands, rubbing them with chloramine mixed with snow.

The news that a soup was being cooked spread rapidly through the crowd of the semi-living; a throng of starved faces gathered at the door. Charles, with ladle uplifted, made a short, vigorous speech, which although in French needed no translation.

The majority dispersed but one came forward. He was a Parisian, a high-class tailor (he said), suffering from tuberculosis. In exchange for two pints of soup he offered to make us clothes from the many blankets still to be found in the camp.

Maxime showed himself really able. The following day Charles and I were in possession of a jacket, trousers and gloves of a rough fabric of striking colors.

In the evening, after the first soup, distributed with enthusiasm and devoured with greed, the great silence of the plain was broken. From our bunks, too tired to be really worried, we listened to the bangs of mysterious artillery groups apparently hidden on all the points of the horizon, and to the whistle of the shells over our heads.

I was thinking that life was beautiful and would be beautiful again, and that it would really be a pity to let ourselves be overcome now. I woke up the patients who were dozing and when I was sure that they were all listening I told them, first in French and then in my best German, that they must all begin to think of returning home now, and that as far as depended on us, certain things were to be done and others to be avoided. Each person should carefully look after his own bowl and spoon; no one should offer his own soup to others; no one should climb down from his bed except to go to the latrine; if anyone was in need of anything, he should only turn to us three. Arthur in particular was given the task of supervising the discipline and hygiene, and was to remember that it was better to leave bowls and spoons dirty rather than wash them with the danger of changing those of a diphtheria patient with those of someone suffering from typhus.

I had the impression that the patients by now were too indifferent to everything to pay attention to what I had said; but I had great faith in Arthur's diligence.

January 22. If it is courageous to face a grave danger with a light heart, Charles and I were courageous that morning. We extended our explorations to the S.S. camp, immediately outside the electric wire-fence.

The camp guards must have left in a great hurry. On the tables we found plates half-full of a by-now frozen soup which we devoured with an intense pleasure, mugs full of beer, transformed into a yellowish ice, a chess board with an unfinished game. In the dormitories, piles of valuable things.

We loaded ourselves with a bottle of vodka, various medicines, newspapers and magazines and four first-rate eider downs, one of which is today in my house in Turin. Cheerful and irresponsible, we carried the fruits of our expedition back to the dormitory, leaving them in Arthur's care. Only that evening did we learn what happened perhaps only half an hour later.

Some S.S. men, perhaps dispersed, but still armed, penetrated into the abandoned camp. They found that eighteen Frenchmen had settled in the dining hall of the S.S.-*Waffe*. They killed them all methodically, with a shot in the nape of the neck, lining up their twisted bodies in the snow on the road; then they left. The eighteen corpses remained exposed until the arrival of the Russians; nobody had the strength to bury them.

But by now there were beds in all the huts occupied by corpses as rigid as wood, whom nobody troubled to remove. The ground was too frozen to dig graves. Many bodies were piled up in a trench.

Only a wooden wall separated us from the ward of the dysentery patients, where many were dying and many dead. The floor was covered by a layer of frozen excrement. None of the patients had strength enough to climb out of their blankets to search for food, and those who had done it at the beginning had not returned to help their comrades. In one bed, clasping each other to resist the cold better, there were two Italians. I often heard them talking, but as I spoke only French, for a long time they were not aware of my presence. That day they heard my name by chance, pronounced with an Italian accent by Charles, and from then on they never ceased groaning and imploring.

Naturally I would have liked to have helped them, given the means and the strength, if for no other reason than to stop their crying. In the evening when all the work was finished, conquering my tiredness and disgust, I dragged myself gropingly along the dark, filthy corridor to their ward with a bowl of water and the remainder of our day's soup. The result was that from then on, through the thin wall, the whole diarrhea ward shouted my name day and night with the accents of all the languages of Europe, accompanied by incomprehensible prayers, without my being able to do anything about it. I felt like crying, I could have cursed them.

The night held ugly surprises.

Lakmaker, in the bunk under mine, was a poor wreck of a man. He was (or had been) a Dutch Jew, seventeen years old, tall, thin and gentle. He had been in bed for three months; I have no idea how he had managed to survive the selections. He had had typhus and scarlet fever successively; at the same time a serious cardiac illness had shown itself, while he was smothered with bedsores, so much so that by now he could only lie on his stomach. Despite all this, he had a ferocious appetite. He only spoke Dutch, and none of us could understand him.

Perhaps the cause of it all was the cabbage and turnip soup, of which Lakmaker had wanted two helpings. In the middle of the night he groaned and then threw himself from his bed. He tried to reach the latrine, but was too weak and fell to the ground, crying and shouting loudly.

Charles lit the lamp (the battery showed itself providential) and we were able to ascertain the gravity of the incident. The boy's bed and the floor were filthy. The smell in the small area was rapidly becoming insupportable. We had but a minimum supply of water and neither blankets nor straw mattresses to spare. And the poor wretch, suffering from typhus, formed a terrible source of infection, while he could certainly not be left all night to groan and shiver in the cold in the middle of the filth.

Charles climbed down from his bed and dressed in silence. While I held the lamp, he cut all the dirty patches from the straw mattress and the blankets with a knife. He lifted Lakmaker from the ground with the tenderness of a mother, cleaned him as best as possible with straw taken from the mattress and lifted him into the remade bed in the only position in which the unfortunate fellow could lie. He scraped the floor with a scrap of tinplate, diluted a little chloramine, and finally spread disinfectant over everything, including himself.

I judged his self-sacrifice by the tiredness which I would have had to overcome in myself to do what he had done.

January 23. Our potatoes were finished. For days past the rumor had circulated through all the huts that an enormous trench of potatoes lay somewhere outside the barbed wire, not far from the camp.

Some unknown pioneer must have carried out patient explorations, or else someone knew the spot with precision. In fact, by the morning of the 23rd a section of the barbed wire had been beaten down and a double file of wretches went in and out through the opening.

Charles and I left, into the wind of the leaden plain. We were beyond the broken barrier.

"Dis donc, Primo, on est dehors!"

It was exactly like that; for the first time since the day of my arrest I found myself free, without armed guards, without wire fences between myself and home.

Perhaps 400 yards from the camp lay the potatoes—a treasure. Two extremely long ditches, full of potatoes and covered by alternate layers of soil and straw to protect them from the cold. Nobody would die of hunger anymore.

But to extract them was by no means easy work. The cold had made the surface of the earth as hard as iron. By strenuous work with a pickaxe it was possible to break the crust and lay bare the deposit; but the majority preferred to work the holes abandoned by others and continue to deepen them, passing the potatoes to their companions standing outside.

An old Hungarian had been surprised there by death. He lay there like hunger personified: head and shoulders under a pile of earth, belly in the snow, hands stretched out towards the potatoes. Someone came later and moved the body about a yard, so freeing the hole.

From then on our food improved. Besides boiled potatoes and potato soup, we offered our patients potato pancakes, on Arthur's recipe: rub together raw potatoes with boiled, soft ones, and roast the mixture on a red-hot iron-plate. They tasted of soot.

But Sertelet, steadily getting worse, was unable to enjoy them. Besides speaking with an ever more nasal tone, that day he was unable to force down any food; something had closed up in his throat, every mouthful threatened to suffocate him.

I went to look for a Hungarian doctor left as a patient in the hut in front. When he heard the word diphtheria he started back and ordered me to leave.

For pure propaganda purposes I gave everyone nasal drops of camphorated oil. I assured Sertelet that they would help him; I even tried to convince myself.

January 24. Liberty. The breach in the barbed wire gave us a concrete image of it. To anyone who stopped to think, it signified no more Germans, no more selections, no work, no blows, no roll-calls, and perhaps, later, the return.

But we had to make an effort to convince ourselves of it, and no one had time to enjoy the thought. All around lay destruction and death.

The pile of corpses in front of our window had by now overflowed out of the ditch. Despite the potatoes everyone was extremely weak: not a patient in the camp improved, while many fell ill with pneumonia and diarrhea; those who were unable to move themselves, or lacked the energy to do so, lay lethargic in their bunks, benumbed by the cold, and nobody realized when they died.

The others were all incredibly tired: after months and years of the *Lager* it needs more than potatoes to give back strength to a man. Charles and I, as soon as we had dragged the fifty pints of daily soup from the laundry to our room, threw ourselves panting on the bunks, while Arthur, with that domesticated air of his, diligently divided the food, taking care to save the three rations of *"rabiot pour les travailleurs"* and a little of the sediment *"pour les italiens d'à côté."*

In the second room of the contagious ward, likewise adjoining ours and occupied mainly by tuberculosis patients, the situation was quite different. All those who were able to had gone to other huts. Their weakest comrades and those who were most seriously ill died one by one in solitude.

I went in there one morning to try and borrow a needle. A patient was wheezing in one of the upper bunks. He heard me, struggled to sit up, then fell dangling, head downward over the edge toward me, with his chest and arms stiff and his eyes white. The man in the bunk below automatically stretched up his arms to support the body and then realized that he was dead. He slowly withdrew from under the weight and the body slid to the ground where it remained. Nobody knew his name.

But in hut 14 something new had happened. It was occupied by patients recovering from operations, some of them quite healthy. They organized an expedition to the English prisoner-of-war camp, which it was assumed had been evacuated. It proved a fruitful expedition. They returned dressed in khaki with a cart full of wonders never seen before: margarine, custard powders, lard, soya-bean flour, whisky.

That evening there was singing in hut 14.

None of us felt strong enough to walk the one mile to the English camp and return with a load. But indirectly the fortunate expedition proved of advantage to many. The unequal division of goods caused a reflourishing of industry and commerce. Our room, with its lethal atmosphere, transformed itself into a factory of candles poured into cardboard molds, with wicks soaked in boracic acid. The riches of hut 14 absorbed our entire production, paying us in lard and flour.

I myself had found the block of beeswax in the *elektro magazin;* I remember the expression of disappointment of those who saw me carry it away and the dialogue that followed:

"What do you want to do with that?"

It was inadvisable to reveal a shop secret; I heard myself replying with the words I had often heard spoken by the old ones of the camp, expressing their favorite boast—of being hardboiled, "old hands," who always knew how to find their feet: *"Ich verstehe verschiedene Sache."* I know how to do many things. . . .

January 25. It was Sómogyi's turn. He was a Hungarian chemist, about fifty years old, thin, tall and taciturn. Like the Dutchman, he suffered from typhus and scarlet fever. He had not spoken for perhaps five days; that day he opened his mouth and said in a firm voice:

"I have a ration of bread under the sack. Divide it among you three. I shall not be eating anymore."

We could not find anything to say, but for the time being we did not touch the bread. Half his face had swollen. As long as he retained consciousness he remained closed in a harsh silence.

But in the evening and for the whole of the night and for two days without interruption the silence was broken by his delirium. Following a last interminable dream of acceptance and slavery he began to murmur: *"Jawohl!"* with every breath, regularly and continuously like a machine, *"Jawohl,"* at every collapsing of his wretched frame, thousands of times, enough to make one want to shake him, to suffocate him, at least to make him change the word.

I never understood so clearly as at that moment how laborious is the death of a man.

Outside the great silence continued. The number of ravens had increased considerably and everybody knew why. Only at distant intervals did the dialogue of the artillery wake up.

We all said to each other that the Russians would arrive soon, at once; we all proclaimed it, we were all sure of it, but at bottom nobody believed it. Because one loses the habit of hoping in the *Lager,* and even of believing in one's own reason. In the *Lager* it is useless to think, because events happen for the most part in an unforeseeable manner; and it is harmful, because it keeps alive a sensitivity which is a source of pain, and which some providential natural law dulls when suffering passes a certain limit.

Like joy, fear and pain itself, even expectancy can be tiring. Having reached January 25, with all relations broken already for eight days with that ferocious world that still remained a world, most of us were too exhausted even to wait.

In the evening, around the stove, Charles, Arthur and I felt ourselves become men once again. We could speak of everything. I grew enthusiastic at Arthur's account of how one passed the Sunday at Provenchères in the Vosges, and Charles almost cried when I told him the story of the armistice in Italy, of the turbid and desperate beginning of the partisan resistance, of the man who betrayed us and of our capture in the mountains.

In the darkness, behind and above us, the eight invalids did not lose a syllable, even those who did not understand French. Only Sómogyi implacably confirmed his dedication to death.

January 26. We lay in a world of death and phantoms. The last trace of civilization had vanished around and inside us. The work of bestial degradation, begun by the victorious Germans, had been carried to its conclusion by the Germans in defeat.

It is man who kills, man who creates or suffers injustice; it is no longer man who, having lost all restraint, shares his bed with a corpse. Whoever waits for his neighbor to die in order to take his piece of bread is, albeit guiltless, further from the model of thinking man than the most primitive pigmy or the most vicious sadist.

Part of our existence lies in the feelings of those near to us. This is why the experience of someone who has lived for days during which man was merely a thing in the eyes of man is non-human. We three were for the most part immune from it, and we owe each other mutual gratitude. This is why my friendship with Charles will prove lasting.

But thousands of feet above us, in the gaps in the gray clouds, the complicated miracles of aerial duels began. Above us, bare, helpless and unarmed, men of our time sought reciprocal death with the most refined of instruments. A movement of a finger could cause the destruction of the entire camp, could annihilate thousands of men; while the sum total of all our efforts and exertions would not be sufficient to prolong by one minute the life of even one of us.

The saraband stopped at night and the room was once again filled with Sómogyi's monologue.

In full darkness I found myself suddenly awake. *"L'pauv'-vieux"* was silent; he had finished. With the last gasp of life, he had thrown himself to the ground: I heard the thud of his knees, of his hips, of his shoulders, of his head.

"La mort l'a chassé de son lit," Arthur defined it.

We certainly could not carry him out during the night. There was nothing for it but to go back to sleep again.

January 27. Dawn. On the floor, the shameful wreck of skin and bones, the Sómogyi thing.

There are more urgent tasks: we cannot wash ourselves, so that we dare not touch him until we have cooked and eaten. And besides: ". . . *rien de si dégoutant que les débordements*" said Charles justly; the latrine had to be emptied. The living are more demanding; the dead can wait. We began to work as on every day.

The Russians arrived while Charles and I were carrying Sómogyi a little distance outside. He was very light. We overturned the stretcher on the gray snow.

Charles took off his beret. I regretted not having a beret.

Of the eleven of the *Infektionsabteilung* Sómogyi was the only one to die in the ten days. Sertelet, Cagnolati, Towarowski, Lakmaker and Dorget (I have not spoken of him so far; he was a French industrialist who, after an operation for peritonitis, fell ill of nasal diphtheria) died some weeks later in the temporary Russian hospital of Auschwitz. In April, at Katowice, I met Schenck and Alcalai in good health. Arthur has reached his family happily and Charles has taken up his teacher's profession again; we have exchanged long letters and I hope to see him again one day.

SALA PAWLOWICZ WITH KEVIN KLOSE

The Wache

The days and nights were warmer, and soon it would be summer. I did not shiver from cold at night, though there were more lice now because it was warm. I had learned from the earlier days to be careful of drinking water and of open cuts. I tried to keep as much to myself as possible and to keep the lice from biting my legs too much. My feet were covered with boils, and I did not want an infection to start.

In June 1943, we were given new machines to help speed the inspection of shells. Before *Appell* one night, some girls mentioned that they had had to work sitting on the floor that day, as new equipment was being installed in our department. When I went to the factory, a long row of strange machines had taken the place of our old, simple tables.

"These will speed your production a great deal," shouted Clara. "I will expect exactly double the amount you normally produce by this morning. You will each give me 10,000 shells by seven in the morning, or you will go to the *Wache* without fail." She assigned us to new places. The new rata would total 150,000 shells a day.

The machines were run by two girls. One filled a hopper with shell casings, while the other sat in a chair, looking into a long wide mirror that reflected the shells as they passed inside the sorting machine on a long, continuous belt. A bright light inside the machine illuminated the casings. It was my job to keep track of the shells in the mirror and to pick out any bad ones, as before. However, the machine was not controlled by me; I could not stop it if something went wrong, but had to reach in quickly and pick out the defective pieces from the belt.

My machine was at the end of the line, nearest the control room. I looked up there from this short distance and watched as women in white smocks and caps inspected the shells with microscopes and powerful lights. I prayed that their instruments would not find any mistakes made by me.

The mirror of my machine was distorted and seemed to give a slight double image. At first I thought this was the way it was supposed to work, but the more I used it the more convinced I became that the mirror was not functioning correctly. Clara strode by, and I raised my head. She walked over. "What's your problem, Jew?"

I was not allowed to speak to her, but had to indicate by signs what was wrong. She pulled me from the chair and sat down. A few seconds later she got up and called for Max, her assistant. The tall man came over and they talked for a few seconds, then he sat down and stared at the mirror. "There's something wrong with this," he said, getting up.

"Well, so what?" asked Clara. "Here, Jew, maybe this will help you!" She slapped me in the face several times. "Can you see things any better now?" She went away and I was left to do the best I could and risk the *Wache* because of the defective mirror.

By concentrating, I was able to get through the first day, and by the second day at the new machine I had learned the trick of using the double-imaged mirror. I had little trouble making the quota, but my eyes smarted from strain when the shift was over.

I lay on my bunk, with my hands cupped behind my head and watched the long black insect with large feelers scurry here and there across the boards above me. It poked into cracks and nosed about in the dark places between the boards. I was rather fond of it. Next to Rysia, it was the only friend I had. I wondered if insects had any feelings. In the weeks at Hassag-Pelcery I had learned to deaden myself to thoughts. I could keep them in control by concentrating only on the need to work and not torturing myself with memories. It was the most successful way to live, and the longer I did it the easier it became.

As I lay there waiting for sleep a new pain which I could not place was stabbing lightly at me, making me uncomfortable. I turned on my side and folded my hands between my legs and the pain subsided. Perhaps it had something to do with my shoulders. I fell asleep.

I had been at my machine for several hours the next night when the first deep pain hit me. It seemed to come from under my arms and to work its way up across my chest. A cold wave passed through me and my hands seemed hot and sticky. I looked at them; they were swollen and inflamed, and I could not move the fingers easily. How had this come so suddenly? What could I do? If Clara found out that I was too sick to work, she would put me to death in a second.

Slowly I filled the boxes with my work. Clara came by in the morning and weighed the production. *"Du arbeitest gut, verflucht!"* she commented as she hit me in the face.

I pulled myself up the stairs and sat on my bunk, trying to discover what was wrong with me. The pains still stabbed from under my arms. I wished Rysia were there to look, but she was working. I was too frightened to ask anyone else, so I sat alone, feeling my chest for sores. In each armpit I discovered an abscess about the size of an egg. They were hard and firm and did not seem "ripe" enough to be drawn. There was nothing to do but try to sleep if I could. At least the worry was relieved, if not the pain. As long as the disease stayed on the outside where I could take care of it, I felt calm enough to cure myself.

But sleep did not come to me. My temperature mounted during the morning and I shook from chills. As the day progressed, it became a nightmare of heat and torture. I writhed on the hard boards and worried about how I was to make the *Appell* on time—only a few hours away. If I did not appear, they would come for me and shoot me. Stieglitz would stand over me, grinning and laughing. I fixed my mind on his face, and in my fevered brain I saw his twisted mouth and scrawny neck swim before me. The hate I had for that single being was enough to propel me to the *Appellplatz* when the trumpet sounded.

I was saved that day by Clara's absence: she did not come in, and her assistant, Max, took pity on me. "Start working," he said the first time I collapsed. The second time, he shook me roughly, trying to wake me, but it did no good. "Try to make your normal production then, Jew, if you can," he said.

I slowly started the machine again and began working as hard as I could. Clara arrived toward the end of the shift, when the pain had lessened a little and I was able to operate the machine effectively.

To my great amazement, when Clara weighed my work I had made the production quota. When that was announced, I suddenly felt as though there was nothing that a human being could not accomplish when aware that death is at hand.

The next night I barely made *Appell* before Stieglitz appeared. He looked suspiciously at me, then went on down the line. I was determined to get through the shift if I possibly could, but just before midnight I collapsed over the machine. The room spun about me, and my body was burning with fever. I staggered up from the chair and dragged myself toward Clara, to beg her to kill me. As soon as she saw me dare to move from my chair, Clara ran over and pounded me with her fists and beat me across my arms. She shrieked at me, but I could not understand her. I tried to raise my arms, to show her what was wrong, and at last, she looked more closely at me and pressed her hand under my arm. When I screamed, she jumped back, startled. "What's wrong—what's wrong with you!" she shouted in a frenzy. "Why do you scream so? Are you sick, you filthy Jew? Do you want to be shot?"

"My arms . . . hurt," I said weakly.

"Get out of my sight then! Go on! Crawl up to that sty and take care of yourself! I don't want to *touch* you," she cried, and started to swing her stick again. I ducked, and the blow glanced off my shoulder. "You have ten minutes, foul thing!" I got to my feet and stumbled up to the barracks.

It was very dark in the room. I bumped into several bunks until I found my own place. The deep sounds of exhaustion filled the room. Rysia was curled into a small ball of rags and arms; that was all I could see of her. I did not wake her, but started to look around for a sharp splinter. At last, I found one in the wall.

I wiped it as clean as I could on my dress, then shut my eyes and drove the splinter deep into the sac of pus under my left arm. Before the pain hit me, I clutched the wet point and with all my remaining power shoved it into the hard, smooth abscess under my right arm.

Pus and fluid spurted and dripped down my sides. I pressed both arms tightly to my sides and felt the pressure go down as the fluid cleared. The pain did not seem to leave, but when I raised my arms I was not wracked by the stabbings as before. My head was clearer, and I could feel sensation in my hands now. I forced myself to go down to the factory and back to my job.

I sneaked in unnoticed by Clara and started to work. I knew

it would be impossible for me to finish my quota. It would have been a relief just to break down and let the tears flow, but there were no tears at all. I worked on in horror, and by morning I had not made the quota. I was sure that Clara would send me to the *Wache,* but she only looked wildly at me and said, "You're lucky, you dirty Jew! I loathe touching you." She kicked me as I tried to get out of the chair and I fell. "I'll get you another time!" she shouted and stalked off.

Stieglitz bothered us again during the day, but I was so relieved by the draining of my abscesses that his actions meant little to me. When *Appell* came, I felt better, though I still had pain. My hands were back to normal, and the fever had left me. All I could think of was that I had survived my first bout with sickness, and would have to survive other sicknesses in the future.

Several nights later, when I went to my machine, Clara immediately came up to me. "If you slack off tonight, as you have been doing all this week, I will kill you," she said evenly. I looked at her blankly, trying to make her words mean something. I should hate this woman, I thought. Clara hates me and I should return her hate. Everything that is ugly in the world is in that woman. But I had no feeling one way or the other. If she wanted to kill me, that was her right, for wasn't Clara a German?

I looked at my partner standing beside the hopper, ready to feed shells into the machine. She motioned to me that this was a good batch of material. The machine started and the first shells rattled down the chute and started across the mirror. Soon, I had settled down to the routine, and as the night advanced I noticed that I was well ahead of my schedule.

However, when the shift was almost over, my machine suddenly stopped. I looked in the mirror—the shells were not moving on the belt any more—it really was not working! I could not believe it. The machine could not break—it was a piece of steel, part of the Germans, part of Clara! It worked as it always had, as it always would, until long after we were gone. Machines did not break—we did.

I stared at my partner. She had not noticed that the machine had stopped, and slowly the hopper filled and overflowed with shells that spilled and clattered on the floor. She looked blankly at me, and I motioned that the belt was no longer moving. I could hear something whirring unevenly inside the machine. I peered hard at the mirror, but I could not see what was wrong.

Down the line, Max stood with his back to us, looking across the factory. How could I get his attention? What would happen when Clara came back and found the machine broken down? I shuddered and called, "Help!" Again I called, and slowly Max turned around, an outraged look on his face. He started up the line, looking at the girls as he went past. "Help!" I called again and he walked on faster and stopped in front of me.

"What is wrong, you impudent bitch?"

"My mach—" I started to say, but he hit me in the face.

"Don't *ever* speak to me, foul one. *Show* me. Do you think you are human?"

Max stepped behind me and tried to force the belt to start, but nothing happened. He listened closely, then he ordered a *Werkschütz* to shut off the power to the machine and he went to call a mechanic. I sat hunched in my chair. It seemed to me that my life was useless now, for my machine was useless. I could not hope to make my quota tonight, and Clara would certainly not listen to reason.

"He's coming back," my partner whispered. I looked up to see Max approaching, followed by a man carrying a tool kit. The second man was a mechanic, I knew, for I had seen him among that group at the *Appellplatz* when I was on the day shift. Max roughly pulled the other girl away from the machine and the young man spread his tools on the hopper. He looked inside, removed a plate from the back, and began working there, pulling wheels and strange cogs back and forth, and finally removing a piece of the machine. He held it up and then, as he was inspecting it in the light, he slowly looked at me and then back at his work.

He was young, perhaps a few years older than I. Idly, I gazed at him as he knelt on the floor, making adjustments. Had the Nazis treated him badly? How did a man accept their humiliations? He was not dirty and wore fairly new clothes. I assumed this was because he was a mechanic, and very valuable to the Germans. I envied him because he did not seem to be afraid of Max. The *Meister* stood above us, watching suspiciously and asking the man questions from time to time. The mechanic answered quickly, in a low, firm voice. It had been so long since I had heard anything but shouting. This had been wrong, that did not function correctly; he counted off the things on his fingers to the *Meister,* then replaced the covering and gathered his tools. He looked at me again. I was not sure, but it seemed as if he wanted information, as if he wanted me to tell him something, or say something to him. I was confused; I suddenly wanted very much to say hello to this man and have him say hello to me, as simply and as strongly as he could. The mechanic stood up and turned to Max.

"This will work now," he said. "I have fixed it quite well enough. But it is a poor machine, you see. It may break down again."

"Start the power," said the *Meister,* and suddenly the belt roared to life in front of me and I turned to the mirror once again. The shells jiggled and spun in the double-imaged glass. The mechanic leaned over my back and looked into the mirror.

"This mirror is defective, too. It should be changed. I will change it if a new mirror ever comes." The *Meister* said nothing to this, but merely nodded. I looked up in gratitude. The mechanic abruptly turned away, picked up his tool kit and walked off across the factory. The casings rattled on and on.

In the morning Clara came and weighed our production. To my astonishment, I had just made the quota. All the finished boxes were sent to the control department and Clara lined us up and gave her daily speech: "If any work is found to be unsatisfactory, you will all be taken to the *Wache.*" With that reminder, we were sent upstairs.

I lay back, feeling my underarms. The swelling had almost disappeared and I felt much stronger than I had a few days before. I was still amazed that I had made the quota. It had seemed so impossible a few hours before. I tried to judge how long it was that the machine had been broken down. During the minutes of waiting, it had seemed as though an hour had gone by. Yet I was safe for another day, and the mechanic had said that he would fix the mirror if he could.

"Get up! Get up! The rata from the night shift of the *Augenschein* has come back! Get up! *Raus!*" I started from my bunk and ran to the stairs and stood there as the girls from our shift streamed by and clattered down. I was numb with horror and would have simply watched them go if a girl had not seized my hand and pulled me along with her.

Dazed and groggy, I felt myself being dragged through the factory. It was a long way through that dim room of noise and bitter smells. Machines danced past me and a girl's pale face looked strangely at me. I squinted, trying to recognize a familiar face. Rysia was here somewhere. The Ukrainian pushing me was shouting something. The *Wache!* It meant nothing to me until the first scream pierced the dullness of my brain.

I found myself standing in a line of girls from the *Augenschein.*

Several were ahead of me, and from the room in front of us came screams and the slap of leather on flesh. Slowly, the line advanced as girl after girl was taken inside. Clara appeared in the doorway. She was smiling, and beads of perspiration rolled down her forehead.

"You're next, pretty one! You'll enjoy the sting of that whip!" Her hands were covered with blood. She pushed me through the door into the room.

The walls were covered with whips, several dozen of them, each coiled carefully and hanging from its own nail. A heavy leather curtain was stretched across one half of the room. From behind the curtain came a deep groan, then the slap of a whip and a piercing scream. Then silence.

"Pick one," said a Ukrainian standing by the door. "Pick a whip." I gaped at him. *"Pick one! Pick one!"* he snarled, seizing me about the throat. "Pick one—quick!" I reached out blindly and took the first thing my hand touched.

"That's fine! You'll like *that* one!"

From the other side of the curtain came grunts of strain as men dragged a heavy weight across the floor and threw it outside. Then silence filled the small room and I could hear them breathing heavily from their exertion.

"Next."

The Ukrainians pushed me forward. "That means you, Jew." I went around the curtain.

The floor on the other side was slippery with blood. The walls and curtain were splattered. A table stood in the middle of the room and four Ukrainians, stripped to the waist, stood by it. The four men looked at me and one of them wiped his head with a cloth.

"Well, don't stand there, swine," he said. "Take off that rag."

I fumbled with the buttons and dropped my ragged dress at my feet. One of the men grabbed the whip from me.

"This is a good one. On the table! On your stomach, unless you want it there instead." I climbed on the table, put my hands under me and closed my eyes. I dug my nails into my thighs.

"Clara!" called a voice.

"Give her twenty-five to start. If she screams, give her more," Clara said. "This one is a lazy Jew, a real bitch! She deserves every lash!"

The four men surrounded the table.

"Anytime you're read—!" began Clara and the first lash struck me. My breath whistled in surprise. Again! I started to scream and it was cut short by the third lash. I fainted.

The shock of cold water brought me to and the beating continued. "The more you scream, the more you'll get!" a man shouted in my ear. "Now shut up!" And the pain came again, searing my back, filling my brain with agony. I remained silent listening to the slap of the whips against my skin and to Clara's voice counting each blow. I passed out again and they brought me to.

"Twenty!" I felt myself shrinking, and retreating from my body. I could not breathe from the strain of holding back my screams.

"Get out of here! *Move!*" The words came in waves, and some men pummeled me, but I could not move. They opened the door and threw me into a hallway. I did not know where I was or what to do. I lay with my head against the wall and tried to tell myself that they would only beat me again if I did not move. But nothing happened. My body refused to respond.

After many minutes, I gained enough strength to feel about me. I discovered that I still was clutching my dress. Slowly, in an agony, I pulled it on and fumbled with the buttons. I could not get up, for my hands were slippery with my blood and did not help me. I could feel nothing but pain surrounding me. I tried to pull myself up, but the walls seemed to lean toward me, and I sat back exhausted. I knew I had to get to the factory and then upstairs, but there seemed to be no way to get there. I began crying then, and when I could not hear my voice, I started crawling along the floor and came to the door to the factory. I pulled myself up, opened the door and stumbled through.

Someone was watching me. I shook my head to clear it and looked again. It was the mechanic who had repaired my machine. He was kneeling on the floor, a wrench in his hand. He was surprised, I saw, then he blinked and looked at the tool in his hand. I noticed everything he did, as though I were watching a slow-motion movie. I crawled past him and leaned on a machine to catch my breath. Far across the factory, Clara was striding back to the *Augenschein*. I could not rest any longer. I glanced at the man. He seemed to be deep in thought as he worked.

Holding to the machines, I crept along the wall to the stairs outside and crawled slowly up them. I could not open the door to our barrack; I scratched at it and tried to say, "Let me in," but my words escaped in a low groan. I listened in horror to it. The door opened and someone looked out at me.

"Help me . . . help me," I cried, but nothing came except the animal's groan. And then unconsciousness.

I woke to find myself in my bunk. The morning sun was slanting through the filthy windows. My dress was sticky and caked with blood, and it stuck to my back. Pain stabbed through me. At last, I managed to turn on my stomach and relieve the agony a little.

The past two days spun before my eyes, and the coming night loomed threateningly before me. What keeps me alive? What makes me strong? I wondered. The Germans must think we are all animals—but an animal would die before we died. I did not see how this could keep up. We could not survive too much longer; these people were bent on destroying us completely. Nothing but a miracle could save any of us.

The day moved on slowly. I lay trying to concentrate on getting up for *Appell* in the evening. It did not seem possible. I tried to imagine what the pain would be like when I tried to pull myself from the bunk as the trumpet sounded, but when the time came the actual pain was beyond belief. Somehow, I found my way to the *Appellplatz* and stood between two girls who helped support me while we were counted and then sent off to our jobs.

Clara greeted us with smiles, as if she had never seen us before. Her passions had been satisfied by the beatings she had counted, and now we were in her good favor once again. Disbelieving, I eased my aching body into the chair and took a deep breath. A shudder passed through me at the thought of having to get through this night. It seemed so hopeless, so pointless. It made no difference whether I produced the shells or someone else produced them. In the end I would die, and this machine would still go on, and then the next person would die. But Clara would live and the Germans would have their rifle shells.

I adjusted the receiving box for the flow of shells. There was something resting in the bottom of the box. Slowly I bent over and endured the pain stabbing in my back. I picked out a wad of dirty paper. It seemed to be a package of some sort. I dropped it in my lap and looked more closely at it. The brown paper had been written on. I unfolded it carefully and looked around. No one was near. And then I read the note written in Polish:

"I pity you. I know who you are. I will share my last morsel of bread with you. Don't look for me. Don't try to find out who I am. You know the danger. I will do all I can to help you."

A small piece of black bread dropped on my lap.

ARNOST LUSTIG

Stephen and Anne

TRANSLATED FROM THE CZECH BY GEORGE THEINER

He lay there quietly.

The beam he was gazing up at had a dark, nut-brown color. On it somebody had scribbled the word "quarantine." It struck him as funny that the walls here inside should be the same red color as the outside walls. He already had his bed—a narrow strip of the paving-stone floor. In the semi-darkness he could make out the rounded shapes of the women, who were getting ready to lie down in the uncertain, flickering light of the candles. He had been lying here in this way for many seconds, in the grip of a fever he was not even aware of, and full of tantalizing thoughts.

Then he fell asleep. He would come awake, wild with desperation, thinking that it was almost dawn, would close his eyes again, desiring to protract the delicious darkness in which he dropped, rose and dropped anew.

He awoke early in the morning.

Astonished, he looked around to find out where he was.

Next to him slept a girl, covered by knapsacks and a dark blanket, on his other side an old man who snored with the exertion of sleep.

He narrowed his eyes and saw her clearly like the white summit of some snow-capped mountain. Her brow was smooth and her skin well-nigh transparent, she had loosely flowing golden hair, and an equally fair nape. The violence with which her image kept returning to him frightened him.

He waited for her to wake. Her hair was like autumn leaves, her lips were pale and half-open. He felt a current pass through him, a current in which there was the light of dawn and the quiet of night.

She sat up, slightly startled.

She covered her face with her long fingers.

"Good morning," he said.

"Good morning."

"Please don't be angry that I am lying here," he said. "I didn't see properly last night."

"It doesn't matter," she replied.

She looked across him to where the old man was lying.

"Are you getting up?" he asked.

"Yes, I am," she said.

"Have you been here long?"

"A week," she replied.

And then: "I was already asleep when you arrived."

"We came in the night," he said.

"Some transports do come at night," she replied.

"We don't even know each other," he said.

She smiled, and he could see both bitterness and embarrassment on her lips.

"My name is Stephen," he said.

"Mine is Anne," she replied. And she repeated it: "Anne."

An official appeared on the threshold of the wooden staircase.

"It's one of ours," she said. "He has got a star."

A wave of silence swamped the attic.

"What's he want?"

"He is going to read out the names," she said.

"Our names?"

"Yes, perhaps our names, too," she replied.

The official stopped a few paces away from them. He spread out his papers like huge banknotes. Then he said that those whom he was going to read out had been selected by the Council of Elders —entrusted with this task by the German H.Q.—and would go and live in the ghetto.

"And the others?"

"Elsewhere," she said.

"Where?"

"Nobody knows," she replied.

And then: "In the East," she said.

The old man next to them was awake now. He was holding a wrinkled, sallow hand to his ear, so as to hear better. "My name is Adam," he said. "Adam," he mumbled.

"Haven't you been read yet?" Stephen asked her.

"No," she said.

Suddenly she felt ashamed that they had not read her yet.

"My name is Adam," murmured the old man.

Then Stephen's name was read out.

"That's you," she said. "Stephen."

"Perhaps he'll read you, too," he said.

He did not.

"Be glad," she said.

He was silent, frightened suddenly by the infinitude of leave-taking that clung to him.

"Don't cry," he said.

"I'm not crying," she replied.

The official announced that those whose names had been called were to go downstairs into the courtyard within ten minutes.

"Just those I've read out—neither more nor fewer," he said curtly.

Then he added: "I've not thought this up—it's orders from H.Q."

"Adam," the old man repeated.

The official left.

"Are you thinking about it?"

"No," she answered.

"They'll read you tomorrow," he said. "Or some other time."

He could not make himself stand up, yet he knew he would have to.

He took her hand.

"Come and see me, won't you?" she said.

"I'll come," he replied.

"We have known each other so short a time," she said.

"I'll come for sure," he said again. "I'm alone here. We can be friends."

"If they leave us here," she said.

"Why?"

"I've heard things."

"What things?"

"That we are to be sent on," she said. "Maybe within a week."

He helped her with the knapsacks.

"You're lucky," she said.

He was looking at her, unable to reply.

The current rose up in him from somewhere deep inside, right to the top and back again to his finger tips with which he was touching the palm of her hand.

"Perhaps," she said quietly, "I shall still be here."

"You will," he muttered.

And then he added: "Certainly you will."

"Go on, then," she said.

He looked at her, and he again felt the current, being drowned in it. Then he got up, letting her hand slip out of his, and something stopped inside him; he felt it in the contraction of his chest and the smarting of his eyes that increased with each step he drew farther away from her.

"Adam," mumbled the old man.

Then he ran along L Avenue; everything that had enveloped him like a spider's web and that alternately burned and went out inside him, alternately driving him forward and drawing him back to the attic of the quarantine, turned over inside him and reverberated like the echo of those words.

He put down his knapsack on the bed assigned to him.

Then he ran back the way he had come, not caring what would become of him and his things.

He dashed inside. He saw her, so slim, on the gray palliasse.

"Stephen," she said.

Then: "It's you."

And finally: "So you've come." She lowered her eyes.

"Annie," he said.

"I didn't really expect . . ." she said.

He ignored the old man, whose snoring disturbed all who were near him. He sat down at her side on the mattress, out of which the straw projected like so many arrows. He did not feel any need to say more than that one word he had said already.

"Annie," he repeated.

He embraced her shoulders and felt the current surging up from inside. The feeling that he was protecting her with the hand that touched her stifled him.

He sat silently next to her, in front of the barrier of stone that was the old man, whose glassy eyes did not take them in and whose sallow neck, resembling a human tree trunk, shielded them from view.

Suddenly his eyes met those of the old man.

"What is it?" she asked.

"Nothing," he replied.

He could feel that she was afraid. She pressed herself closer to him.

Then she saw the old man's gaze and she was frightened by what she read in it—a wild, imploring insolence and an inquisitive envy.

"My name is Adam," the old man muttered.

He kept holding his hand up to his face to catch the sound of words that did not reach him.

"Let's get away from here," said Stephen.

"Yes, let's," she said.

Then she added: "What if the official comes?"

"Why should he?"

Her eyes fell and she looked at the floor.

"Let's go, then," she said.

She did not dare to look again into the dark pools of the old man's eyes. She rose. She had on a coat of some warm, blue material.

Looking at her, the coat and everything else seemed to him to be as clear and clean as the sky.

He had to step across the old man's mattress.

He knew he would speak to him.

"Look after Anne's things," he said.

And to Anne it seemed as if only these words really woke the old man. He dropped the hand that had acted as a hearing aid. His almond-brown eyes grew wide and soft.

"Adam," he said.

Then he added: "Right-oh! You run along, children!"

She had to lower her eyes once more.

"Is that your brother?" the old man asked.

They looked at each other. He felt the current again running through him.

"Yes," he replied for her.

They went out, and it seemed to them that everything they looked at was without shadow.

And Stephen wished that the current should pass through the tips of his fingers to Anne, that she might feel in that touch the sun, and hope, and the rosy rays of day and its light.

"Brother and sister," he said.

And then: "More than that."

They walked round the blacksmith's shop. On the other side of the slope that towered above the town they saw the rambling building of the Council of Elders.

"If only I had an uncle here," she said.

"Has he gone?" he asked.

She turned her face to his and, with her finger quite close to him, tapped her forehead.

"Silly," she said, "I was thinking of an uncle who does not exist."

"Are you alone?"

"Completely," she replied.

"Are you hungry?"

"What could you do about it?"

"Do you know where I live?"

"No," she said.

"Here," he said. "Wait a second."

He ran upstairs and pulled a piece of cake out of his knapsack; this he broke in two, leaving one of the halves to the boys who were watching him.

"For your hunger," he said when he was downstairs again.

"Thanks," she said.

Suddenly they both laughed.

"Let's go back there," she said then.

"There?" he asked.

"Yes," she said.

"Yes," he repeated.

When they were sitting down again, he said: "They'll read you tomorrow."

"Oh, I'm not thinking about it," she said.

"There are other things apart from that," he said.

"What things?"

"Other things," he repeated.

Then they went out, but they only had time to walk once round the town.

The darkened trees began to merge with their own shadows, the twilight toying with the leaves.

"Come," she said. "I'll accompany you."

He gazed into her eyes, so close to his. He put his arm around her shoulders, which were frail and gentle, making him think it was up to him to protect her. The strong feeling that seemed to have a life of its own inside him and rose in waves up to his throat and farther, both the light and the dark curve of her silhouette, that which at once constricted him and released him from the shadows, holding out the promise of a sensation of freedom, all this flowed into the single word which he now uttered:

"Anne!"

"Stephen!"

He kissed her on the mouth.

"I've never . . . been like this before," she said.

It was his first kiss as well as hers.

And he again felt those waves returning, clean and fragrant, and he kissed her lips and eyes, which were now filled with tears, and felt a desperate longing that he need never, even at the price of death, live otherwise than at this moment.

They walked a little way from the door, to the spot where a yellow, wooden fence divided off the ghetto from the H.Q.

They shivered with the chill of evening.

"It's not so late yet," she said.

"Annie," he said.

"Where shall we go?" she asked.

"Annie," he repeated.

"We'll have to be going," she said, and stood still. He felt the irrevocability of the hour that closes the day like a thin sword-blade having the power to cut even the invisible current somewhere deep inside where no one can see.

He led her wordlessly round the block of houses next to Q 710. He was aware that some outside influence was disturbing that current inside him, and yet he was glad he was walking by her side and feeling her warmth, and at the same time unhappy because he knew what was coming; his throat was constricted by the same huge hoop that was encircling his chest and pressing against his eyes.

"Annie," he said.

"Yes?" she replied.

And then, after a long silence: "If you want, Stephen," she said, "come and see me in the night."

"I will," he whispered. He felt as though she had cut through ropes which had until now bound him.

"Yes, I will," he said again. "I'll come for sure."

"You can go across the courtyards," she said.

Then she added: "That's how they do it here."

"Yes," he said.

"We'll be moved soon," she said. "I feel it."

"I'll come," he repeated.

"I feel it somehow," she said.

And then, "I'm terribly afraid. It's even worse now."

"Don't worry," he said. "I'll come for sure."

"It's not far across the courtyards," she said.

"Yes," he said.

He took off his coat and threw it over her.

She returned it to him.

Then, all at once, she ran off, suddenly and unexpectedly. She tore herself away from his hands, regretting that she had said what she did. She knew the laws of the ghetto a week longer than he. He only heard her steps, receding into the darkness.

A fraction of that moment was before his eyes every second that passed by, deepening the darkness, these fractional parts of the picture composing a huge mosaic which contained the current and her half-open lips and her tears.

Then the boys became quiet and went to sleep.

He knew he would stay awake. He pieced together the fragments of the night, and only when it seemed to him that the stillness was going to overwhelm him with its immense, unbearable weight, did he steal from his bed.

He jumped over the knapsacks and shoes lying in the middle of the room, and stood by the door. He reached out for the handle. In the instant in which the cool contact poured a whole ocean into his brain, the shining brass growing dull under the imperceptible shadow of his palm, he was again conscious of the warm waves and heard the creaking of the wooden stairs that led up to the attic. At that moment he heard his heart beating, a bronze bell tolling inside him. He pressed down the handle, cautiously but firmly.

The ocean poured itself out into emptiness.

The room was locked.

He felt the soft blow. The earth fell away beneath him. He swallowed his tears. Now he could see the emptiness, and in it a small face and the transparent skin of her forehead, that indescribably fragile something that filled him with a feeling that there was a reason for his existence, those frightened eyes and that breath bitter like almonds.

He crept back to his bed, and then again to the door.

The white square, full of an overpowering silence, gave back a mute echo of the brotherhood he felt for her, a brotherhood that from that moment elevated him above this world and at the time flung him down to its very bottom.

He rattled the handle.

"Be quiet!" someone shouted.

And added something else.

He tried to make himself believe that she could see him all the way from where she was, through the silken web of the night, that it was all one great window, and that behind it was she.

Then he lay on his back, his eyes fixed on the gray ceiling, upon which was her image, indistinct and hazy, but clear in all its details —her eyes and lips. Her hair fell loosely down in the shadows and her voice sounded in the stillness.

His eyes smarted. He was aware of this only every now and again, in the intervals of his imaginings in which he heard every word a thousand times and once, as a single word, and then as one great silence.

She penetrated everything: the white door and the stillness of the night.

She returned to him in his feverish visions, and he walked with her, his hand on her shoulder, and the waves rose and fell in him and filled both of them.

In the morning he ran, breathless, through the town.

He flew upstairs.

All he found was an empty attic.

The transport to the East had left in the night.

LEON WELLS

The Death Brigade

During this part of my imprisonment I was able to keep a diary. Thus I am able to give, to some extent, and as far as it proves useful here, a day-by-day account of what happened to me. Of course, if I had been caught keeping such a record I would have been shot. Later I shall explain how it happened that I was able to keep this journal of my experiences in what we inmates called the "Death Brigade"—that group of Jews the Germans forced to burn the bodies of their countless victims.

Perhaps I should say here that on my return I found Janowska Concentration Camp much larger and far more thoroughly organized for work than it had been when I had escaped. Now special work brigades were sent into the city daily under complete guard to do all manner of work. These brigades were returned to the concentration camp each evening. Other brigades worked in shops within the camp. Instead of going to work, however, often a whole work brigade was taken out to be shot. There seemed to be no method or reason for such executions—work ill done, the members too weak to carry on, and so on. The Germans seemed to decide such matters completely arbitrarily. Every male individual in the camp never knew when he woke up in the morning whether he would be going to work or to death that day.

Only infants and children, the old, the sick and, for the most part, women, could be certain the Germans would kill them as soon as they arrived at Janowska. For these there was for the most part no respite.

But now to begin my diary, the step-by-step account of how I got into the "Death Brigade" and what happened therein.

June 15, 1943.

Reveille sounds at 4:00 A.M. This means getting dressed quickly and rushing out of the barracks where we sleep through the crowd of bedraggled, emaciated inmates. Everybody hurries because soon it will be time for formation. On the way voices call out in all directions; these are the voices of prisoners hawking their wares. They yell: "Hot coffee"; "Sugar"; "Salami"; "Bread." Because of the lack of money among the "business people" as well as among the customers, bread is sold in portions of about three ounces. This portion is the standard ration that an inmate received per day.

With the others, I am in a hurry to take care of the necessities. A long line has already formed at the toilets. The situation here is chaotic. It is a struggle to get in and a struggle to get out. At last I am able to get inside, where there is more confusion than at the entrance. There is a constant yelling: "Don't piss on me!" "Don't knock me over!"

Close to every temporary toilet occupant there is a long, disorderly line. Everybody who waits in line is holding his pants, ready to go. They quarrel over who came first. In unison they yell at the one who is squatting: "Hurry up; you can finish it later at work!" A few even threaten him: "If you don't get up right away, I'll push you right into it." Or, "If you don't get up right away, I'll piss right on you."

The next line is preparing to squat when someone suddenly says to the man in possession of a toilet hole, "I'll give you a piece of paper if you'll give me your place." An agreement is made, and the bickering starts anew.

Finally I manage to leave the latrine and begin pushing through the mob to the washroom. Here there is nothing but confusion. For a few groshen (pennies) one can buy a canteen of water from a ragged inmate who has managed to push through the mob at the camp's single water faucet several times to obtain an extra supply. He cannot keep this water for his own needs, but must sell it for the few pennies that it will bring him. Three ounces of bread and a quart of watery soup with a few beans in it daily are not enough to keep him in working condition, so he helps himself in this way. He is helped, too, by the fact that he works in one of the "camp brigades" (the people who work outside the camp and can smuggle things in to the inmates). When the man has a "good day," and gets his hands on five or six canteens of water and also finds customers with enough money, he can earn the price of a portion of bread.

I buy a canteen of water and wash myself. After washing, I buy a portion of coffee for half a zloty. Standing in line to get coffee is impossible. The very poor have monopolized this line, and it is necessary to buy from them. Even by passing near the kitchen one can get hit over the head by the camp police, who assume that you are trying to get to the kitchen window for the second time. The very poor are willing to run this risk.

Now I hurry to find the foreman of my work brigade to get my bread ration, since he is in charge of the supply for his whole group. I find the foreman (a prisoner like myself, of course) in the yard, where the inmates are formed into groups of five. Each brigade has its arranged place. The camp police, with rubber truncheons in their hands, herd the inmates to formation.

"Foreman, please, my bread portion," I say.

"You didn't get it yet?" He checks a piece of paper where he has the names of those who have received their portion—for some try to get a second helping.

I get into formation, and at the same time I start to eat. I hardly have the first bite in my mouth when an inmate begs me for some. He doesn't care that the formation has started and he is liable to get hit over the head with a club.

Finally the men are organized in formations. An ominous silence prevails. We are standing in fives, in separate brigades in the form of a U. Everybody is facing inward.

On the right side of each brigade a single inmate stands alone; each has a yellow, blue, red, or white armband on his left arm. These are the foremen of the different work brigades. From the faces and clothing of the men one can easily recognize where and what kind of work the brigade is doing. The brigade that is working on the *Ostbahn* (East Railroad) always looks black from the soot, and they are very lean. The work there is very arduous, and the men are constantly beaten. Because it is very hard to do any "business" on the railroad, they have no additional income and must subsist on the standard camp rations. Other brigades look better dressed and cleaner. They work some place or other in the city and under better circumstances. Impatiently we wait for the moment when we shall be leaving the camp.

Outside the gate music starts to play. Yes, we have an orchestra, made up of sixty men, all inmates. This orchestra, which has some known personalities in the music world in it, always plays when we are going to and from work or when the Germans take a group out to be shot. We know that for many if not all of us the music will someday play the "Death Tango," as we call it on such occasions.

At last the gate opens, and three S.S. men come in with Tommy guns on their left arms and whips in their right hands. They are accompanied by a large dog.

We hear the command "Attention! Hats off!" Like a precision drill team, we all take off our hats with our right hands and hold our breath, waiting for the next command. Everyone's face is frozen; for one motion or simply for a caprice of their own, these murderers can shoot tens or even hundreds of people.

Suddenly we hear the command, "Down!"

Everyone falls down. We are commanded to get up again. Then down. This is repeated many times. After this, there is a long pause, and we hear the call for the first brigade to march out. After the first comes the second, third, and so on.

Everyone is waiting impatiently to leave the gate behind him. At last we are in line, and we hear: "Left turn and forward march!" We march like soldiers. After we go through the gate, the brigade I am in hears, "Brigade, stop!" My brigade stops. The murderers are standing in front of us. There is ironic laughter on their faces. Next to them the *Askaris* are standing in their black uniforms, looking into the face of the concentration-camp chief.

Wilhaus is still Chief of Janowska Camp. He still has the secret smile always on his face. At a given signal from Wilhaus, the *Askaris* may very well, for no reason at all, suddenly encircle a brigade and lead it off to be shot. They had done it to thousands before us.

We are lucky this time; it doesn't happen. Our foreman now reports the number of inmates in our group. One S.S. man checks to see if the number is correct, and we get our command to march forward. We march to the place where they assign us to work. There a few brigades are already waiting. I am one of seventy-five selected from all the waiting brigades. We are told to wait for a truck that will take us to build a road between the towns of Kulikov and Zolkiew. We wait for a few minutes, but the truck does not arrive. We get an order in the meantime, to carry bricks, and are instructed that when we hear the call, "Highway construction, Zolkiew," we must gather at a designated place. Our new foreman is a well-known heavyweight boxer named Gross; he has been saved from death several times by Wilhaus, who favors him.

It starts to drizzle.

I go to the plumbing shop where I usually work. The foreman allows me to work there instead of carrying bricks, but when the truck comes I will have to go on it to build the road. This is just a temporary respite.

Now I discuss with others in the shop the possibility that in telling us we are going to the town of Zolkiew to work the Nazis may be up to some kind of trick. I keep looking through the shop window where I can see the place we are to gather, but the truck does not arrive. Through the window I can see my comrades walking in a line with bowed heads and sad faces, each carrying five bricks. I can also see the hands of the clock, which hangs above the camp gate, moving slowly forward.

Time passes. The lunch hour is nearing, and it is still drizzling. The raindrops are falling on the faces of the men carrying the bricks, and they roll down their cheeks like tears. It looks as if nature is crying through these people.

It is twelve o'clock. The foreman gathers everybody for lunch, and we shuffle back toward the camp. Suddenly we hear the word *sechs*. It means an S.S. man is approaching. Within seconds, without turning our heads, we form groups of fives. We hear the voice of the foreman, "Attention! Hats off!" We take off our hats, and march like soldiers. After a short while we hear, "Hats on!" We put our hats back on, and for a while longer we march in formation until the S.S. man disappears.

Back at the gate through which we had gone earlier, the guard counts us and gives the foreman a slip with the number to be fed. We return to that part of the camp yard where we live and eat. It is clean everywhere. The barracks in which we live are surrounded by small gardens. Here and there one can see the cleaners; they carry sticks and are in charge of keeping the camp spic and span. One can hear the tread of our feet. The roads are made from headstones from the Jewish cemetery. You can see the lettering on these stones. The so-called *Friedhofskolonne* (cemetery brigade) works at the Jewish cemetery, bringing the gravestones that are used here for road construction.

We approach the building where the kitchen is. Here we line up in front of a window with our canteens in our hands. The foreman stands beside the window, checking each one so that nobody can return for a second helping. Everyone is staring at the cook's soup-spoon to see if one is to get a bean or a piece of potato.

I have my soup now, and I am hurrying to see if I can buy a piece of bead. The soup is nothing but a pint of boiled water, but very few of us can afford to buy anything additional. Then, too, it is hard to get anything to buy. At last the cemetery brigade comes back. I buy a piece of bread from one of the marchers. In the meantime, my "soup" has cooled off. Like everyone else I sit down on the ground near the kitchen building, and eat. An inmate passes by who succeeded in getting a second portion of soup; he is looking for a customer who will buy his soup so that he in turn can buy a portion of bread. I finish eating my lunch and go to the washroom to wash the canteen. It is empty here now, too. I hang the clean canteen on my belt, as everyone else does. The half-hour lunch is over. We gather to leave again for work. We pass the gate. Here there is a tower that contains a guardhouse. Across one side of this guardhouse a boy about eighteen years old is spread-eagled. He is black and blue, and silent. He is tied so that his feet do not touch the ground; he hangs in the air. Before he was tied up he got twenty-five lashes. This is his end; as a result of his punishment he will be unable to work; he will be *kaput,* shot. Everybody goes back to his morning job; but before we leave, our foreman reminds us that when he calls us we should gather quickly so he will not have to wait for us.

I return to the plumbing shop. Here I discuss again what I should do, go with my group or not. Is this a trick? If they are going to take us to the "sands," why haven't they done it, as with everybody else, in the morning? Why do they need a truck, and couldn't we walk to the "sands" like everybody else?

Everyone advises me to go with my group because they know that at the first opportunity I intend to escape. They know me of old—I had escaped before. Leaving camp and the city, the truck will give me my best chance to escape.

While we are talking in the yard in front of the shop, two trucks arrive. Our brigade gathers and we start to board the trucks. I look out of the window of the plumbing shop; I can see what is happening, and again I ask myself, Should I go or not? I finally decide that if Gross, who has been saved from death so many times by Wilhaus, is going, I, too, can take the chance. It is a fateful decision.

I run out of the shop to where the trucks are loading, and board the same truck that Gross is on. A tall, slim S.S. man with the rank of *Scharführer* steps out of the cab and asks which one of us is a carpenter. Everyone raises his hand and yells what he is, a carpenter, bricklayer, a painter, and so on. From another side I hear a voice say, "Enough! Enough!" I look at the man who has spoken. He is a heavy, good-looking man with the rank of *Untersturmführer*. He is to be our future boss. He counts us, but instead of being seventy-five we are only forty-four. He says, however, that he has enough men for the time being and that tomorrow he will get more. He gets into the cab of the truck and we start to roll.

The heavy iron gate opens in front of us. We are now on the main road, but no one is certain whether we are actually going to Zolkiew. It is still drizzling. Everyone tries to figure out where the truck is taking us. At the approach of Pilichowsky Street, which leads to the "sands," the directional signal of the truck shows that we are turning into that street. We begin to stare at each other, and simultaneously say, "Let's jump!" Gross, our foreman, jumps first. After him a second man, then a third. I have one foot over the tailgate of the truck when out of nowhere a large truck appears carrying about eighty *Schupos* (German soldiers on police duty in occupied territories). We hear shots, and our truck stops. The two men that jumped off the truck after Gross leap back on the truck. I ask myself why they have come back when we are being taken to the "sands" anyway? Isn't it better to be killed attempting to escape than to get undressed and see in front of you the fire that consumed the previous victims—for we know that the Germans burn our bodies right after they shoot us. The truck moves forward, the *Scharführer* standing on the step of the cab, pointing his pistol over our heads. The truck with the *Schupos* follows. We are trapped.

Raise your head, man, and spit into the faces of these murderers! Nobody does; it will bring only torture before death. Still, perhaps one shouldn't give up so easily. Miracles do happen, and we may be saved. Hundreds of thousands have waited for a miracle in the past two years, but it never came. Stop hoping!

During the truck ride all kinds of thoughts go through my head. What is my guilt that I have had to witness the deaths of my parents, my brothers, and sisters first? Why didn't I go with my two little brothers instead of now, all alone? Was I a coward, afraid of death? Had I "saved" myself, watching as my two brothers undressed themselves to be shot, only to end up here, twelve days later?

Torturing questions. Yet, like everyone else around me, I bless every moment that I am still alive, and hope each second for salvation.

It is still drizzling. The truck stops. We are at the "sands." The *Schupos* and the S.S. men with machine guns surround us. The *Untersturmführer* gives us the command, "Get off!" Everyone jumps off the truck, and we fall into formations of five. A thick, greasy black smoke rises from a deep ravine that is over a thousand feet long. We look into the ravine. It contains an open mass grave with thousands of bodies visible to us. On the side of the hill are large piles of wooden logs. At the bottom of the ravine stands a machine, operated by a *Schupo* in a black fatigue uniform. The machine is connected by a hose to a barrel of oil. The machine pumps oil through pipes into the fire. The fire is hissing. Perhaps the burning bodies are hissing? Perhaps they burn these people alive? In a few minutes I shall know.

"Don't be afraid," the *Untersturmführer* begins his speech. "You will work here, and when the work is finished you will go back to camp."

We listen to him with mistrust. We know these speeches by now. Weren't all those who were killed told they were on their way to work? We are told that we must give up everything we have in our pockets except our handkerchiefs and cigarettes. They tell us that they know how to search and where people hide things. They advise us to give everything up and not to risk being shot. We throw everything on the ground in front of us, even our handkerchiefs and cigarettes, because we are sure that we are going to be killed. We are then asked, "Which one of you has been a foreman?" One young blond youth, Herches, in his twenties, our future *Oberjude* (Jewish brigade leader), steps out, and another man, named Lustman, about forty years of age, comes forward.

Who doesn't know the Germans' tricks? There are two fires. I am sure that one man will lead one group to one fire and the second to the other fire.

"Which one of you is a carpenter?" the *Untersturmführer* asks. Without thinking I raise my hand. I have nothing to lose. Maybe they will send me to Pelczynska Street, where the headquarters are, to work; dead bodies don't need a carpenter. Later on, I shall think about taking the next step. In any case I shall not be there long, as I shall attempt an escape at the first chance. A few of the other inmates raise their hands along with me. Because I am the tallest one in the group, the Germans choose me first and then select two others. Guarded by two *Schupos* and the *Scharführer* carrying a Tommy gun, we volunteers are led to the working place, leaving the others behind us. I have been wrong in volunteering, I suddenly realize. Nothing could be worse than this! Now it will be impossible to escape!

We stop.

"Here," explains the *Untersturmführer,* "we shall build the bunker where you will live."

The spot he indicates is near the edge of the ravine. Enclosing half of this spot are the sides of two very steep hills about fifty feet high. Flat terrain extends for a few thousand square feet between the two hills and the ravine.

When we get there we notice that somebody has already started to build; part of a bunker has been set up. There were three brigades here before us, but none of them had worked more than three days (I was told this in the concentration camp). Now I know exactly where I stand. The *Scharführer* tells us that we must build carefully because we shall have to live here. I know the whole truth now—we shall build as much as possible in three days and then we shall be burned to death. After us, a new brigade, new victims, will be told that they are going to Zolkiew or Boberik, and they, too, will end up in this accursed place.

We are issued tools and given general instructions by the *Scharführer* as to how the bunker should look. We look at one another questioningly. Our looks say: Maybe you are a carpenter? It seems that everyone had the same thought in his mind when he volunteered: Perhaps the other man will be a carpenter and I'll be able to pass as a helper. But not one of us is a carpenter. Suddenly one of the men addresses the *Scharführer,* who has discovered by now that none of us has the slightest knowledge of carpentry. The man tells him that one of the other men in the brigade is a real carpenter. The German asks the name of the man, sends for him, and in a few minutes he arrives. Under his supervision we begin to build. The new man doesn't know too much about carpentry either, but somehow we make some progress. We are all curious to know what has happened to our other comrades, but we are afraid to ask since we are forbidden to speak. We hear the carpenter murmur, "It's hell back there in the ravine."

Suddenly the *Scharführer* tells us to interrupt our work and gather up the tools. We form a line, and under guard we go down to the ravine, to the huge open grave, in formations of fives. The fire is burning; the smoke stings our eyes and the smell chokes us. The fire crackles and sizzles. Some of the bodies in the fire have their hands extended. It looks as if they are pleading to be taken out. Many bodies are lying around with open mouths. Could they be trying to say: "We are your own mothers, fathers, who raised you and took care of you. Now you are burning us." If they could have spoken, maybe they would have said this, but they are forbidden to talk too—they are guarded. Maybe they would forgive us. They know that we are being forced to do this by the same murderers that killed them. We are under their whips and machine guns. They would forgive us, they are our fathers and mothers, who if they knew it would help their children. But what should we do?

> Father, if you came here
> Couldn't I have gone together with you
> And have everything behind me?
> I wouldn't have been standing alone
> on your grave
> And burning your body before my death.

We are standing between the bodies in puddles of blood. We wait, but for what? Perhaps we are waiting for death, or perhaps we shall be sent back to the "Death Cell" where we will sleep as the brigades before us have slept, waiting only for death.

On the hill the *Schupos* are standing with Tommy guns in their hands. They are armed as if they were waiting for an attack. We overhear one of them ask the other, "Do you have enough bullets?" We stare at one another. Do they mean this for us?

Our leader, the young blond boy Herches, reports how many of us there are. The number is forty-two. We hear the command "Right turn!" Everyone turns to the right. The turn is not so precise as in the concentration camp because of the bodies we are standing on.

There is a command, "Link arms!" In fives, we climb back up the steep, slippery ravine. They tell us if anyone releases the arm of the other he will be shot. In a little while we are at the top of the ravine where we were three hours before. Now, however, we have courage enough to breathe. The commander of the *Schupos* gives us instructions we must adhere to while walking. For the slightest error we can be shot.

1. Each must link arms with the other.
2. The distance between each group of five must not be more than one and a half feet.

3. It is forbidden to look around.
4. Everyone must walk with bowed head.
5. It is forbidden to talk.

The head of the *Schupos* reminds us again that for the slightest infraction of these regulations, or even any suspicion of it, we shall get a bullet.

Now we are counted again, and the head *Schupo* yells, "Forward!" He adds to it—"but slowly." We are walking with slow step, in fives, on the slippery clay and road. With bowed heads and arms linked we shuffle as if we were walking after a hearse. We are not going the same way as we came this noon, by truck. The road we are on is the one that connects the concentration camp with the "sands." The road is hilly, and contains puddles of water. The whole place is a mass grave.

We move forward. It is still drizzling. One can already see a camp tower on which an *Askari* stands. Maybe they are taking us back to sleep in the concentration camp? In that case they won't see me anymore—somehow I will escape.

We approach the concentration-camp yard. Here we find inmates sitting on the ground, sorting potatoes.

Among the inmates are some who were supposed to go to Zolkiew with us but had been smart enough to get out of it somehow.

We are told to turn our heads the other way. The Germans have forbidden anybody to see the faces of inmates who have seen the "sands."

We stop in front of the barbed-wire fence of the concentration camp. Then we are led into a special part where I had not been before. The barracks in this section are about three feet apart, all in one line. This is where the women prisoners live. They work in D.A.W. (*Deutsche Ausvuestungswerke*—German Army Supplies) and in the laundry. Each barrack is about forty-five feet long and eighteen feet wide, and each in turn is divided into three sections. Each section has a door and three windows. The windows of the first barrack facing the gate though which we entered have gratings of iron bars. This is the so-called "Death Cell." The Jews caught in the city are brought here, where they wait until the next morning. Shooting usually takes place in the morning hours, and when enough people have been collected.

Anyone who lands in the "Death Cell" is certain to die. These barracks stand on pillars, so that there is about a twelve-inch separation between the floor and the ground. There is a space fifty feet long and ten feet wide between the barracks and the barbed wire. Here we are told to sit down on the ground, in the mud, with our feet tucked under us.

I think: Should I try to escape right now by crawling under the barracks? No. I decide to wait until late at night. I plan to pull out a piece of board from the barracks floor and crawl out in the space under the barracks. I hope that the guard won't stay with us all night and that they will lock us up and leave.

One *Schupo* leaves to get water so we can wash up. We sit and wait. From the second and third sections of the "Death Cell" barracks, frightened inmates, their eyes blackened, their faces swollen and with black and blue marks all over them, can be seen looking out through the iron bars of the windows. These are people brought in from the "Aryan side." (The whole city is now, in reality, the "Aryan side"—the Jewish side is now the concentration camp.) This means they had been caught hiding in Lvov, trying to pass as non-Jews. When captured they are brought to the concentration camp, where they are questioned and tortured until they lose consciousness. When the victim falls on the ground, nearly dead, the Germans revive him, and when he gains consciousness the torture resumes. The Germans want to find out if the victim knows where others are hiding. While we sit there one S.S. man, tall, slim, with only one arm, by the name of Heine, rank of *Scharführer,* brings over a tall, heavy-set prisoner. One can see that he had once been elegantly dressed—though his clothes are now in shreds and he has been beaten to a point beyond recognition. Heine is known by all as the worst sadist here. His greatest pleasure is derived from cutting people up with his dagger. He is the chief interrogator here.

The *Schupo* who had gone for the water returns. With him are two women carrying buckets of water for us. These are from the group who clean the women's barracks. They stop for a moment and stare at us, with that special look given new victims. We wash. While sitting, we strip from the waist up and in formations of five we go to the basins and wash. The second group of five does not approach the basin until the first group has finished and is seated.

Now we are finished washing. Our dinner arrives on a wagon. It is placed outside the barbed wire because the drivers are forbidden to come in. The dinner wagon leaves, and four of us go out, under guard, and bring the food back. One of the *Schupos* commands, "The fire tender and the tabulator will give out the food." I think to myself that I know practically all the occupations here, but I never heard the names of these two before. I am to find out.

Everybody receives half a gallon of soup, much thicker than the soup in the concentration camp, a five-ounce portion of bread, and a spoonful of marmalade.

We finish dinner and go into the third section of the "Death Cell" barrack. It is empty. The door is locked behind us.

Our cell is about seventeen feet wide and twenty feet long, and it has three iron-barred windows. Because the wooden partition dividing our cell from the one next to it doesn't reach the ceiling, it is possible to climb from one cell to the other. Around the walls are sacks filled with straw. Near the door are two buckets. Everyone rushes to the buckets, since none of us had taken care of his needs since lunchtime. We had been afraid to ask for permission. In a few minutes the buckets are overflowing, spilling all over the floor. The whole cell becomes one big puddle. We hear the voice of the *Schupo:* "What is happening here? Instant quiet!" Two shots are fired that hit the ceiling of our cell. "Everyone lie down immediately!" An ominous silence prevails in the cell. Two of us share one straw sack. We lie silently. From the other side of the wall we hear children crying. Perhaps they are crying because of thirst or hunger. We hear men and women moaning. They cannot sit, stand, or lie down because they have been beaten so badly. They have been in the cell for three days already, and now they are just waiting for the S.S. men to bring them to the "sands."

After a few minutes I begin to talk to my neighbor. He has a foul odor about him because of his work with the corpses. We can't even smell the stench from the buckets because the smell on the clothing of the people who work with the bodies is much stronger. (When we came into the cell we had heard from the neighboring cell: "Pfew, it smells!" "What smells so terribly here?")

I start a discussion with my neighbor with the question, How can we get out of here? Little by little we fill each other in on details of what has happened in the ravine. He has seen much that I have not, because I worked on the construction on the top of the ravine.

"It was real hell," he says, and tells me that when his group had got to the bottom of the ravine two among them were called back up the hill. There was a truck, and on it was a corpse riddled with bullets. It was Gross, our foreman. Two of the prisoners were told to take Gross by the legs and pull him down the ravine and toss him in the flames. At the same time, my companion went on, a doctor who was in his group committed suicide by taking a capsule of cyanide. He died instantly. So of forty-four persons only forty-two were left.

They then were put to work in earnest, my neighbor now told me. One group worked with shovels—this meant digging out the bodies that had been buried or partly buried after former mass murders. Another group worked with the corpses directly. This was a terrible job. One had to grab the hands or feet of a corpse and pull it out from a veritable mountain of dead bodies. Very often the corpse slid out of their hands, or the skin of the body came right off and was left in their hands. Voices from the top of the hill constantly screamed, *"Los, warum so langsam!"* "Quicker, why so slowly!" "Come here quickly!" The one called was frightened, and went up the hill quickly. He knew that twenty-five lashes were waiting for him. It was not his fault that the corpse slid out of his hands. But there were no excuses. So in twos they pulled the corpses out, one holding the hands and the other the feet. Each corpse weighed 150 to 200 pounds. These were relatively fresh bodies—about two weeks old. That meant they were from the final liquidation of the ghetto. I think: Perhaps my two brothers were among them.

The bodies were tossed into the fire, my neighbor says. On one side the fire tender was standing. (He was one of us prisoners, too.) His work was to see that the bodies were put in right and that the fires burn at the right heat and are not extinguished. He must add wood and shovel away the ashes. On the other side of the fire the tabulator was standing. He held a piece of paper and a pencil in his hands. His task was to keep count of how many bodies were burned each day. This is a top-secret job. It is forbidden to tell even the *Schupos* how many are burned each day. In the evening the tabulator reports the exact number to the *Untersturmführer*. Even the tabulator must forget the amount after he reports to the *Untersturmführer,* my neighbor tells me. When the *Untersturmführer* asks him the next day, "How many bodies were burned yesterday?" the tabulator must answer, "I don't know."

The corpses are called "figures" here, my neighbor continues. To toss in the bodies one has practically to go into the fire oneself. Those on this job have their hands, face, and hair singed. Once the first body is thrown in the fire, they run for the next corpse, because even fast walking is dangerous here. Everyone is afraid of hearing the familiar phrase: "Faster! Why is the work going so slowly?"

"Another day like today and nobody will be able to endure it," my neighbor says. "They won't need to shoot us."

He falls silent. We look at each other. Neither one of us has the courage to interrupt our silence now or the other's thoughts. Perhaps he is thinking of his parents or family. These are always the last dreams of the doomed men. If the Germans were to ask any of us for a last wish, I am sure it would be to see once again our deceased father, mother, wife, children, brother, sister.

Mother . . . Mother, you who sold your gold teeth to buy food to send packages to the concentration camp so that your son might not hunger.

From a distance we can hear the sound of music. The Germans always play it for the inmates who are returning from work. Slowly one and then another of us gets up and quietly and carefully starts to move around the cell. Some of us cannot lie down any longer because we are starting to feel the pains from the whippings we had received that day. Nobody chases us away from the window. The head of the *Schupos* is gone. The *Schupos,* once they are alone, come near the windows. They look around to see if any of the S.S. men are watching them. They give us cigarettes and try to calm us down. They tell us not to worry, that we will not be killed.

Maybe they are telling us this to prevent us from trying to escape?

Across from our cell are the women's barracks. Women look out of their windows. They would like to pass something to us but are afraid of the *Schupos*. The *Schupos* notice this, and approach these women, asking if they want to give us bread. We indicate with our hands that we do not want any bread but that we would prefer cigarettes. Some of us call out our names. We want them to give our names to friends or relatives in other parts of the camp.

Night falls. Everybody lies down in his place. Two *Schupos* keep guard around our cell. Should I try to break through the door? They will start shooting. But there are only two guards and only some of us will be shot; the others will escape. But what will happen after we get out of the cell? We have the barbed wire to contend with. This barbed wire is closely woven, and about ten feet high. Two feet from the first fence is another identical fence. It would be hard to climb over it. Every six or seven feet there is a pole with a searchlight on it. And if one could break out of this section, there is still another where the workshops are located. It is very well lighted, and on each corner there are guard towers.

But we *have* to do something! For we are certainly going to go from this "Death Cell" to the "sands."

The two *Schupos* are still guarding us. Perhaps later they will leave. With these thoughts I fall asleep. I dream about my father and mother. They are crying because their last child is going to be killed by the same assassins that killed their other children. I awaken. I must try to escape. I approach the window and I hear the *Schupos* talking. I try to wake up my comrades, but they are sleeping soundly. Lying down again, I think about what could be done. After a while I fall asleep. I dream again about my parents, about my mother, when she was taken away to be killed. I dream about her telling that she is leaving seven children. In my dream I know it is eleven months later and that I am nearing the same end as all her other children. I dissolve in self-pity and I start to cry. I wake up and fall right back to sleep, continuing to dream about my mother, my father, my brothers, my sisters.

JOSEF BOR

The Terezin Requiem

TRANSLATED FROM THE CZECH BY EDITH PARGETER

"This day will be inscribed in letters of gold in the annals of the S.S. garrison of Terezin."

That was how the camp commandant put it in his reply to Eichmann's speech, and it expressed what he really felt. This was indeed a happy day for him. Even in the morning it had been a great relief to him when he had seen Eichmann stepping out of the car. And then, the later events! They had proceeded to the celebratory parade, and still no one had had the slightest idea what they had to celebrate. An award of decorations! Today, in this ticklish situation, when for a long time there had been no distribution of decorations to the *Wehrmacht*. And, indeed, Eichmann in his speech had made witty reference to that very fact.

"Distinctions are not handed out lightly nowadays," he had remarked ironically, "but this time they are awarded as by right. To the worth of the S.S. statistics, bear witness. Here there's no need for reflection: the successes in reaching the prescribed military targets are shown in positive figures, and the language they speak is clear and convincing."

So they had distributed today, for "military merit," decorations, medals, and crosses, KVK, KVK II, even KVK I; and finally Eichmann had pinned on the breasts of Günther and the camp commandant, these two alone of all the company, the *Kriegsverdienstkreuz* with sword. It was Himmler's order that they should be awarded here, he said, in Terezin, in the important military sector of the S.S., so that everyone would realize the significance of the action that was hastening to its culmination on the territory of the Protectorate of Bohemia and Moravia.

Eichmann was a beautiful speaker, and it was a pleasure to listen to him when he came to hang a KVK II with sword on your tunic. The camp commandant congratulated himself. He had not received any distinction for two years now. Eichmann was right: they weren't giving away war-service crosses for nothing these days; they had to be earned laboriously. And it was just at this moment that they had remembered, in such a period of strain, and everyone was delighted about it. Everybody liked it here in Terezin. Just look at Eichmann: amiable, friendly, a changed man; not even among his subordinates was his pleasure dimmed today.

"Every time a company of S.S. sits down to a meal," he joked when they took their places at the table, "it breaks some regulation or other." And promptly he went on to invite the camp commandant to sit at the head of the table with the highest.

So here sat the commandant at the head of the table between Eichmann and Moese, in sheer delight; and he had already given orders for champagne to be brought, for this glorious day must certainly be celebrated.

"And how are we going to finish the day? What are these Jewish artists of yours going to perform for us?" asked Moese with interest.

"Verdi's Requiem," replied the camp commandant, as he had been taught.

"I beg your pardon?" Eichmann blurted out in astonishment. "Jews singing the Requiem in Terezin?"

The company of S.S. had fallen silent, every one of them watching Eichmann with strained attention. The man was twitching, trying to keep his gravity, but it was more than he could manage. He could not get over the surprise, that Jews, sharp and cunning Jews, should be singing a Requiem, never dreaming that. . . . Fools, fools, if they had had the slighest suspicion of what awaited them now, they would hardly have found it any singing matter. Eichmann could no longer control himself; the laughter he had been restraining by force convulsed his face in a spasmodic grin and tore his throat in a yell of mirth.

His table companions stared stupidly at one another, without a notion of what was amusing him; but their chief was laughing, and that was an order. The company of S.S. men burst into loud and lusty laughter.

But Moese did not laugh. He alone remained grave and silent, for he alone understood and knew what Eichmann found so amusing in the idea of the Requiem. The Jews would be singing it for themselves, as though tolling their own death knell; that was what Eichmann found so funny. But Moese did not agree with Eichmann. The Jews surely knew very well for whom the bell was tolling now throughout Europe; even in the camp they received reliable reports of what was happening outside, and they were not fools. Let's wait, rather, until this evening; then we shall know what there is to laugh at here.

Nor was the camp commandant amused. Never before had he seen Eichmann laugh aloud, and what the devil was he laughing at now? And at whom? At the Jews or at him? What could there possibly be so ridiculous in this program? Pure art, the Jewish elder had assured him, a unique performance such as you're never likely to hear again, Jews singing the ancient Catholic prayers from the twelfth century. Surely there could be nothing improper in that. And the Jewish elder would never dare to make a fool of the camp commandant; besides, he didn't even know why he had asked him to arrange this show, and had no suspicion that he was composing a program for the S.S. But trust a sly Jew and he'll jerk your feet from under you when you least expect it.

But Eichmann had already calmed himself, and he clapped the commandant amiably on the shoulder: A splendid idea, my good friend, excellent, we shall be very glad to hear the Jews sing the Requiem.

"Gentlemen," he said, raising his voice, and everyone at the table rose. "I give you our host! To the camp commandant of Terezin!"

A drawn curtain veiled the stage. A fortunate idea of the commandant's, to have that hung. He wanted to have everything here properly appointed: gleaming footlights, dimmed auditorium, everything as in a real theater. And he had no suspicion that this arrangement suited everyone; the S.S. always preferred to stare out from darkness, and the singers at least would not have to look at the faces of their audience.

The stage was full of the sound and commotion of musical instruments being tuned. The singers were already in their places. Schächter wiped his forehead and cheeks with a handkerchief; he did not feel well, and breathing was difficult. This would be a strange performance; they had not even been able to rehearse or make any other preparations. Perhaps it was better this way; he would not even have known what to say to them. Somehow they must surpass themselves tonight—hold together as one and maintain the tempo.

He glanced at Jirka, the tympanist; Jirka would have to help him out tonight. An orchestra always has two conductors; the one with the baton may sometimes flag and lose his concentration, but the tympanist must never weaken. Who could tell what surprises this performance would spring, what the music would conjure up? Perhaps nothing, absolutely nothing, and that would be the very best way, simply to play numbly and keep time; such music today's audience would understand best.

He waved a hand at Jirka: you'll have to help me today, I can't manage a performance like this single-handed, and don't forget, in the last bars there's a change. Choir and orchestra fortissimo, and especially you, see to it! Three strokes short, one long!

He looked at his choir and soloists, and now he felt a little better; he knew every one of them, he knew what they could do, he could rely on them. His only fear was for Maruska; she had the most difficult task today, and to her alone he had spoken in advance. "You must not think of parents and brother and lover," he had told her. "Remember the others, too, all those beaten and tormented and massacred, they will unite for you into one great mass, you will not even recognize individuals among them, and so much the more clearly you will be aware of the true face of the murderers. For today you will have the murderers before you. You must not show fear or weakness before them. Today you will be singing to the murderers, don't forget that."

The Jewish elder entered the auditorium and went straight to the conductor. They talked together agitatedly. Tonight's performance must not last more than an hour at the longest, so the camp commandant had just ordered. He would have to shorten the Requiem somehow, leave out some part of it.

Schächter stormed and gesticulated. "Scoundrels, villains," he shouted into the hum of the tuning instruments, "they ruin everything they touch, they can't even keep their hands off a work of art." This order hit him like a blow, but perhaps even that was just as well; let them all see what sort of an audience they had today.

Red in the face, he mounted his rostrum. "We're shortening the Requiem, by order of the camp commandant."

The orchestra fell silent, waiting confusedly for their conductor's decision.

We'll cut the beginning, thought Schächter, and begin somewhere in the middle. And already he knew where. *"Confutatis maledictis. . . ."* Yes, we'll begin there, damn you, that very verse we'll hurl into your faces. He longed to give the signal on the spot, but he hesitated. No, it wouldn't do; he couldn't begin like that. Better if they warmed up and sang themselves in first. He must not begin like that, he admitted on reflection; he was answerable for tonight's performance to the artists and their families. And Moese was here, and he understood music; there would be a terrible revenge for an insult so transparent. All the same, he wouldn't let them off that verse; he would yet throw it in their faces.

He heard the murmur of movement and voices from the auditorium, the penetrating announcement of the commandant, and that was sign enough; in another moment the auditorium would be darkened and the curtains would swing apart. How should be begin? Whom should he choose, on whom should he call to stand up and be the first to overcome the paralyzing cold emanating from the dark auditorium?

"The *Recordare,*" he whispered.

"Schächter's gone mad," muttered the choir. "He's chosen the women, he's beginning the same way as *that day!*"

The curtain parted, and uncovered menacing, repellent darkness. The footlights gleamed. The conductor stood erect, facing his choir. No one moved.

On the stage the Jewish elder entered. Thin and pale, he walked slowly to the edge of the stage. And bowed deeply.

> "Weary he sank, seeking me."
> The crucificial way of humanity.

Tonelessly, in a veiled voice, Maruska forced out the individual words; Betka joined her, and together they fixed their eyes fervently upon the conductor, seeking help and strength. He should have been guiding and directing them, but Schächter's face was white; he stood motionless, hardly living. You're singing accurately, only go on, go on numbly and keep step. So much they'll understand, those down there in the dark. Only go on and keep step.

The duet closed, the orchestra was hushed, and now came the tenor, beginning alone, without accompaniment. Rosenfeld was an experienced operatic singer; often in his career he had salvaged an unsuccessful performance. Calmly he stepped forward from the row of soloists, for this was his solo; his grand aria was beginning.

"Groaning 'neath my sins I languish, Lord, have mercy on my anguish . . ." the tenor's full voice rang, and Schächter listened attentively. You're not groaning, boy, he thought to himself, you're giving a brilliant performance of an operatic aria. That isn't how we rehearsed it. The orchestra suddenly felt where their conductor was leading them, and the singer amended his course. His voice softened and changed; he was praying passionately now.

> *"Spread Thy grace behind, before me*
> *Lest the flames of hell devour me."*

That isn't Rosenfeld singing, they marveled, that's someone else pleading and praying in deep penitence; his desperate groaning has penetrated even here out of the dark torture chamber under the earth. Your humble prayer didn't help you, child, Haindl got you, and he killed you—Haindl, who sprawls there now in his armchair, stupidly listening.

Schächter had drawn himself erect. He was conducting again; he was in command. Bass!

"Confutatis maledictis," thundered through the hall. Listen, you murderers there in the dark, damn you, you and those others a thousand times damned! Moaning could not move you, but soon now, soon, we shall speak to you in a language you'll understand better.

The singers were with him; they understood. The music exalted them; they drew deep, panting breaths, struggling to subdue their fierce passion, to hush their tormenting hatred. The tempo faltered; the orchestra waited. The storm was approaching. They yearned for it, waiting thirstily, until lightning slashed out of the baton, and the kettle drums thundered terribly.

The storm broke, but it did not sweep them away in its fury, for Schächter subdued it. He could not unleash the rage of elemental forces; his heart was constricted. There was one verse he had not remembered in time, but he thought of it now and his head reeled. *Lacrymosa!* He had not said one word of warning to Betka; he had forgotten her.

The storm passed, rolling away into the distance; already the last murmur died away in the violins. Silence fell. Even silence is music; it sharpens the awareness. Schächter fixed his eyes upon Betka, and saw no one else. The silence fettered and bound him; he could neither move nor speak. Feel my need, Betka, he implored, look at me, let me cry out to you, at least with a look, that you must not cry now, Betka, before them you must not!

But Betka did not look at him; she began the quartet of soloists alone. She stared into the darkness, straight before her, where danger was lurking. She was accustomed to danger; every day she looked into its face, always she lived and endured with the mad in their dark, closed cells. She felt the same perilous challenge now; something glittered there in the dark, and she had recognized it. Madmen! These were madmen she had before her, decked out in their tawdry finery, with jingling tinsel draped on their breasts, strutting out their fantasy as heroes.

Sharply she launched herself against them, and Schächter exulted: yes, yes, that's how it should be pronounced, and now that hard "cry" again, and the broad "o," spit in their faces, cast your lightnings at them. I need not teach you how to pronounce that word, you know best how you must sing.

The first part of the Requiem hushed to its close, but the director stretched out his hand at once, and bore his artists onward with him. The very music drove them forward now. Listen, you there in the dark, how solemnly the music cries, listen well to what the ancient book of humanity has been proclaiming for thousands of years.

I will multiply thy seed as the sands of the earth, I will bless him who blesseth thee, and curse him who curseth thee.

Do you hear, you there in the dark? You have marked us as the seed of Abraham, and now we, prisoners in a Jewish camp, exult before you. You have not broken us, you will not break us!

Joyfully they sang the glorious ode, but the conductor's gesture again calmed and silenced them.

The orchestra stilled, the choir was hushed. They drew a deep breath and watched with passionate concentration every move of the conductor's hand. The finale began.

"Libera me, Domine, de morte aeterna," sang the choir. As though indeed they prayed for the dead, Schächter thought to himself, and was not aware that he himself had willed it so. Dread had him in its grip now, and was draining the strength from him; he could not even lift his glance to gaze before him. Somewhere there Maruska stood; he was summoning her now to the inescapable moment when she would take her stand alone, fragile and slender, face to face with the inhuman murderers, as once, twice, three times before, in Munich, Vienna, and Prague.

The singing of the choir stilled into an awe-stricken whisper, and then even that died in a sudden, despairing cry. Schächter held his breath.

"Tremens factus sum," Maruska measured out coldly word after

word, slowly pacing out her crucificial journey of terrible memories, and again transcending them. There was no one to help her, and she did not tremble. Slim and white she stood, erect, like a statue carved in marble; only her eyes burned, great, dilated eyes, seeing and sorrowing. Again she returned to the theme, again repeated it in a deep, chilling recitative. This was no longer song; this was an impartial judge pronouncing a stern and just judgment. And now the cello softly joined her, took up the melody and sang it in a grieved tremolo, quivering and afraid, Meisl's cello, which had earned bread for his four children and now lamented and wailed its desolation.

But enough of lamentation, the conductor's hand ordered, and he raised it high. Without the baton now, clenched into a fist. And struck.

The drum rolled, the kettle drums rattled, the brass blared, the singers yelled from full throats, the soloists giving voice with them; they could not be silent now. Schächter's fist held back the choir but could not hold back himself; he shouted aloud with the tumult. The last *Dies Irae!* The day of wrath is come, the day for which we have waited so long, and not in vain. Your armies are torn to pieces as you have torn and trampled us, streams of blood gush from your deep wounds, and your country is rent and tattered in the thunder and smoke of thousands of bursting bombs. And this is right and due, not for revenge, not for hatred, only for the sake of human justice.

The storm passed; passion and hatred were stilled. We are remembering you now, our dear ones, an eternal memorial to you who have died for us. And you, prisoners in the concentration camps, be strong and courageous in invincible faith and hope. They sang fervently now, their voices mingling in rich harmony and fusing into a mighty, sublime chorus that ceased abruptly. Deep silence. Their nerves were quivering with expectation.

Like the stroke of a bell, Maruska's crystal voice rang out: *"Libera me!"* Everywhere the bells pealed in answer. *"Libera me!"* resounded the voices of the choir. "Deliver us! Deliver us!" clamored altos and tenors, sopranos and basses, from all sides. "We want liberty!" the orchestra replied to them. And the kettle drums rolled and thundered: *"Libera nos! Libera nos!"*

Schächter started in consternation. No, not yet, Jirka, you're changing the rhythm, that's not here, what are you doing? But Jirka took no notice; he was directing the orchestra now.

"Li-be-ra nos! Li-be-ra nos!" he beat from the kettle drums. Under-

stand, Raphael, three strokes short, one long; no one who has once heard it will ever forget it. Beethoven's stroke of fate!

Schächter drew himself to his full height.

"Libera me!" slashed Maruška's passionate cry.

"Libera nos!" thundered the gigantic choir for the last time.

The last roll call of the tympani had ebbed away. The footlights outlined the conductor's figure sharply as he stood erect, his back turned upon his audience. Nothing stirred. Only the curtain slowly closed.

Eichmann sat crouched deep in his armchair, and strange thoughts tossed and eddied in his brain, as strange as the music that had called them up. "Interesting, very interesting!" he observed to Moese.

"Unique. I've never before heard such a performance of the Requiem," Moese agreed.

Eichmann applauded. Not too lavishly, since the artists were Jews, not too faintly, for the performance had certainly been unique, and praise was due to the camp commandant, too, for the exemplary arrangements.

Eichmann was applauding, and that was a signal for the S.S. Applause rang through the hall. Out before the curtain stepped the Jewish elder, thin and pale. And bowed deeply.

The summer drew to its close, and the time of the transports began again. The commandant had promised that Schächter's company would not be separated. The promise was kept. All together they ascended into the first wagons of the first transport.

JAKOB STENDIG

Execution in Plashow

TRANSLATED FROM THE YIDDISH BY MOSHE SPIEGEL

About 4 P.M., a caravan of railroad cars with approximately eight hundred passengers set out from the work camp, which was destined later to become an extermination center. This time, no holy Scrolls of the Torah were carried by those in the vanguard, as the artist Hirshenberg has depicted it, although such Scrolls were undoubtedly hidden in the knapsacks of some of the travelers. But more remarkable is the fact that children were hidden in the luggage of some of the fathers. The little smuggled passengers had undoubtedly been drugged, so they would not betray their presence by crying. In those tragic days, ordinary fathers and mothers often attained the stature of heroes. I chanced to witness a dispute between a couple, husband and wife, who had formerly agreed as to which ones would remain with the child in the ghetto and which would proceed to the work camp. The mother was anxious to convince the father that one victim was enough; that he would be able to weather the storms all alone, and that her parting from the child was uncalled for. And so, why should both of them be sacrificed? The argument seemed to proceed without any conclusion being reached.

We are already accustomed to death; it is an everyday occurrence with us. The best and noblest among us are seized suddenly and at the least provocation. It might be for taking a breathing spell, for leaning on one's shovel or for a moment's rest on the dumpcart containing a tombstone, which one trundles with superhuman effort. Or it might be for a "perspiring face," an offense for which Gett had once passed judgment on two young Jews who were standing in the line, ready to go to their work detail. During the roll call, Gett commanded them to step forward, whereupon he shot them dead in the presence of thousands of inmates of the camp.

Once a sixteen-year-old lad, named Haubenstock, hummed under his breath, in all likelihood unconsciously, the melody known as "*Tchubchik.*" Someone overheard it and, assuming it to be a communist tune, denounced the boy to the authorities as a communist. The unfortunate lad was thrown into a cell with another Jew; and within a few days the carpentry shop erected a gallows for two, with two hooks fastened to the crossbeam three meters in height, alongside the western wall of the Abraham Cemetery, facing the men's barracks. Directly beneath the gallows a platform, with a passageway leading to it, was constructed. That evening the workers were barred from the barracks, and ordered instead to assemble for roll call. An ominous silence pervaded the camp. The people awaited the imminent tragedy, with fear and trembling. Before a throng of ten thousand, lined up in a square formation, a group of Gestapo officers headed by *Oberführer* Scherner, appeared. A detachment of Blackshirts deployed in a semicircle, to protect the officers. Scherner then produced a document from which he read two sentences to death by hanging: the sixteen-year-old Haubenstock, for communism; and the engineer Krautwirt, for sabotage. Within a few moments, the young lad was escorted to the platform, where the noose was placed around his neck. When the foot support was removed the doomed victim was left dangling in the air; when the rope was later cut, the body would drop into a box.

I stood at some distance from the execution, and could not observe the face of the victim. But even if I had found myself close enough, I could not possibly have brought myself to gaze into those glassy eyes that desperately searched for some sign of hope. The boy dropped into the container, still alive. Gett called down curses on the head of the executioner; and the latter hurriedly extricated the boy and proceeded to fasten the noose on him again. The victim pleaded with Gett for mercy, but the officer commanded that the "job be disposed of." This time the task was successful and the body remained dangling in the air. The engineer Krautwirt, the second victim, decided to do away with himself before his turn came. He refused to be such a horrible spectacle before his ten thousand fellow-men. Cutting the veins in both of his wrists with a razor blade, he slumped to the ground in a faint. His dead body was then strung up on the gibbet.

And once, at twilight, a group consisting of sixty young men and women returned to the barracks from the work camp known as *Banarka,* lugging provisions for the other inmates of the barracks in their knapsacks. They were detained and inspected by the Gestapo, one of whom, named Will, reported to Gett that the inspection had yielded positive results. Whereupon Gett ordered that the entire group be "liquidated." A detachment of Blackshirts then surrounded the sixty unfortunates and marched them, five abreast, to the hill known as *Hoiawa Gurka* where they were all put to death.

In 1944, after most executions, the bodies were cremated. Those flaming funeral pyres came to be a daily occurrence in the camp. The inmates, performing their daily tasks nearby under the eye and club of the S.S. men, had become so accustomed to the scene that the burning of eight thousand victims that had been disinterred from the graves of Plashow did not interfere with anyone's work.

ADOLPH WOLFGANG

Scoundrels' Entertainments

The torture camp of Schebnye is situated ten kilometers from Jasle. The S.S. *Oberführer* Scherner, and his representative, the S.S. *Sturmführer* Haas, had established the camp and there had satisfied their sadistic desires at the expense of thousands of young lives. I was the first to be deported to Schebnye and am perhaps the only living witness of their crimes. The commandant of the camp, S.S. *Untersturmführer* Sheidt, a human beast, who has on his conscience countless murders, issued a decree that all Germans were to carry a knout. That same day the tanner was ordered to weight each knout with five metal rings fastened to the ends of the tongs.

I will describe only a few of the atrocities practiced in the Schebyne camp. Around the camp there were erected observation towers, on which machine guns were mounted and a strong guard maintained. In the middle of May, a transport of about a hundred railroad cars, loaded with clothing, shoes, underwear, furniture, various machines and implements, and all manner of used utensils and other objects, all pillaged after the liquidation of Jewish ghettos, arrived. Facilities were set up for repairing torn garments and broken furniture.

The mansion of the Princess Gorejski was renovated and turned into palatial apartments, which were occupied by the commandant of the camp and the deputy S.S. leader Scheidt. They also served as occasional headquarters for the German military high command of the Cracow district, headed by the *Oberführer* Scherner and the S.S. *Sturmbanführer* Haaze. The Gestapo of Cracow also used to meet and concoct their future plans. Orgies and debauched revelry were frequent occurrences there. Thousands of bottles of champagne and brandy were kept on hand and drunken exhibitions were common. When Scherner, Haas, and Gett, the commandant of the Plashow camp, along with other Nazi worthies got together, the carousals sometimes went on eight or ten days. Great quantities of liquor were consumed. Chefs and bakers, assisted by a score of helpers, worked around the clock. Each of those revelries would takc a toll of several score of lives, mostly women. During these periods, corpses were carried out every day from the mansion. The daily morning roll call was nothing compared to the one in the evening. In the morning we would be given fourteen decas of bread and a cup of coffee and then assigned some work chore, whereas the evening roll call was associated with floggings. The least infringement brought forth twenty to fifty lashes, whether the offender was a man or a woman. Scores of bloody victims would be removed from the square where the roll call took place.

The S.S. officers Berndt and Hubert were specialists in torturing the prisoners. Whoever fell into their clutches suffered hell on earth until merciful death at last freed him. They seemed to delight in torturing their victims; when the latter would faint, they were revived only to be tormented again. These officers also used a trained dog, who mutilated the unfortunates it was set upon. After the roll call, the two commandants, the chefs, and the rest of the participants in the drunken carousals would pick beautiful young girls, ostensibly to clean up the headquarters. Racial prejudice was no deterrent here. Following such "cleaning chores," the girls who survived would return home humiliated and disgraced. Those who resisted paid with their lives.

As another attraction of those debaucheries, a certain F.M., of Cracow, who served as barber to the German military staff, was ordered to bring a girl with him, so that they might serve as models for pornographic photographs. There were quite a few of such revelries, at the end of which the celebrants proceeded to break up the furniture and aim their revolvers at lamps and mirrors, thus wrecking the elaborately furnished chambers. Then trucks were dispatched to the ghetto to requisition furniture, and the headquarters was renovated and refurbished.

Anyone who entered our camp was initiated into a life of martyrdom. For instance, a popular pastime of the Germans was to force a prisoner to shoulder a "matchstick"—actually a wooden beam weighing a hundred kilos—and to run around the block with it. One usually stumbled under such a burden; whereupon he was flogged and then removed unconscious to the barracks. There were no sick people in our midst—they were shot. The prisoners would therefore disguise their ailments and carry out their chores in spite of high fevers and severe pain. There were many deaths. Pregnant women were usually shot. During an epidemic of typhus, a barrack was converted into a hospital, where a score of afflicted persons were "isolated"—and dispatched to Kingdom Come. There were also instances of escapes from the camp. As a "punishment," three prisoners were executed for the flight of one Pole and ten for the flight of one Jew.

When a new transport of Jews arrived they were closely scrutinized and subjected to ugly perversions, tortures, and murder. This task was usually carried out by a group of twenty Germans, under the command of the notorious Berndt and an assistant, who had had considerable such experience in the Dachau concentration camp. Those inspections were more painstaking with women, especially with the young and the beautiful. They were stripped and made to dance and go through all kinds of contortions. Occasionally Scheidt, the commandant of the camp, a creature of the lowest animal instincts, and his entourage visited the barracks of Jewish women and picked out the beautiful ones—for a "personal inspection." He would introduce original pastimes—such as target shooting with a Jew as a target. He also forced men and women to have public intercourse. Two sisters from the town of Bilitz, both proficient office workers, were employed by the bureau of the *Kommandatur*. I heard the Nazi official, Pospich, tell them, "You'll be among the first to be shot." On being asked why, he answered, "For one thing, because of your work, you have learned some confidential information about our affairs. Besides, we've got to kill off all the Jews." He kept that promise: he shot the two girls down. But the real reason, it was rumored, was that his propositions to them met with no success.

In July and August, 1943, thousands of Jews were brought into the camp. With the arrival of each transport, the young adults were ushered into the camp. The older people and the children were driven in trucks to a meadow, located between the forest and the stream, some two kilometers away, where they were shot and cremated. The charred remains of the human bones were cast into the river. Then the earth at the scene was ploughed under, in order to erase all traces of the slaughter. The scenes of children being torn from their mothers' arms, of married couples being separated, were heartbreaking. Every few moments lorries which carried the unfortunates away returned only with the clothing of their human cargo. Mothers recognized the clothing of their children; men and women, that of their mates. The prisoners were beaten mercilessly. From the heaps of garments, the Germans appropriated the best for themselves; the others were turned over to the tailor shops for repairs. After such an "Action," the Gestapo officials would call upon the shoe shiners to clean the bloodstained boots. Nightlong sprees, in which Jewish girl dancers were forced to join, would follow, during which Gestapo officials would tenderly kiss their hands; the following morning the dancers were among the first to be shot. Trucks loaded with lumber and barrels of kerosene would be dispatched to cremate the bodies. The flames of such a funeral pyre were visible for a distance of several kilometers. S.S. officer Josef Gzimek, a tall broad-shouldered man with shifty eyes, assumed command of the camp. The former official had been dismissed because he had smuggled out gold taken from the Jews. Gzimek surpassed his predecessors in atrocities. He organized a jazz band, which performed during the "Actions" and muffled the groans of agony. Scarcely a day passed when he didn't kill some two score of the unfortunates. On one occasion when Gzimek shot two women, Yehiel Zimerman, from Bochnia, knocked him down with one blow to the face. A struggle to the death ensued. Three Germans came upon the scene, freed their chief, and strung the Jew up by his hands. Before the latter breathed his last, he muttered, "May my suffering atone for the Jewish people." Quite a few Jewish men were executed for attacking German persecutors. In some instances, the victims were strung up by their feet, to expedite death.

An action on a larger scale took place on November 2, 1943. Six hundred soldiers of the *Wehrmacht* arrived at the camp, ready to suppress the resulting rebellion of the prisoners. Three thousand Jews were assassinated. On the following day, the warehouses were filled with the clothing of the victims, some of which we recognized. On the sixth of November, the action was renewed: the last trucks, carrying some two hundred Jewish unfortunates, did not reach the point of execution. Though each truck was guarded by twelve Germans with machine guns, the captives engaged their torturers in a desperate fight. Most of the mutineers paid with their lives. Thus the road of martyrdom of the Jews of Schebnye came to an end.

ESTHER GARFINKEL

Maidanek

TRANSLATED FROM THE YIDDISH BY MOSHE SPIEGEL

In Lublin, we were taken from the train and divided into groups. Skilled workers were dispatched to work details in the towns of Ponyatow and Trawnik. But I was not a skilled worker and, moreover, had two children. I was not accepted anywhere, and remained with the largest group, made up of women and children. I thought that it would be best that way. We were ordered back into the train. But at dusk we were ordered out again, and were marched, men and women in separate columns to an unknown destination. As darkness set in, we were flanked by Germans carrying electric lamps. Leading one child by the hand, I carried the other, until I was so exhausted that I felt I would slump to the ground at any time. For a moment I was tempted to sit down by the side of the road, no matter what the consequences. But I realized that I must make a superhuman effort to save my two precious children.

On finally reaching the camp, we found the men already there. Husbands and wives were reunited amid tears of joy and hopes for a respite, since this was a work camp. Actually, though, this was the notorious Maidanek camp. In the morning, when I saw my haggard-looking children, I cried bitter tears. But I was already weary unto death, and lacked the strength even to fight for a drink of water. The Germans then proceeded to line up the elderly, the young men, and the children in three distinct columns. Before I could realize the seriousness of the situation, I was shunted to the other side of the camp, where we were directed to the baths.

I did not believe then that the Nazis would stoop to murdering children. We women were lulled into the false hope that while we were working our children would be taken care of separately. Still I was trembling all over, and deeply concerned about them. As we emerged from the baths, we anxiously asked a robust looking German in civilian attire about the children.

"Have no fear," the German reassured us. "They are being taken care of properly. They are in no danger. They'll be given milk and whatever they need."

Credulous and naive, we believed him. But that same day, as we were being marched to work, some Poles asked us, "Are you women so stupid that you don't understand that there are ovens in Maidanek? All the children and all the elderly men and women have already been cremated alive."

I can never convey what I felt at that moment. I am a simple woman and lack the words for it. I had endured privation, had done my utmost, in the hope of saving my children. For a time I wept and mourned this, my greatest loss, and I implored the Lord for strength; then I became too numb to feel anything. I even lacked the courage to commit suicide. I just dragged on listlessly like a cow in the herd, working in the *"Scheiskommando"* gardening. We hauled baskets of fertilizer from the latrines to the gardens. What a task! After being steeped in stench for twelve hours, one becomes filthy beyond description.

I spent two weeks in Maidanek. Every day, during roll call, young, healthy women were ushered into the gas chambers. If one had a bandaged leg, or had blisters as a result of sunburn, or a simple sore, or was too tired to report for roll call, she was doomed. During the biweekly inspection, an S.S. doctor, waving a cane, would direct his victims to their doom according to his whim, since he didn't trouble to examine each one individually. As they paraded past him, merely pointing his stick to the right or left and uttering *"Hier, hier,"* he sealed the doom of some, while sparing others.

S. B. UNSDORFER

The Yellow Star

TRANSLATED FROM THE YIDDISH BY JOSEPH LEFTWICH

The minutes passed, and still we knelt. Then with common accord we rose from the ground. To me, it seemed that we had just arisen from *Shiva,* which is our traditional form of mourning. We ventured outside, where we found thousands of prisoners walking, dancing, marching in formation, singing, crying, and shouting in celebration.

By now the main body of tanks and armored vehicles had trundled well ahead, pushing and crushing the nation that had disgraced humanity to a just, final, and irrevocable defeat. Here and there, some prisoners, the old Buchenwaldians, were moving ahead and leaving by the main gate, armed with rifles and revolvers. Their faces were white masks, but their eyes burned with a fierce light. They were not trying to escape, nor were the intent on assisting the victorious Americans. Their one objective was to track down the murderous S.S. guards, those killers who in the hour of retribution had made a cowardly escape into the thick forest which lay close to the nearby city of Weimar. The pendulum had swung round, and now the prisoners were after the blood of their captors. Revenge, just punishment for the uniformed beasts who had slaughtered millions of innocent victims, was not to be denied.

As the avenging Buchenwaldians hurried out of the main gate, the first U.S. armored car drove into the camp proper. We rushed towards it, kissing, patting, and stroking its bulletproof body, and when the first man, an officer, thrust his steel-helmeted head out of the turret, he was pulled out by the mass of men and lifted shoulder-high. Accompanied by jubilant thousands, he was carried about the camp despite his incessant protests and demands to be returned to his troops. He was hailed by the Buchenwald prisoners as the symbol of their freedom and victory.

The great day was drawing to its close. Darkness fell. By now the camp was in possession of about one hundred S.S. guards who had been dragged in by the armed inmates. Some still wore their hated uniform; others had already donned civilian clothes which they had prepared months ahead. These erstwhile Nazi bullies were confined to a separate block near the main gates, surrounded by a posse of armed *Haeftlinge*.

They cried like lost children, shouting and protesting their innocence to the angry mass of prisoners milling around the block. Some pleaded passionately that they had never been near the camp; others insisted that they were "only guards." The more inventive types claimed that their grandparents were Jews. Never has there been such a swing round from captor to captive.

When morning dawned, camp loudspeakers passed on their messages in a dozen languages, warning the liberated prisoners that the retreating S.S. had blown up the water system. It was an act of God that they did not manage to carry out their other projects, such as exploding the mines which were found all over the camp.

A week elapsed before the U.S. Army managed to take charge of the camp, which included thousands of *Mussulmänner*—living corpses who were no longer able to move or even talk, so injured and seriously ill were they. Arrangements for food and water supply were made, and steps taken to dispose of the barrack full of captured S.S. men.

Buchenwald was a tragic and pitiful sight in these postwar days. Day after day, new pits and huts were discovered into which thousands of dead bodies had been dumped waiting to be taken to the camp's huge crematoria. The yards inside the crematoria were packed with huge piles of dead bodies stacked twenty feet high, while scores of blocks were filled to overflowing with *Mussulmänner,* the ghastly cripples and starved-out men whose only possible salvation was a mercifully quick death and burial.

Hundreds of prisoners who in their wild hunger had rushed the kitchens and stormed the food stores, died the next day sitting on the toilets or lying on their beds. Long, long after the Nazi captors had deserted their prisoners, death raged throughout the camp and took its toll in thousands. There seemed no end to the misery and wretchedness of Buchenwald. Liberation Day had brought its own tragic end, and it broke one's heart to see that now, when aid and assistance were beginning to arrive from all parts of the globe, for many thousands of prisoners, beyond human help, they had come too late.

Meanwhile, German civilians by the hundreds were brought in daily from the nearby city of Weimar. Their task was to work in the huge kitchens, to clean and disinfect the barracks, and to dig mass graves on a steep mountain slope which stood about a mile away from the camp, and which overlooked Weimar.

I picked up a few English words and commercialized them by becoming a guide and showing visiting troops over the death camp.

"May I show you the concentration camp?" I would ask the soldiers as they streamed through the main gates. Then I would guide them around the camp, beginning with the crematoria whose stoves still held charred but recognizable bodies, on to the hospital, the *Musselmänner's* block, the punishment barracks, the dog kennels, and so on.

My reward consisted of cigarettes, chocolates, soft sweet biscuits, tinned food, and other delicious delicacies which I shared with Benzi, Grunwald, and other friends.

After "working" in the mornings, I would spend the afternoons at the cemetery watching over the Germans as they dug the graves, and myself joining other inmates who volunteered to assist in the burials.

Thousands of victims were literally chucked like old rags into the gaping mass graves. There was no time for identification attempts or even for religious rituals, in spite of the tragic scenes that frequently occurred when inmates recognized their relatives or close friends among the mass of corpses, and prayed over them.

The worthiest service I could think of performing in this huge holocaust was to say a few words of prayer. It was, indeed, all I could hope to do. Each of my visits was concluded with a quiet recital of the traditional mourners' *Kaddish.*

"May His great Name be exalted and sanctified throughout the world. . . ."

As I walked back to the camp across the broad concrete roads, built in the center of the thick forest by Jewish blood and lives, I pondered the words of the *Kaddish.*

What would happen to our Jewish nation, to our religion and heritage, after this great and tragic disaster? The face of every Jewish inmate in the camp mirrored a vivid picture of the Jewish people: a crippled and shrunken people, a race which had suffered the most tremendous spiritual, as well as physical, onslaught in the history of mankind; a race of orphans, widows, and widowers; a race of mourning fathers who had lost their sons; of saddened mothers who had their babies snatched away from their breasts; of sons who had seen their fathers, brothers, and sisters burnt to ashes while still half alive.

We had not the heroic glamor of soldiers who had died on the battlefield, or sailors drowned in the ocean; we were prisoners who had been humiliated and scorned, and now that we were free, what did the future hold?

We had lost our noblest and finest, our dearest and most precious, in the course of a callously prepared program of cold murder, destruction, and annihilation; we were a nation whose blood was shed in every country under Nazi occupation, far away from battlefields and air attacks.

Who, I wondered, would again care to hear of God, of religion, of rituals, and of observances?

I knew that the Germans would now have to supply us with food, that the British would bring drugs and medical aid, that the Americans would flood us with cigarettes, chocolates, and vitamins. But who would provide the religious serum which was so necessary to instill some spirit of Godliness into a hopelessly crushed people?

I felt the great need of my father's guidance and precept to put me on my feet again. I needed him so much, for he always knew the answers to my problems. I felt sure that he would be able to assure me that there was still a God over us, that everything that I had learned to hold and treasure was still true. But my father was dead, burned by the Nazis. Yet even now I could feel his influence.

Now that the dreadful nightmare that had started at Sered had come to an end, I had to start life afresh. How would I fare? Where should I go? Certainly I could not stay in the Devil's Chambers of Buchenwald, nor could I face the vast unknown of a foreign land.

So it came that when I was asked by the authorities after V.E. Day whether I would like to return to Czechoslovakia or emigrate to the West, I decided to return home. Maybe there was still a very faint ray of hope in me that some of my kinsmen had managed to survive. I had met people who had saved themselves at the very gates of gas chambers. Could there be? . . . Perhaps? . . . Who knew?

There were my sisters, Paula and Golda. I cherished the hope that by some miracle they might have survived the holocaust inside their bunkers in Nitra, and that I would find them safe with their families.

Bratislava was the town of my birth and my youth—the place which I loved and for which I longed whenever I left it, even for a short trip; the place where I learned to become a Jew and suffered inhuman hardships for being one. This, I felt, was the only place where I could start my life again and face the future with hope and confidence.

But strangely enough it was on the pyre of the camp, in that hellhole of Buchenwald, that I received my first injection of vitamin R—Religious Revival.

A few days before our scheduled departure for Czechoslovakia, the camp loudspeakers blazed out an announcement that the Jewish chaplain to the U.S. forces would be conducting religious services in the evening to mark the festival of *Shavuoth*—the anniversary of the receiving of the Law by the Jewish people on Mount Sinai.

Having lost my handwritten diary, as well as my *Haggadah,* during the march from Nieder-Orschel to Buchenwald, this announcement came as a pleasant yet disturbing surprise.

Since my childhood I had always looked forward eagerly to the arrival of our wonderful and inspiring festivals, and particularly so in the tragic war years. But I wondered whether we weren't being put to a test too soon. Who among those thousands of physical and mental cripples would want to attend services and prayers so soon after their tragic experiences? The Festival of the Receiving of the Torah! Within a few weeks after liberation, religion which had seemed to do so little for us, was now challenging us and our loyalties.

But just as you cannot measure the physical strength of an oppressed people, so you cannot gauge its spiritual wealth and power.

On that evening, Buchenwald staged a fantastic demonstration of faith and loyalty to God. Thousands upon thousands of liberated Jews crowded into the specially vacated block for the first postwar Jewish religious service to be held on the soil of defeated Germany. The *Mussulmänner,* the cripples, the injured, and the weak came to demonstrate to the world that the last ounce of their strength, the last drop of their blood, and the last breath of their lives belonged to God, to Torah, and to the Jewish religion.

As Chaplain Schechter intoned the Evening Prayers, all the inmates in and outside the block stood in silence, re-accepting the Torah whose people, message, and purpose Hitler's Germany had attempted to destroy. Jewish history repeated itself. Just as our forefathers who were liberated from Egypt accepted the Law in the desert, so did we, the liberated Jews of Buchenwald, re-accepted the same Law in the concentration camps of Germany.

ISRAEL KAPLAN

In the Sick Hut

TRANSLATED FROM THE YIDDISH BY MIRIAM HOFFMAN

A Package Arrives

"Food! Hunger! Bread, Bread! . . ."

"It's the gypsy again!" the awakened, pain-filled voices moan.

"Quiet him, Binder," the pleas waft through the darkness to the sick man who is lying near the Jew from Hungary, because Binder knows already how to put a stop to the raving of the helpless one.

It is difficult for them to fall asleep again in the bitter cold. It is mid-March and the days are sunny, but the nights here still feel like winter. The hut has not been heated since yesterday. The frost glitters through the low ceiling boards that are but thinly covered on the outside with moss. It must be midnight already—perhaps even around one o'clock, the inmates surmise. Since all their timepieces have been taken from them, they can only guess at the time. The Hungarian is quiet. Binder probably fed him something. Using the Hungarian nickname he has given the man, he makes him repeat:

"Yacobfy, remember . . . the bread-soup was tasty yesterday? Aha, it smelled good! . . . Then remember, Yacobfy, that you are two bread rations behind. I borrowed those for you, yes? . . . We must figure something out. Besides, you know, your eating utensils were lost. I laid out five cigarettes for a bowl for you. Yes? . . . Then I must get it back from your package! You are so weak that I'm constantly stuffing you with sugar. You know. I borrowed that also, yes?"

"It's all the package," grunts Boruch Blit from his pallet where he has spent several weeks already and knows practically everyone. "That small package doesn't even let this Yacobfy sleep—he who can't stay alive—and that head!"

It is more than a week since the Hungarian was brought to the hut all cut up. He is a newcomer in camp. His wife and six children were killed only recently. The thinking pattern of a camp inmate was therefore difficult for him to absorb. Both his posture at the "distribution center" and the manner in which he paced did not appeal to the S.S. The officer, therefore, took it upon himself to "straighten out the Jewish backbone" and to "cure" this creature. During the night Yacobfy was placed between the electrically charged wires that encircled the camp. When the fellow emerged at dawn he was so dizzy that he fell on his head. In addition to the head wound, he was shaken with convulsions and started jumping in the narrow passageway.

"Binder has no scruples about doing business even with such a person," mutters Yosef Groyer, an elderly fellow from Luthuania. "He shuts him up with a bit of bread and tries to brainwash him about a multitude of debts."

"However, he takes cognizance of people, even of those in our hut, the *Mussulmänner* . . ." retorts Boruch weakly, and, true to his nature, tries to justify Binder's conduct. A person like Binder worries that when the contents of the package will be distributed someone will intercede and not allow a helpless person to be robbed.

Binder is well known in camp. Polish Jews who know him from home tell that for years he had been a helper in a market and that he used to drag customers over to his stall. Later, he had advanced himself to the position of traveling salesman and part-time broker. He was one of the first policemen in the ghetto in Lodz and his glib tongue was particularly noticeable during the "transports." He assured the Jews that they were being transported to easy jobs, and hundreds of them believed him. His wife and children disappeared in Auschwitz, and their fate is unknown to him. It was there, in camp, that he had become so friendly with the S.S. and a big shot with the *Kapos,* a big "wheel."

Here, in Dachau, Binder had risen to the position of block leader. Suddenly one day, Einstein, the dog belonging to the *Raportführer,* with whom Binder was friendly, jumped him. Einstein, the clever dog that never left his master's side, leaped across the *Appellplate* and bit into Binder who, half nude, had been sunning himself. The amazed expression on his master's face and the motions of his hands were of no avail; the dog bit a hunk of flesh off Binder's arm, and bit into several other parts of his body as well. Binder keeps consoling himself that the *Raportführer* immediately apologized and even sent him a big hunk of salami with a note saying: "Meat heals meat."

"Whether it was the *Raportführer* or the dog, one of them did pull something out of him." This is the conclusion that Blit has arrived at about Binder in the past few days, and keeps repeating it now, in the dark, in his dull voice.

"A person doesn't change," whispers a Jew from a nearby pallet. "Binder tries to do business even here, in the sick hut. Wait until the package arrives. Gee, when will we finally get to see this wonderful treasure!"

There has long been talk in camp about food packages—individual packages from the Red Cross for each inmate! Finally, they arrived. The cardboard box was not too large but, for the first time since they had been incarcerated, they saw meat, fish, cubes of white sugar, biscuits and Swiss cigarettes! Almost every block had received these packages already, but the distribution had stopped more than a week ago. The three huts that are designated for the sick, and a fourth hut, alongside the ambulance, where the doctors reside and examine the patients as well, did not receive the packages. The Germans refer to this block as "ka-be," an abbreviation for *"krankenbau"*—sick bay. The Germans don't step foot in this pestilent corner and the entire authority there lies in the hands of the Jews themselves—the doctors, the nurses, the supervisors. This hell hole is even referred to as the "Jewish State." The Jews here are restless and unnerved because the distribution of the packages halted with them, the very sick!

Many see the explanation for this state of affairs in the entertainments that are lately in full swing. Besides the S.S. who are entitled to everything and who are on a continuous round of parties and orgies, the Aryan *Kapos* and their aides, too, have been on quite a "bender" since the packages arrived. Now the Jewish *Kapos* and other big shots have started having a good time also. They have found more security in this secluded area in the "Jewish State." Several hours ago it was even quite lively in the ambulance with one-time performers entertaining. The artists, who had been rounded up from amongst the camp inmates, were compensated for their work with food products. Who knows, therefore, what havoc has been wrought at the expense of the sick.

The later it gets, the colder it gets. Several panes are missing in the window at the end of the hut, beneath the roof, and the rusty tin that's been covering the holes has been ripped off by the wind. The bit of straw under one's body affords little protection against the frozen ground. Not everyone can tighten his covers because some have wounds that can't be touched. People try to huddle even closer to one another in the already crowded hut, if but to get a whiff of someone's warm breath. Joseph Groyer is so disappointed that no warmth emanates from his neighbor by the wall. Ice-cold air seems to waft from him. Soon Groyer realizes that his neighbor has expired. The latter had been brought here three days ago, deathly ill. One of the "masters" had broken a board across his back. Lacking the necessary instruments, all that the doctors here could do upon discovering that the man's bones were broken, was to send him to the hut where those that needed surgery lay. There were more than fifty patients there already, so Joseph couldn't contain himself and took this new patient over next to himself. The man had left Slovakia just a short time ago. He was still wearing his civilian clothing because he was one of the more recent arrivals and the S.S. had not managed to take it fom him. He had a bag of food with him as well as the package which he had received before leaving his block.

Joseph can barely turn from side to side because of his bandaged knee. Terribly upset, he whispers about his neighbor's death to Boruch Blit whose body is all lacerated and foul-smelling.

"Meilach," murmurs Boruch as he awakens. It is the surname of a father and son who recently died together, on the same day, and whom he often mentions.

Soon he is wide awake.

"Is that one no longer here? Joseph, all his things belong to you! The man was suffering for three days and who helped him? Did Binder? You did everything for him. You can hardly move yourself, and yet you helped him and waited on him. Why, only yesterday you insisted that the doctor do whatever he could to alleviate the man's pains. Only you have a right to them, Joseph, they're yours!"

"Rights," exclaims Groyer reproachfully, "I just couldn't bear to see him suffer. What does that have to do with rights?"

The expression on the face of this short person with the high forehead—Blit would so much want to catch it here, in the dark! Time and again he had seen Joseph refuse gifts of bread or other food from a German, no matter how hungry he might have been, nor how insulted the donor. Everyone knew that it was a matter of principle with him. He was not very young. Before he was confined in the ghetto, and later in camp, his entire world had centered somewhere in Latvia. He had attended a *cheder* in his town and a *yeshiva* in a nearby town. He was about to become a *shochet* [ritual slaughterer], but the sight of blood frightened him. For years he had worked in a mill—had even become an executive there. He had been the breadwinner for his mother and a divorced sister with children, who had all expired already. Despite all this, however, Blit still can't submit to Groyer's incredible, "Even under these circumstances not to avail oneself of leftovers!" So, he tries to influence him with: "Joseph, you are peculiar, a paradox. . . ."

The murmuring of Groyer and Blit is interspersed with the howling of the wind through the windows. Suddenly, there is the sound of a gay little tune from the center of the hut where the stove stands:

"Inte lek, Inte lek, Telek, Telk, Tel, Tel!"

Many are awakened by the singing. However, seldom does anyone talk to Ludz or to Fill, not even Binder, their neighbor and protagonist. Ludz and Fill are the "housekeepers" in this hut and have many friends among the S.S. and the *Kapos* in camp. Everyone knows that these seventeen-year-old boys learned the song from their Germans. It's been years since the two youngsters came to this camp. Here is where they grew up and they hardly know of any other world. When they were children they flattered the S.S. men, the *Kapos* and the other officials, in order to fall into their good graces. Now they even try to mimic their manner of speech. They just sang this song to chide Blit, who is an "intellect," or a *"Telek,"* as the Germans call people like him, and whom they particularly hate. "Their eyes bulge because they are bookworms," jeers Zilke; "their brows wrinkle at the sight of a letter, and they seek an explanation for everything. . . ." From time to time the "intellectuals" really are fresh and do grimace. Roshman, an *Untersharführer,* used to call it "Jewish *chutzpa*" and, during an "action," they were the first to go. Boruch Blit has been here a long time. It is known that he was once a school principal. Since Groyer has been next to him, respect for the *"Shtubendinst"* has fallen.

Ludz and Fill keep repeating in the dark: *"Telek, Telek, Tel, Tel! . . ."*

Disregarding the youngsters, Blit continues his discussion, and now he has new motives:

"Listen, Joseph, they won't keep you here too long. The doctor gave you medication more than a week ago. In a day or two, you will return to work. . . . The *Kapo* poked you while you were working and you fell on a rusty wire. That's how you got your infection. If you hadn't worn wooden shoes, and ragged ones at that, you wouldn't have fallen so clumsily. Had you worn heavy woollen trousers, and not those tattered pajamas, the iron would not have bitten so deeply into your knee! Shoes! With me, it all started with walking. At first I scraped my foot and couldn't bandage it; then I got frostbite, which turned into abscesses. Now I have them all the way up to my armpits. Take my shoes, Joseph." He placed the shoes above Joseph's head and, next to them, his trousers, too. "Take it. And take the other things also. Fill your heart with the package! You've been saved! What are you dreaming about?"

Blit continues whispering for a while and then, again perplexed by Groyer's words, says:

"How can you, in any case, right now, explain it?"

"I used to read many books. Philosophy held little interest for me. I do believe, however, that there is such a thing as a moral obligation. Yes, there must be such a thing as respect for a human being. Only a while ago he was alive. To grab his belongings so quickly. . . . How can one do such a thing!"

"Ha, ha!" There is a sound of laughter from the pallets of the privileged characters near the stove. And the *Stubdiner* shouts: "Quiet, you disgusting, ill-bred creatures. Go to sleep immediately, damn you!"

Groyer keeps Boruch's mouth covered with all his strength. Today is not the time for him to cope with this group, nor with Binder, particularly because of the abscesses that have appeared all over his body. Groyer has his own excuse for not criticizing the two uncouth characters. He has been accustomed to say that he fears the dangers of an obscene word. And, any conversation with people such as they are can result in the use of the worst kind of language. It's just against his principles to engage in that kind of talk.

In the quiet of the night he tells Blit about his first day of forced labor. The sudden German occupation and the tragic changes threw the Jews into a panic. As Blit undoubtedly knows, the people lost their equilibrium and gave vent to their grief upon one another. Tongues were loosened and one heard curse words everywhere. Joseph, miraculously, escaped the slaughter in his hometown and, after many hardships, he reached Kovno. One day, the Germans nabbed him and made him dig together with the other Jews. "Immediately, there were arguments among the people and a flood of obscene language spewed forth. The most outstanding among them was an elderly man. He kept arguing: This one doesn't hold his shovel properly; the other digs slowly; because of someone else the ditch will be crooked and the entire group will be punished.

"The replies were sharp, and the language obscene:

" 'Hey, you trickster, you underworld character, where did you creep in?!'

"Apparently he had argued with everyone already, so now the old man caught hold of me. However, I restrained myself, and kept quiet. This incensed him terribly. In a flash he was next to me and his anger knew no bounds. Finally, I replied quietly:

" 'Uncle, no matter how many obscene words you will use, you won't hear one from me.'

"The man quieted down. His hands dropped convulsively over his face and, quivering, he left.

"In that moment I knew that principles must survive this suffering; the more difficult and bitter the times, the more one must guard one's speech. During the years in the ghetto, as well as here in camp, I was often enraged and tempted to be led astray by bad language. But I was immediately restrained by a foreboding that I might be punished, that my belief in surviving these sufferings would come to naught and I would not live to see freedom!"

Groyer is pleased that his whispering hasn't awakened anyone. It is good, too, that Boruch is dozing again. Sleep is the only antidote to pain. He can't forget, however, that tomorrow morning Boruch must undergo surgery again. These new swellings must be opened, and he is so weak. Besides, he has nothing with which to bandage him. They only give a small piece of linen, in the ambulance, for each wound. The first thing to do in the morning is to find something among the remains of his neighbor.

The stillness in the hut doesn't last long. The Hungarian again whines:

"Food! Hunger! Bread, Bread!"

"Filthy Jew, shut your mouth!" yell Ludz and Fill. "It's the package that's already tempting you. . . . Keep still!"

This command brings no quiet. One Jew reminds himself that Fill's parents (their real name was Feivel), together with their younger children, were taken away during an "action" about three years ago. Fill knew German at that time already, and that was of help to him. So the Jew groans in the dark:

"These two may one day meet with this 'filthy Jew' in one piece of soap. . . ."

"Is it possible that our camp, too, will turn over its corpses?" murmurs someone from another pallet. "There is a rumor that a nearby soap factory is demanding raw material."

"It is quite evident that these two boys are no longer favorites with the Germans," whispers another Jew. There is many a youngster here in camp who, for a mere kindly glance from the authorities, would become their lackey. After all, one can become a *"Pipel."* The masters use these *Pipels* for their most depraved gratifications. These youngsters don't even know that this can render them incapable of enjoying a normal life at any future time. And, lo and behold, the good Germans banished their favorites here, outside the Pale!

"Is it true that Ludz has a venereal disease?" whispers another, "He has been expecting to become a *Kapo* shortly. Binder has been his advisor. . . ."

"Quiet! Stop the mumbling!" the *Stubdiner* yells again. "You don't want to get well because you are slackers, but when there is an 'action,' a transport, you are the first. . . !"

When they are done reprimanding, the two sing again:

> "In London by the Thames
> Lies a big British swine;
> His name, this disgusting one is
> Mr. Neville Chamberlain!"

Halfway through, Fill stops singing. When Ludz screams, he gets hoarse and every German word he utters sounds ludicrous. Fill reminds Ludz:

"*Untersharführer* Laskar always ridiculed your accent!"

"And what did Kunze say about your crooked nose?" retorts Ludz.

The howling wind is laden with bright white snowflakes that scratch one's face. The inmates burrow deeper under their covers and try to sleep. Binder's grumbling can be heard from the vicinity of the cold stove: "Yacobfy, remember . . . three portions of bread, fifteen cubes of sugar, yes?"

RESISTANCE

PHILIP FRIEDMAN

Jewish Resistance to Nazism: Its Various Forms and Aspects

Introductory

During World War II over 8,300,000 Jews came under the rule of the Nazis, as well as of Nazi-controlled or dominated countries. The bulk of this Jewish population was concentrated in eastern Europe (5,650,000), while over a million lived in the Balkan countries, almost one million in central Europe, and 600,000 in western Europe and the Scandinavian countries.

One could argue that at least part of the Jews, particularly in western and central Europe, were so integrated in their countries of origin that it makes no sense to deal with the phenomena of Jewish life apart from the historical fate of their fellow countrymen.

Whatever the merits of this reasoning, it can by no means be applied to the Nazi period. No matter how much the Jews were integrated in the life of a country, the Nazis marked them as a separate racial unit, segregated from the rest of the community and submitted to special discriminatory legislation, and later on to annihilation. And just as the Jewish predicament stood out as something special and different, so was the Jewish reaction to Nazi persecution. Jewish resistance to Nazism was, therefore, different from that of the non-Jews. There were, of course, similarities between Jewish and non-Jewish resistance. But there were far more dissimilarities. We will try to deal with both.

There were several basic conditions for a successful resistance movement. One of them was a favorable strategic basis. The inaccessible mountain regions of France, Yugoslavia, or Greece, the thick forests and the marshes of Poland, Lithuania, Byelorussia and western Ukraine formed a favorable strategic basis. The Jews were denied this advantage from the very beginning because, in eastern and partly also in central Europe, they were herded by the Nazis into hermetically sealed ghettos where their every move could be controlled and which they were prohibited to leave on pain of death. This made it extremely difficult for them to start a conspiratorial movement. Liaison among scattered Jewish underground groups could be maintained only at considerable risk and difficulty by daring couriers. Weapons and explosives had to be smuggled into the ghettos, slipped in through heavily guarded ghetto gates, brought in through sewers and by other ingenious means. In a later period the Jewish underground tried to get its fighting groups out of the ghettos to the woods and mountains. They did not always succeed. In many cases they were caught and executed. Thus, the Jewish underground was not able to prepare the necessary strategic basis for its future outside activities.

But there were also other obstacles. In the Jewish underground of Warsaw, Bialystok and other ghettos, a passionate discussion was going on: What were they to do? Stay in the ghetto or leave it for the woods? It was primarily a moral issue: Were they entitled to leave the ghetto populace to face the enemy alone or did they have to stay on and to take the lead in the fight when the crucial moment of the extermination actions arrived? After heated debates, the opinion prevailed to stay on in the ghetto as long as possible, despite the disadvantages of this position, and to leave it only at the last moment when there was no longer any chance to fight and to protect the ghetto populace. The minutes of one of those dramatic debates in the Bialystok underground were saved and were published after the war.

An important element of the strategic basis was to have the friendly cooperation of at least a part of the nonfighting population, in order to secure vital information and the supply of food, to shelter the sick and the wounded, and in time of retreat to hide the partisans or their weapons. But in many Nazi-occupied countries the general population did not identify itself with the Jewish resistance movement and had a rather equivocal, sometimes even a hostile, attitude to it. In many instances the peasants were unwilling to suffer for a cause they did not consider their own. On the one hand, they were urged to supply food, fuel and transportation to the Jewish partisans; on the other, they were savagely punished by the Germans for doing so. In addition, the Jewish partisans in eastern Europe sometimes had to maintain the so-called family camps in the woods for their children, elderly people, and women threatened by Nazi annihilation. The peasants were particularly unwilling to support with supplies those family camps in addition to the fighters. One of the biggest family camps attached to Tovie Bielsky's fighting group in the forests of Byelorussia was called "New Jerusalem" and harbored about 1,200 inmates. Bielsky used to tour the peasant country campaiging for his camp and delivering speeches to the villagers.

Arms and Leadership

A steady, uninterrupted supply of arms is a condition *sine qua non* for resistance operations. Most of the non-Jewish underground movements had received vast supplies of arms and other material from their governments-in-exile and from the Allied governments. But in no country was the Jewish underground treated on an equal footing with the recognized national underground organizations. Whatever the Jewish underground was to receive had to go through the national channels and the amount of supplies eventually allotted often came too late or in ridiculously small quantities. Sometimes Jewish requests for weapons were refused outright, as, e.g., in Bialystok and in Vilna. In Warsaw, after long negotiations, the Jewish underground received, in February 1943, a small supply of arms. fifty revolvers, fifty hand grenades and four kilograms of explosives. Thus, the Jews had to resort to other sources of supply, to buy at black market prices from peasants, from illegal arms dealers, from deserters, all kinds of arms, or to produce their own weapons in small clandestine factories and repair shops. Eventually they managed to scrape together some meager and obsolete equipment that was no match for the powerful German arms.

Another great disadvantage of the Jewish underground was the shortage of competent leaders. The seasoned leaders of the pre-war period were no longer there. Many of them had been evacuated before the outbreak of the Polish-German war in 1939, or were deported during the period of the Soviet and German wartime occupation. A particularly ruthless process of eliminating the Jewish leadership was carried out by the Nazis. Jewish intellectuals, professional, political and trade-union leaders, former Jewish soldiers and officers, were sent to labor camps or exterminated under various pretences.

Fortunately, the Nazis did not, in the first period, pay too much attention to the youngsters and so both the leadership and the rank and file of the youth organizations survived the initial stages of the extermination of leadership. Those youth organizations became the cradle of the Jewish underground. But they had to learn all about underground warfare from scratch. The non-Jewish underground movements, too, had trouble because of the shortage of leadership, but they had more possibilities of replenishing the losses. In the years 1942–45, 6,700 persons of eighteen various European nationalities were clandestinely brought by boat and aircraft to the European underground. The Soviet authorities left during their retreat specially trained leaders for underground warfare and later constantly flew in new cadres of instructors and officers.

From these efforts to bolster the guerrilla leadership the Jews benefited only in a very small degree. Many young Jews in Palestine volunteered for the parachutist units to be dropped by the British in Nazi-occupied areas and hoped in this way to get in touch with the Jewish underground. The British reluctantly drafted and trained 240 of them, and after much delay agreed to send to Europe, in the spring of 1944, only 32, who reached their destination. This was too late and they were too few to be of much help to the Jewish underground.

The Element of Time and of Timing

Jewish underground groups were formed in almost every Nazi-occupied country. There were many groups, of various political persuasions, initially with very little or no contact between them. In general, the resistance movement of the European nations was a grass-roots growth, not organized from the top by a central organization, except perhaps in the Soviet territories. Time was, therefore, necessary for a long educational campaign for training in underground tactics and in the use of weapons, for welding the small scattered groups into a centralized efficient fighting body. But the Jews had much less time than the others for these preparations. The Nazi campaign of mass destruction against them started in the fall of 1941. By the fall of 1943 the ghettos of Europe were almost depopulated. The Jews who survived those massacres had to disregard proper timing and to act instantly. They could not expect considerable help from the non-Jewish underground. Thus, e.g., the Polish underground told them that it was too early for the Poles to launch a revolt in 1942 or 1943 because it might jeopardize the attainment of their ultimate goal. Polish parties were opposed to a step they considered suicidal and futile. But for the Jews in the ghettos this was the last moment. A similar situation prevailed in the concentration camps, such as Auschwitz. It was only with great difficulty that the Jews of the *Zonderkommando* secured permission for the revolt from the underground leadership in Auschwitz, in which, however, the general underground movement did not take part.

The Objectives

The operations of the Jewish and non-Jewish underground movements had different objectives. In the case of the latter, the purpose was to regain political freedom; in the case of the Jews, it was a hopeless fight against biological destruction.

Hope is an important psychological factor in every struggle. If a definite goal and a terminal point of the struggle can be indicated, it bolsters the movement and the morale of the fighters. But there was no hope, no *terminus ad quem,* and no encouraging objective in the Jewish underground movement. Its only objective was to die with honor instead of dying in infamy, a desperate suicidal struggle.

Different Traditions and Moral Values

The patterns and forms of reaction to the Nazi occupation and persecution developed differently in each nation, manifesting particular national traits, modeling the educational campaign, the propaganda and other activities after its own national historical experience, traditions, and moral values developed through the centuries. France had its tradition of revolution since the end of the eighteenth century and a recent historical experience of German occupation in 1870, and partly in 1914–18. The Belgian underground was in many ways conditioned by the vivid memories of the ordeals of the German occupation during World War I. The Poles had an old insurrectionist tradition going back to 1794, 1812, 1831, 1863, 1905, and cadres of leaders had been brought up in those traditions. The elaborate Polish underground state during the Nazi occupation resembled in many ways the underground state they created in 1863.

The Ukrainian underground thrived on the traditions of the Cossack rebellions and the Haidamack revolt, and frequently used these symbols to kindle the imagination of its countrymen. The Yugoslav partisans were in a way a direct continuation of the legendary fighters against the Turks. But there were also other traditions. Thus, the Czechs, facing complete political isolation after the crushing defeats of the Hussite rebellion, developed during the centuries of Hapsburg domination methods of passive resistance, which in their case may have been a more subtle and effective course. This attitude, so graphically symbolized in the immortal character of *Der Brave Soldat Schweyk,* they also adopted against the Nazis.

Different and peculiar in their own way were also the Jewish traditions. They were not uniform because the Jewish group was greatly differentiated, both culturally and socially.

The intelligentsia, the acculturated part of the middle class and the working class adopted the traditions and values of their host-nations. But the large mass of Orthodox Jews, particularly in eastern and south-eastern Europe, had quite a different attitude to those problems. Whereas most other nations have legacies of heroism in which heroism meant physical and military prowess, in the case of Orthodox Jewry the concept of heroism is interwoven with the idea of spiritual courage, of sacrifice for the sake of religion known in Hebrew as *Kiddush Hashem* ("Sanctification of God's Name"). This was the main form of resistance carried on by the Orthodox Jews. It was a resistance stemming from religious inspiration and it contained a deeply rooted ancestral heritage epitomized by the saying "not by force but by the strength of the spirit." This attitude had been maintained during many centuries of religious persecution. Its essence is epitomized in the idea that the evil of the world should not be fought and cannot be defeated by physical force, because the struggle between good and evil will be decided elsewhere, by Divine Providence; it will by no means be decided by physical warfare. In accordance with this view the true weapon is the weapon of conscience, prayer, religious meditation and devotion and not armed resistance. The Orthodox Jew did not believe that it was possible or even desirable to resist the Nazis in any other way. They believed that the recital of a chapter of the Psalms would do more to affect the course of events than the killing of a German—not necessarily immediately but in the infinite course of mutual relations between the Creator and His creatures. There are no doubt similar attitudes among other nations. It would perhaps be a rewarding study to establish, for instance, the similarities, if any, between the "non-resistance" of the Orthodox Jews and the passive resistance or "non-cooperation" of Gandhi and his followers in India. Although different in their backgrounds, these attitudes are in both instances based on a definite philosophy. There is no question here of tactics or of strategy. It is a normative philosophy of life holding that this is the way it should be done. In various periods in human history there were many religious sects which acted in this manner.

Forms and Patterns of Jewish Resistance

(A) PASSIVE RESISTANCE

There were many different forms in which resistance to Nazism was carried on by various groups and nations. There were also intermediate forms between one and another resistance pattern and sometimes it is not easy to draw a clear line between them. This is particularly true when we come to define the forms of spiritual or moral resistance, sometimes also called symbolic resistance.

In French postwar literature and also in other languages an argument developed over these subtle distinctions and definitions. Several writers refused altogether to recognize any form of spiritual or moral opposition to Nazism as a manifestation of resistance. After all, they argued, moral or spiritual resistance did not involve any active fight against Nazism or contribute anything to its defeat. Nor did moral resistance involve any particular danger to its upholders. Therefore, they concluded, these forms of passive opposition could not be considered manifestations of resistance. This derogatory attitude to passive resistance is in many ways not justified.

In fact, there were many forms of spiritual and moral resistance which involved risk of life. There was also spiritual resistance of groups of people who, for reasons of principle, religion, or because of particular views, could not and would not engage in armed resistance, preferring to suffer, or even to die, rather than comply with the demands of the enemy or carry out his orders. As an example we may mention the sect of Jehovah's Witnesses, many of whose members died in Nazi concentration camps.

There is a great amount of documentation on the forms in which Jewish religious resistance manifested itself. We have records about prayer groups that would congregate in ghettos and concentration camps in spite of the heavy penalties, including the death penalty.

We also have accounts of other acts of courage, of attempts to rescue Torah Scrolls from burning synagogues, although many persons were killed in the attempt. We have heard about Hasidim, a Jewish pietist sect, who assembled and prayed and danced in religious ecstasy until the last minute of their lives. There are many accounts of religious self-sacrifice *(Kiddush Hashem)* performed by groups and individuals, by rabbis and laymen. But spiritual resistance is not necessarily bound to be derived from religious inspiration only. There were various instances of moral resistance by non-religious people. The action of the famous educator and writer, Janosz Korczak, of the Warsaw Ghetto, who voluntarily went to his death with the children of his orphanage and refused to be exempted from the deportation, was secular in character. The matter was argued for and against in Polish postwar literature, and several writers seriously criticised Korczak because they saw in his deed a sign of passive surrender instead of resistance. I mention Korczak only as an example. Many other educators did likewise.

Various other forms of passive resistance may be noted, e.g., a clandestine Jewish group in Lodz systematically listening to Allied broadcasts, and spreading the news until they were caught and deported or executed; or the artists in a ghetto theater who poked fun at the Nazis or their collaborators; or indulged in veiled satire; or the clandestine education of children.

There were other forms of passive resistance. Escape to the woods and hiding, both in specially prepared hideouts or in Christian homes, or bearing forged "Aryan papers," were some of these forms. In several ghettos of eastern Europe the Jews, before a German extermination operation, set their ghetto afire and attempted to escape in the ensuing confusion. In several ghettos and camps the Jews managed to build, during long weeks of secret labor, underground tunnels which led them to freedom. It happened that Jews rounded up for deportation refused to board a train, until the Germans opened fire on them. In the town of Marcinkonis, near Grodno, this organized passive resistance involved the entire Jewish population. In Slovakia all the young men of a small town lay down on the railway tracks when the deportation train arrived.

A widespread form of passive resistance was the building of various, sometimes very ingenious, dugouts, usually called "bunkers." There were bunkers in almost every town and the Germans sometimes had great difficulties discovering and "conquering" them. In Warsaw alone General Stropp's troops had to blast, during and after the

Warsaw Ghetto Uprising, 631 bunkers. General Katzman, the S.S. and Police Chief in Galicia, describes in his report a net of veritable underground fortresses in Rohatyn and tells of his difficulties in liquidating the numerous bunkers in Lvov. Sometimes, Jews succeeded in building elaborate underground networks as, e.g., in Baranowicze and Vilna.

(B) UNARMED ACTIVE RESISTANCE

Unarmed active resistance was in many cases only the first phase of the underground work, later to develop into armed resistance. However, in many cases unarmed underground work became a goal in itself.

The work of *La Sixième* in France is one example. This was a group of Jewish youngsters of the Scout movement, and perhaps of some other youth movements as well, who joined them. *Inter alia,* they organized a network of small "factories" for the manufacture of forged "Aryan" documents, which were then supplied to Jews. In western Europe, among a friendly and helpful Christian population, this was in many cases enough for evading the Germans. They also founded a network of bases for the rescue of children and, indeed, saved many of them. Mention should also be made of the illegal frontier crossings frequently practiced in France, Belgium and Holland. This work required extraordinary courage; it meant traversing Belgium and France and escorting groups of children and youths as far as the Pyrenees, to neutral Spain and Portugal. The leaders of this underground work were eventually caught by the Germans and killed. Children and youths were also smuggled across the frontier into Switzerland. There were hundreds of such cases. A great deal of illegal frontier crossings also went on in Poland. There was a kind of "underground railroad" from southern Poland through Slovakia, Hungary and Rumania aided by the efforts of Jewish underground organizations in those countries. There also were escape routes from Hungary and Rumania through Bulgaria and the Black Sea to Turkey and Palestine, and from Greece to Turkey.

An intermediate form between passive and active resistance were the acts of sabotage. Slowdown and sabotage in factories was in most cases carried on individually or collectively, without preliminary planning or organizational preparation. However, some acts of sabotage were distinctly the result of careful preparation and were carried on from a focal underground center as, for example, the arson strategy against the German armament factories in 1942 by the underground in Warsaw. The Germans accused the Jews also of starting gigantic fires in Daugapils (Dinaburg) and other centers of Latvia, in Kaunas, Kiev, Ushomir, Zhitomir, etc. It is possible, however, that the Germans exaggerated or even manufactured those charges to use them as pretexts for their mass slaughter of Jews.

(C) ARMED RESISTANCE

Spontaneous acts of individual or collective armed resistance have been recorded in numerous memoirs, eyewitness accounts of Jews and non-Jews, as well as some German official reports. There were also preparations for armed resistance carried on in various ghettos by the Jewish underground. Jewish underground organizations existed in Warsaw, Vilna, Bialystok, Cracow, Czestochowa, Bedzin and many other Polish towns. We also know of organized Jewish undergrounds in other countries and cities, e.g., in Kaunas, Riga, Minsk, in countries like Slovakia, Holland, Belgium, France. Not all of these groups were able to carry out their plans. Some of them were discovered and destroyed by the Germans before they had a chance to accomplish their schemes. However, in addition to the Warsaw ghetto uprising in April 1943, there was armed organized resistance in Bialystok, Lachwa, Minsk, Mazowiecki, Slonim, Nieswiez, Kleck, Braslaw, Glubokie and a few other places. Jewish underground groups also organized uprisings in the concentration camps of Treblinka, Auschwitz, Sobibor, Koldyczewo, in the camp at Janowska Street in Lvov, etc. In Paris, Jewish underground groups managed to ambush and kill several high German officials; in Cracow they succeeded in blowing up a café where several German officials were killed.

As time went on many Jews who escaped to the woods and mountains began to join together into guerrilla units. Until the beginning of the Soviet-German hostilities, general partisan warfare was still in its infancy. Thus, the small Jewish groups were also in their infancy. But they were still able to play a considerable role, particularly in Poland and France.

In France, the Jews joined the *Maquis* wherever this was possible or formed their own small guerrilla groups uncoordinated and not unified in central organizations until very late.

In Poland, the Jewish guerrilla groups were too weak for military operations, except in self-defense, and they did not have the cooperation of the native population and of the Polish underground. As usual in underground organizations, the authority of central bodies was weak in the field and the local groups often behaved as they liked. In addition, various "wild" groups developed, sometimes only loosely connected with the legitimate underground Home Army. At times even simple brigand groups assumed the guise of fighters for independence. The Jews in the woods, both individuals as well as guerrilla fighters, were often persecuted by those "boys of the woods" and sometimes annihilated. The democratic and socialist Polish underground was in general too small to be of real help to the Jews. Thus, many Jewish underground groups simply disappeared before long.

These conditions gradually changed, particularly after the outbreak of the Soviet-German war. Soviet prisoners escaped to the woods and formed bands and guerrilla units. Later on a steady flow of Soviet supplies and officers welded these groups into a well-organized guerrilla army. In the initial stage of World War II the communists were almost entirely passive. But after Russia had gone to war against Germany, they became very active. Furthermore, although they were numerically small in the beginning (that is, in 1941–42), they carried greater weight than their numbers justified, especially in eastern Europe. The reason was that they were operating at a distance of only a few hundred kilometers from the Russian army, which was attacking the Germans and advancing daily. Russian partisans and parachutists within a short time virtually took over the command of most of the existing guerrillas that were not already a part of the nationalist Polish or Ukrainian underground. Jews in the underground movements of the western countries were able to draw support in one form or another from the sympathy of a large section of the population, whereas in eastern Europe, dependence on the left-wing underground was, in many cases, the only way left to them. There have been published many memoirs of Zionist or Orthodox Jewish guerrilla fighters who deplored the fact that they had to join communist-led or influenced partisan units; but they had no other choice if they wished to survive and to fight the Nazis.

(D) JEWISH RESISTANCE: ÉLITE OR MASS MOVEMENT?

The underground movements in some countries, e.g., Poland, Belgium, France, Holland, Denmark and Yugoslavia were, in the second phase of the war, mass movements with many well-organized members and a large number of sympathizers. In some countries, however, as in Czechoslovakia, the underground was rather a secret group with limited membership and tenuous contacts with the masses, and emphasis was laid there on the development of a tightly-knit revolutionary élite. Both definitions do not correspond to the situation in the Jewish underground. In some way the Jewish underground developed as a secret élite group. The Orthodox masses, for reasons already mentioned, could not be won to the idea of armed resistance. But in other groups, too, the German terror generated an attitude of complete apathy. The number of people who wanted only to adjust and survive was very great. Thus, the underground groups in the ghettos were rather isolated, lonely small islands.

A different situation prevailed in the Jewish guerrilla movement. It was not an èlite movement because many of the best people and underground leaders were annihilated before they even got a chance to leave the ghettos for the woods. Neither was it a mass movement because a mass escape from the ghettos was impossible. It was rather an accidental gathering of various elements, many of them, of course, people with a spirit of enterprise and courage, who managed by chance to find their way to the woods. In only a few cases was a Jewish partisan unit the result of a carefully planned move stimulated by purely ideological pursuits. There were relatively more of such planned Jewish guerrilla formations in western Europe than in eastern Europe.

(E) COMPOSITION OF THE JEWISH UNDERGROUND

While the partisan units in the woods sometimes were a result of a haphazard gathering of fugitives from the ghettos, without clear political objectives and leadership, the underground groups in the ghettos were from the beginning to the end closely-knit ideological groups formed along party lines. The share of each party in the underground and in the guerrillas varied in each country. At any rate, on the basis of the literature available to date, it would seem that there were underground movements sponsored by General Zionists, Socialist Zionists, *Hashomer Hatzair,* Revisionists, *Mizrachi* and the Socialist Bund. In several countries there were also other groups politically less clearly defined, such as, the Jewish Scout Movement *(Les Eclaireurs Juifs)* of France. After the outbreak of the Soviet-German hostilities there was a communist underground as well.

Jewish Participation in the General Resistance Movement in Various Countries

In addition to the specific Jewish underground, Jews were also represented in the general non-Jewish resistance movements. In some countries this was the rule. Thus, for example, there were no special

Jewish underground organizations in Italy but a comparatively great number of Jews were active in the general Italian underground. The same is true also of some other countries, e.g., Bulgaria and Greece. In other countries, such as France, many Jews were active both in the general resistance and in special Jewish units. Jewish and non-Jewish groups sometimes cooperated in special joint enterprises, for example, in the rescuing of children in France, Belgium, Holland. In Belgium the Jewish and the non-Jewish underground joined forces to attack a deportation train from the camp at Malines (Mecheln) and rescued several hundred Jewish deportees. Some groups, opposed to Nazis but not yet definitely organized, developed to meet the challenge of an unexpected emergency. The Amsterdam anti-Nazi riots and the strike of February 1941 are a case in point. In Brody, eastern Galicia, a Jewish fighters' organization maintained close relations with the leftist Ukrainian underground in Lvov which helped them with arms' supplies and by sending instructors.

Jews participated in the Polish democratic and socialist resistance movements. However, in the principal Polish resistance force, the Home Army, there were few Jews.

In eastern Europe, generally speaking, the Jews succeeded in joining any nationalist resistance group only in such cases where they were able to pass themselves off as non-Jews by having possession of "Aryan" documents. There were a number of such cases but they are not always easy to discover because of the concealed identity. Several Polish authors, for example, mention the activities of some of those camouflaged Jews, individuals or groups, without mentioning their Jewish descent. Sometimes the author does it in good faith as a result of ignorance, sometimes he does it deliberately, or he just disregards this as being a matter of minor importance. Sometimes only the leaders of the guerrilla units knew of the true identity of their Jewish members, and after both the leaders and the rank and file of the Jewish fighters perished, they took the secret with them to the grave.

The Psychological Factors and the Problem of Self-restraint

The German terror mechanism kept both Jews and non-Jews alike under stress and the large mass of the population was perforce made cooperative, and kept by sheer fear from any anti-German activities. But the Nazi terror hit the Jews much harder than the non-Jews. The rigors of forced labor, of camps, prisons, and various penalties were applied with much more vigor and ruthlessness against Jews.

The physical and moral isolation generated among them a feeling of hopelessness and lethargy. The methods of discrimination employed against Jews, the compulsory resettlements and deportations and the systematic starvation produced a feeling of degradation and humiliation which broke the spirit of many. On the other hand, the Germans used tactics of deception. It took much time before the people learned what was the real meaning of the "working assignment" to the camps and plants, the sending of children to alleged children's homes or colonies, the resettlement, and so on. In a kind of self-deception people used to cling to the last straw of hope and did not want to jeopardize the "German truce" by any imprudent act of resistance. In many places there was pressure of public opinion on the underground movement to stop their dangerous game. The Nazis knew how to utilize these psychological factors by applying the system of collective responsibility in the most ruthless way. Thus, for example, the assassination of a particularly brutal S.S. guard in Lvov by a Jewish worker resulted in the retaliatory killing of 1,000 Jews taken at random from the ghetto by the S.S. The sense of responsibility and of family ties, particularly strong in the Jewish population, thus became a deterrent to underground activities. Of course, this was self-delusion. Several authors who have written about Budapest and Theresienstadt have made the claim that Jewish self-restraint rather than prowess saved the lives of the inhabitants of those two areas. If a resistance movement had arisen in Theresienstadt, they contend, it would not have been possible to save its last 17,000 Jews and if the underground movement in Budapest had tried to provoke a revolt as in the Warsaw Ghetto, the 100,000 Budapest Jews would have suffered the same fate as the last Jews of Warsaw. It is, however, highly disputable whether the self-restraint on the part of the Jews was the main factor responsible for saving these two communities. It is rather more reasonable to assume that they were saved thanks to a combination of various circumstances connected with the general political and military situation. Jewish self-restraint could only delay the deadline for annihilation by the Nazis, but could not prevent it.

Conclusions

Jewish resistance manifested itself sometimes in ways and methods similar to those of other nations under Nazi occupation. However, there were also other forms of religious and moral resistance innate in (and more suited to) the mentality and philosophy of the large Orthodox Jewish masses of Eastern Europe. Various factors handicapped the development of Jewish resistance: the lack of a strategic basis, the absence of the operational and tactical media for an underground struggle, the lack of outside support and of an ultimately practical available objective, the poor timing. Nevertheless, there were Jewish underground groups in almost all Nazi-occupied countries, and various individual and collective acts of armed resistance.

In many cases it is not easy to discover Jewish participation in the general resistance movement because of the general rules of anonymity and conspiracy applied by the underground. It is also not easy to estimate how much the Jewish or any other resistance movement contributed to the war effort in general. The military effectiveness of the guerrilla war is still a controversial issue. Thus the historian of the Greek resistance movement, C. M. Woodhouse, believes that the effect of guerrilla operations was out of proportion to the great suffering caused by it to the civilian population. We take exception to this view and believe that the partisan movement in some places, e.g., in the Russian hinterland or in France, considerably harassed the German armies. On the other hand, the underground can never be a decisive and final strategic weapon, only a complementary one—and this only if it has powerful outside support. Where this is not the case, and the fate of the uprisings in Banska Bystrica and in Warsaw in 1943 and 1944 is a case in point, it is doomed to defeat. As a matter of fact, history knows more examples of heroic defeat than of victory of the isolated and lonely resistance movements.

However, the psychological effect of a resistance movement can be long lasting regardless of how much it accomplished in terms of warfare operations. A Polish sociologist, Felix Gross, makes the excellent point that both the Serbians and the Poles celebrate national defeats as days of victory(the Kosovo battle of the Serbians and the Polish uprisings of 1831, 1863, 1944). But this observation should also be applied to other nations and epochs. Thermopylae is perhaps the most striking and celebrated example. In the Jewish community it has become an almost religious observance to celebrate every year the anniversary of the Warsaw Ghetto Uprising as a symbol of Jewish resistance in the Nazi period. It is a celebration of resistance without victory. Heroism cannot be measured only by its ultimate achievements. Jewish resistance was more hopeless, anyhow, than any other resistance could be. It is the decision of a handful of men and women to take up an unequal and hopeless struggle against the most powerful and ruthless force of their times, a decision requiring suicidal sacrifice and strong moral values, that is being celebrated and revered.

SHMERKE KACZERGINSKI

The Girl in Soldiers' Boots

TRANSLATED FROM THE YIDDISH BY MOSHE SPIEGEL

Major Brodkin glanced at his notebook and was reminded that he had to be at headquarters at precisely two o'clock.

Just then, the guard announced:

"Someone by the name of Sonya Kotlovska."

"Oh," the major exclaimed, rushing to the door, "please come in, Comrade Sonya."

They both sat down on the window ledge, their eyes fixed upon the marching columns of soldiers below.

"One must not ignore the truth," Brodkin remarked. "Right now the Fascists are winning. True . . . but in the long run no one has ever defeated us." He caught Sonya's eye, and, as one, they exclaimed:

"And no one ever will defeat us!"

"I realize that a diversionary movement in the enemy's rear is not the easiest thing to manage," Major Brodkin drawled. "I also realize that crossing the front line is a pretty difficult task. . . . Yes. All the same, dear Sonya, I think that if you keep your head you'll achieve your goal. Try to get to your hometown and the nearby villages, where you grew up, where you know every peasant, every inch of the highways and byways, every single little hut, where the scent of every bush is familiar to you. Once there—if you are willing (Sonya glanced impatiently at him)—you could render us great service. . . ."

Then, aware of her mounting annoyance, the major took her face in his hands and spoke more affectionately:

"Don't be mad at me, Sonya. It isn't that I doubt your willingness to help. But you know how it is—we're all only human. Anything could happen to you." Groping for further words for a moment, he finally remarked, "Well, Sonya darling—do you promise?"

On July 10, 1941, several pedestrians suddenly halted on the main street of the ghetto in the town of Kimelishki as they caught sight of a girl hurrying by.

"But the Kotlovsky girl," one of them said in surprise, "was supposed to have gone off with the Russians."

"And if she has stayed here instead do you think that means she's deserted them?" another rejoined.

2.

He was seated in a wide leather armchair on a silk pillow, peering through the thick cigarette smoke.

She, a small tight-lipped creature, stood in a corner of the room near the door, staring at him.

He was Heinrich Raabke, chief of the Gestapo of the Vilaik district; *she,* Anna Lovskovska, one of the thousands of peasant women of the neighborhood.

"So you say that you were beaten up so that you can't sit down," he said, with a smile. "Hmm . . . you got a beating from someone, all right. But Germans don't beat people, my child," he went on, straightening his legs and stretching his right hand toward her in an exaggerated gesture. "That's a joke; no one will believe you. Germans don't inflict such punishments, especially on young women like you." He reached out to touch her, but she brushed his hand angrily aside.

"Hmm. . . . Indignant. . . . I barely touch you and right away you get on your high horse." He began to puff nervously upon a cigarette, lighting one match after another. Finally, flinging his cigarette away, he rapped out disdainfully:

"Little one, if I had given you that beating, you would be lying crumpled up on the floor, as limp as that cigarette butt."

"You've got good pupils, chief," Annushka rapped back.

"And you, Lovskovska, are still arrogant," Raabke raged. "I'll show you how to associate with such trash as communists, prisoners, Jews, and the Ukrainian soldiers. You're even poking your nose into German affairs." He paced up and down the room, biting his lip in anger, and muttering under his breath, "What am I to do with her?"

After considering for a few minutes, he decided to let her go for the time being, but to keep her under surveillance, so that he could find out whom she met and where, and round them all up. He then began to turn over in his mind how he would deal with her gang, once he had taken them into custody. He could starve them first, he thought, then hand them over to his adjutants for some real punishments. But no—that Lovskovska girl he would hand over to no one—her he would save then for himself. He would make her talk, all right. He'd get her to tell him everything about undercover atrocities in the district. He would destroy all the traitors.

Once again he paused near her. His heart pounded, and with a leer, he murmured, "Oh, you, Anna." He put his hand on her back, and his fingers slowly moved toward her graceful white throat, toward the satin-smooth face. "Oh, you, Anna."

"I did not expect such a thing from you, sir," Anna mocked him, removing his hand. "Is that how polite you are to your prisoners?" she asked with a sarcastic smile. "I must say it is hardly in character."

Raabke again flew into a sudden rage and slapped her face, shouting, "Get out, you damned bitch!"

"Now, *Herr* Raabke—that I did expect," she exclaimed in a tone of proud anger.

Several days later, twenty-eight soldiers of the Ukrainian battalion, accused of murdering Raabke, the chief of the Gestapo of Vilaik, were jailed in the Gestapo dungeon there.

Niccolai Rudenko, one of the accused, assumed full responsibility for the crime. And despite all the torture to which he was subjected in an effort to force him to implicate others, he adamantly refused to change his story. When Rudenko, beaten almost into a trance, stood in the dugout, he could discern but one thing through the haze: the dreamy blue eyes of Annushka, who had rescued him from the meaningless and ignoble life of his pre-partisan days. And although he was now face to face with the Angel of Death, he felt unburdened and at ease. He had carried out the mission Annushka had entusted him with—he had put an end to Heinrich Raabke, the Gestapo fiend.

3.

The community was in a state of turmoil; the people were frightened and didn't know which way to turn. There were rumors that the local inhabitants would be deported to Germany; that the partisans had been apprehended; that all the Jews would be seized and taken away. . . .

Quite a few men wearing new German army overcoats and boots had arrived. Some of the natives maintained that they were not Germans at all, but Russians.

As for Annushka, she had been in rather poor health lately; her hitherto animated face now wore a look of melancholy, and she was constantly biting her nails.

She was being urged by the underground organization to learn the purpose of the new arrivals and to take necessary measures to the best of her ability.

Annushka strolled out to the city park where the soldiers strolled about in an effort to pick up girls.

"Where are you headed, all alone, beautiful?" a soldier asked of her in Russian.

"I'm out for a walk," Annushka answered, and then added in a casual tone, "How is it that a German like you speaks Russian so well?"

"Only my clothes are German, I myself am a Russian," the man replied.

"You—a Russian! Tell that fairy tale to someone else," she answered.

He motioned to several other soldiers, and when they had joined him, he said, "She doesn't believe that we're Russians. You tell her."

As Annushka continued to laugh skeptically, one of the men asked, "What are you giggling at?"

"What am I giggling at?" Annushka replied in surprise. "You claim to be Russians—that's a laugh, all right."

"So help us God," one of the men protested, "We're Russians—we don't even understand German."

"You're not really Russians—no one could believe that."

"Why not?" they demanded.

"Why not?" she repeated and then added, accentuating each word, accusingly, "Because you who claim to be Russians are really planning to fight your own brothers."

The soldiers were dumbfounded. And one of them asked, "So what are we then?"

"Murderers—you're traitors!" Annushka replied. It was as though she had dropped a bombshell.

A sensation. All sorts of things were being rumored in town. The newly-arrived militia seemed to have vanished as rapidly as it had arrived. What could that signify?

And the rumors had some basis. On the road leading to the town of Tcheremshitze, several partisans of the Voroshilcov Brigade lay in hiding, hidden by the underbrush.

"The devil knows what's going on. We could be walking into a trap," Kolya observed. "It's certainly a report that's hard to believe," another remarked.

Just then another said in a low voice, "Hush! I hear footsteps. . . ."

Then they saw scores of armed men in German uniforms plodding along the sandy road. Had it not been for the presence of Annushka, whom Kolya recognized at a distance among the German soldiers, who knows how it might have ended? Actually, one of the two military detachments encamped in the town had come out to join the partisans in the woods, with tears of repentence in their eyes at having served the Germans. All the soldiers greeted and embraced the delegation of partisans that had been sent to meet them. Anna Lovskovska, their savior, was in a transport of delight.

4.

Picture a heavy wicker basket, covered with hay as though it were packed with eggs, but actually containing copies of the latest issue of the partisan bulletin with an appeal to the soldiers. As she lugged that basket through villages and settlements, Annushka familiarized the peasants with what was going on in the outside world and with the dangers surrounding them.

Annushka seemed to be quite fearless. On entering a town, she made her way to the marketplace, thrust bulletins into the wagons and whispered to the peasants, "Read it and then pass it on to others!" She slipped into the local community center, thronged with peasants, and posted appeals and rallying calls on the bulletin board. Sometimes a peasant would protest, "What sort of new bulletins are these?" But Annushka would already be out of sight. . . .

The Germans unexpectedly surrounded the village of Shaulaske. One of the officers accosted Annushka and, looking suspiciously at her and her basket, inquired:

"Ham—eggs?"

The valiant Annushka retained her composure in this sudden predicament and, taking hold of the officer's arm, asked with a smile, "Is it ham that you wish? Come along, *Herr* officer?"

The pressure of the girl's hand sent a warm glow through the soldier's body. She gripped his arm harder now, and he gazed down at her and laughed foolishly.

"You're a real soldier—gallant and full of life. Beautiful, too. Come over to us," and he helpfully took hold of the basket.

"You're a real gentleman," she said, laughing.

"All Germans are gentlemen," he answered slyly.

"Of course, they all are," she agreed.

The officer strolled along with her, happy as a calm at high water. He was too occupied to return the salute of passing enlisted men. Annushka agreed to meet him at the fence near the church at eight o'clock that evening.

The German officer, burning with impatience, paced up and down at the rendezvous, glanced at his watch and muttered, "It's already fifteen minutes past eight and there's no sign of her."

A little girl came running toward him from the main street and said to the officer, "Here's a letter for you."

The officer unfolded a large printed bulletin, at the top of which was written, "Are you waiting, my dear Fritz? Keep on waiting. Read this bulletin, meanwhile, until I get there. Death to the German army of occupation!"

5.

Weapons were to be had near the city of Vilna, and Annushka was urged by a commander of the partisans to go there and procure some arms for his unit.

Upon her arrival, she located a former classmate, the Lithuanian garrison officer, Kapotis, in the town of Podbrodz. Wasting no words, she said:

"Listen, Julek. I realize that you're a commissioned officer; but I can't believe that you are serving the Germans wholeheartedly."

Kapotis stared at her sternly.

"Julek, you seem to be thinking, 'How does she dare talk to me like that!' But I know you, so it's you I come to for help. Listen, Julek. I need some weapons."

Kapotis suddenly felt a deep respect for his daring ex-classmate, and he recalled the way she used to be able to hold her own with their teachers.

"I'll give you arms, and then you'll turn them on me," he said ruefully.

"Julek, there are worse rats than you that I could shoot, as you very well know."

"Annushka, you're going a little too far. You know, jokes have their limits, too." Then, after a momentary silence, he added, "But I suppose I can let you have, as a sort of souvenir from me, two rifles and my own automatic." He unsheathed his shiny revolver, remarking, "I'll tell you where I'm going to hide the rifles; and you fly just as soon as you've got them. A German echelon is due to arrive here in an hour, and it would complicate things if you were caught."

Within an hour and a quarter, Kapotis was instructed by telephone to deploy his military unit to the local railroad station, where the arriving echelon had suffered a considerable number of casualties.

"A girl-bandit, indeed. . . ." he mused. "How careful one has got to be with her! I happened to mention casually the arrival of a military unit and she lost no time in organizing an attack!"

6.

Some of the natives informed against her in the town of Lopenko. Annushka and two companions managed to get out of town in the nick of time. Annushka became aware of a pursuing posse while it was still some way off, and the three fugitives managed to hide themselves in the underbrush. The German squad surrounded the spot and leveled a barrage.

Annushka assumed command; her companions looked at her silently, awaiting her orders.

"Those ghouls will not take us alive," flashed through her mind. And she heard again in her mind the rallying cry, "Death to the German conqueror!"

"Annushka, Annushka—remember our massacred people," it seemed to remind her.

Signalling her companions and aiming her own automatic, she shouted, "Fire!"

Usually calm and unruffled, Annushka was now filled with the rage of battle. "Let 'em have it! Take good aim!" she urged on her fellow partisans.

As the trio rained death upon the German unit, whose men fell like sheaves, Annushka and her two companions felt as though they were riding on the crest of a wave of joy.

The surviving officer of the pursuing troops later apologized at headquarters:

"Our unit consisted of thirty-two men; but that Annushka had under her command a hundred and fifty. . . ." But the report Annushka gave later to her fellow partisans was somewhat different.

And always when I look at the proud Sonya, or Annushka, as she was known among the partisans, in her kerchief that blends with the blue of the sky, with her knapsack, and with the automatic snug at her side, I recall the song, "The Girl in Soldiers' Boots." I envisage then the heroine of a novel or of a poem that has its origin in real life. . . .

SAMUEL BORNSTEIN

Dr. Yehezkel Atlas, Partisan Commander

In spring 1942, when Hitler's forces reached the gates of Moscow, Dr. Yehezkel Atlas, a young Jewish physician, lived in the small town of Kozlowszczyzna, in the Slonim district of western White Russia. About twenty-eight years old, he had arrived in this distict in September 1939, fleeing from the Nazi invader after the occupation of Lodz, his birthplace. His parents and his seventeen-year-old sister Celina had also fled eastward with him, to the territory annexed by the Russians; but in summer 1941, when the Nazis invaded Soviet Russia, the Jewish refugees again faced the Nazis.

A harsh and bitter period of persecution began. Decrees were issued at lightning speed, one after the other, which stupefied the Jews. After about nine months, the Gestapo began an absolute liquidation of the ghettos in the vicinity of Slonim. Kozlowszczyzna was one of the first marked for liquidation. One night the notorious Heyk, the Gestapo leader in Slonim, arrived here with a squad of Lithuanians. All the Jews of the town, including Yehezkel's parents, were cruelly murdered in cold blood, but Dr. Atlas himself was left alive because he was a physician. When the murderers asked who the young woman in his house was, he replied that she was his sister. She was also taken out and shot. Thereafter, Dr. Atlas could not rid himself of the thought that they might have left her alive if he had claimed that she was his wife.

The Germans transferred the stupefied and despairing young man to the village of Wielka Wola, which lies on the river Szczara, surrounded by large dense forests,—the Pushchas of Ruda Jaworska, Dombrowszczyzna and Lipiczany. This was a period of magnificent victories for the Germans, and it seemed as though no power in the world could stand against them. From the peasants Dr. Atlas learned that in the neighboring forests there were former Russian soldiers who did not wish to surrender to the enemy. These had been joined by a few active local communists, including the Jew Abraham Kopelowicz. The peasants related that these people, the partisans, killed every German and policeman who fell into their hands.

The young Jew, whose world had collapsed about him, began to weave plans of resistance and vengeance. He contacted the forest dwellers and regarded himself as one of them, though he remained in the village. As time went on he began to serve those first partisans as a doctor. At the time there was no organized partisan movement. The individuals who roamed through the forest were not yet prepared for a planned and continuous struggle against the enemy, and rested satisfied with petty operations. For the moment Dr. Atlas did not join any group. At the time he thought that his task was to obtain arms for them. The peasants of the neighborhood, who became very fond of him, informed him of caches containing large quantities of arms abandoned by the Russians at the time of their retreat.

On the 24th July 1942, the Dereczyn Ghetto, about 30 kilometers from the domicile of Dr. Atlas, was liquidated. Hundreds of Jews, including old folk, women and children, were cruelly murdered by Lithuanians, German gendarmerie and local police. This time, however, and unlike the Jewish community at Kozlowszczyzna, who had all been slaughtered, several dozen Jews succeeded in escaping.

That night, after the dreadful day, the Jews who had succeeded in escaping slaughter by hiding in bunkers fled through field and swamps toward the hoped-for forests. Their hearts were filled with despair, fear and uncertainty about the morrow. The first group reached Wola, Dr. Atlas's village. It included the three brothers Lipszowicz, their sister Teiba, Yekutiel Chmelnitzky, Bella Hirschhorn, Isaac Rosenthal, Israel Kviat and another few refugees. In the wood, near the village, the Jews from Dereczyn found a man who seemed to belong to another world. He was a lean but handsome young fellow, with kind blue eyes and a head of curly brown hair. When he spoke his lip rose a little, showing two rows of white teeth. He spoke quietly but strangely and convincingly. From time to time he would lift his glasses a little and raise his eyebrows. He was wearing a shirt with high boots on his legs, and in his belt was a Nagan pistol.

Atlas listened to their sad story. They only had one request: to be admitted to a partisan group in order to avenge themselves on the Germans. Atlas led them deep into the forest and ordered them to stay there. He disappeared, and then came back several times carrying food and weapons. Each rifle and bullet was welcomed with roars of victory. Little by little the despairing men and women began to feel hopeful once again.

Atlas encouraged them, and told them a great deal about the partisans, the possibilities of fighting, and taking vengeance. A few days later the young men undertook their first action to obtain food supplies under his leadership. Then they understood the power of arms. When they had fled from slaughter, broken and in a state of collapse, the peasants closed their doors to them. Now that they had arms in their hands, they aroused fear and respect. Day by day Atlas added new members, especially selected from the refugees in the forests.

Atlas worked feverishly. He knew that his time was limited, and that he must create a company worthy of the name and capable of engaging in military action in the shortest possible time. He saw his primary function in the organizing of a fighting group He did not disregard the existence of the dozens of helpless Jews left from the Jewish community of Dereczyn. In his opinion, the fighting group had to provide their brethren with food for sustenance and arms for defense; but its real purpose was fighting. He displayed exceptional organizing talent and working capacity, so that it seemed as though he never slept or rested at all. He was on the move by day and night, attending to everything, bearing everybody in mind, obtaining arms, setting out on foraging expeditions, and establishing contact with the partisan command. Dr. Atlas the physician was replaced by Dr. Atlas the partisan commander, whose mission was to lead his men to fight against the enemy.

Atlas desired only to liquidate the garrison at Dereczyn and execute judgement on the Germans and their helpers. At that time the Ruda forests changed. The few who had once hidden from the Germans had become many. Besides the Jews, scores of Russian soldiers from the Red Army, who had hitherto lived in the villages, now began to take to the woods. A command was established, and partisan units began to organize themselves. Atlas put pressure on Boris Boolat, the Chief of Staff, to proceed against Dereczyn. His efforts bore fruit. One day he appeared in camp and said, "Boys, our time has come, we are attacking Dereczyn!", and he set out at the head of his men to join the partisan forces. Fearing that he might have to act as a doctor and provide first aid and medical treatment, which would remove him from actual fighting, he took the field nurse, Bella Hirschhorn, with the company when they set out for action. About three weeks after the slaughter, one August evening, the partisans went into action against the Dereczyn garrison, with the company of Dr. Atlas in the lead.

In the battle that followed, they showed unusual bravery. They were the first everywhere. The unit found an outlet for its feeling of vengeance and gave the enemy what he deserved. On the mass grave of the Dereczyn Jews the Atlas men executed 44 policemen. Several lads fell in the battle, and a few were wounded. The seriously wounded included David Dombrowski, one of the leaders, who ordered his brother Nioma, before his death, "I am dying, and didn't manage to take proper vengeance. Remember that you have to avenge our kinsfolk."

After the battle of Dereczyn, which ended with a brilliant victory for the partisans, the fame of Commander Atlas and his company spread throughout the forests. The Russians, who used to regard the fighting talents of the Jews wth great scepticism, now looked at the Atlas lads with respect. The Jewish doctor, who had never before engaged in military matters, became widely known as a brave and gifted commander. The command began to ask his advice on everything. And where they had hitherto put pressure on him to engage in medicine, on account of the grave shortage of doctors, they now understood that they could not spare him as military man.

It was hard to recognize his men. Even their appearance, dressed as they were like the Russian partisans in high boots, leather knapsacks and shirts (some of which had fallen into their hands during the assault in Dereczyn), and well-armed, was evidence of the tremendous change. The despairing men had become desperate and fearless fighters, prepared for any action. Atlas found the time ripe to spread a special doctrine among his men, the doctrine of struggle and revenge. He repeated again and again: "We must not settle down and take things easy, lads. Our struggle only began when we defeated the German garrison at Dereczyn. Your lives came to an end in the slaughter during the 24th July. Every additional day of life is not yours, but belongs to your murdered families. You must avenge them." Henceforward every candidate who wished to enter the company was asked by the commander, "What do you want?" and had to answer, "I want to die fighting the enemy." These phrases possibly sounded high-flown, but it was all quite understandable and regarded as normal and straightforward.

So far there was no contact with Russia nor with the partisans in distant forests. The function of the partisan movement was not quite clear. The idea of sabotaging movements of the German army from the rear, that is, derailing trains, burning bridges, etc., had not yet ripened in the minds of the commanders. But Yehezkel Atlas foresaw the future. He already saw clearly that the partisans must strike at the enemy while they were transporting equipment and manpower eastward to the front; but as yet the partisans did not have the resources for this task.

One day Atlas fetched two large shells to the camp. In accordance with his instructions the explosives were removed, and it was then possible to handle them with the aid of ordinary grenade fuses. Dr. Atlas set out with his unit to take sabotage action near the Rozhanka Station. As a result of this operation a train was derailed for the first time in the whole region. This served as a signal for all the units in the neighborhood, and they began to engage in similar actions. Atlas' men went on derailing trains, and were very successful. They were also the first to burn bridges. The Jewish commander set out with a few fighters to a place which was dozens of kilometers away in order to burn a bridge near Belitza town on the river Niemen, over which the Germans transported military equipment eastward. On the way the Atlasites met people who had escaped from the slaughter in the small town of Zhatel (Zdzientziol), and had just run away from the slaughter to the Lipiczany forests. The sight of Jewish fighters, armed, well-dressed and erect, gave rise to tremendous excitement among these unarmed and hopeless folk. Atlas promised them his help, and kept his word in due course. He told them of the life and activities of his company. In that action the bridge was set on fire, and the fame of Atlas again spread far and wide.

He did not give his lads time to rest. There was a tacit agreement among them not to speak of actions that were past, but to plan fresh operations instead. One action followed another. Life in the camp was lively and boiling all the time. Atlas turned the cooking over to the girls, and gave older men or those of limited fighting capacity the task of supplying equipment and food. The others went out and fought. The commander's influence on the youngsters, whom life had turned from bakers and shoemakers into fighters, was unchallengeable. Atlas was surrounded by glowing affection. He was regarded as both commander and father. The youngsters obeyed his orders without hesitation; and under his influence they engaged in a kind of competition in brave deeds. Individual and group courage, and an absolute unflinching stand in the face of death, were characteristic of most of them. And the personal exemple was given by the commander himself, whose brave deeds boundlessly inflamed his young followers.

On one occasion Atlas disappeared from the camp for a long time. Somebody had remembered that he had said several times that he wished to say *Kaddish* on the anniversary of the death of his parents and sister at their graves. Now their graves were in Kozlowszczyzna, where there was a German garrison. They felt gravely concerned for their courageous and beloved commander. His men knew that he was capable of anything. A few days later he reappeared in camp together with Berik, one of the fighters. They were both quiet and very thoughtful. Atlas had fulfilled his vow. He and Berik, whose family had also been killed on the same occasion, entered the little town by night and said *Kaddish* at the graves of their dear ones under the very noses of the Germans; while they held their weapons at the ready in their hands.

Dr. Atlas was the symbol of uprightness, justice and truth. It was strange how this delicate intellectual from the big town fitted in with the simple boys, adopting their habits and way of speech. He felt like one of them, and they also regarded him as one of themselves. Atlas never shouted at any of his men. In personal relations he set out to explain and convince. But if anybody ever broke any of the accepted laws of forest life, and had to appear before his commander, he felt worse than he would have done if he had had to stand before a court martial. His high personal morality was like a light for the feet of the lads who tried to imitate him in every way. In the fights and actions many of them were as brave as their commander, and became generally known in the forests. Among them were the late Elik Lipszowicz, the late Asher Bogdosh, the late Abraham Lewkowicz, the late Berik, the late Chaim Aglonick, Munia Kovalevsky, who is believed to have fallen as a soldier in the Red Army after leaving the forest, Elijah Kowensky, who lost his hand in a battle and is now in Israel, and many more.

Atlas and his company took an active part in the attack on the Koslowszczyzna garrison, in which the partisans were defeated. In the fighting his liaison officer Izu Rosenthal, one of the first members of the company, lost his life. He was fetching shells for the partisan cannon. In order to save time he ran directly from one post to another and was shot by the Germans. Chaim Joshua Lipszowicz and his two helpers took a dangerous position, and covered the retreat of the entire partisan army with their machine-gun.

In the forest much was told of the bravery of the Atlasites when the Germans assaulted the partisan area. The Germans fortified themselves in a forest near the river Szczara, on the opposite bank of which the partisans defended their own positions. A large group of Hitler troops tried to cross the river in boats but met with the withering fire of the defenders. Most of the assailants drowned in the river, and the survivors withdrew in confusion. The partisans saw two Ukrainians coming out of the river, and trying to return to their posts in the forest about a hundred metres away. All of a sudden one of the partisans jumped into the river and swimming energetically approached the enemy. A moment later another followed. The two partisans swiftly crossed the river, and weapons in hand pursued the two Ukrainians under the murderous fire of the Germans, who were covering the retreat of their comrades. The partisans shouted from every side, "Come back lads, come back!" But within a few moments the two fellows had overtaken the Ukrainians and killed them. They crossed the river again under an unceasing hail of bullets and appeared in their own positions, bearing the arms of the slain men. The two who had shown this rare courage, self-sacrifice and disregard for death, were Dr. Yehezkel Atlas and Elijah Kowensky, who had decided on the spur of the moment to join in his commander's daring operation.

Soon afterward the staff decided to attack the German guard force at Ruda village, which was in the heart of the forest and paralyzed the movements of the partisans. In this battle as well, the Atlasites distinguished themselves. Asher Bogdosh was the first to reach the enemy positions. He flung a hand-grenade at them, swung the muzzle of the heavy machine gun round on them and compelled them to retreat. This Bogdosh had previously been a *yeshiva* student, quiet and retiring; and nobody had ever imagined that he was capable of brave deeds. Dr. Atlas paid a great deal of attention to him, talked much with him, and had high hopes of him. Nor was he disappointed. In the Ruda battle considerable equipment and first-class arms fell into the hands of the Atlasites.

Atlas also looked after the inner life of the camp. He knew that a fighting soldier requires entertainment and must be kept cheerful. In the camp the lads joked a great deal, sang and played music. An important part was played by the girls, of whom Atlas did not particularly approve. To be sure, he understood that running the household part made their presence necessary, but on the other hand, he was always nervous for fear that some of the lads would become involved with the girls and flinch from action.

In the autumn, Atlas was already thinking about the future of his group during the approaching winter. He feared the bitter winter cold of White Russia, and the snows in which the partisans would leave tracks that the Germans could follow. He was the first to order his men to dig camouflaged caves underground, and store large quantities of food. For some time the men became toilers instead of fighters. Working hard, they prepared their winter quarters. Other units followed the Jewish commander, and the humming of saws and other tools was to be heard everywhere in the forests. In the morning the woods echoed to the songs of lads returning to their camps with wagons loaded with sacks of flour and meat. By the time the company was well advanced in its winter preparations, the commander was already planning fresh operations. This transition from camp life to fighting life and movement was easy for the Atlasites. They willingly and enthusiastically went about ambushing Germans, blowing up bridges, etc.

On the 21st November, 1942, tremendous German forces engaged in a concentrated attack on the partisans. Heading his fighters, Atlas approached the points facing which the attackers had taken up their positions. In order to save time and commence early action, he seems to have decided, as usual, not to act in accordance with the rules of ordinary military strategy. He ran ahead erect. The Germans saw him and opened fire. Dr. Atlas was badly wounded. He managed to whisper to the fellows beside him, "Lads, I appoint Elik Lipszowicz to take my place. Pay no attention to me and go on fighting!"

Dr. Yehezkel Atlas fell, but his name remained together with the Atlas tradition which required his men to follow in his footsteps.

The Atlasites were attached to a Russian regiment in which they continued to be among the most outstanding and distinguished members. Dr. Atlas served as a partisan commander for only half a year, yet his activities in the earliest period of the entire partisan movement left behind a clear line of moral struggle for the Jewish fighters, and led them along the paths of partisan bravery and fame.

RACHEL AUERBACH

The Jewish Uprising in Warsaw

TRANSLATED FROM THE YIDDISH BY MOSHE SPIEGEL

Sunday, April 18, 1943

The militia is already in Warsaw. An S.S. detachment has arrived with 400 men and six officers. There is also an *ersatz* detachment of S.S. cavalry, with 450 men and ten officers; a police unit of 160 men and six officers; a *zonderdienst* unit of 48 men and two officers; a Ukrainian *Hilfsdienst* unit of 151 men; a 55-man security police unit, and a police unit of 471 men and officers.

The *Wehrmacht* supplied these weapons and special units: four cannon and operators; a flame thrower; a pioneer unit of 16 men and two officers; a sanitation unit and ambulance; a heavy French armored wagon and crew; two German tanks and crews; 166 Polish firemen with equipment; an artillery battery and crew; and special engineering-sapper units for mining and demolition.

The other military units are to be reinforced later. There is now a fully trained and equipped army in Warsaw, ready to attack the ghetto fortress.

Also in the city is Jurgen Stropp, a pillar of the Nazi hierarchy. An S.S. brigade leader and major general of police, he has been sent here by Himmler himself. S.S. and Warsaw police leaders conferred at 11 A.M. today to plan the attack.

News of the conference reached the ghetto in the evening, greatly alarming the Jewish population. The Jewish Fighting Organization held a council. Each group was alerted for battle, and final orders were issued.

It is Passover eve. On this night mothers and grandmothers, busy with household tasks, were wont to work far into the night. Fathers would tour their homes with a goose wing to dust away bread crumbs, the ritual of removing leavened bread.

But tonight families are busy carrying bundles into bunkers. Men pace the courtyard nervously. Windows are darkened, but there is feverish activity inside. People talk in whispers.

It is midnight. The Jewish Fighting Organization is emerging. Curfew is not observed tonight. Armed Jewish troops in German uniforms appear in the streets, banging on doors and gates. The residents watch with mixed consternation and enthusiasm.

Oh, you Jewish children! Dear little boys! Oh, you fighters!

A chapter of Jewish history, as well as that of Poland, marches in the streets tonight. . . .

They rouse and alert. They call upon their brethren to resist. The announcement of the uprising has already been posted on the ghetto walls. Now comes the last appeal, the cry, "To fight, to die, for the honor of our people!"

It is now 2 A.M. and the ghetto is being surrounded, for the third and last time. Armed police are posted every 25 kilometers to complete the encirclement. Now the squads of the Jewish Fighting Organization are in position.

It is 4 A.M. German infantry and motorized units enter the ghetto, followed by armored cars, weapons and ambulances. They enter the "no man's land" between the ghetto and the workshops in small groups, then re-form into their regular units. All sound is muffled. Their motored vehicles are run as quietly as possible.

But all their cautious vigilance is in vain, for the ghetto does not sleep. It harkens to the footsteps of those who tread stealthily in, like savages bent on plunder and pillage, like beasts homing in for the kill.

TOVIA BOZHIKOWSKI

In Fire and Blood

TRANSLATED FROM THE YIDDISH BY MOSHE SPIEGEL

Monday, April 19, was the day before Passover, and the first day of spring. Sunshine penetrated even to the cheerless corners of the [Warsaw] ghetto, but with the last trace of winter the last hope of the Jews had also disappeared. Those who had remained at their battle stations all night were annoyed by the beauty of the day, for it is hard to accept death in the sunshine of spring.

As members of *Dror,* we were stationed at Nalevskes 33. I stood on the balcony of a building on Nalevskes-Genshe with several friends, where we could watch the German troops who stole into the ghetto. Since early dawn long lines of Germans had been marching—infantry, cavalry, motorized units, regular soldiers, S.S. troops and Ukrainians.

I wondered what we could do against such might, with only pistols and rifles. But we refused to admit the approaching defeat.

By 6:00 A.M. the ghetto was surrounded. The first German detachment advanced toward Nalevskes. As it neared the crossroads of Nalevskes-Genshe-Franciskaner we opened fire with guns, grenades and small homemade bombs.

Our bombs and grenades exploded over their heads as they returned our fire. They were excellent targets in the open square, while we were concealed in the buildings. They left many dead and wounded. The alert, confident attitude of our men was impressive. The youthful Jacob shot his pistol continuously, while Abraham Dreyer and Moshe Rubin commanded from windows. Zachariash, *Dror* commander, moved among the men, building their courage.

Liaison officers scurried between positions with messages. The battle went on for two hours.

Rivka, an observer, watched the enemy retreat. There were no more Germans on the front street. Zachariash returned beaming from his survey of the battlefield; 40 dead and wounded Germans were left behind, but we suffered no losses.

But even in our satisfaction we realized we would eventually be crushed. It was, though, a triumph to gladden the hearts of men who were about to die.

Quite a while passed without a sign of returning German troops. We discussed the battle, and some of us slept, our fingers firmly on our guns. Then our observers reported German tanks on the Maranovski side and German troops crawling along the Genshe walls.

Zachariash had hardly ordered battle readiness when heavy cannonading began. The Germans had set up a barricade on the corner of Genshe and Franciskaner and attacked from its shelter. We shot only on target, for bullets were dear.

During a lull we ascertained dozens of German casualties. Our formations remained intact. We threw a flaming jar of gasoline on their barricades. They replied with incendiary bombs, and we decided to pull back.

Our way led through attics, the avenues of communication in the ghetto. We learned that Genshe 6, which was to be our second position, was surrounded. Our Nalevskes 33 position was flaming. We were cut off. The floors beneath our feet were beginning to burn and the smoke was suffocating.

We had sent out a patrol earlier to find an escape route, but they had not yet returned. The Germans had begun to reach the roofs. We fired at them, and Moshe hit one. The others ran off. We stripped the dead German of his weapons, conscious that we would pay for this with our lives but determined to take as many Germans as we could with us.

Our patrol finally returned and led us back. We continued operations from Kozie 4.

On Wednesday, April 20, I was stationed on Mila 29 under Berel Broida. With me were men who had fought on Zamenhoff Street. For the first time since the fighting began I learned what had happened on other fronts.

After their defeat at Nalevskes-Zamenhofa the Germans no longer approached the ghetto with pomp. Now they moved cautiously, one by one, seeking shelter behind buildings. They massed their strength against our forces concentrated at 28, 32, 38 and 50 Zamenhofa. Our defense was coordinated among groups from *Dror, Hashomer Hatzair,* P.P.R. and Bund. We let the first German troops pass into the ghetto and met them with a hail of bullets and grenades at Zamenhofa and Mila. We surrounded them, and soon the street was littered with German dead.

For the first time since the occupation we watched Germans run in panic. We had suffered one casualty, Yechiel of *'Shomer Hatzair.*

The Germans then tried new tactics. They burned everything in sight. The ghetto was in flames, and the fires spread to the basements, which sheltered many Jews in hiding. Those who were not burned died of bullet wounds. Our people's panic and confusion was overwhelming. We wept not for those who had died but for those who yet lived.

We should have adjusted our strategy to their new methods, but instead of mass resistance we organized isolated, sporadic attacks on German patrols and small units. We attacked at night, when the ghetto was comparatively free of large German detachments. Our losses were heavy, but our spirit remained high.

In the dark, the Germans wore rubber-soled boots to muffle their steps. We wrapped our shoes in rags and were able to sneak up on them. As the German offensive progressed our condition deteriorated. It was impossible to breathe in the cellars, under burning houses. People ran from one refuge to another, but the fire was everywhere. There were often a hundred Jews in cellars which could accommodate ten. A deep fear contributed to our physical and moral decline, fear the Germans would soon locate the *"Malinas."* The cries of infants often put the Germans on the trail of the hidden ones.

On April 24 we were evacuated to a new fighting position at Mila 9. The transfer, under Lutek Rothblatt of Akiva and Pavel of P.P.R., was accomplished in perfect order. At Mila 9 was now concentrated the meager remaining fighters—2,000 men.

We spent the night in the open, waiting for the German assault. We were divided into several groups, guarding the various entrances to the street. Suddenly reports came of Germans at Kozie 24, and we sent more men there. After a brief exchange of shooting several Germans fell and the others set fire to the entire street. It spread to Mila 9. Thousands ran in panic to nearby homes, but there were flames everywhere.

Eight of us gathered to lay plans in one of the burning homes. We knew we could not hold out for long, and decided to send a patrol of four men to the Aryan side to organize an escape route for the others.

At dawn the next day, Sunday, April 25, Haliner and Yeshya of *'Shomer Hatzair,* Dorca of P.P.R., and I set out for the sewerage system. I cannot forget those first moments as we waded into the canal. Hundreds of Jews stood in the filthy, putrid water, doubled up in despair as their little ones lay unconscious at their feet.

We edged our way amid dead and dying. It took us six hours to reach the Aryan side. But at the exit was a booth filled with German guards and Polish police. The police caught the fleeing Haliner and Dorca and turned them over to the Germans. Jeremiah was caught as his foot touched the soil, and shot as he tried to escape. As I stuck out my head a policeman began firing. Luckily, he missed and I ducked back into the canal. I was the only one to return to the ghetto.

I found my unit battling at Kozie 3. We killed six Germans. We fought through the night at Mila 5 and 17, amidst fire, bullets and exploding mines.

On the nights of May 7 and 8 a few of us tried the canal again. This time we headed for Smotcha Street, but at the exit were again met with shooting and had to turn back. On the way back we had to pass the corner of Walynska and Zamenhofa. We stopped, and Mordecai of *'Shomer Hatzair* went ahead to ascertain the situation. He signalled us to follow, but the minute we entered Zamenhofa shots rang out. We scattered, tossing hand grenades as we ran. The fighting lasted an hour, and a few Germans died. Seven men succeeded in breaking through to Mila 18, but four of them were seriously wounded. Myself, Mordecai and Israel Canal were cut off from the others. The Germans pursued us until 6 A.M.

After 20 hours of roaming amid ruin and devastation we managed to reach Mila 18. There was not a living being there.

The Germans had apparently made a concentrated attack on these last positions a few hours before our arrival. Rather than surrender the last of our comrades had committed suicide. The sight broke us completely.

We roamed together through the burned out streets, over corpses and shattered homes.

That night I joined another group looking for a canal exit on Franciskaner 22 and Nalevskes 37. This time we had better luck. After much wandering we met Kozhik, who headed several emissaries from the Aryan side. They had been searching for us for more than a week. P.P.R. had readied a place for us on the Aryan side.

We returned to the ghetto for our comrades. After forty-eight hours of wandering through the canals, forty of us reached the Aryan side on May 10. From there we were taken by truck to the nearest forest. Had we made contact earlier, the tragedy of Mila 18 would never have happened.

ZVI GOLDFARB

Hehalutz Resistance in Hungary

At the beginning of 1944, after the large-scale massacre of Jews under Nazi occupation, Hungarian Jewry had still been spared, and that country, together with Rumania, were as yet isolated islands of refuge. The Jews of Hungary, who until that year had had no direct experience of Hitler, continued to delude themselves into a state of unfounded complacency. "Hungary," they said, "is not Poland, and we shall be spared the fate of Poland. What happened there will not happen here." They relied on Horthy and regarded with dissatisfaction the incursion of Jewish refugees rescued from the catastrophe, fearing that by offering them assistance they would only cause their own position to deteriorate. I still remember how difficult it was for me to find a room to stay in after I crossed the frontier into Hungary. One Jewish householder even threatened to call the police if I did not leave his premises immediately.

That was the general atmosphere among the Jewish population, with the exception, of course, of the pioneer movements, the few members of the Zionist movement and other individuals here and there. There was but little scope for activity among this population, devoid as it was of any heritage of independent national activity and lacking in public backbone. From time to time Jewish refugees were caught crossing the frontier and sent back without scruple. It was only after months of half-hearted activity, during which contact was established with the organization at Istanbul through emissaries of the political movements, that the hitherto narrow limits were exceeded, and in the course of time activities of extensive range developed.

At the beginning of 1944, when the Nazi invasion of Hungary threatened on the horizon, preparatory measures began to be taken with increased vigor by the pioneer movements acting in co-ordination—especially the *Dror-Habonim* movement *(Hakibbutz Hameuhad), Hashomer Hatzair* and *Maccabi Hatzair*. We began to brace ourselves and prepare for the new imminent disaster, of which we gave warning from the very first days, calling on the Jews not to delude themselves; but the majority turned a deaf ear.

The policy of the pioneer movements was to prepare the ground for rescue work and at the same time to equip themselves so that the hour of need should not find them unarmed. The energetic activity which now began was aimed at rescuing as many Jews as possible by every available means in the existing circumstances. We undertook the smuggling of Jews on a large scale across the frontiers into those countries which had not yet fallen into Hitler's clutches—at that time mainly Rumania. In spite of the oppressive laws there, the position of Jews in Rumania was incomparably better than in Hungary after the invasion, and even Slovakia could at that time be used as a temporary shelter, since the Jews there had already been exterminated and were no longer being sought out.

Simultaneously with smuggling across the frontiers, we engaged in the wholesale production of forged papers, an undertaking in which we attained incredible results. Hundreds of thousands of Jews were provided with documents of this type and were accordingly able to move about unmolested, at least for the time being. The third objective to which we devoted ourselves was the construction of bunkers for shelters, for storing arms and equipment and for the final stand. We began this work even before the German invasion.

We contacted our comrades in Carpatho-Russia in good time, elaborated plans of operation with them, provided them with money to construct bunkers, store food and acquire arms. We were resolved to hold out as long as possible, under no circumstances to be herded into the death trains and finally, when no alternative was left to us, to meet the murderers arms in hand.

Immediately on the German invasion the mass-extermination of Hungarian Jewry commenced at breath-taking speed, beginning in the provinces. Hundreds of thousands of Jews were transported daily to the death camps. We therefore increased the rate at which Jews were smuggled across the border into Rumania, calling this operation an "excursion." Emissaries were sent in advance to make contacts, prepare hiding-places, obtain guides, etc.

The whole area was ablaze. The mass extermination was in full swing. Every group crossing the border was augmented by children and young people; the fugitives from Carpatho-Russia also joined the convoys. Of those who managed to cross the frontier, some succeeded in reaching *Eretz Israel* while others were drowned in the Black Sea as "illegal immigrants." Britain was none too eager at that time to allow these fugitives to enter the country. When Rumania joined the anti-Nazi powers, the frontier was blocked, virtually becoming the front line, and the smuggling was rendered incomparably more difficult.

We concentrated our activities mainly, however, on the capital and the resistance movement. We who were active in the movement were "protected" by our home-made forged documents. Matters were generally thrashed out at prearranged meeting places and at definite times—morning, afternoon and evening—in the main thoroughfares, at street corners, in the municipal park, etc. In addition, we had rooms in the Red Cross building in Boross Street at our disposal, virtually working under the protection of this organization. At these meeting places instructions were given and documents handed over for distribution, and from them liaison workers would set out for their respective sectors.

I myself used to move about the city bearing an Italian identity card and I had a typical Italian name, Maria Marchese, although I did not know a single word of Italian. Naturally, the Hungarians and Germans did not know any Italian either, and this saved me more than once when I was required to produce my papers for inspection. I walked about the streets with an official air, wearing boots and a semi-military greatcoat, thus appearing beyond suspicion. The Nazi and Hungarian detectives soon got wind of my activities, however, and they began to seek me out. They knew my name was Zvi and that I came from Poland. From comrades who had been arrested, interrogated and released I heard that the Germans knew my distinguishing marks, and was accordingly compelled to change my dress and facial appearance from time to time in order to mislead them.

Other members of the local pioneer resistance movement also moved about the streets freely, some of them wearing the uniform of the Fascist Party or the Fascist Youth and, of course, carrying suitable papers. They would travel openly on their motor-cycles, going wherever required in our service. And here it is worth noting that when Szalasy was on the point of seizing power in Hungary, our members immediately received orders to take up arms. Many of them donned the uniform of the Fascist Youth on that day and took advantage of the chaotic situation to seize weapons.

These uniforms and forged papers opened up to us considerable opportunities for carrying out rescue work. When the Jews started being herded into the ghettos our lads would go out in uniform, enter houses and bring out Jews, ostensibly to transfer them to the ghetto, but in actual fact they took them to our hiding-places and bunkers and especially to the foreign legations whose aid we were receiving. Other Jews were taken to the woods in the vicinity of the city.

On the eve of the Fascist coup I happened to be in one of the woods outside the city where members of our movement were engaged in arms drill. It was a Sunday. On the same day we heard over Radio Budapest that Horthy was severing his ties with Nazi Germany. I returned to Budapest without delay in order to be on the scene of events, but on the next day the Fascist Szalasy seized power with the help of the Germans and we were obliged to adapt our methods to the changing situation.

One day, when Nashka and I were travelling by tram along one of the main streets, we noticed two leaders of *Hashomer Hatzair* being marched along under escort of two uniformed comrades of ours. The "prisoners," followed by their "captors," were not on the pavement but in the middle of the road, and the spectacle astonished us so much that we jumped off the tram and followed them. After some time they turned off into a small back street, where they parted company. They told us that the *Hashomer Hatzair* men had been recognized by Hungarian passers-by while walking along the street, and that the latter had begun shouting, "Jews!" They were immediately surrounded by an angry crowd, but it so happened that our two uniformed friends were passing by at that very moment. They approached the enraged mob and took the two men away, declaring that they would conduct them to the right place. The crowd believed them and all four walked off together, one pair as prisoners and the other as their escort.

Onc day, arriving for a prearranged meeting in one of the parks on the outskirts of the town, I was informed that one of our men had been arrested in the street although wearing uniform. He had simply been recognized by Hungarians, who alerted a crowd in order to capture him. There had actually been two of them walking along the street, but one managed to get away and recount the disaster that had befallen the other. I knew that the captured man had arms and papers in his room which had to be cleared out immediately in the event of any untoward occurrence, as otherwise an infinitely greater disaster awaited us. Accordingly, I rushed straight away to one of the bunkers to fetch his friend who, residing in the same house and therefore known to the owners of the apartment, would no doubt be given access to the room. We proceeded with the utmost caution. First we made sure that the police had not already crept in and prepared a trap for us. Anyhow, we managed on that day to salvage the arms and transfer them to a place of safety.

Looking back today, more than ten years later, over the activities of the pioneer resistance movement in Hungary, I am astonished myself at their scope and proportions. It must not be forgotten that the Jews were completely estranged from Zionism, *Eretz Israel* and active Zionist work. On the one hand, assimilationism was rampant, while on the other, the religious Jews, petrified in their orthodoxy, were strange to Zionism. As a result, Hungarian Jewry was at a loss during the days of the disaster. I still remember how angrily Nashka was driven away from the *Kehilla* in the Budapest Ghetto when she went there to offer them rescue papers. There was no link between the pioneer movements and the majority of Jews in the country, and the movements there grew and expanded mostly during the days of the disaster, which kindled the Hebrew pioneering flame in the hearts of the youth; but it was lacking in the active, fighting pioneer heritage. In these conditions, the achievements and range of the underground activities may well be wondered at.

STANISLAW KOHN

The Treblinka Revolt

Before I arrived at Treblinka, in other words before October 1, 1942, cases of rebellion on the part of Jews had been reported. Thus, for example, a Jewish youth from Warsaw who worked in one of the death companies, having seen his wife and child escorted to the gas chamber, attacked the S.S. man, Max Bill, with a knife and killed him on the spot. From that day the S.S. barracks bore the name of this Hitlerite "martyr." Neither the plate on the wall of the barracks nor the massacre of Jews after this attack deterred us. This episode encouraged us to fight and take our revenge. The Warsaw youth became our ideal.

A desire for revenge burned within us as we witnessed Hitler's extermination methods, and ripened each day and began to concretize into something precise, particularly from the moment when the fifty-year-old doctor, Choronzicki, of Warsaw, began to be active. The doctor worked in the camps as sanitation adviser, a task invented by the Germans to mock the humiliated victims even more vilely before despatching them to the gas chamber. He was a calm, cautious man who, on the surface, appeared very cold. He wandered around in his white apron with the sign of the Red Cross on his arm as in the olden days in his Warsaw consulting room, and seemed completely disinterested. But beneath his apron beat a warm Jewish heart, burning with desire for revenge.

After the infernal experiences of the day, the four instigators of the revolt met by night around his wooden bed and discussed the plans. Their first preoccupation was to get hold of dynamite and the necessary arms. These four men were the above-mentioned

Dr. Choronzicki, the Czech army officer Zielo, naturally a Jew, Korland from Warsaw and Lubling from Silesia. After a short time, when an enlargement of the organization committee was needed, we were joined by Leon Haberman, a Warsaw artisan; Salzberg, a hatter from Kielce; Marcus, a twenty-two-year-old youth from Warsaw and the Warsaw agronomist, Sudowicz. We could procure arms either inside or outside the camp, stealing them from the German and Ukrainian S.S. We tried both methods. We began to make a study of the camp armory and the headquarters barracks. But they were guarded by Germans and there was no means of entry. At first we thought of digging a subterranean passage, but this was difficult to carry out because of the continual danger of discovery. Then we decided at all costs to make a key to the armory. This could only be done, however, if one of us could approach the iron door. It was merely a question of waiting for the propitious moment.

An opportunity soon presented itself. Something broke the lock of the armory door and the Germans were obliged to have recourse to one of the Jewish mechanics in the camp.

The Germans took the greatest precautions. The door was carried out into the laboratory, but the mechanic managed to distract the attention of the German guard for a moment and took an impression of the key in cobbler's wax. After a few days our group received a key to the armory. We hid it with the greatest care, watching for a favorable opportunity to use it.

The task of acquiring weapons outside the camp was entrusted to Dr. Choronzicki. He managed to get in contact with a Ukrainian guard who consented, naturally for a large sum of money, to buy light arms. A few of our purchases were safely smuggled in, but then something happened which put an end to our supplies and cost the life of Dr. Choronzicki. On one occasion, when carrying a large sum of money destined for the guard, he met the camp vice commandant, S.S. *Untersturmführer* Franz, a bloody murderer notorious for his sadism. By pure chance he spotted the packet of banknotes peeping out of the doctor's apron.

"Here with the money," roared the S.S. man, suspecting that the doctor was planning to leave the camp. Choronzicki lost no time and attacked him with a knife, puncturing him in the neck. Franz managed to leap out of the window and to call for help. Choronzicki, well aware of the tortures that awaited him and the dangers that threatened the whole conspiracy, swiftly swallowed a large dose of poison which the conspirators always carried on their person. The S.S. men rushed up and tried to restore him in order to take their revenge, but in vain.

In this way the instigator of the revolt died, but his death did not put an end to the matter. On the contrary, it encouraged the others to continue.

If Dr. Choronzicki had been the instigator and the head, the title of Chief of Staff must be given to Captain Zielo. The participation of this well-trained soldier greatly facilitated the realization of a task which was both difficult and complicated. In difficult moments when many of us fell a prey to resignation and abandoned all hope of a revolt, Captain Zielo continued to encourage and to incite us to carry on. When he was transferred to another part of the camp, all the plans and decisions went to him for approval, notwithstanding the danger involved in this liaison.

Engineer Galewski of Lodz was chosen to replace Dr. Choronzicki, and he, too, dedicated himself to the cause with all his heart. He was a very cautious and reserved man, typical of many of those who proved useful to our cause.

The date of the revolt was postponed several times for various reasons. The first date was fixed in April 1943, while Dr. Choronzicki was still alive. And then the last transports of the Warsaw Jews were brought to Treblinka. From them we learned about the ghetto revolt. The Germans treated them with particular savagery; most of the trucks were full of corpses of ghetto combatants who had refused to leave the ghetto alive. Those who now arrived were no longer resigned and indifferent creatures like their predecessors.

The group decided that the hour for the revolt had arrived. In the camp were a number of so-called "court Jews," those who humiliated themselves in the service of the Germans. Some of them had a certain freedom of movement within the camp. At times they even found it possible to approach the armory. These privileged individuals were all very young. The command decided to entrust to these boys the task of expropriating a hundred hand grenades from the armory on the day of the revolt.

They proved to be well chosen for the task. Huberman, who worked in the German laundry, the shoe-black Marcus, and Jacek, a Hungarian boy of eighteen, managed to get a certain number of hand grenades. Exceptionally lithe and skillful, the fourteen-year-old boy, Salzberg, son of the above-mentioned leader, took a huge pile of S.S. uniforms as though they were being taken to the tailor, whereas the pockets of these uniforms were filled with hand grenades. The bombs had to be concealed and only appear at the last moment if the revolt was to succeed.

In the meantime our activities increased. Dr. Leichert Wengrow, chosen by the Nazis from a new batch of Jews to replace Dr. Choronzicki, eventually became a member of the committee. A Czech also joined us: Rudolf Masaryk, a relative of the late President of Czechoslovakia. He had refused to abandon his wife, a Jewess, and had accompanied her to Treblinka. Here he was among the privileged and was attached to a working party. With his own eyes he had seen his wife, who was pregnant, taken to the gas chamber. Masaryk became one of the most active members of the committee. We must also mention Rudek, the mechanic from Plok, who worked in the garage. His job was very important for our action because it was there that we hid the weapons.

Months of tension and waiting passed in this way. We looked death in the face. Thousands of men and women, completely nude, arrived daily in long files at the "Jewish State," as the Germans with their usual cynicism had christened the building which contained twelve gas chambers. *Untersturmführer* Franz continually made significant speeches in our presence: "The gas chambers will continue to function as long as a single Jew remains in the world."

The desire for revenge increased continuously. The terror-stricken eyes of the Jews being led to their death and thrust into the gas chamber called for revenge.

At last the leader, Galewski, gave the signal for the revolt. The date fixed was for Monday, August 2, 1943, at five o'clock in the afternoon. This was the plan of action: to lay an ambush for the chief murderers, to liquidate them, to disarm the warders, cut the telephone wires and then burn and destroy all the extermination plants so that they could never function again; to free the Poles from the detention camp of Treblinka a mile away, to join up with them and flee into the forest to organize a partisan band.

An atmosphere of great tension lay over the camp that Monday morning. The leaders needed all their efforts to calm people's spirits. Finally special inspectors came to see that the normal quota of work was carried out as usual in order not to arouse suspicion. Only the sixty people who had planned the coup knew the details. The activists were divided into two groups and as soon as the signal was given each group was to occupy the position assigned to it.

At one o'clock in the afternoon we got into file, as on every day, for the roll call, the last roll call in this camp because there was never to be another. But when the head of a group of workers, Galewski, told us that today work would finish an hour earlier than usual because *Scharführer* Rotner was going to Malkinia to bathe in the Bug, he winked his eye slightly as though alluding to the "bath" we had prepared for the Nazis.

At two o'clock in the afternoon the distribution of weapons began. Young Salzberg and the other boys searched their employers' huts for weapons and took them to the garage. It was very difficult to purloin the hand grenades from the armory. That day a pile of refuse was being removed from near the armory. This was very convenient but it disturbed the camp administrator, S.S. Miller, who had just arrived and wanted to sleep. The agronomist, Sudowicz, responsible for the garden, called on him with the excuse of making some decisions about plants. At the same time Marcus and Salzberg took up the carpets and beat them in front of the armory. The guards were obliged to move away for a while. At that moment the door of the armory was opened with our key and Jacek, the Hungarian boy, slipped inside, climbed onto the window sill at the end of the room, cut out a small square in the glass with a diamond and handed out the bombs and other weapons to Jacob Miller from Wlodzimierz Wolynski, who put them on his refuse cart. The arms were carried to the garage. This time the hand grenades acted as a spur.

Spirits grew agitated and no one could keep the secret. The leaders therefore decided to start the revolt an hour before the agreed time.

Punctually at four o'clock in the afternoon messages were sent to all groups with orders to assemble immediately in the garage to fetch their weapons. Rudck from Plotzk was responsible for the distribution.

Anyone coming to fetch weapons had to give the password, "Death," to which the reply was "Life." "Death-Life," "Death-Life!" Cries of enthusiasm arose as the long-hoped-for guns, revolvers and hand grenades were distributed. At the same time the chief murderers of the camp were attacked. Telephonic communication was cut and the watchtowers were set on fire with petrol. Captain Zielo attacked two S.S. guards with an ax and made his way to us to take over the command.

Near the garage stood a German armored car, but Rudek had

swiftly immobilized the engine. Now the car served as a lair from which to fire on the Germans. Our gunfire felled the *Sturmführer* Kurt Majdkur and other German dogs. The armory was taken by assault and the weapons distributed. We already had two hundred armed men. The others attacked the Germans with axes and spades.

We set fire to the gas chambers, burned the faked railway station with all the notices: Bailystok-Wolkowisk, Office, Tickets, Waiting Room, etc. We burned the barracks which bore the name of Max Bill.

The flames and the reports of the firing roused the Germans who began to arrive from all sides. S.S. and police arrived from Kosow, soldiers from the nearby airfield and finally a special section of the Warsaw S.S. Orders had been given to make for the neighboring forest. Most of our fighters fell but there were many German casualties. Very few of us survived.

SALOMEA HANNELL

Revolt

TRANSLATED FROM THE YIDDISH BY MOSHE SPIEGEL

In June 1942, a horrible "Action" occurred in Oustriki-Dolni. All the local Jews were rounded up. Half of them were killed and the others ran for cover to the woods. A few months later, the second and last "Action" took place. Several hundred townsmen were marched out to a deep ravine, and a Gestapo official addressed them thus: "Do you see how the sun is shining, and how wonderful the world is? But as for you, all of you are about to die!"

One child said a prayer for all the unfortunates. After the execution, the Jews remaining in the town were placed in railroad cars and deported to the death camp of Sobibor, near Vlodawa. The horrible journey lasted three days and three nights. Some of the deportees went out of their minds and many wished for a quick death. On one occasion, when a child was shot at a railway station, the other mothers envied the mother of the victim, because her child was already dead, whereas their children still had to face torture and finally death in the gas chambers. The captives paid two hundred zlotys for a handful of snow to cool their parched throats.

When the human cargo consisting of three thousand people reached its destination, the prisoners were stripped of all their pitiful belongings by the camp officials. Out of all that throng, but seven women and eighteen boys were chosen to be spared; all the others were doomed to death. The women were ushered into a barracks known as *Kasa,* where their heads were shaved and their clothes removed. They were handed tickets to the baths, as well as receipts for their clothes and shoes. The Gestapo men informed them that they would be given baths and deloused. In one instance, when something went wrong with the mechanism of the gas chambers, the naked unfortunates ran out, screaming.

The Germans asphyxiated their victims with chloric acid. The bodies were usually cremated at night. The workers in the camp used to welcome the arriving deportees with song. Ukrainian Fascists belabored their doomed victims with whips. The corpses were buried for a year, then their bones were disinterred and burned to ashes. Between January 17 and October 17, 1944, the concentration camp was administered by six hundred servants, among them a hundred and twenty women.

The day's activities started with a roll call at 5 A.M. On one occasion, two men had escaped, and twenty other prisoners were shot to death in reprisal. Five captives volunteered for the supreme sacrifice and the Gestapo selected the other fifteen. Following the roll call, each proceeded to his work detail, in the laundry, the tailor shop, the shoe repair shop, the carpentry shop, or some such department, under the supervision of the Gestapo and their Ukrainian henchmen. A man would be shot for stealing a piece of butter. Should some Gestapo member reward a captive with an extra morsel of food, another Nazi official made short shrift of the victim. The soup served for dinner was not edible. Certain tasks were assigned as punishment. For laxity on a job, one would be assigned to extra arduous chores, such as loading heavy rocks into railroad cars, and so on.

During the weeks prior to the revolt in Sobibor, we became aware that the camp was surrounded by soldiers, and heard considerable shooting. Somewhat later, the *Scharführer* informed us that a hundred and sixty were shot for attempting to escape. We knew that the latest action was a liquidation of the employees who had been attached to the crematorium for a rather long time.

Once three sealed railroad cars arrived in Sobibor. Those who went to unload them found all the prisoners dead. Among the corpses removed from the cars were women in childbirth whose babies, with umbilical cords uncut, were still breathing.

The Gestapo official, Nestringer, who supervised the asphyxiation of the unfortunates, would order a new group of victims, as soon as one group had been given the quietus. At that time the groups arriving were ever smaller in number. After arrival at the camp a few of each group would be left unharmed for a few days. They were urged to address letters to their relatives, telling of their welfare—only to be asphyxiated the following day.

Jews sometimes arrived in passenger cars, wearing their usual attire and carrying baggage, ignorant of the purpose for which they had been brought there. And when the stark truth dawned on them, they wondered in desperation why they had made no effort to escape before their arrival. From time to time there were attempts to escape from the camp. In June a group of Jewish workers from Holland were accused of plotting a revolt and were executed.

But it was only after the arrival of a transport of Russian Jews, among them the Jew Sabuda, that a serious revolt was planned. He selected five intelligent Jews to cooperate with him in the preparations. First of all, weapons had to be obtained; the girls succeeded in filching some from the camp's arsenal. Then Sabuda sought out the leaders of the various workshops, each of whom was to kill the Gestapo chief at his particular shop. The revolt began on March 14, at 3 P.M. Each workshop invited a Gestapo chief, under some pretext or other—and put him to death. At that crucial moment an armed German visitor chanced to enter one of the workshops and, coming upon two murdered Gestapo men, he ran out and sounded an alarm. One hundred and fifty captives managed to escape and hide in the woods; all the others were massacred. I along with a few girls succeeded in getting away through the barbed wire which had been cut. I did not encounter any of the Sobibor townsmen. Throughout the night I heard intermittent shooting. At dawn I trudged over to the village and, thanks to my non-Jewish appearance, was able to make my way to Cracow.

Appeal of the Jewish Fighting Organization to the Polish Population

TRANSLATED FROM THE YIDDISH BY MOSHE SPIEGEL

Poles, Citizens, Soldiers of Freedom!

Through the din of German cannon destroying our homes, the homes of our mothers, wives and children; through the noise of their machine-guns, seized by us in the fight against the German police and S.S. men; through the smoke of the fires and the blood of those murdered in the Warsaw Ghetto, we convey greetings to you.

We are aware that you have been witnessing with anguish and tears of compassion, with amazement and breathless anticipation the war we have been waging against the occupation forces during the past few days.

But you can have seen and will see every doorstep in the ghetto becoming a stronghold and remaining a fortress until the end. All of us may perish in the fight but we shall never surrender. We, as well as you, are burning with the desire to punish the enemy for all his crimes, with a desire for vengeance. It is a fight for our freedom as well as yours.

It is a fight for our human dignity and social and national honor, as well as yours.

We shall take vengeance for Oswiecim, Treblinka, Belzec and Maidanek!

Long live the comradeship of arms and blood of fighting Poland! Long live freedom!

Death to the murderous and criminal occupation forces!

Let us wage the life and death struggle against the German occupation forces until the very end!

JEWISH FIGHTING ORGANIZATION
April 23, 1943

SAMUEL ZYGELBOJM

The Conscience of the World

LETTER WRITTEN BY DEPUTY ZYGELBOJM BEFORE COMMITTING SUICIDE.

Samuel Zygelbojm was one of the leaders of the Bund and a very popular figure among the Warsaw Jews. In 1940 he managed to flee from Poland after the invasion. After spending some time in various non-occupied countries, and later in America, he reached London in 1942. There, as representative of the Polish Jews, he joined the National Polish Committee which eventually became the Polish Government-in-Exile. During his stay in London he did everything in his power to draw the attention of the world to the fate of the Jews under Nazi occupation, but was unable to obtain any reaction. The news which arrived from Warsaw of the revolt in the ghetto, and the ultimate phase of the extermination, led him to commit the extreme act of protest against the indifference of the Allied Governments to the fate which had overtaken his people. He took his life, explaining the motives of his suicide in a letter addressed to the Polish Government-in-Exile, which forwarded it to the British and American governments. It was the deliberate gesture of a strong man, a suicide of the most heroic nature. Zygelbojm rejected the comfortable existence of a politician in the diplomatic circles of the British capital to be united in death with the combatants of the ghetto.

With these, my last words, I address myself to you, the Polish Government, the Polish people, the Allied Governments and their peoples, and the conscience of the world.

News recently received from Poland informs us that the Germans are exterminating with unheard-of savagery the remaining Jews in that country. Behind the walls of the ghetto is taking place today the last act of a tragedy which has no parallel in the history of the human race. The responsibility for this crime—the assassination of the Jewish population in Poland—rests above all on the murderers themselves, but falls indirectly upon the whole human race, on the Allies and their governments, who so far have taken no firm steps to put a stop to these crimes. By their indifference to the killing of millions of hapless men, to the massacre of women and children, these countries have become accomplices of the assassins.

Furthermore, I must state that the Polish Government, although it has done a great deal to influence world public opinion, has not taken adequate measures to counter this atrocity which is taking place today in Poland.

Of the three and a half million Polish Jews (to whom must be added the 700,000 deported from the other countries) in April, 1943, there remained alive not more than 300,000 Jews according to news received from the head of the Bund organization and supplied by government representatives. And the extermination continues.

I cannot remain silent. I cannot live while the rest of the Jewish people in Poland, whom I represent, continue to be liquidated.

My companions of the Warsaw Ghetto fell in a last heroic battle with their weapons in their hands. I did not have the honor to die with them but I belong to them and to their common grave.

Let my death be an energetic cry of protest against the indifference of the world which witnesses the extermination of the Jewish people without taking any steps to prevent it. In our day and age human life is of little value; having failed to achieve success in my life, I hope that my death may jolt the indifference of those who, perhaps even in this extreme moment, could save the Jews who are still alive in Poland.

My life belongs to my people in Poland and that is why I am sacrificing it for them. May the handful of people who will survive out of the millions of Polish Jews achieve liberation in a world of liberty and socialist justice together with the Polish people.

I think that there will be a free Poland and that it is possible to achieve a world of justice. I am certain that the President of the Republic and the head of the government will pass on my words to all concerned. I am sure that the Polish Government will hasten to adopt the necessary political measures and will come to the aid of those who are still alive.

I take my leave of all those who have been dear to me and whom I have loved.

Samuel Zygelbojm

A Manifesto of the Jewish Resistance in Vilna

Offer armed resistance! Jews, defend yourselves with arms!

The German and Lithuanian executioners are at the gates of the ghetto. They have come to murder us! Soon they will lead you forth in groups through the ghetto door.

In the same way they carried away hundeds of us on the day of Yom Kippur. In the same way those with white, yellow and pink *Schein** were deported during the night. In this way our brothers, sisters, mothers, fathers and sons were taken away.

Tens of thousands of us were despatched. But we shall not go! We will not offer our heads to the butcher like sheep.

Jews, defend yourselves with arms!

Do not believe the false promises of the assassins or believe the words of the traitors.

Anyone who passes through the ghetto gate will go to Ponar!

And Ponar means death!

Jews, we have nothing to lose. Death will overtake us in any event. And who can still believe in survival when the murderer exterminates us with so much determination? The hand of the executioner will reach each man and woman. Flight and acts of cowardice will not save our lives.

Active resistance alone can save our lives and our honor.

Brothers! It is better to die in battle in the ghetto than to be

* Safe conduct passes. To deceive and bewilder the Jews, the Germans constantly changed the colors of the passes which were to have safeguarded them against deportation, always further limiting the number of persons entitled to them.

carried away to Ponar like sheep. And know this: Within the walls of the ghetto there are organized Jewish forces who will resist with weapons.

Support the revolt!

Do not take refuge or hide in the bunkers, for then you will fall into the hands of the murderers like rats.

Jewish people, go out into the squares. Anyone who has no weapons should take an ax, and he who has no ax should take a crowbar or a bludgeon!

For our ancestors!

For our murdered children!

Avenge Ponar!

Attack the murderers!

In every street, in every courtyard, in every house within and without the ghetto, attack these dogs!

Jews, we have nothing to lose! We shall save our lives only if we exterminate our assassins.

Long live liberty! Long live armed resistance! Death to the assassins!

The Commander of the F.P.A.

Vilna, the Ghetto, September 1, 1943.

MORDECAI ANILEWICZ'S LAST LETTER

The Last Wish of My Life Has Been Fulfilled

It is now clear to me that what took place exceeded all expectations. In our opposition to the Germans we did more than our strength allowed—but now our forces are waning. We are on the brink of extinction. We forced the Germans to retreat twice—but they returned stronger than before.

One of our groups held out for forty minutes; and another fought for about six hours. The mine which was laid in the area of the brush factory exploded as planned. Then we attacked the Germans and they suffered heavy casualties. Our losses were generally low. That is an accomplishment too. Z. fell, next to his machine-gun.

I feel that great things are happening and that this action which we have dared to take is of enormous value.

We have no choice but to go over to partisan methods of fighting as of today. Tonight, six fighting-groups are going out. They have two tasks—to reconnoitre the area and to capture weapons. Remember, "short-range weapons" are of no use to us. We employ them very rarely. We need many rifles, hand-grenades, machine-guns and explosives.

I cannot describe the conditions in which the Jews of the ghetto are now "living." Only a few exceptional individuals will be able to survive such suffering. The others will sooner or later die. Their fate is certain, even though thousands are trying to hide in cracks and rat holes. It is impossible to light a candle, for lack of air. Greetings to you who are outside. Perhaps a miracle will occur and we shall see each other again one of these days. It is extremely doubtful.

The last wish of my life has been fulfilled. Jewish self-defense

has become a fact. Jewish resistance and revenge have beco
alitics. I am happy to have been one of the first Jewish fighte
the ghetto.

Where will rescue come from?

MORDECAI ANILEWICZ
During the Revolt, 1943
Warsaw

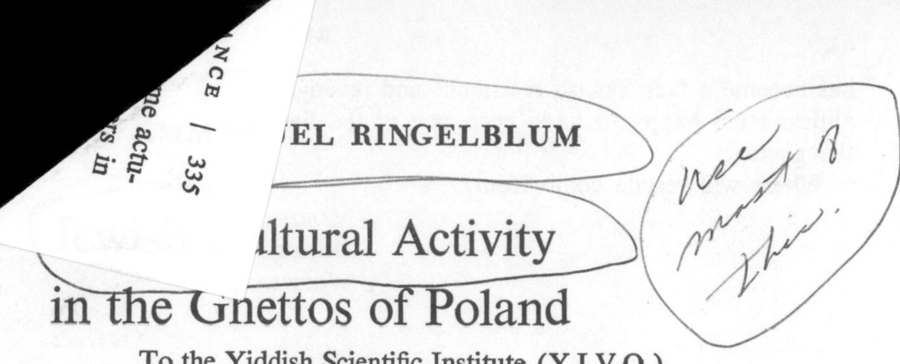

…EL RINGELBLUM

…ltural Activity in the Ghettos of Poland

To the Yiddish Scientific Institute (Y.I.V.O.)
To the Jewish Pen Club, to Sholom Asch, H. Leivick, Y. Opatoshu and R. Mahler

TRANSLATED FROM THE YIDDISH BY MOSHE SPIEGEL

Dear Friends:

We write at a time when 95 per cent of Polish Jewry has been wiped out, wiped out under savage torture, in the gas chambers and charnel houses of Treblinka, Sobibor, Chelmno and Oshpitzin or in the countless liquidations in the camps and ghettos. The fate of our people now painfully rotting in the concentration camps is similarly predetermined.

Perhaps a handful of Jews will survive to live a precarious existence in the Aryan sections of the cities or in the forest, hunted like beasts. It is gravely doubtful that any of us, the communal leaders, will survive the war, working under extremely hazardous conditions as we do.

When Polish Jews fell under the cruel yoke of the Nazis, the independent Jewish communal leadership began its widespread, far-reaching work, dedicated to self-help and resistance. With the active assistance of the "Joint," a colossal network of social welfare agencies arose in Warsaw and the hinterlands under the leadership of Z.H.T.O.S. [Society for Jewish Social Welfare], *Centos* [Central Shelter for Children and Orphans], and T.O.Z. [Society to Guard the Health of the Jewish Population]. O.R.T., too, was active. With the help of these organizations and their committees tens of thousands were able to prolong their lives. The work was kept up to the last, as long as the Jewish community showed a spark of life. Political parties and ideological groups were enabled to conduct their conspiratorial work in secrecy, and cultural activities were shielded.

The watchword of the Jewish social worker was, "Live and die with honor," a motto we endeavored to keep in the ghettos. It found its expression in the multi-faceted cultural program that grew in spite of the terror, hunger and deprivation. It grew until the very moment of the martyrdom of Polish Jewry.

As soon as the Warsaw Ghetto was sealed off, a subterranean organization, *Yikor* [Yiddish Cultural Organization] was established to conduct a wide program in Jewish culture. The program included scientific lectures, celebrations to honor Peretz, Sholom Aleichem, Mendele, Borochov and others, and projects in art and literature. The prime mover of *Yikor* was the young economist Menachem Linder, who was killed in 1942.

Under the mantle of *Centos* kitchens and children's homes there sprang up a network of underground schools representing varying shades of opinion: *Cisho, Tarbuth, Schulkult, Yavneh, Chorev, Beth Yaakov* and others. The secular schools were taught in Yiddish. These schools were established through the work of Shachna Zagan and Sonia Novogrudski, both of whom died at Treblinka.

A furtive central Jewish archive was formed under the deceptive title, "Society for Enjoyment of the Sabbath," by Dr. Emmanuel Ringelblum, who, in collaboration with [six names are mentioned here] gathered material and documents concerning the martyrdom of the Polish Jews. Thanks to the efforts of a large staff, about twenty trunkfuls of documents, diaries, photographs, remembrances and reports were collected. The material was buried in . . . , which even we could not enter. Most of the material sent abroad comes from the archive. We gave the world the most accurate information about the greatest crime in history. We are continuing our work on the archive, regardless of circumstances.

In 1941 and 1942 we were in contact with . . . in Vilna, who, under German control, managed to coordinate and conceal a good portion of the Y.I.V.O. documents. Today there are no Jews in Vilna. This once great center of Jewish culture and modern scientific research is in shambles.

But throughout almost the entire existence of the ghetto practically every Jewish organization participated in underground work, especially youth groups. We put out newspapers, magazines and anthologies. The most active groups in this work were the Bund, which published the "Bulletin," "Current Events," "Voice of Youth," *"Nowa Mlodziez," "Za Nasza i wasza Wolnosc"; Hashomer Hatzair,* which published *"Jutrznia Przewiosnie,"* "Upsurge," and a series of anthologies; Left *Poale Zion, "Nasze Haslo,"* "Proletarian Thought," "Call of Youth," "Vanguard"; Right *Poale Zion,* "Liberation"; *Dror, "Dror Yedios," "Hamadrich," "G'vura," "Pine";* the anti-Fascist bloc, "The Call;" the Communists, "Morning *Freiheit,"* and others. Some publications reached almost all other ghettos despite extreme difficulty in communications with Warsaw.

Centos, the central child care organization, led much activity among the children. Led by . . . and the unforgettable Rosa Simchovich (who died of typhoid contracted from street waifs), teachers, educators and artists, *Centos* founded a central children's library, a theater and classes in Yiddish language and literature. Thousands of adults joined in for "Children's Month," a program of cultural and artistic projects which provided a little happiness far from the hideous realism of their existence. Today there are no more Jewish children in Poland. Some 99 per cent were murdered by the Nazis.

The ghetto even had a symphonic orchestra, under Shimon Pullman. Its concerts and chamber music afforded us moments of relaxation and forgetfulness. Pullman and most of the other musicians perished at Treblinka along with violinist Ludwig Holzman. The young conductor Marion Noitich died at the Travniki camp.

A great deal of young talent was found in the ghetto. The daughter of a director of the Warsaw Synagogue, Marisha Eisenstadt, was called the "Nightingale of the Ghetto." She was killed during the liquidations. There were many choral groups, notably the children's chorus directed by Feivishes, who died at the Poniatow camp. Other choirmasters were Gladstein and Sax, among those who died at Treblinka. Jewish painters and sculptors, living in frightful poverty, organized occasional exhibits. Felix Friedman was one of the best; but they all died at Treblinka.

Our activities continued in the concentration camps. In Ponyatow, Treblinka and other camps we formed secret social societies and even arranged secret celebrations during holidays. Activity continued as long as there was life, in desperate struggling against the barbarism that imprisoned us.

When the deportations began our organizations turned to battle. The youths showed the way in Zionist organizations and all branches of the labor movement. Armed resistance began in Poland. We defended the Warsaw Ghetto and fought at Bialystock. We destroyed parts of Treblinka and Sobibor. We fought at Torne, Bendin and Czestochowa. We proved to the world that we could fight back, and we died with dignity.

That's what we wanted to tell you, dear friends. There are not many of us left. There are ten writers [names follow] we would like you to attempt to contact through the Red Cross; we don't know if they are still alive. Enclosed is a list of the dead who have helped in our work.

We doubt if we will see you again. Give our best to the builders of our culture, and to all who fight for human redemption.

Dr. E. Ringelblum

I Believe

INSCRIPTION ON THE WALLS OF A CELLAR IN COLOGNE, GERMANY, WHERE JEWS HID FROM NAZIS.

I believe in the sun even when it is not shining.

I believe in love even when feeling it not.

I believe in God even when He is silent.

On the Agenda: Death

A DOCUMENT OF THE JEWISH RESISTANCE

In February 1943, Mordecai Tannenbaum, an "inmate" of the Vilna Ghetto, was sent, with a few others, to organize the resistance in the ghetto of Bialystok. The reprint that follows is the record of a meeting held at the time by the executive committee of the Hehalutz, *organization of Palestinian pioneers, Bialystok branch. Six months later, Nazi troops entered the ghetto; they met with fierce resistance, which continued until the middle of September, when the Nazis "won" the battle of Bialystok. Among the estimated forty thousand Jews who fell in the battle was Mordecai Tannenbaum. The record of the meeting, originally in Yiddish, was preserved by a Polish peasant.*

MORDECAI: I'm glad that at least we're in a good mood. Unfortunately, the meeting won't be very gay; this meeting is historic or tragic, as you prefer, but certainly sad. The few people sitting here are the last *Halutzim* in Poland. We are entirely surrounded by the dead. You know what has happened in Warsaw: no one is left. The same is true of Bendin and Czestochowa, and probably everywhere else. We are the last. It's not a particularly pleasant feeling to be the last; on the contrary, it imposes a special responsibility on us. We have to decide what to do tomorrow. There is no point in sitting together in the warmth of our memories, and there is no point in waiting for death together, collectively. What shall we do?

We can do two things: decide that with the first Jew to be deported now from Bialystok, we start our counterattack, that from tomorrow on nobody is allowed to hide during the action. Everybody will be mobilized. We can see to it that not one German leaves the ghetto alive, that not one factory is left standing.

It is not out of the question that after we have finished our task some of us may even be still alive. But it must be a fight to the finish, till we fall.

Or we could decide to escape to the woods. We must consider the possibilities realistically. Two of our comrades were sent today to make a place ready; in any event, as soon as the meeting is over a military alert will be instituted. We must decide now, because our fathers can't do our worrying for us. This is an orphanage.

There is one condition: our approach must be based on an idea, and our thinking must be related to the movement. Whoever imagines or thinks that he has a real chance to stay alive, and wants to use his chance—fine, we'll help him in whatever way we can. Each one of us will have to decide for himself about his own life or death. But together we have to find a collective answer to the common question. I don't want to impose my opinion on anybody, so for the time being I won't express myself on the question.

ISAAC: What we're really debating is two different kinds of death. Attack means certain death. The other way means death two or three days later.

We ought to analyze both ways; perhaps something can be done. I don't have enough precise information, and I should like to hear the opinions of better informed comrades.

If comrades think that they could remain living, we ought to think about it.

HERSHL: It's still too early to strike a balance on everything we've lived through in the past year and a half. Nevertheless, in the light of the fateful decision confronting us, we must form a clear idea of what we have lived through.

Hundreds of thousands of Jews have perished in the last year; with great subtlety the enemy has succeded in demoralizing us and leading us like cattle to the slaughterhouses of Ponar, Chelmno, Belzec, and Treblinka. The extermination of the Jewish communities of Poland will be not only the most tragic but also the ugliest chapter in Jewish history, a chapter of Jewish impotence and cowardice. Even our movement has not always stood on the required high level. Instead of giving the signal for desperate resistance, we have everywhere put off making a decision. Even in Warsaw the resistance would have had a different result if it had been started not at the end but at the beginning of the liquidation.

Here in Bialystok it is our fate to live through the last act of the bloody tragedy. What can we do, what ought we do? The way I see it, this is the objective situation. The great majority of the ghetto, of our own family, have been sentenced to death. We are condemned. We have never looked on the woods as a hiding place; we have seen the woods as a base for combat and revenge. But the tens of young people now escaping to the woods are not seeking a battlefield; most of them are living a beggar's life and will doubtless find a beggar's death. In the conditions in which we now find ourselves, our fate would be to lead the same beggar's and vagrant's life.

Only one thing remains for us: to organize collective resistance in the ghetto, at any cost; to consider the ghetto our *Musa Dagh,* to write a proud chapter of Jewish Bialystok and our movement into history.

I can imagine how others would have reacted if their families had been subjected to what ours have been. The lowest gentile peasant would have spat on his own life, and stuck a knife into the guilty one. The only emotion dominating him would have been the thirst for revenge.

Our duty is clear: with the first Jew to be deported, we must begin our counteraction. If anyone succeeds in taking arms from the murderer and going into the woods—fine. A young person with weapons can find his place in the woods. We still have time to prepare the woods as a place for combat and revenge.

I have lost everything, all those near to me; still, there persists the desire to live. But there is no choice. If I thought that not only individuals could save themselves, but fifty or sixty per cent of the ghetto Jews, I would say that our decision should be to remain alive at any cost. But we are condemned to death.

SARAH: Comrades! If we are concerned about honor, we have long since lost it. In most of the Jewish communities the extermination activities were carried out smoothly, without counteraction. It is better to remain living than to kill five Germans. In a counteraction we will all die, without any possible doubt. On the other hand, in the woods forty or fifty per cent of our people can be saved. That will be our honor and that will be our history. We are still needed; we shall yet be of use. Since in any event we do no longer have honor, let it be our duty to remain alive.

ENOCH: No illusions! We have nothing to expect but liquidation to the last Jew. We have a choice of two kinds of death. The woods won't save us, and certainly rebellion in the ghetto won't. There remains for us only to die honorably.

The prospects for our resistance are not good. I don't know whether we have adequate means for combat. It's the fault of all of us that our means are so small, but that's water over the dam—we'll have to use what we have. Bialystok will be liquidated completely, like all the other Jewish cities.

In the first operation the factories were spared, but no one can believe that the Nazis will let them go this time.

It is obvious that the woods offer greater opportunities for revenge, but we must not go there to live on the mercy of peasants, to buy our food and lives for money. Going to the woods should mean going to become active partisans, but that requires arms.

The weapons we have aren't suited to the woods. If we do have enough time left, we should acquire arms and go to the woods.

But if the Nazi action intervenes, we must answer as soon as they touch the first Jew.

CHAIM: There are no Jews left, there are only remnants. There is no point in talking about honor; if we can, we must try to save ourselves, and not worry how we'll be judged. We must hide in the woods, and maintain systematic communication among the comrades.

MORDECAI: If we wanted to hard enough, and made up our minds that it was our duty, we could make sure our people were safe to the very end, as long as there were any Jews left in Bialystok. I ask an extreme question: do the comrades who are for the woods propose that we should hide and not react at the next Nazi action, so that we can escape into the woods later?

(VOICES FROM ALL SIDES: NO, NO!)

There are two opinions, one represented by Sarah and Chaim, and the other by Hershl and Enoch. Make your choice. One thing is sure—we won't go to the factories and pray to God that the Nazis catch the people who have hidden, so that we can be saved. And we won't watch passively from our factory windows when comrades from another factory are led away.

We can have a vote: Hershl or Chaim.

FANYA (of the Branch): I agree with Enoch. We have to choose between one big action here, or a series of much smaller actions, which in the end will have a much greater significance—I mean escaping into the woods. Because we aren't sufficiently well equipped and don't have the opportunity to go to the woods, and because the situation is very tense, we must emphasize counteraction right here; as soon as the first Jew is seized for deportation, we must attack with all our strength.

But if nothing happens for a few more weeks, we must make every effort to leave.

ELIEZER SUCHANITZKY (of the Branch): Comrades! I think it would be wrong for us to try to work in two directions at the same time. Taking to the woods is a good idea; it gives us some chance to remain alive. But at the present moment, when action is so imminent, going to the woods is an illusion. Even if we have another three or four weeks, we won't be able to assemble all the necessary material and take it with us.

I think there is only one thing for us to do: to answer a Nazi action with our counteraction. I think we should work only this line, so that we can give the most forceful possible answer with the limited means at our disposal.

JOCHEBED: Why is there all this talk about death? It isn't natural. Even a soldier at the front, or a partisan in the woods, in the greatest danger, keeps on thinking about life.

We know what the situation is, but why frighten everybody with all this talk about death? If that's what we should do, let's take to the woods, or remain here and fight it out. That doesn't mean that we must necessarily be killed. Everything we've been saying here is opposed to our most basic instincts.

CHAIM: I don't agree with Jochebed. We must be consistent, we dare not give anyone the moral dispensation to run away. This will be for keeps, not for fun. When we fight, it will have to be to the last. And to fight means to be killed. I think we would be accomplishing more if we remained alive, by taking to the woods.

[He suggests setting up a base outside the ghetto, so that sabotage can be carried on inside the city even after the Nazis act.]

MOSES: In the order of importance, the counteraction comes first; then, if possible, organization of partisan activity in the woods. Everyone here, without exception, should speak his mind, because the lives of all the comrades depend on the decisions made at this meeting. If necessary, let the meeting last until morning.

CHAIM: You want everybody to speak so the meeting should decide against counteraction in the ghetto. (*PROTEST*).

DORKE (of the Branch): I think our position must be the position of people in a movement, of people with full consciousness of what they're doing, who know what has happened to our nearest relatives and friends.

We will die a worthy death. The chances for revenge are greater in the woods, but we cannot go there as vagrants, only as active partisans. Since the necessary preparation for the woods is impossible now, we must devote all our energy to the counteraction.

ZIPPORAH: It's hard to say anything, it's hard to choose the manner of your own death. There's a kind of argument going on inside me between life and death. It's not important for me whether I or somebody else will remain alive. After what we have lived through and seen with our own eyes, we shouldn't have too high a notion of the value of our lives. I am trying to think a little more deeply of the question of our movement.

We're proud of the fact that our movement lived through the most difficult period in the history of the Jewish community in Poland. I was brought here from Vilna, and so were many others. There were certainly more important people to save. It wasn't I who was brought here, and it wasn't you; it was the movement. Now the question has been posed: will the movement be destroyed entirely? Does the movement have the right to be destroyed? We are a movement of the Jewish people; we must, and we do in fact, undergo all the sorrows and persecutions of the people.

When we consider the right to stay alive, I say yes, we have every right. Perhaps our movement may have to be the only one to speak up, when that is needed. Take the example of Warsaw. That was certainly a proud and manly death, but it wasn't the kind of thing a movement should do.

The decision of a movement should be to remain alive.

I don't mean we should hold on to life for its own sake, but for continued work, for extending the chain that was not broken even in the darkest days.

Our chances are as small as they can be, but if we put everything we have into our effort, we can succeed.

SHMULIK: This is the first time we have had to hold a meeting about death. We are going to undertake our counteraction not to write history, but to die an honorable death, as young Jews in our times should. And if our history is ever written, it will be different from the history of the Spanish Jews, who leaped into the flames with "Hear, O Israel!" on their lips.

Now, as to the action. All our experience teaches us that we can't trust the Germans, in spite of their assurances that the artisans will be protected, that only those who don't work will be deported, and so on. They have succeeded in driving thousands of Jews to the slaughter only by deception and demoralization.

And yet we have a chance to come out of the impending action safely. Everyone is playing for time, and so should we. In the short time that remains, we can work to improve our small and impoverished store of weapons.

We should also do what we can about the woods, where we can fulfill two functions.

I don't want to be misunderstood. We shouldn't interpret our hiding while the action is taking place as cowardice.

No! Man's instinct for life is so great, and here we must be selfish. I don't care if others are deported in our place. We have a greater claim on life than others, rightly.

We have set an aim in life for ourselves—to remain living at any cost! We were brought here from Vilna because there was a smell of liquidation there, and living witnesses had to remain. We must therefore do everything we can, if there is no liquidation immediately, to wait and gain time.

But if the liquidation starts now, then let it be all of us together in the counteraction, and "let me die with the Philistines."

SARAH: I want the comrades to know that I will do whatever is decided. But I'm amazed by the calmness with which we're talking about all this.

When I see a German, I begin to tremble all over. I don't know whether the comrades, and especially the girls, will have enough strength and courage. I said what I said before because I don't have any faith in my own strength.

EZEKIEL: I don't agree with Sarah. In the face of death you can become weak and powerless, or you can become very strong, since there is nothing to lose. I agree with Shmulik that we should begin our counteraction only in the event of a definite liquidation.

ETHEL: Concretely—if an action is started in the next few days, then our only choice can be a counteraction; but if we are granted more time, we should work along the lines of taking to the woods.

I hope I can be equal to the duties that will be imposed on us. It may be that in the course of events I shall be strengthened. In any case, I am resolved to do everything that needs to be done.

Hershl spoke rightly. We are going to perform a desperate act, whether we want to or not. Our fate is sealed, and there remains for us only the choice between one kind of death and another. I am calm.

MORDECAI: The position of the comrades is clear. We will do everything we can to help as many people as possible escape into the woods for partisan combat. Every one of us who is in the ghetto when the Nazis start their action must react as soon as the first Jew is seized for deportation. We are not going to haggle about our lives; we must understand objective conditions.

The most important thing is this: to maintain until the very end the pride and dignity of the movement.

HIRSH GLICK

Jewish Partisan Song

TRANSLATED FROM THE YIDDISH BY AARON KRAMER

Never say that there is only death for you
Though leaden skies may be concealing days of blue—
Because the hour we have hungered for is near;
Beneath our tread the earth shall tremble: We are here!

From land of palm-tree to the far-off land of snow
We shall be coming with our torment and our woe,
And everywhere our blood has sunk into the earth
Shall our bravery, our vigor blossom forth!

We'll have the morning sun to set our day aglow,
And all our yesterdays shall vanish with the foe,
And if the time is long before the sun appears,
Then let this song go like a signal through the years.

This song was written with our blood and not with lead;
It's not song that birds sing overhead,
It was a people, among toppling barricades,
That sang this song of ours with pistols and grenades.

So never say that there is only death for you.
Leaden skies may be concealing days of blue—
Yet the hour we have hungered for is near;
Beneath our tread the earth shall tremble: We are here!

Captain Jaquel's Story

The fullest evidence which we have about the activities of the Jewish underground in France during the Nazi conquest is that of Jacquest Lazarus, known by his nickname, Captain Jacquel, who was the head of the Paris group of the Jewish Combat Organization [*Organisation Juive de Combat*].

In February 1943, Jacquel tried to escape from France and join the Free French Forces which were being organized in England. He considered himself as a Frenchman in all respects, and thought of France as his homeland—but in the previous few months he no longer recognized his country. Two desires struggled within him—the desire to remain in France, no matter what, and the desire to join the French Forces taking shape outside the country. He had been in the French army for six years, was an assimilationist, and thought that Jews who took offense when anti-Semitic remarks were made were being oversensitive. When the first anti-Jewish laws were passed, he was also asked to fill in a questionnaire about his origin, and did so without hesitation. He did not imagine that it would have serious consequences. He even asked the Commissariat for Jewish Affairs to be allowed to remain in the army. Several of his ancestors had been in the army also, and had even distinguished themselves in battle. But to no avail. In August 1941, Jacquel was discharged from the army. His fellow-soldiers commiserated with him; his officers were apathetic.

Jacquel went to St. Etienne, to his sister. He worked as an insurance agent for six months. Then he was forbidden to work at this profession, since he was a Jew. Soon after this, he found himself a job in a bank. He knew of the existence of the underground, and even had some weak connections, but deep in his heart, he objected to "irresponsible acts." On the 11th of November, 1942, he woke up. The Germans broke the terms of the armistice agreement and began to persecute Jews and send them to concentration camps, and the Vichy French Government even gave up Jews from the unoccupied French area. He began to make a serious accounting of his position. He was advised to escape to Switzerland, but he refused. For a time, he sought a way to reach North Africa and join the Free French Forces there. In the train, on the way to Perpignan, he met his childhood friend, Ernest, who influenced him to change his course. Ernest proved to him that a brave Jew could do much inside France as well.

Ernest introduced him to a young woman, Anne-Marie, and thus he came in contact with one of the cells of the autonomous Jewish underground organization. One month later, Jacquel was a member of the Jewish Armed Forces [*Forces Armées Juives*], which in the course of time became the Jewish Combat Organization.

This "Jewish Army" had arisen in Toulouse during the first few months after the armistice agreement. Its spiritual father was David Kanot, a Russian Jewish emigré poet. The establishment of the Jewish organization encountered many more difficulties than that of underground non-Jewish organizations, since the latter could hide behind some official front, while the Jews were persecuted, discriminated against, watched, and, in general, severely limited.

At first, the organization was concerned only with aid and rescue. After the expulsion of July 1940, Toulouse became the capital of the South. Many Jews arrived there. On 24th August, 1942, the expulsion of Jews who had come to France after 1936 began. That was the time for the organization to begin to work. It was decided to expand the organization, to increase the smuggling of Jews to Spain and Switzerland, to improve the intelligence service and the forging of documents, and to maintain a department for the housing of homeless Jews. At that time, many people joined the organization and swore their oaths of loyalty and obedience. The secrecy, the devotion and the discipline were exemplary. There was not one case of betrayal by a member of the organization. Provocateurs and spies were unable to penetrate into the organization at all. Those of its members who fell into the hands of the Gestapo did not betray their comrades, even under the most terrible tortures.

After Captain Jaquel had been sworn in, about two months passed before he was called up. He was given the task of organizing youths of under-army-age, who were in the Italian-occupied part of France.

The aim was to train them, so that later on they could form groups and spread out all over France, in every city and town of any importance. The Italian-occupied area was chosen for two reasons: there was a large number of Jews there and the Italians behaved very tolerantly to the Jews. They did not carry out the Germans' orders, and prevented by force the execution of the Vichy Government's order to hand foreign Jews over to the Germans. The first group was organized in Grenoble, and Captain Jaquel began to train its members.

In Grenoble, Jaquel worked at his former "profession" as an insurance agent. In the meantime, he made contact with two young men, ex-students, who became the pillars of the local underground organization. There he became acquainted with the members of the Zionist youth movements, who asked him to train them in the use of weapons. But trouble soon came. The Germans conquered the whole of the Italian area. A reign of terror began in Nice. Mila Racine, who smuggled old people and children into Switzerland, was caught, together with a member of the organization, Roland. The Germans, after they had turned the small town, Vercourt, into scorched earth, burnt Challais, which had served as a hideout and a training-place for the underground organization.

Jaquel continued to meet with a small group of people and taught them the elements of topography and the principles of fighting and field organization. They would often go into the country and do practical exercises in the use of weapons and topography.

Jaquel continued to travel about, in order to organize more underground groups. After some time, he had to change his identity and obtained false papers. Only then did his real life in the underground begin.

On the 8th of September, 1943, Italy signed an armistice. The Germans took the place of the Italians. Matters became much worse. Jews began to flee to Nice, which they considered as the last city of refuge on French soil. They came in trains and lorries, men, women and childen, the ill and the healthy. They created new problems. They had to be housed and fed. The youths who had been organized into the "Group of Nice" volunteered to carry out these tasks.

The Group in Nice

The Gestapo was not slow in appearing. They used to make sudden searches in restaurants, shops, homes, public institutions and in the boulevards. Every Jew who was caught was sent to Drancy, and from there to an extermination camp. The group in Nice was the only one which was at all active, and it rescued hundreds of people.

Its main activity consisted in the preparation of false documents. At first, the members of the group used to produce four hundred false identity-cards every night. Later on, with the aid of a printer, they managed to prepare thousands of birth-certificates, baptismal-certificates and identity-cards. Since it was difficult to procure the stamps necessary for their completion, many of these documents were sent to other parts of France for their final stages of preparation.

The girls used to rush around from house to house where whole families were hiding in most unsanitary conditions in fear of going out into the streets. They would bring them sugar, chocolate for the children, and food-cards, etc.

As a result of betrayal, several members of the organization were caught. It became more difficult to acquire arms. The girls had to help at that too. They maintained contact with Marseilles, and used to return from there with arms.

At the same time, an intelligence service was established, whose task it was to discover who was telling the Gestapo who their members were, and to find out facts about them in preparation for punishment.

It was necessary to discover the person and to familiarize oneself with his habits, in order to be able to choose the most suitable moment for his elimination. This work demanded great patience, and efforts were not always crowned with success. Once it was necessary to be in ambush for eleven days in order to catch the police chief on whom a death sentence had been passed.

According to the plan, the members of the organization had to mingle with the crowd: one group would identify the man and another would shoot him. For ten days they waited for him to appear and he did not. After the action, the members of the organization were supposed to mingle with the crowd again, and to begin to villify "those terrorists"—and to note the reaction.

The intelligence service also had a long list of people who collaborated with the organization without belonging to it.

One day at the beginning of October 1943, Jaquel was called to Toulouse for fifteen days. There he met Maurice Ferer, who gave him an important task—to train the first underground group

(Maquis) in the area. He went to the headquarters of the secret army in Tarne and received permission from the regional head to establish a Jewish underground group. The members were young people who had come from all over the country. Their hiding-place was a deserted farm near Albis. Jaquel was fearful that the large amount of traffic would draw attention, but to their great luck, it was the time of the annual fair, and no one noticed them. At the farm, there was a small armory of out-of-date weapons. Modern weapons were parachuted to them. The training was carried out in a comradely spirit, but the climate, the mud, etc. did not allow for large-scale exercises. After a fortnight, they returned to Toulouse.

In Grenoble, in the meantime, the difference between the Italian and the German occupation had begun to be felt. But the local underground movement did not sit with its arms folded. One day, the arms stores of Polygonyeux were blown up. The Germans panicked. They began to shoot at everyone they saw in the street. They feared that a general uprising had begun and that they were hemmed in. A curfew was established from midnight, but special permission to move about was given to those who could prove that because of their work they had to be in the street after twelve. In spite of that, two newspapermen were killed, two railwaymen and a baker who had not taken care and had gone to the door of his shop.

The Germans then established a curfew every day from 7 P.M. and on Sundays from 3 P.M. But it did not help. Three weeks later, a barrack was blown up. This was ascribed to Czech soldiers, who had been called to the German army. The underground became more daring. They began to shoot at German officers and militiamen. The Germans increased their repression: they forbade the use of bicycles after five. The curfew, which had been abolished, was reintroduced. All cinemas and coffee-houses were closed until further notice. German guards patrolled the streets at all hours of the night.

On 24th December, 1943, the Germans combed a large area. They encircled it and arrested all the men and women. The women were released, while the men were divided into Jews and non-Jews. The Jews were sent to extermination camps and the non-Jews to work camps. The searches continued, but the members of the Zionist movement did not despair. They continued their work, mainly social and the preparation of forged papers. With the aid of a printer, they were able to manufacture all kinds of documents—even work-cards and Gestapo documents.

There were two kinds of false documents. The first was documents prepared, not very thoroughly, with imaginary numbers and imaginary signatures of non-existent people. They were for people who were not in danger of being caught in a serious search. The other kind was called "synthetic" and was prepared with real details of town councils, etc. and could stand up to a thorough examination. The third way—used later—was called "reproduction"; that is, the details were copied in full from the real identity-card of a living person. In this manner, many Jews received "Aryan" French documents.

At the same time, people were being smuggled to Switzerland—especially Jews persecuted by the police, and children. The children were concentrated in groups of 20–30, in a school building in Nancy, until they were able to cross the border. After they had crossed the kilometer of no-man's-land they were well received by Swiss customs officers.

Arms for the Fighters

On 1st January, 1944, Jaquel left Grenoble and went to Lyon where there was an important branch of the Jewish underground quartered behind the front of a well-known newspaper stand. Most of the members would go there on their way from place to place, in between various "jobs." From there, orders went out all over France, and that was where all those who intended to reach North Africa and join the Free French Forces used to meet. Jaquel was told to organize the underground in Tarnes. Not far from Albis there were two abandoned farms and that was where the various groups began to train. The first group consisted of Jews who had come from Holland via Belgium. At first, they completely lacked arms, but a few days later arms arrived from Toulouse.

One evening, airplanes appeared and parachuted packages to them. However, they did not land near the underground's farm, but near another farm in the area, which was showing lights. Jaquel did not despair. He went there, and since the farmer was afraid he would be reported, he allowed Jaquel to remove the packages and the parachutes. In this way, the precious arms were saved. Jaquel gave the parachutes to farmers in the district, so as to ensure their silence—and took the parcels to the underground base.

In the meantime, the Germans had begun a reign of terror in the area of Nice. Bruner, head of the Drancy concentration camp, engaged in a Jew-hunt, aided by collaborators from among the White Russians who showed "physiognomic" abilities. Sergei Muzharov was at their head. The underground decided to do away with him. It was not simple. The man was cunning and careful. He knew that his death sentence had been passed by the secret court of the underground, and took all precautions. There was a German guard of thirty soldiers around his home. He hardly ever left the city. When he went to and from Gestapo headquarters, he was accompanied by his bodyguard. In spite of all that, it was decided to follow him and to wait for the opportunity to carry out the sentence.

One day, Muzharov left his house alone, and rode away on his motorcycle. Here is the full story as told by Jaquel himself:

"Our people were four in number. Roget and Ernest were in front, ready for action. Raymond stood behind them to cover them, and Marc was a long way from them near the railway crossing. He had to 'deal' with Muzharov if the latter should manage to escape, or to tell if the road was not clear. Not far away, in the fields, peasants were working.

"Muzharov arrived. He saw Ernest and Roget before him and realized immediately what was going on. He quickly tried to escape—but it was too late. He was struck by five revolver bullets. He continued on his motorcycle. He was out of range. The farmers came closer. Ernest and Roget slipped away. Half an hour later, they met Marc, and he told them the rest of the story.

"Muzharov was hit but did not fall. He managed to go another two hundred yards, in a zig-zag. When Marc saw him dripping blood, he went up to him. The farmers and passers-by also came forward to him. Muzharov began to scream, "Terrorists! Terrorists!" Marc tried to shoot him—but in the meantime German soldiers had arrived. Marc then coolly supported Muzharov—helped him to stand, and said, "You are wounded: my poor friend." The German soldiers did not know what was going on before their eyes. Marc told them of a terrorist attack on Muzharov and pointed in the wrong direction. He told them that Muzharov had to be taken to a hospital immediately. . . ."

Muzharov did not die; but he ceased his activities. Many of the people who worked for him left Nice the following day. His second-in-command took his place—Georges Karakayeff.

The underground began to deal with him too—but it quickly became clear that it would be very difficult. The intelligence branch could discover no "habits." But the opportunity to kill him occurred by chance. One day a small accident took place. A girl, a member of the underground, while riding her bicycle in the Boulevard de Victor Hugo, was struck by a man on another bicycle and fell. The man apologized politely and smiled. He fancied the girl. She, for her part, sensed that he was a Gestapo agent. When he asked her to meet him in a café, she agreed. She then ran and told her friends in the organization.

At the appointed time, she entered the café, while her friends were waiting outside. She met him and agreed to spend the day with him but said that she first had to run a message for her mother. She arranged to meet him later—but Karakayeff decided to accompany her. They rode out of the city on their bicycles. Robert followed them, also on his bicycle. When they were alone, he drew his pistol and fired two shots. Karakayeff did not fall. He pulled his pistol out and tried to shoot Robert: but Robert was faster than he and shot him twice in the head. Karakayeff's body was found later at the crossroads near his bicycle.

Members of the Jewish underground used to wear the Star of David on their shoulders. This was their answer to the German order according to which all Jews had to wear the yellow patch. They wanted to demonstrate that they were fighting the Nazis as Jews.

THE
NON-JEWS

THE NON-JEWS

The Jews who lived on the Aryan side were exposed to special kinds of danger, and were constantly in peril. They could be recognized by former friends; carelessness might arouse suspicion of German officials or collaborators; they were persecuted by underworld characters who blackmailed them and then betrayed them to the Nazis.

Some of them had Aryan papers—false documents. Many had no such identification and were compelled to play the role of Catholics by speaking fluent Polish and having "good" features. Sometimes Aryan papers were obtained for huge sums, but many were forged by the underground, and held by members of the Jewish Socialist and Nationalist organizations who were active during the occupation and maintained contact with the Polish anti-Nazi underground.

This chapter in the struggle for survival is marked by extraordinary heroism in the face of treachery and brutality. It is illuminated by shining examples of humaneness, idealism, and even self-sacrifice by Polish intellectuals, priests, laborers, and plain people.

SOFIA NALKOWSKA

At the Railroad Tracks

TRANSLATED FROM THE YIDDISH BY MOSHE SPIEGEL

At the break of day, the woman with the crippled knee sat on the moist grass, beside the railroad track. Someone nearby managed to escape; another lay motionless at some distance, beyond the forest. A few more got away; two were mowed down. Only she lingered on, neither dead nor alive.

When he stumbled upon her, she was alone, but gradually other people appeared in this lonely spot. Workingmen, women, and a young lad, they approached from the direction of the brickyard and the village, then halted apprehensively, and scanned the scene from a distance.

Every now and then, a knot of people assembled, looked about uneasily, and then departed. They spoke in whispers, sighed, huddled together and were on their way. What had happened was clear enough. Her curly, crow-black hair was dishevelled; her eyes beneath the half-closed lids were glazed. No one spoke to her except when she asked if those lying sprawled out beyond the woodland were dead; they answered, "Yes."

Day was breaking; she sat in an open space, visible from a distance. News of the tragedy spread. It was a time when terror gripped every heart, and when anyone lending a hand to a victim was subject to the death penalty.

A younger man who had lingered longer than the others trudged off a few paces, then retraced his steps. She asked him to get her some veronal from the druggist, and offered him money, but he refused.

She lay prostrate with closed eyes for awhile. Then she sat up, moved her leg, hugging the knee to her body, and then covering it with her skirt. Her hands were bloody as she moved them from her knee. The death sentence that lurked in the shattered joint was like a spike that impaled her to the earth. She lay quiet for a time, her dark eyes closed. When she finally opened them, she became aware of new faces—and of the young man, who was still there. She begged him to buy her whisky and cigarettes. This time he didn't say no.

The group assembled in the clearing on the hill attracted attention, and others joined it. The woman lay prostrate, in full view of the onlookers, like an injured animal that the hunter has injured but failed to kill. She lay there, drunk now and dozing, looking to no one for help.

Before long, an old peasant woman who had trudged away, came back; panting, she unwrapped a small can of milk and some bread from a kerchief and thrust them into the hand of the prostrate girl. As she walked away, she glanced back to see whether the injured woman would rouse herself and eat. But when she caught sight of two policemen approaching, she covered her head with her kerchief and quickly disappeared. The others trudged off, too. Only the gallant young man who had brought the whisky and cigarettes lingered on. But she asked nothing more from him.

The policemen took in the situation and began a whispered discussion. She begged them in a weak voice to shoot her instead of turning her over to the enemy. They hesitated for awhile and then started away. After a few steps they paused, evidently undecided what to do. But they finally went away without carrying out her request. The young man tried to light a cigarette for her, but his lighter refused to work. He then told her that one of the two men lying dead beyond the woods was her husband. His voice was husky with pity as he uttered the sad words.

She tried to drink a little milk but was too weak.

It was a cold, windy spring day. A few cottages were scattered along the opposite side of the barren field. Some small scraggy pines swept the sky with their needles. The woodland into which she longed to escape was situated beyond the railroad tracks. This patch of wasteland was her whole world now.

The young man, who had gone away, now returned. She took another sip of liquor and lit a cigarette. A soft semidarkness, spreading from the east, veiled the sky; and from the west clouds billowed upward.

Other spectators, homeward bound workers, stopped at the scene and learned of the tragedy. They conversed in loud tones, as though she could not hear them—as though she were already dead.

"The dead man over there is her husband," a woman remarked. "They escaped from the train toward the woods, but were shot. She was hit in the knee, and could not run any farther.

"If it had happened in the woods, we could move her easily," chimed in the old peasant woman who had come back for her tin can, as she looked sadly at the milk spilled on the grass. "But with people watching we don't dare do a thing."

Thus it was that no one was willing to move her before dark, or call a doctor, or get her to the railroad station from which she could be transported to a hospital. The inhabitants were not prepared to cope with such an unforseen tragedy. And so it was just a matter of her dying—one way or another.

When she opened her eyes again at dusk, the two policemen had returned, and the young man still lingered on. She begged again to be shot, though she did not dare hope that they would do so. But she covered her eyes, so as not to watch whatever might befall.

The policemen conferred again on what to do, each urging the other to carry out the stricken woman's pathetic request.

"Then, let me do it," the young man said.

After some further argument, from the corner of her eye she saw one of the policemen take his revolver from its holster and hand it to the stranger.

The people still lingering at a distance, watched as the young man bent over her. A shot rang out. As the people turned sadly away, someone said, "It would have been better if we had called for help. To shoot her like a dog. . . ."

Under cover of darkness, two men came from the woods to remove her. Not knowing of the young man's action, they at first thought she was asleep, but realized that she was dead when they started to lift her.

She lay there until noon of the following day, when the village bailiff and other men arrived and ordered her buried, together with the other two who lay dead along the railroad tracks.

"But why did he shoot her? That's what puzzles me," the man who reported the incident to the authorities wondered aloud. Then from someone came the answer, "There is such a thing as compassion."

"WLADKA" (FEYGL PELTL-MIEDZYRZECKI)

Polish Friends

TRANSLATED FROM THE YIDDISH BY MOSHE SPIEGEL

It would not be right to suppose that all the gentile Poles with whom we were in contact were unreliable people, provocateurs, or mere mercenaries at best. True, most of the gentiles with whom we dealt accepted money for the least service rendered. But not a few of them were kindhearted, with much sympathy for our tribulations. There were even some who risked their lives to rescue Jews from danger.

Even though their number was few, it must be acknowledged that without the cooperation of this handful of friendly gentiles, we, the members of the Jewish underground who carried out our work outside of the ghetto, could not have accomplished much. At crucial moments, in times of great risk, these friends enabled us to carry out our important missions.

I have previously mentioned the part played in our misfortune by Polish villains, informers, and provocateurs, as well as by the indifferent majority of the Polish population. Therefore, I am duty-bound to refer as well to those who stretched forth a helping hand to us then. I shall mention only a few of these, with whom I was in close contact.

Wand Wnorowska was one of the first gentiles with whom I had anything to do after I left the ghetto. The widow of a Polish officer, she was in her forties, a gentle aristocrat, and a member of the so-called better Polish society. She ran a ladies' tailoring establishment, and I found employment with her as soon as I crossed to the Aryan side. To have a job and warm quarters during the winter was good in itself and an important camouflage for my underground work.

When I was called upon to devote all my time to illegal activities, and therefore had to give up my job as a seamstress, the gentile Wanda gladly accepted in my place friends of mine who had just succeeded in getting out of the ghetto: Khautche Werktzeig-Elenbogen, Rivka Rosenshtein, Zoshka Kersh, Helenka and Bronka of Piotrkov. She welcomed them all warmly, paid them relatively good wages, and made every effort to ease their lot. Wanda soon made friends with her Jewish girl employees, took an interest in their hardships, and endeavored not only to give advice but to help them through her contacts with gentiles. She was gradually drawn into our little world, and became one of our confidantes.

The new quarters at 39 Vspulne to which Wanda had had to move had already become a clandestine rallying point for the Jews, frequented primarily by those who came from Piotrkov in various sorts of disguise. Wanda had an open hand as well as an open heart for everyone. The downtrodden and desperate came to seek her counsel and help. Whether it was living quarters, documents, or anything else that was needed, Wanda could usually find the right connection to solve the problem.

Whenever I appeared, Wanda would take me aside to discuss "her" poor Jews. This gentile woman would confer with me, insisting that more help must somehow be obtained for "her people." She could not comprehend the difficulties which limited the scope of action possible by us. One thing was uppermost in her mind: to render help to the needy.

I was the one who managed to transfer considerable sums of money from the underground organization to Wanda, and she, in turn distributed these funds in accordance with our instructions. She never wanted anything for herself. When we offered her money to ease her own strained circumstances, she felt offended and refused to accept the offer.

"You are in more trouble than I am," she would answer modestly.

She was most happy on her birthday, when her house overflowed with flowers from her Jewish friends. Proudly she pointed to the various bouquets and showed the notes attached to them. That was the only compensation this splendid woman would take from us.

Juliana Larish, a young gentile girl who before the war had

worked as a bookkeeper for the Jewish family of Zilberberg in Prague, was another Polish "woman of righteousness."

When the deportations to concentration camps began in the ghetto, some Jews turned for help to their gentile friends of former days. And the kindhearted Miss Larish responded. Moving with caution, she succeeded in enabling twenty-one of her Jewish friends to escape from the ghetto. She concealed ten Jews in her own house at 7 Bzeske; she sent a three-year-old little girl named Iza Blokhowitz to a friendly Polish family in Radzimin; and one Jewish woman with Aryan features was put up in a newly bought house.

Juliana had a thriving meat supply business, and most of its profits went to Jews in hiding. She provided them not only with a refuge but also with such things as clothes and books. This gracious woman was constantly preoccupied with Jewish affairs, running from one secret hiding place to another as she endeavored to lighten the burden of the unfortunate. She helped them observe the Jewish holy days, and even lent a hand in baking the *matzoth* for Passover!

To distract the attention of her neighbors from the huge baskets of provisions she provided for those in hiding, Juliana began frequently to invite her Polish and German customers in for a snack. This brought the respect of the neighbors who observed her from the courtyard.

Through the thin walls of their hideouts, the Jews used to eavesdrop on German conversations, occasionally overhearing venomous anti-Semitic remarks.

In this way weeks and months went by, and everything seemed to be going smoothly. Then, one early morning, the German police knocked on Juliana Larish's door at 7 Bzeske. Fortunately the Jews in hiding managed to conceal themselves in time.

Juliana's courage and presence of mind were admirable. She slipped away from the gendarmes on some pretext, and contrived to telephone her friend of the imminent danger. Thus no incriminating evidence was found there when the police burst in. Later, Juliana learned that her own employees had denounced her to the authorities. Undismayed by the police raid, she continued her work of mercy until the end of the war, sheltering the refugees until new places of concealment could be found for them.

I used to make the rounds of all of Juliana's hideouts, supplying the Jews there with forged documents. Of the hidden Jews, twenty-one survived: three of the Blokhowitz family, three of the Zifferman family, four of the Zilberbergs, four of the Miendzizhetski, three of the Goldsteins, and four of the "Hotel Polski" group.

The gentile Pero, a middle-aged clerk in a Polish hotel on Marskalkovska Street, was another hero. Through a Jewish woman named Malie Piotrkovska and her thirteen-year-old daughter, Bronka, he became our ally.

The extent of his generosity is attested by the harrowing story related to me by Mrs. Piotrkovska, who came from Lodz. Compelled to leave her hideout at 36 Krochmalnia in broad daylight, Mrs. Piotrkovska, who could not pass for an Aryan, wandered about with her daughter in search of lodging for the night.

At one point a group of gentile youngsters had recognized poor Mrs. Piotrkovska as a Jewess, for they pursued her with shouts of *"Zhidowa, Zhidowa!"* (Jews, Jews).

When they tried to snatch her pocketbook, she started to run. The Polish police then took the woman and her daughter into custody and brought them to the German authorities.

It now seemed clear to the mother and the daughter that their doom was sealed. The fate of every Jew who fell into the clutches of the Germans was well known. But since the Piotrkovskas possessed false documents attesting to their antecedents, they decided to play the role of gentiles, even if their cause was a lost one anyhow. They were interrogated about their origin and about their knowledge of Christian prayers, customs, and so on. The daughter replied accurately, but the mother fumbled. The German examiners were at a loss, but they suspected the two of being Jewish. The accused were jailed overnight, and were told that they must produce a Pole who would vouch for having known them as Christians before the war—or else they would be liquidated.

Pero was the only Polish friend the Piotrkovskas had who might be able to save them. It was evening. There was no telephone in Pero's home. He had to be reached by phone at the place where he worked. And there was no guarantee that he would care to risk his life on their behalf. He could be put to death if he perjured himself for them. However, to reach him was their last chance—their only hope!

They racked their brains for the telephone number of Pero's employer, and at last they remembered it. Now everything depended on whether Pero would stand by them. The authorities of the

German headquarters telephoned Pero to learn whether he knew Frau Piotrkovska and her daughter. They were suspected of being Jewish—an accusation which they denied. Could he vouch for them? If so, he was to report in the morning for questioning.

Mother and daughter await Pero with shuddering hearts. Will he dare come? He arrives at last, and is subjected to interrogation. Pero sticks to his guns, maintaining that he has known the Piotrkovskas as Christians since some time before the war began. The Germans remind him that perjury is punishable by death. In his flawless German Pero assures them he would take no such risk, again asserts that the Piotrkovskas are good Christians, and at last convinces the dubious officials. The accused women are cleared, and the authorities actually apologize to them for the trumped-up charge. The interrogators urge Frau Piotrkovska, in the event of future inconvenience, to report to the German authorities, since the accusation of being Jewish is no trifling matter!

Though his own home was under surveillance, Pero then let the Piotrkovskas stay with him. Later we even persuaded him to give shelter to still other Jews. He cooperated with us until the very end.

All the Jews who found asylum with Pero have survived. Ironically enough, as a Polish officer he himself died in the Warsaw uprising in 1944.

Helena Schiborowska of 36 Krochmalnia was another dedicated worker for us. She was a small, dark-skinned widow with children who hardly took time to bother with her own household chores because she was so busy helping persecuted, browbeaten Jews. When a hideout became unsafe, its occupant would call upon Helena for help. Her house had been raided as a result of tips supplied by informers, yet on occasion she would shelter a desperate Jew. She also tried to persuade her gentile neighbors to accommodate Jews, refusing to be daunted by their coolness toward the suggestion. When she did manage to enlist the cooperation of some neighbors, she would come to our secret meetings to tell us joyfully of her new achievement.

Helena Schiborowska did accept money for her efforts; however, she would then spend it on the unfortunate Jews under her care. All of us admired her generosity.

She herself lived in poverty. She sold her jewelry and donated the money to needy Jews. Not a few Jews owe their survival to the efforts of this benevolent little woman, who rendered help in so straightforward a manner, and with such understanding. She is still alive, and now lives in Warsaw.

These are a few of the "good Poles," with whom I chanced to come into contact during the Nazi regime. Unfortunately, the number of such commendable and kindhearted gentiles was rather small. Our relief and rescue mission would have been greater, and more Jews would have survived, if in their midst, the Polish people had had more individuals with such heart and conscience.

CAROLA SAPETOWA

A Polish Woman Relates Her Story

TRANSLATED FROM THE YIDDISH BY MOSHE SPIEGEL

Our family* consisted of parents and three children: Samush Hochheiser was the youngest; a little girl named Saliusha; and Izio—the oldest. I raised the children.

The father was shot during the first year of the war. I became separated from the family when all Jews were segregated into the ghetto.** But I used to visit the ghetto every day, and bring whatever things I could. I missed the children dearly, and thought of them as my own.

When things got out of hand in the ghetto, the children would come to me, where they felt at home. In March 1943,*** the ghetto was liquidated. The youngest chanced to stay with me.

On that day I approached the gate of the ghetto, and it was surrounded by S.S. men and Ukrainians. People ran about, woebegone. Mothers and children were struggling to reach the gate. Suddenly I caught sight of the mother with Saliusha and Izio. The mother saw me too, and whispered to the little girl: "Go to Carolcha." Without wasting a moment, the little girl glided miraculously through the heavy, high boots of the Ukrainians, and ran toward me with outstretched arms.

The two of us, together with my aunt, made our way to our village of Vitonowice, near Vodowice. The mother and the little boy were sent to the "transport"—both of them perished.

It was a hard life. If the children have survived, then one must

* Characteristic description of a family in which she served.
** In Cracow.
*** The 18th.

believe in miracles. At the beginning, the children would go outside, but as time went on things became worse and I had to keep them indoors. But that didn't help either. The local community knew I was hiding Jewish children, and I was threatened and hounded from all sides. Everyone insisted that I hand the children over to the Gestapo—otherwise, the village would be ravaged and burned, and its people would be killed. The *soltis* of the village was friendly to me, and this calmed me a bit. Others were much more adamant and aggressive. I had to bribe them with gifts.

But that situation didn't last long. The German S.S. officers went about sniffing and prying. I ran into adventures with the peasants, who declared that the children should be moved to the granary and have their little heads chopped off while asleep.

I went around as though in a daze. My old father was worried. We racked our brains about how to save the children. They themselves knew what was going on, and before going to bed pleaded, "Carolcha, don't kill us tonight! Not tonight!" I had the feeling of becoming numb and petrified and resolved not to betray them, come what might.

A novel thought occurred to me. I seated the children in a wagon and, as I drove through the village, assured the peasants that I was going to drown them. They believed me. At night I brought the children back and hid them in a neighbor's loft.

It was a hot, sultry July, and the children lay huddled on a heap of dust half-a-meter thick. The unfortunate youngsters began to suffer from all kinds of sores; the nails on their hands and feet began to fall off. They were simply rotting away. It broke my heart; I thought I could not bear it any longer, but I kept on. I had to earn some money for their food. And I had to pay for their hiding place.

The children suffered thus for three months. I managed somehow to cure their festering sores, but they were deathly pale, especially the little girl, who was endlessly frightened. The little boy seemed to hold his own.

When my money gave out, I could not pay for their hideout any more, and hid them in our stable.

Once, during an inspection, an S.S. man entered the stable. For a moment it looked as though they were finished. But Samush instinctively spread straw under the cow and busied himself with similar chores. We were flabbergasted. How had such a youngster conceived of such a trick? Salusha stood in a corner, unnerved. The danger was over, the children saved.

After that, things calmed down until the Red Army arrived. The children are happy and I am even more so. I would never part from them even if they were to go to the ends of the earth. I regard them as my own children. I love them and would go through fire and water for them.

WLADYSLAW BRONIEWSKI

To the Polish Jews

(In Memory of Samuel Zygelbojm)

TRANSLATED FROM THE POLISH BY ILONA RALF SUES

No cry of despair rose from Polish cities and towns.
The defenders of Warsaw's Ghetto fell like a gallant battalion.
A wandering Polish poet, I steep my words in blood
And my heart in a deep sea of tears
To write of you, oh, Polish Jews.
Not like men did they come, but like bloodhounds.
Not as soldiers they came, but as butchers—
To murder you, murder your children and wives,
To choke people to death in gas chambers,
To burn people alive in vans filled with lime,
And to jeer at the agony of their terrified victims.
But you picked up cobblestones from the street
And hurled them at their cannoneer who loaded his gun
To blast your house off the face of the earth.
Sons of the Maccabees—you know to face death,
like your fathers.
You joined us in that battle which began in September,
Though you knew there was not a chance to win.
Here are the truths to be carved in stone
And engraved forever in all Polish minds:
The house they destroyed was our common home;
The blood we both shed has made us brothers;
Our union was sealed at Execution Walls;
Our union was sealed by Oswiecim and Dachau,
By each nameless grave, by each prison bar.
Our common roof over war-smitten Warsaw

Will be a bright sky when Victory crowns
The long years of bloody and heartbreaking struggle:
Every man will be free and have bread and have rights,
And there will be one single race, supreme—
The race of noble human beings.

DONALD LOWRIE

Chambon-sur-Lignon

In some sections of France a village is either wholly Protestant or wholly Catholic. This distinction prevails in most cities as well: if you are a Protestant, you trade usually with Protestant shopkeepers, or the reverse if you are Catholic. One of the best-known Protestant villages in southern France is Chambon-sur-Lignon, in the hills above Lyon. The most important institution in the town is the Collège Cévenol, a top-grade preparatory school. And both school and town have always accepted the leadership of the local Protestant clergy, who are also part of the college teaching staff.

Chambon was already well acquainted with refugees before the Jews began to come. When the remnants of republican armies in Spain began to pour over the border into France, two years before the 1940 debacle, they were apportioned out to different parts of the country, and Chambon welcomed its share. The Spanish refugee families made themselves useful in the town, and left their monument there, in one of the best-built camps the French Y.M.C.A. possesses, constructed by these unwilling guests from Spain.

Then, at the outset of war, thousands of families were evacuated from frontier sections of Alsace. Every southern French town had to take in its quota of these homeless people and find the necessary housing. The resultant clash between French citizens of German background and citizens in small French villages who had never been outside their own communities, produced many problems for social work agencies. Chambon accepted its portion of Alsatians, most of them Protestant, which made adjustment easier.

When the deportations began, besides several children's homes there were three centers for refugees in Chambon, managed by three of the different organizations belonging to our Coordination Committee. Among the residents in these homes, the majority of them people liberated from internment camps, there were over a hundred Jews.

Most French Protestants have never ceased protesting since Huguenot days. Chambon was outraged by the reports of Jewish arrests and deportations. Almost as if it had been planned, Vichy soon gave the townspeople a chance to register their opinions.

Late in the summer of 1942 the Vichy Minister for Youth, Lamirand, making a propaganda tour of the region, came to Chambon accompanied by the préfet and called a meeting of youth organizations. His speech extolling Marshal Pétain was received politely, but afterward a delegation of thirty senior students at the college, with their two pastors, waited on him to present their formal protest against what Vichy was doing with the Jews. "And we must tell you, Monsieur le préfet," they said, "that if any attempt is made to molest the Jewish guests in our village, we will resist, and our teachers too."

This was something new in the préfet's experience. He spluttered that the deportations were not anti-Semitic "persecution" but simply a regrouping of European Jews in Poland. Then he inadvertently admitted that he had received Vichy orders to take the Jews from Chambon. Growing more angry and red-faced with every minute, he turned on the two pastors: "Be careful! I know what you've been doing here. I can show you letters I've received. When the time comes, we'll get your Jews, and you'd better let them go peaceably." And he stalked out of the room.

That same week the pastors and their students made plans to hide their Jewish guests. If refugees were not a novelty in Chambon history, neither was their concealment. Some of the hideouts chosen had been used three hundred years before by the Huguenots. The whole countryside was alerted, and scarcely a farmer refused to take in a refugee should this become necessary.

On a Saturday afternoon a fortnight after the first visit the police came again, this time with two large khaki-colored buses which drew up in the village square. The police captain called on Pastor M. in his study: "We know you know all the Jews in this town—give us a list."

"But of course you don't really expect me to do that," the pastor replied. "Would you, in my place?"

"Well, then, you can at least sign this," and the captain held out an official poster: "Appeal to Jews." The notice urged all Jews in Chambon to turn themselves in to the police, quietly. This would avoid all risk to families which had been sheltering Jews and prevent any disturbance of public order. By this time the other Chambon pastor had joined Pastor M. "But we cannot sign this," they assured the gendarme.

The police captain wasted no more words. "You'll sign it by tomorrow noon or I'll arrest both of you. Tomorrow noon," he growled, as he slammed the door behind him.

That night was a busy one for Chambon. Something went wrong with the town's lighting system, but darkness seemed not to hinder considerable movement. The police, waiting for their ultimatum to expire, slept in their buses. The Sunday morning church service was tense and the pastors expected to find the police waiting to arrest them as they went out into the street.

Instead, the gendarmes had begun their house-to-house search. Every house in the village, as well as most of the nearby farms, was rigorously inspected from cellar to attic. They found one Jew who had not hidden because half his ancestors had been Aryan. Villagers could scarcely keep from smiling as they passed those twenty gendarmes sitting in their two buses with their one captive. Someone brought the prisoner a homemade cake. Others quickly took the hint, and before long the meek-looking little man had a heap of presents that filled more space in the bus than he did. This was one way of showing complete solidarity with the pastors.

On Monday morning the shamefaced police had to release their sole captive, who had presented documentary proof that he was half "Aryan." However, they began a new combing-over of the town and the country around it that continued, on and off, for more than a fortnight. Although twenty gendarmes hunted the woods and made countless surprise house searches in the town, not a single arrest could be made, and at last they departed in their two army buses.

I said not one person had been arrested in Chambon, but there was one exception which proved very interesting. Madame Durand (that is not her name), "grande dame" of the village, had taken one of the Jewish refugees, a girl student, into her home. When first she heard of impending police action, Madame Durand went to the commissaire of police at once. "I give notice," she said, "that I have a girl named Greta at my house and I assume complete responsibility for her." That was that, and Madame Durand and the entire family went peacefully to bed. At three in the morning the police took the girl, despite Madame Durand's outraged protests. At six o'clock Madame Durand was in the train for Vichy. Before the day was over she had interviewed the Minister of Foreign Affairs and the Chief of Police, a man almost as hard to see as the Pope. In the meantime the girl had been put into a train and was on her way to Germany. Fortunately she was taken out of the car before it crossed the demarcation line, and so was saved, at least for this time. From then on Madame Durand addressed reams of letters to all her friends telling of the terrible thing that had happened to her. As propaganda for further resistance the incident was most fortunate.

La Maison des Roches, the European Student Relief home for refugees in Chambon, experienced particularly dramatic episodes. Its residents were all university students who had been released from various internment camps through the efforts of the Nîmes Committee. The students were of nine different nationalities: ten of them were Aryan, twenty-one were Jewish. Here in the Collège Cévenol these young men could continue their studies. To help them with the French language, four French students from the Collège came to live with them in La Maison des Roches.

After German occupation of southern France, the residents of La Maison des Roches, like the rest of the people of Chambon, lived in a state of constant alert. Time and again there would be a rumor that the Gestapo were about to search the house, and there would be a general exodus to the woods. Since most of the police raids seemed to take place at night, students would sleep in the woods and come back to the house by day. A red-checkered towel hung in a certain window informed them that the coast was clear.

This uncertainty so disrupted any orderly study that the young French director of the house made a special trip to Vichy to explore the atmosphere there. To his discreet inquiries the authorities gave assurance that no arrests in his house were contemplated. This assurance turned out to be as good as most of Laval's promises, and within a fortnight, possibly because the director's Vichy inquiry had called attention to Les Roches, the house was suddenly visited one summer morning by the dreaded Gestapo, demanding entrance. The courageous young director stalled with them at the front entrance, while all the Jewish students escaped by a rear door.

Of course the whole village was concerned about what might be happening in the student home, but how could anyone manage to pass the police cordon? A retired clergyman finally hit upon a scheme. He told the Gestapo men he was afraid something might happen to a valuable book he had lent one of the students, and so was permitted to enter the house. He returned to tell the townsfolk that Les Roches was in terror. The police were using their customary method of questioning plus physical coercion. It looked as though the whole group of students, all refugees but none of them Jews, would be carried away, and apparently nothing could be done to save them.

Here a pastor's wife intervened. She knew that one of the Austrian students at Les Roches had saved the life of a German soldier who had been stricken with cramps while swimming in the little river and who would have drowned without the young Austrian's timely help. As the pastor's wife she could and did call at the local German army headquarters, demanding to see the officer in charge. "Would you let that student who risked his life to save one of your men be arrested by the Gestapo?" she asked him. When he said no, the pastor's wife insisted that he accompany her to Les Roches and tell the story. Now, no minor officer would ever of his own accord cross swords with the all-powerful Gestapo, but such was the lady's persistence that this one reluctantly went with her. She managed to pass the police line by saying she was the cleaning woman, come as usual for her work. Inside, she put on a blue apron and took over in the kitchen, serving coffee to the Gestapo inquisitors. Once in their presence, she was able to insist that the German officer tell the story of the Austrian student and the rescue. As a result, he was the only man of the residents to escape deportation. The Gestapo, realizing how they had been tricked by the director at the entrance, took him away with the other students and for good measure the four French students also. The young director never returned.

Neither did most of the other Aryans. The case of one of the four French students was particularly distressing. Of Jewish origin, he was himself a Christian. Foreseeing possible interrogation, he had once asked his pastor what he should say about himself under questioning. The pastor had said that he need not mention his Jewish parents: he should simply insist that he was a Christian, his French nationality and his membership in the Christian church should assure his safety. . . . The Gestapo in Chambon did not discover the young man's racial ancestry, but once he was in a concentration camp in Germany—with full knowledge of what was happening to Jews all around him—his conscience so plagued him that he went to the commandant and revealed his Jewish parentage.

He was immediately shipped out of that camp and was never heard from again.

The day Les Roches was raided the two pastors also were arrested and interned in Gurs. However, powerful intervention secured their release within two months, and they were able to continue as the center of activity in Chambon.

If the local Chambon police had ever sympathized with Vichy's plan to eliminate the Jews, German occupation certainly changed their minds. The long drawn-out anguish of hiding hundreds of Jews for months on end could never have been as successful as it was without the secret collaboration of friends in the local police office. Before almost every raid word would be passed around indicating what houses were to be searched. Somehow this system failed in the case of Les Roches.

Chambon was an outstanding example of the feeling that had developed across the whole of France. Everywhere Christian people were helping Jews to escape the Nazi clutches. One man I knew lived for weeks with four other refugees in a cellar whose entrance was concealed under a trash pile. Another walked for six days along the railroad track posing as a workman, tapping the switches with his hammer, often passing police checkpoints undetected. A fascinating story could be written about disguises and subterfuges that helped Jewish refugees to elude their pursuers. Near Marseilles the children held in a detention camp learned that the age limit for exemption from deportation had been lowered from eighteen to sixteen, whereupon the fourteen boys between those two ages left for the woods before the police should come to get them. They were adopted by a troop of French Boy Scouts, and for weeks lived in the woods like Indians, fed secretly by their Scout protectors. In Chambon one day a large group of children from the Swiss Aid home got through the police cordon thrown around the village by donning Scout uniforms and marching out, singing French Scouting songs they had been practicing for weeks for just such an emergency. Scores of Jews, particularly children, found escape from the Chambon area impossible and never left it until the end of the war.

To their indiscretions in hiding Jews, the people of Chambon added the crime of helping the Resistance. Chambon became a minor headquarters for the *Maquis,* the secret Resistance army, and the symbiosis of these two groups, the one led by the pastors refusing, as a matter of principle, the use of violence and the other existing principally to employ force against the Germans, was one of the exciting experiences of those years. Each group respected the other, each trusted the other's devotion to the same cause. Finally, as one of the pastors later told me, they could scarcely decide which group did more to protect the other. It was a double spy of the *Maquis*—a man the Nazis employed for espionage who was secretly reporting to the French—who warned the Chambon pastors so that they were able to go into hiding just before the Gestapo came a second time to seize them.

When, a little later, the American O.S.S. began dropping parachutists into southern France the Chambon churchyard was a favorite target. One American who broke a leg in the operation was cared for in the local hospital until he was able to travel, although the Germans, now in full control, made frequent visits in the town looking for suspicious characters.

By the time the Germans occupied all of France the fame of Chambon had spread far and wide. The whole countryside became one vast clandestine organization, with practically every farm sheltering a Jewish family. After the war, Jewish relief agencies estimated that more than a thousand different Jews had spent some time in this brave and hospitable community. To the Jews the word Chambon meant helpfulness; to the police, and particularly to the Gestapo who came in with the Nazi army, the name was odious. Time and again they struck at this hated symbol of resistance.

One day the pastor was being questioned by the Gestapo about his activities in caring for Jews. He told them that it was his duty as a Christian, adding that he would do the same for Germans should the occasion arise. It did: at the end of the war a large prisoner-of-war camp was established just outside Chambon, and in the face of somewhat violent criticism by local citizenry the pastor began at once to minister to the Germans there.

RIVKA KWIATKOWSKI-PINKHASIK

Gallows in the Balut Market

TRANSLATED FROM THE YIDDISH BY MOSHE SPIEGEL

Three dead Jews are dangling from a gibbet. A sentry with drawn bayonet paces to and fro, as though apprehensive lest the corpses break away from the gallows and escape. . . .

The marketplace in Balut was still steeped in slumber when the three Jews were brought to the gibbet. Isaac the butcher, who had come in from a neighboring village lugging a slaughtered calf, was the first to notice the dead men. He was stunned by the sight, and it seemed to him that only a superhuman effort enabled him to reach a gate where he could sit down, breathing heavily.

"Woe, woe to us. . . . Three Jews on a gibbet! Why? Why?"

Isaac, the strong man among butchers, for whom lifting a heifer in the slaughterhouse was mere child's play, staggered under his burden of veal when he resumed his journey. At last, eyes bulging with fright, he slumped into a chair at home, and lamented to his anxious wife:

"It's bad, Berachah. . . . Three Jews strung up on the gibbet at the marketplace. . . ."

At the sound of Berachah's wailing, the Jewish neighbors came running, and they hardly believed their ears as she told them the sad news. Then they all headed for the marketplace to see for themselves.

The crowd of spectators around the gibbet grew ever larger, standing like a mute array of witnesses before heaven and earth. Now and then, however, a muffled protest could be heard from the glassy-eyed, trembling throng, a mutter about avenging the outrage.

"What will come next?" others groaned. "Good God, what do they intend to do with us now?"

The German sentinel with the deep-set, watery eyes and a face as blue as though his blood had congealed, paced up and down in silence. There was a wry, fiendish smile on his face, as if this were an omen that all Jews would soon be dangling from gibbets.

Isaac was plodding home once more, on legs still numb with fright. Dense clouds of smoke from burning synagogues seemed to be hovering before his eyes and nostrils. He lifted his eyes to the heavens, which were their usual summer blue, as though to invoke there the justice that was bound to come. Ordinarily Isaac was not pious, and he attended services at the House of Study regularly only because this put him right with his customers at the butcher shop. Now, however, he saw an awesome sign from above in the smoke billowing from the synagogues. The enveloping darkness became so impenetrable that he had to grope his way home.

On his return, Isaac was met in the courtyard by the womenfolk, their eyes so red from weeping that it might have been blood instead of tears that trickled from them.

"Where are we to go with our children?" the women wailed. "Such a dreadful decree . . . to leave our home in two hours. What are we to do now?"

The Germans had chosen the house with the newly refurbished school for their barracks and had ordered the Jews to vacate it immediately. The floors of the classrooms were being strewn with straw on which the soldiers were to sleep. Girls were seized in the courtyard and ordered to clean the windows and scrub the woodwork. The courtyard was filled with the soldiers' crude jeers and profanity.

Each of the Jewish householders picked up a few pitiful belongings, and carried them off to acquaintances for safekeeping. There could be no talk of getting other living quarters—hundreds of Jewish refugees were arriving every day. In their abject fear, women now simply grabbed their children and hastened away from the courtyard full of soldiers. . . .

But what had suddenly happened? Why were the German soldiers now carrying back the straw from the classrooms to the waiting cars? Why were they cursing and spitting in disgust?

"Gracious sir," the housekeeper told the German officer, placing her hands on her swelling bosom, "they have dirtied up the whole place; all the walls are covered with filth, and the roaches are crawling everywhere. And the rats—they're the size of horses. I've been working for these damned Jews for years, trying to keep this building clean, but it was a waste of time. Dear sir, there's no end to the filth here!"

"I didn't like the place to begin with!" the officer replied, spitting again in disgust. "It's a shame, though—such a fine school building. . . . Take out the straw!" he commanded the fatigue detail, and then bellowed, as a parting shot, "We'll get even with those mangy Jews! They've poisoned the whole world!"

The Jewish mothers embraced the housekeeper and whispered excitedly, "You've saved us—you must be God's messenger. How are we to thank you?"

"How else was I to deal with those pigs?" Wanda the housekeeper demanded, beaming triumphantly as she wiped the perspiration from her face. She despised these Nazi soldiers with the bulging red necks above their khaki uniforms, who had swooped down like locusts, plundering and pillaging. And what those murderers had done to the Jews! Had they no fear of God? . . .

The Jewish women showered their savior with gifts of all sorts, linen sheets, towels, a woollen kerchief, boots for her son, and so on, some still murmuring, "Such a miracle!"

Isaac glanced at the sack containing the slaughtered calf and deliberated: perhaps I should give the meat to the inhabitants of this courtyard to celebrate this event.

But better days did not lie ahead; there were only more harsh decrees over and over again.

Warnings to the Germans, "Beware of contagious diseases!" were posted on telephone poles.

And for the Jews these rallying cries were posted on all the buildings:

"Whoever leaves the Jewish ghetto will be punished by death!"

"Whoever appears in the street without the Jewish yellow badge will be punished by death!"

Death! Death! Death!

"Is this the end? Is our doom sealed?" was the thought that ran repeatedly through the stunned minds of the shaken Jews.

"This is only the beginning! This is only the beginning!" the Jewish spirit, conditioned by the fear of centuries, would reply.

BENJAMIN ELLIS

The Fugitives

TRANSLATED FROM THE YIDDISH BY MOSHE SPIEGEL

The Sandler brothers with their wives and aged mother were registered as residents of Polish birth, but they were not. Their identity cards were not bona fide documents. Such expedients were common in those difficult times. When they moved into their new apartment in Warsaw they would not employ anyone of Polish blood to help them clean up the terrible mess that met their eyes. It was a sorry sight, a shambles. Not one piece of furniture was in place. It was like a scene from some adventure or battle film, with unmistakable evidence of a bloody finale.

It was chaos. The floor of what must have been the dining room was a mass of debris—broken utensils, bits of broken porcelain dishes and crockery smashed as though by the senseless fury of a madman.

There were shredded bits of paper and blood-soaked rags scattered about everywhere, and the walls were smeared with blood, the crimson of which was an appropriate color for such a scene of horror. The beds had been pushed into the center of the rooms from their accustomed corners. They were of brown wood, and they stood like operating tables, with blood-soaked mattresses and soiled red-flecked linen, torn as though a surgeon had performed an emergency operation on some mother who had given birth to new life and had left her tell-tale sacrifice of blood.

When they ventured fearfully into still another room, it was even more of a wreck than the others. Here the furniture was not merely pushed about in a confused mess; the floor not just littered with filth and blood-soaked rags; it contained worse than overturned tables that made one think of a dead horse on its back, with its stiff legs upthrust in the obscene gesture of carrion indifferent to the sensitivities of man.

The walls were in keeping with the other signs of demonic destruction that met their eyes. They were scarred and defaced as though some desperate victim had sought to tear them down and escape. The Sandlers stood and took in the scene of carnage, appalled and silent. This sorry place brought back memories. It reminded them of another wrecked home from which they had fled long ago; or perhaps of one from which they had set out on a peaceful voyage and to which they returned to find it in ruins.

After several hours of hard work they succeeded in repairing the walls to some extent. The landlord had grudgingly offered them such material as he had. They swept out the debris scattered about and returned each piece of furniture to its proper place. The beds and tables had been placed where they had been before the holocaust, and they were ready to settle down for a rest when the short, corpulent landlord appeared. His tired, watery eyes roamed over the repaired walls, the covered gaps, the furniture restored to its proper places in each room. In fact, he was much more interested in his property than in the Sandlers themselves. After looking everywhere and apparently being satisfied, he turned to his new tenants and assuming a weary, resigned expression, he said, "I am deeply sorry, my dear *Herrschaften,* but I cannot permit you to remain here. You must find yourselves another flat." "Another flat?" cried the older Sandler brother in a shocked and fearful voice. "Another flat? What is wrong?"

"This business is too risky for me," answered the landlord, who had not disguised his satisfaction at the improved condition of his property. He leisurely examined the repaired walls and the various pieces of furniture. Then he continued, "You see, and I hope you will understand my position, Jewish people lived here before and the Gestapo came after them. It didn't take long either. Just eight days ago they were all taken away." He sighed deeply. "You should have seen them. They were beaten almost to death. They were scarcely breathing. Nothing left of them but human wrecks. Lord, Lord, you should have seen them. It's too risky for me—too risky—you can see that for yourselves. If it were not for your brother here," he continued, turning to the pallid younger Sandler, "I might take a chance and keep you here—the rest of you are more or less like the rest of us, like Christians. But your brother, I'm not so sure he really belongs to you. But if he is one of you, I'm sorry, my *Herrschaften*."

"God! God, dear God!" burst out the old mother; and she wept loudly and lowered her face into her hands. "Please don't cry, Grandmother," said the pot-bellied landlord, who could not resist another satisfied glance at the improved appearance of his apartment. "Please calm yourself." The old lady wept bitterly, her body shaking with grief. Unable to hide their feelings, the sons and their young wives were pictures of despair and helplessness. They were like so many other fugitives who had found refuge for a moment and then once again found themselves pursued and hounded.

As though in an endless nightmare they were once more on the run and heaven alone knew when and where the chase would end. Since they had fled Lemberg, with their false identity documents, they had had three hideouts in Warsaw, counting this one. After five or six nights in the first one, the landlord had given them a gentle hint to find another refuge. They had been in the second place two weeks when a peculiar character carrying a black-leather overcoat the worse for wear and weather-beaten leather cap to match, knocked, and then pushed his way in. His black clothing harmonized with the black, shifty eyes beneath the visor of his cap. Without the slightest effort to identify himself, he counted the number of Sandlers in the place, and then demanded to be paid for his silence. And not just for the lot of them. They were helpless and at his mercy. He returned again and again. Every day or so he appeared to collect his bribes. Then he began to linger an hour or two, and made himself at home. After receiving his money, he would sit and boast of the many Jews whose lives he had saved and the number he had helped to escape from the ghetto. In addition to boasting of his acts of charity, this kind-hearted gentleman, his beady black eyes like those of some untamed jungle beast, poked into every corner, behind each wardrobe, and the hangings on the walls, on the hunt for hidden refugees—more victims to exploit.

And now the old woman, unable to control herself, wept convulsively as she thought of the continual wandering and flight from one flat to another. "How much better it would have been for me had they sent me off to the crematorium—how much better than this agony, all this suffering, this weariness. How much can one bear—how much?" Shaken with grief, she tottered about the room. The landlord answered, almost apologetically, "What a time we live in! But I am not to blame." He did not appear to be entirely indifferent to the old woman's grief. He glanced toward the younger women and said, "Now these young ladies here—one would never say they were Jewish." And he pointed to each in turn. "And for you, Grandmother—well, I might chance it. But I wouldn't risk anything for you," he added, addressing the youngest Sandler son, who stood pale and speechless.

One might have thought the young man was a hardened criminal who had been caught in the act of escaping from prison, and so he himself felt after the brutal frankness of the landlord. He had realized very early that these endless flights from one place to another were beyond his strength. And he also knew that even the first flight from his familiar Lemberg to Warsaw had been made for his sake. But only now did he fully realize to what extent he was responsible for all their hardships—that he was the loose wheel that was endangering the family vehicle.

"You can't blame me. All this is no fault of mine," repeated the landlord, as though eager to remain an innocent party to the tragedy. "My own nest is in danger. I can't take the chance."

"And suppose I leave the others here?" asked Marc, feeling a sudden tightening about his heart. "Suppose I left and went off alone somewhere, would you let my family stay? Can they stay here without me?" With a smile of relief, the landlord replied, "That's up to you. You can have until morning to decide. Until tomorrow, my *Herrschaften*."

When the landlord left, all his loved ones gathered about Marc—his young wife, his sister-in-law, his brother, and his mother. It was as though a bed-ridden invalid had suddenly begun to speak of dying.

"I'll go to the ghetto—the ghetto," cried Marc, pale as a ghost and trying to push his way past his family. "I'll be just one more Jew among the thousands there."

His mother shrieked, "Not the ghetto! Oh, God be with us—dear God, dear God. After all the time we have spent in hiding in order to keep out of the ghetto, now you would go there and walk into the trap of those murderers. After all our suffering would you surrender to our killers?"

"It's madness," cried the older brother, furiously. "Those in the ghetto are dying in caves and holes in the ground and filthy sewers infested with rats. Some remain in their terrible underground bunkers rather than live in the ghetto—and now you want the ghetto. And how will you get there? Do you think you can just walk over the line and into the accursed place? Don't you realize it's just as hard to get into the ghetto as it is to get out?"

Each one argued with the pallid, trembling Marc. Each one offered his own counsel and tried to show Marc how mad his idea was of making his way to the walled-in city of the Jews. He was treated as though he were a weaker child who had to be given more counsel and attention to keep him from choosing the wrong path. But like an obstinate youngster, he remained silent in the face of all their entreaties. The black despair that had enveloped him became more poignant, there was a sense of tightness about his heart, and his breath came in gasps. The always pallid face turned deathly white. He staggered and clutched at his chest. He was in a state of shock, like one who has remained too long in the steam room of a Turkish bath and on emerging is breathless from the sudden change.

As the Sandlers sat helpless around Marc, silent, self-reproachful, and filled with an even greater guilt as they saw the alarming change in his face, the fat landlord burst into the room as though pursued by the devil himself and ordered them to pack up and get out immediately. They did not remove their eyes from the bed, where Marc now lay covered with heavy blankets. A damp cloth was folded across his forehead. When the landlord saw the grave change in the young man, he hesitated a moment, and said more quietly, "Tomorrow morning then. You must leave the flat tomorrow morning."

As he made his way out, the Sandlers all turned to watch him. The expressions of impotent hatred on their faces seemed to threaten that tomorrow's dawn would be the last he would see on this earth. But when he had closed the door behind him they were face to face with their helplessness. They did not dare to go out to search for a doctor or to attempt to call one in.

They were forced to stand by with their hands tied and watch Marc's suffering. As his fever mounted, he tossed from side to side. They had no thermometer with which to take his temperature, but knew he had a raging fever by the flushed and mottled skin on his sunken cheeks, his delirious mumbling, and by his hot, restless hands picking at the covers. All they could do for him was to replace the unclean cloth on his forehead with another dipped in cold water. They could only hope that with the passing of the night hours and the coming of the dawn there might be some improvement, if only a drop in his temperature. But meanwhile, the night was unrelieved suffering for the stricken man, and his anxious family moved about like so many condemned prisoners awaiting execution.

The old mother dragged herself from room to room, muttering to herself, "We must leave before daylight. Where can we go? What will become of us?" From time to time she would drop into a chair and doze off, and then awaken with a start and begin her weeping again. Then she would again drag her tired old legs from room to room, to keep from falling asleep again. She trembled all over as she walked on and on as one might tramp up and down the corridor of a hospital after a loved one has been left in the hands of the surgeon for an extremely dangerous operation.

"Where can we go? Where can we take him?" she cried over and over. All through the rest of the night she avoided the sickroom and sought refuge from the sight of his suffering in the other part of the flat. She seemed to shrink within herself and to grow thinner before one's eyes, and her hair turned from gray to white overnight.

When the dawn's feeble light showed through the shutters, Marc's breathing had improved slightly. The blond young women who "didn't look like Jews," in spite of their own exhaustion after a sleepless night, gently helped him to a sitting position. Then the doorbell clanged like a signal from hell and the portly landlord was banging on the door. He was more excited than on the evening before, and one might have thought someone was pursuing and threatening to expose him to the common enemy. Without another look at the sick man, he cried "My *Herrshaften,* this is it. You must pack up at once and get off the premises." Although the Sandlers had known since the day before that he intended to get rid of them, now that the time had come they were paralyzed. It was as though they were hearing the landlord's sentence for the first time and that it was unexpected. The old woman gave a strangled sob and collapsed into a chair. Forcing himself to action, the older brother busied himself with gathering together their few effects. The sick man moaned and whimpered as the young blond sisters-in-law helped him into warm clothing, including two suits of long underwear. Even though everyone's face betrayed the horror and terror in their hearts, as though they were in the midst of an air raid, they managed to get their stricken loved one dressed. Although their hands trembled as they worked, they handled his pitifully emaciated body as gently as though he were a newly born baby.

When the old woman heard the whimpering of her helpless son

she raised her fist to her mouth in an effort to suppress her cries of "O God! O God!" which seemed to be wrenched from her over and over against her will.

A spirit of darkness seemed to hover in the room. Everything was dark before her eyes as she listened to the heavy breathing of her older son as he feverishly worked at tying up their meager belongings, to the excited voice of the landlord, to the unending whimper of the sick one—all the sounds clashed in a nerve-wracking, deafening babel of voices such as might come from people trapped in a dark echoing tunnel and struggling to escape by climbing one over the other in their despair. All about her was darkness, merging with another darkness much blacker and more terrifying as they prepared to leave the flat and as the younger women, fearfully and with trembling hands, led Marc down the stairs. To the mother it was all like a fantastic vision of some unreasoning and useless struggle. They were all hopeless participants in this dreadful scene as they made their painful way slowly down the steps. They were like passengers on a wrecked ship sinking in the dead of night into the frightful oblivion of the unplumbed ocean depths.

FELIKS KANABUS

Address at the J.N.F., September 20, 1965

Ladies and Gentlemen:

It is very difficult to go back in thought to the time I am supposed to talk about. It is difficult for many reasons. For one, after twenty years my memory is not able to retain everything, for it is hardly perfect. Secondly, because my memory revolts against going back in time and bringing to light the pictures and memories of that horrible era. Thirdly, and primarily, because the memory that the martyrdom of both nations, the Jewish and the Polish, took place in my native land is extremely painful.

Nazi Germany, because of its quest for world domination, intended to destroy other nations, one by one. The first victim of their lust was the Jewish people. The second was the Slavic nations. Not everyone during the war realized that the Nazi terrorism was planned with a diabolical, cold accuracy and reason.

The Germans planned on scattering the conflicts between their victims. They knew about the existence of anti-Semitic feeling in pre-war Poland. This anti-Semitism flourished during the pre-war period of political flirtation between the German and Polish governments. Because of this, the plan of extermination of Jews in Poland was based on a collaboration of German and Polish forces. It was a fiendish plan. For these reasons, the Nazis selected Poland as the site of the planned total annihilation of Jews.

As a Pole, I am forced to admit in deep sorrow and shame, that some Poles, whom I hesitate and resent calling Poles, helped the Germans in their brutal and destructive activities.

Reactionary Polish groups accepted the racial inequality slogans and the ghettos that were formed. Yet, I must stress the fact that most of the Polish society did not accept the ghettos. Most of the Poles held in contempt Polish anti-Semitism and helped the Jews whenever possible in proportion to the opportunity. However, giving aid to Jews in Poland was extremely difficult and dangerous, more so than in any other country occupied by the Germans. Hiding Jews in the Polish sector, outside the ghetto, was punished by death. In no other country were the penalties as stiff. Also, in no other nation were there as many Jews who needed and sought help. I do not exaggerate when I say that all the Jews who survived the war in Poland owe their lives to the aid and friendship of Poles. Without this aid, it was absolutely impossible for a Jew to survive the war in Poland. This aid was given in many various ways. One of these was to supply a Jew with a counterfeit *Kennkarte,* which made life possible outside the ghetto and also gave one a chance to find a job. However, this was a realistic escape only for those Jews who did not look like Jews, and who did not have any outstanding characteristics which automatically classified them as Jews. A problem arose of destroying Jewish characteristics.

With this, it became imperative for doctors to remove the Jewish characteristics via operation. There were two basic types of operations involved: a) operations on the nose, b) operations which removed all traces of circumcision, the so-called anti-ritual operations. Because I had always fought against anti-Semitism, even before the war, when I was a student, I decided that I would help Jewish people in any way possible during the war. I hid Jews from the Nazis in my apartment, and helped them find hiding places in the houses of my friends and relatives. I gave Jews *Kennkartes,* the identification papers. I supplied the Jews in the ghetto with food and drugs. I also supplied food and drugs to Jews hidden on the Polish side. I found employment for Jews, and placed them in hospitals under false names in order to cure them. But the most specialized form of my help to Jews was the anti-ritual operations. As a surgeon I can say that these operations were without a past and I hope that they are without a future.

When I started performing these operations, I was unable to look up the correct procedure in a surgeon's notebook. I was also unable to ask for advice from an older, more accomplished surgeon. A surgeon performing such a circumcision, or actually an anti-circumcision, was dependent only on his own skill and imagination, especially since these operations had to be performed secretly. My assistants during the operations were my wife, Irene, or my brother-in-law, both doctors. However, neither of them was a surgeon. After a few months, I found out that two other surgeons were also performing the same operations, each one separately. They were the following surgeons: Dr. Andrew Trojanowski, who died last year, and Dr. Jan Grocholski, executed by the Nazis in 1942. We decided to exchange our experiences between us, in order to choose the best operating technique. Unfortunately, Dr. Grocholski was executed soon after we formed our agreement, but I exchanged information with Dr. Trojanowski until the end of the war.

I performed about seventy anti-circumcision operations. Dr. Trojanowski performed about the same number. Satisfactory results were obtained in more than half of these cases. Many of my patients lived through the war. Some are in Poland, while others are scattered throughout the globe. In the majority of the cases, I did not know the names of my patients. Some changed their names after the war. Practically none of the patients knew my name. They came to me through recommendation of a group of trusted people who acted secretly. Some of them were Edward Gutgieser and Adolf Berman (Borowski), who is now a resident in Israel.

I performed these operations either in my office or in the homes of my patients. It was impossible to perform these operations in a hospital. Operating conditions were very poor and primitive. The dressing on the wounds had to be changed and consequently it demanded visits after the operation. Sometimes, when I came to a patient after the operation to change the bandages, I did not find him, for he had had to change his apartment and hide. I had many adventures at that time, from which I was luckily able to escape. For example, at one time while I was in the middle of an operation, I heard the shouting of Germans through the window. They came in a large group, closed the gate, gave orders that no one was to leave his apartment, and started searching all the apartments one by one. My patient, my assistant and I found ourselves in a trap without an exit. I had to stop and destroy all the signs that indicated I had been performing an operation. The patient was under anesthesia and was bleeding. The location of the wound would have been proof for the Germans that they had caught us performing an anti-ritual operation. Quickly, I placed a bandage on the wound, put the patient in bed and attempted to awaken him before the Germans came. Fortunately, the Germans called off the search before they came to our apartment because they had already found their victim. It was fate that they found him before they searched our "operating room." For our escape, the person the Nazis did find paid dearly. It happens like that very often in life and even more often during war.

In the last world war, it was not only the soldiers and the armies who fought. It was a war of nation against nation. This war was thrown upon Europe by Adolf Hitler in the name of happiness and well being of his nation, for which he wanted to get *"Lebensraum."* Only a few intelligent people observed not only the madness but the precision of the plan. There was a planned devilish method in the madness. The one defense against this brutal plan for supremacy of one nation was the solidarity of nations in the face of adversity, and the simple brotherhood of individuals. I have always believed that this brotherhood is part of people, regardless of political schemes, national intrigues and the different governments of various nations. The war did not change this, and I still believe that brotherhood is an integral part of the structure of man. I deeply believe that in future generations the path of life will be controlled by the human mind and the human conscience.

Glossary

ACTION. Mass herding of Jews for transportation to concentration and/or death camps, or in the camps to liquidation in gas chambers.

A.K. [*Armia Krajowa*]. The Underground Polish Military Organization, comprised of various elements, some rabidly anti-Semitic. In several instances German Jews in hiding were terrorized and others were killed.

ANNIHILATION CAMPS IN POLAND. Auschwitz; Belzec; Treblinka; Chelmno; Maidanek; Sobibor. See individual entries.

ARBELTS-EINSATZ; ARBEITSAMT. Branches of the ghetto administration which supplied workers for German forced labor.

ARYAN SIDE; ARYAN PAPERS. The section of the city outside the ghetto limits where Jews were forbidden to live. Some Jews managed to obtain false Aryan papers through connections and money, but these did not always prevent them from being caught. Aryan papers were also held by agents of the Jewish underground organizations, to facilitate their making contact between the ghetto and the outside world.

AUSCHWITZ. [Polish: Oswiecim]. One of the most notorious Nazi concentration and death camps, which imprisoned about four million people during its existence from June 1941 to December 1943. Documents submitted at the Nuremberg Trial revealed that two and a half million persons were killed there, or died of starvation, overwork and illness. These included more than half a million Jews from all over Europe, but the majority were Polish Jews. Auschwitz had gas chambers and four crematoriums to incinerate the corpses, with a capacity of 24.000 people per day.

There was a central camp (*Stamlager* Auschwitz #1), Birkenauf (Auschwitz #2) and Manowic (Auschwitz #3, with a factory for synthetic rubber *"Buna-Werke"*). The *Stamlager* incorporated 40 smaller camps.

AUSSIEDLUNG. Described by the Germans as "resettlement"—in reality the deportation of Jews to annihilation camps or to central ghettos in the big cities.

BALUT; BALUT MARKETPLACE. The poor Jewish section of Lodz which was part of the ghetto during Occupation.

BELZEC. A concentration camp in the General Government of Poland, near Lublin. In 1940 it was a labor camp, after March 1942 an annihilation camp. The corpses of the asphyxiated Jews were cremated on bonfires.

Five thousand a day were brought from Calicia and Lublin. By December 1942 the camp had liquidated at least 600,000 Jews from Poland, Germany, Austria, Czechoslovakia, Rumania and Hungary.

BIRKENAU. [Polish: Brzezinki]. A division of Auschwitz.

BLOCKAELTESTER. A barrack leader chosen from the prisoners by the German officials who was responsible for the administration to the S.S. Many of these group leaders were criminals.

BUCHENWALD. One of the first concentration camps in Germany, formed in 1937 near Weimar, Thuringia. After Herszl Grynszpan's assassination of Von Roth, 10,000 German Jews were imprisoned here.

BUND. The General Jewish Labor Union of Poland [*Allegemeiner Yiddisher Arbeiter Bund*], and part of the Socialist International. It was active in the underground. Also included the youth organization *Zukunft* and the children's organization SKIF [*Sozialistischer Kinder Farband*].

BUNKER. An underground hiding place in the ghettos, forests, and fields. Also, a fortified fighting position, such as the J.F.O. center in Mila 18.

CHAPUNES. [Catchers]. Jargon used in Vilna and other cities to describe Nazi aides who seized Jews in the streets or dragged them from their homes for forced labor.

CENTOS. Jewish relief organization in Poland: *Centrala Opiekie nad Sierotami* [Orphan Care Center]. See T.O.Z.

CHELMNO. [German: Kulmhof]. A village near the Polish town of Kala, and the site of an annihilation camp equipped with gas chambers and five crematoriums. The camp was established in December 1941.

People murdered here numbered 370,000: of these 340,000 were Jews from Wartegau; 25,000, Jews from Germany, Czechoslovakia, Luxembourg, Bulgaria, Belgium, France and Italy; 5,000, gypsies who were living in Lodz, and officers of the Polish and Soviet armies.

CRYSTAL NIGHT. [*Kristallnacht*] German name for the pogroms carried out November 9–10, 1938, in Germany in revenge for Grynszpan's slaying of Von Roth. Hundreds of synagogues and stores were burned and plundered. The name was derived from the glass fragments of broken windows which littered the streets of the German towns.

DACHAU. One of the first concentration camps in Germany, established near Munich in March 1933 immediately after Hitler's assumption of power. In September 1939 it was closed and its prisoners taken to Flassenburg, Buchenwald and Mathausen. Many of the inmates were Jews.

DROR. [Hebrew]. Freedom. Name given to *Freiheit Hehalutz*—Youth Group of the Right *Poale Zion*.

FLASSENBURG. A concentration camp in Germany which absorbed Jewish survivors from Polish ghettos and camps.

F.P.O. *Fareinikte Partisaner Organisatzye*—United Partisan Organization, founded in the Vilna Ghetto in 1942 with a membership of Zionists, Bundists and Communists.

GENERAL GOVERNMENT. Name given by the Nazis to western and southern occupied Poland, which consisted of four districts: Cracow, Lublin, Radom and Warsaw. After the outbreak of war between Germany and the Soviet Union, Galicia was added. The Governor-General was Hans Frank.

GESTAPO. Initials of *Geheime Staats Polizei*, Nazi Secret State Police. Established in Prussia in 1933, after 1936 its power spread throughout Germany. Its chief aims were the persecution of Jews and dissident political parties. Under Himmler's rule, the Gestapo was a prime factor in the murder of six million Jews.

GHETTO. Walled section of a city where Jews were secluded and patrolled, and prohibited to leave under penalty of death. This was a medieval system revived by the Nazis. The inhabitants were crowded into a small area in the worst part of town, with a minimum of hygienic facilities.

The first ghetto in Poland was established in Lodz in 1939, and one of the largest was that of Warsaw, established in 1940. The ghettos served as collection centers of inhabitants of neighboring small towns, and facilitated subsequent deportation to death camps.

GROSS-ROSEN. [Polish: Rogoznical]. A concentration camp in Silesia for the Jews who had survived liquidated ghettos and camps in Poland.

GRYNZSPAN, HERSZL. German-born son of Polish-Jewish parents who in October 1938 were returned to the Zbonszyn refugee camp in Poland. In revenge, Grynszpan in November 1938 shot Von Roth, German Juridical Advisor in Paris. In retaliation, the Germans carried out the Crystal Night.

HASHOMER HATZAIR. [The Young Guard]. A Socialist-Zionist movement of Jewish youth, formed in 1913, that vastly increased its activities in many countries after World War I. Its members were trained to live in a kibbutz; by 1935, 2,500 training centers had been established in the United States and Europe, with a membership of 100,000. Prior to World War II *Hashomer Hatzair* became a political party in Palestine, and founded *Mapam*.

HEYDRICH, REINHARD. Group leader of the S.S. and commander of the S.D. One of the initiators of anti-Jewish actions, he organized the Crystal Night. He was murdered on May 27, 1942 by the Czech underground. To immortalize him, the Nazis named an extermination action of Polish Jews "Action Reinhard" and the groups who executed it were called *"Einsatz Rein."*

H.K.P. *Heers Kraftfahr Park*. The headquarters of the military motorized communications agency which employed Jewish slave labor.

HOTEL POLSKY. One of the most treacherous German ruses. Nazi officials announced that foreign citizens or those possessing foreign passports would be allowed to leave Poland. These people were temporarily housed in the Hotel Polsky on the Aryan Side in Warsaw to create the impression that they would be sent abroad. Then they were murdered.

JANOW C.C. Situated on Janow Street in Lemberg. A forced labor and transit camp from which transports were sent to Belzec Death Camp and where 200,000 persons, mostly Jews, lost their lives.

JEWISH SOCIAL SELF-HELP. Established in Warsaw in September 1939. It functioned in the ghettos under various names and opened public kitchens, conducted children's nurseries, etc. It was independent of the *Judenrat*.

"JOINT." Familiar term for American Jewish Joint Distribution Committee, founded in New York in November 1914 as a relief agency for Jews overseas. It is the foremost U.S. Jewish agency for help and rehabilitation abroad, working with the Jewish Agency for Palestine and O.R.T. to sustain surviving Jews in Europe. During the Nazi occupation, J.D.C. succeeded, by official or underground means, in sending funds to support the various institutions which Jews had formed in the ghettos.

JUDENRAT. [Council of Jewish Elders]. Official body of Jewish representatives organized by the Germans in the ghettos and camps to administer the occupied Jewish communities. Established in September 1939 on order of Reinhard Heydrich.

KAPO. Trustee or overseer in charge of work detail or branch of concentration camp, such as hospital, kitchen, etc. *Kapos* were drawn from among the camp prisoners, usually German criminals. The name derives from the Italian capo "head," or a contraction of "*Kamp Polizei.*" After liberation many *Kapos* were slain by the prisoners or jailed for collaboration by special courts formed for this purpose.

KARAITES. [Hebrew: *Karaim*]. A heretical Jewish sect from the eighth century which rejects post-biblical rabbinic traditions and accepts only the teachings of the Bible. Their settlements were concentrated in the Crimea, Galicia, Turkey and Lithuania. At present only 4,000 Karaites remain in the world, with 1,500 in Israel.

LITZMANSTADT. The German name for Lodz.

MAIDANEK. Formed in 1940 near Lublin as a camp for prisoners of war. In 1942 it became an annihilation camp. In May of that year the method of murder was changed from mass-shootings to gas chambers. It destroyed a total of 500,000 victims, mostly Jews. The camp was dissolved in July 1944.

MATHAUSEN. A concentration camp formed in 1938. It had 60 divisions and imprisoned many Jews from occupied Europe.

MELINA. Hiding-place on the Aryan side for people and merchandise. Derived from the Hebrew word *"Molin"*—a place to spend the night.

MILA 18. The building in the Warsaw Ghetto which housed the bunker and headquarters of the J.F.O. [Jewish Fighting Organization].

MUSSULMAN. Camp jargon for inmates who were totally exhausted or afflicted with incurable dystrophia and were unable to work. These were the first candidates for selection by the Nazis.

ONEG SHABBAT. [Hebrew]. Celebration of the Sabbath. Pseudonym of the organization secretly established by the historian Dr. Emanuel Ringelblum to assemble the Ghetto Archive in Warsaw. Also called the Ringelblum Archive.

PARTISANS. Underground fighters against Nazi occupation forces, operating mainly in the forests. There was a general partisan movement which included Jews; also Jewish partisan groups in White Russia, Poland and Lithuania.

PASSYAKES. Jargon of Polish camp inmates to describe their striped prisoners' uniforms.

PLASHOW. Concentration camp erected on the grounds of the Jewish cemetery in Cracow. It functioned between March 1943 and July 1944, with 10,000 murdered. The survivors were transferred to Auschwitz, Gross-Rosen, Mathausen and Flassenburg.

PONAR. Annihilation center on the outskirts of Vilna. Began operations in July 1941, with a total of 60,000 victims among the Jews of Vilna and environs.

P.P.R. Initials of *Polska Partija Robotnicza*—Polish Labor Party, formed in January 1942 as the renewed communist organization of Poland after the old one was dissolved by the Comintern in 1938 as a spy organization.

PUNKT. [Yiddish]. Point. A haven in the Warsaw Ghetto for refugees, homeless children, etc. Usually administered by the Jewish Social Self-Help.

S.D. *Sicherheitsdienst*—the Nazi Security Police.

SELECTION. Choosing inhabitants of a ghetto or camp for deportation or death.

SKIF. See BUND.

SOBIBOR. Annihilation camp in Lublin region erected in 1942. Prisoners were Jews from Poland, Soviet Union, Austria, Czechoslovakia, France and Holland; 250,000 were killed. In October 14, 1943 the inmates rebelled and destroyed the camp.

SOLTIS. Administrative head of a Polish village representing the government.

S.S. *Schutzstaffel*. The Nazi Elite Guard, formed in 1925 to "protect" the *Führer*. Later it was responsible for liquidating anti-Nazis and Jews. Its chief function was the supervision of the camps and ghettos.

STROPP, JURGEN S.S. Brigade Commander and Major-General of the German police, who quelled the Warsaw Uprising of April 19, 1943. After the war a Polish court sentenced him to death.

T.O.Z. Jewish Relief Organization in Poland: *Towarzystwo Ochrony Zdrowia* [Protection of Health]. See CENTOS.

TREBLINKA. One of the Nazi death-factories in Poland, where 750,000 persons, mostly Jews from Warsaw and environs, perished in gas chambers. The camp was established in 1940 and destroyed in a prisoners' revolt on August 2, 1943.

UMSCHLAGPLATZ. A collecting point in the ghettos for deportation, usually near a railroad siding.

WARTEGAU, OR WARTELAND. The territory in western Poland, near the Warta River, encompassing Posen, parts of Lodz, Kalisch and Pomern, which was incorporated into the German Reich on October 8, 1939. Most of its 460,000 Jews perished in the Chelmno death camp.

WOYT. See SOLTIS.

ZBONSZYN. Site of refugee camp in Posen, on the German-Polish border, to which German Jews of Polish origin were transferred in October 1938.

Z.O.B. *Zydowska Organizacja Bojowa,* the Polish name for the Jewish Fighting Organization in the Warsaw Ghetto.

ZONDERKOMMANDO. Jewish prisoners in camps assigned to deal with the corpses: extracting gold teeth, transferring from gas-chambers to crematoriums, etc. Or S.S. men and police detailed for liquidation actions. The *Zonderkommando* in Auschwitz revolted and dynamited some of the crematoriums.

ZUKUNFT. See BUND.

Biographies

Ilse *Aichinger* was born in Vienna in 1921, and was forbidden to continue her education during World War II. After the war she wrote *Herod's Children*. The novel was published in Germany in 1948 and has become a classic there. She has written short stories and several distinguished radio plays. She now lives with her husband and children in Bavaria.

Mordecai *Anilewicz* was Commander of the Jewish Fighting Organization in Warsaw and a leader of the Hashomer Hatzair in the underground. He was active in the Jewish National Committee and Jewish Coordinating Committee. During the Warsaw Uprising in April 1943, he was in the JFO bunker at 18 Mila Street. On May 8 when the Nazis surrounded the bunker and escape was impossible, Anilewicz and others committed suicide rather than fall into enemy hands.

Rachel *Auerbach* started her literary career before the war. During the Nazi occupation, she was one of the Jewish National Committee's agents on the Aryan side. She wrote several studies about the Holocaust. She now lives in Israel and works for Yad Vashem. The chapter published here is a fragment from her book *The Jewish Uprising in Warsaw, 1943*, Warsaw, 1948.

Josef *Bor* was a lawyer in pre-war Czechoslovakia. In 1942 he was sent, together with his family, to a concentration camp in Terezin. Of his entire family, he was the only one to survive. He now lives in Prague, where he remarried and has two children.

Samuel *Bornstein* was born in Lodz, Poland. During the occupation, he escaped and joined the partisan group organized by Dr. Atlas. He was liberated by the Red Army and now lives in Israel.

Tuvia *Bozhikowski* was one of the organizers of the Zionist youth organization, Dror, in the Warsaw Ghetto. He was active in the Jewish Fighters Organization in the ghetto and participated in the April revolt. His book *Between Crumbling Walls* has been published in both Yiddish and Hebrew. He died in Israel in 1959.

Wladyslaw *Broniewski* is a Polish poet.

Rachmil *Bryks* was born in Poland. During the occupation he was in various concentration camps. He lives now in New York with his wife and five daughters. He is the author of several volumes of stories depicting Jewish life in the ghetto and camps. His *Cat in the Ghetto* has been translated into several languages.

Jacob *Celemenski* was born in Warsaw in 1904. During the Nazi occupation he was active in the underground as a representative of the Bund. He was sent to Auschwitz in 1944. He came to America in 1950, where in 1963 his book *Mit Mein Farshnitenem Folk* appeared.

Abraham *Eisen* was born near Lublin. He spent the occupation in a labor camp near the Vilna Ghetto, where he wrote *People of the Ghetto,* published in New York in 1949. His second book, *The Spiritual Face of the Ghetto,* was published in Mexico in 1950. Eisen died in Canada.

Benjamin *Ellis* was in a camp during the occupation. He is now in the United States and is a free-lance writer. His several volumes of stories relate to the central theme of Jewish life during the Holocaust.

Abraham *Foxman* was born in Poland in 1940. During the occupation, he was on the Aryan side in Vilna. He was brought to America in 1950. He has written in English and Hebrew about the Holocaust. He now lives in New York where he is director of the Department of the Middle East of the Anti-Defamation League (B'nai Brith).

Anne *Frank* was a child of German Jewish parents who fled in 1933 to Holland. When Holland was occupied, she, her parents and some of their friends were hidden by Christian friends. They were discovered by the Germans and sent to a concentration camp. All of them perished except Anne's father. The diary which Anne kept in her hiding place was found after the war and was hailed as a great human document and translated into many languages.

Philip *Friedman* was born in Lemberg, Eastern Galicia, in 1901. He was an educator and historian, and during the war was active in the underground in Poland. In 1944 he organized the Central Jewish Historical Commission in Poland. He was cultural director of JOINT in the American zones in Europe. In 1948 he came to the United States where he lectured on Jewish history at Columbia, was dean of the Jewish Teachers Seminary, and was director of the Bibliographical Department of YIVO and Yad Vashem (for the documentation of the Holocaust). He died in 1966.

Esther *Garfinkel* was an inmate of Maidanek, where her two children were killed.

Mordecai *Gebirtig* was born in 1877 in Cracow. He worked all his life as a carpenter in Cracow, and became one of the most popular folk balladists in Poland. He was put into the Cracow Ghetto under the Hitler occupation and was killed there in 1942. His poem "Our Town Is Burning," written in 1938, became one of the most popular songs in the ghettos and concentration camps and among the survivors in the D. P. camps.

Shaye *Gertner* was fourteen when he was deported from Lodz. He was sent to a number of concentration camps: Poznan, Dachau, Birkenau-Auschwitz. He participated in the Zonderkommand revolt in Auschwitz.

Hirsh *Glick* was born in 1920 in Vilna. When the ghetto was liquidated, he was sent to a concentration camp in Esthonia. He escaped from the camp and joined the partisans, and died while fighting as a partisan. His partisan song, "Zog Nit Kainmol," became the hymn of the underground organization.

Zvi *Goldfarb* was a member of the Zionist youth organization, Dror, in Poland, and arrived in Hungary during the war years. Together with other representatives of Zionist youth movements, he figured prominently among the leading participants in Jewish rescue and resistance work in Hungary.

Bernard *Goldstein* is author of *Five Years in the Warsaw Ghetto* (originally published as *The Stars Bear Witness*), New York, 1961. One of the great organizers and leaders in the history of the General Jewish Socialist Labor Organization—the Bund—Goldstein was widely admired and respected by Jewish workers for his various abilities, principled conduct and immense courage. When Hitler began marching eastward, Goldstein took an active part in defending the Jewish populace against attacks by Polish anti-Semitic hooligans. After the Nazis occupied Warsaw, he joined the Jewish underground. He was fated to survive the destruction of the ghetto. His book records events which transpired in the ghetto of Warsaw from October 1939 to June 1945.

Julian *Gross* was a witness to the atrocities committed in the Cracow Ghetto.

Salomea *Hannell* was deported to Sobibor. He escaped to Cracow where his "Aryan appearance" enabled him to survive the Holocaust.

Captain *Jaquel's* episode appears in various anthologies but nowhere is there any information regarding the author.

Eliezer *Jeruschalmi* was born in 1915 in White Russia. At the outbreak of the war he was a member of the Central Committee of the Poale Zion in Lithuania. He escaped from the ghetto and fought with the partisans, then with the Red Army. After the war he lived in Israel and wrote about the Nazi atrocities in Lithuania. He died in Israel.

Shmerke *Kaczerginski* was a poet who belonged to the pre-war literary Young Vilna group. He was a member of United Partisan Organization in Vilna. He perished in an airplane disaster in Argentina in April 1954. This chapter is from his book *Partisans Are Coming*, Munich, 1948.

Feiga *Kammer* was born in 1906 in the town of Lubaczon. During the occupation, she managed to hide, with her three children, on the Aryan side.

Israel *Kaplan* was in the Kovne Ghetto during the occupation. After the war, he compiled and edited documents relating to the extermination of Jews. He now lives in Israel.

Stanislaw *Kohn* was an inmate in Treblinka where he helped to organize an uprising against the guards of the camp. He managed to escape.

Abba *Kovner,* a leader of the Hashomer Hatzair, was one of the founders of the United Partisan Organization, and its last commandant. He now lives in Israel.

Regina *Landau* was rescued from Lancut concentration camp.

Primo *Levi,* an Italian Jew, was deported with a group of Italian Jews from an Italian camp to Auschwitz. In his book *If This Is Man* he relates his experiences.

Donald A. *Lowrie* was born in Wooster, Ohio. He has spent over forty years in Europe. During the First and Second World Wars he was in France, and he worked to allay the suffering of refugees, internees and prisoners of war. He now lives in New York City.

Arnold *Lustig* was born in Prague in 1926. He was sent, together with his parents, to Auschwitz, where his father died in the gas chambers. He was then transferred to Buchenwald. After the war he returned to Prague. He has since written several volumes of short stories and novellas. He is now married (his wife was also at Terezin) and is the father of two sons.

Maurice *Meier* was born in Germany. After the Nazis usurped power, the Meier family led to Switzerland and then to France. Maurice Meier was sent to a detention camp and later to "Free France." He escaped to Switzerland. After the war, he learned that his entire family had been exterminated, and he left for America.

Marga *Minco* was a child at school in Holland in 1940. She was the only member of her family to escape arrest.

Alexander P. *Mintz* was a member of the Bund in Poland. During the Occupation he worked for the French Underground and edited the Bund's illegal newspaper, *Unzer Stimme* (Paris-Lyon-Grenoble 1942–1944). He died in Buenos Aires in 1962. The chapter published here is from his book *In the Years of Jewish Destruction and Resistance in France,* Buenos Aires, 1956.

Sofia *Nalkowska* is a Polish writer. She is the author of a book entitled *Medallions* (Warsaw, 1953), and of other works.

Hanna Mortkowicz-*Olczakowa's* description of Yanosz Korczak's "last walk" is included in many books.

Perez *Opoczinski* was born near Lodz and began writing at an early age. During World War II he was postman in the Warsaw Ghetto, and active in the Oneg Shabbat (Sabbath joy), the pseudonym of the organization founded by Emmanuel Ringelblum to assemble secretly the ghetto archive. He died of typhus in the ghetto. His writings about the ghetto were found in the archive under the ruins of Warsaw. This is a chapter from his book *Reportage from the Warsaw Ghetto,* published in Warsaw in 1945.

Sala *Pawlowicz* was a slave laborer in an ammunition factory in Poland, and then was an inmate in Bergen-Belsen and other concentration camps. She was liberated in May 1945. She is now in America, is married and has a daughter. She became an American citizen in 1955.

Rivka Kwiatkowski-*Pinkhasik* started to write in the Lodz Ghetto. She was a member of the Socialist Zionist movement. After the liquidation of Lodz, she was sent to a labor camp in Germany. Her first book about the Nazi era, *From Camp to Camp,* appeared in 1960 in Buenos Aires. She now lives in Israel. This chapter is from her book *Hands,* published in Haifa, 1957.

Emmanuel *Ringelblum,* social historian, teacher, scholar and archivist of the Warsaw Ghetto, was the founder of the Oneg Shabbat, the secret archive of the ghetto. Ringelblum and his fellow archivists collected some 100 volumes of memoirs, German official documents and various reports on the resistance movement in Poland. He also wrote accounts of the underground movement, which were smuggled out of the ghetto and dispatched to Jewish communities around the world, so that they might be alerted to the tragedy of Polish Jewry. His journals cover day-to-day events in the ghetto from January 1940 to early 1943. Although he had a rare opportunity to be rescued by the Polish underground, Ringelblum refused to leave Warsaw because of his commitment as the chief archivist in the ghetto. He believed that by continuing to serve in this role he was fulfilling his obligations to his people; and he hoped that his journals and the records of the Oneg Shabbat would be preserved as a legacy for posterity. The Nazis murdered him and his family in 1944. He was then 44 years old. After the war, Ringelblum's notes were found in rubber-sealed milk cans under the ruins of the Warsaw Ghetto.

Reuben *Rosenberg* was eleven at the outbreak of the War. After the liquidation of the Jews in his town, Lublin, where his family lived, he was sent as a slave laborer to a number of camps: Buchenwald, Flossberg, and others. He was liberated by the American Army.

David *Rubinovich* lived in the village of Krajnie, Poland. During the occupation he was deported, along with all the Jews of the vicinity, to an unknown place. He kept a diary from 1940 to June 1941. It was found in 1957 and published in 1960.

Leon *Salpeter* was in the Cracow Ghetto at the time 10,000 Jews were deported.

Carola *Sapetowa*—a Polish peasant woman. During the occupation she hid two Jewish children. She had worked in their parents' home in Cracow as a servant prior to the war.

Levi *Shalit* was a writer before the war. He was a prisoner in the Sianliai Ghetto in Lithuania and now lives in South Africa. The selection published here is from his book *So We Died,* Munich, 1949.

Isaiah *Spiegel* was a member of the young literary group in Lodz. He was sent from the Lodz Ghetto to the concentration camps and after the war returned to Poland. He now lives in Israel. The selection published here is from his book *The Kingdom of the Ghetto,* Lodz, 1947.

Jacob *Stendig* was an inmate in the Plaszow concentration camp.

S. B. *Unsdorfer* was born in Bratislava. He was fourteen years old when Czechoslovakia was occupied. He was sent to several concentration camps and after the liberation wrote *The Yellow Star.*

Leon Welickzer *Wells* was born in Poland in 1925. During the occupation he was in the Lemberg Ghetto, later in the camp on Janowska Road, from which he escaped. He is an engineer and inventor. He has lived in the United States since 1949, is now married and the father of two children. *The Janowska Road* was written in English, and was first published in France where it received excellent reviews.

Eliezer *Wiesel* was born in 1928 in Hungary. He studied in Paris. He returned to his birthplace during the Nazi occupation and was sent to a concentration camp. He was liberated in April 1945. He writes in Yiddish, English, French and Hebrew. He is the author of a number of novels which have established for him an international reputation.

Yankel *Wiernik* was born in 1889 in Poland. He was active in the Bund. He was sent to Treblinka by the Nazis where, in 1943, he organized the resistance against the Ukrainian guards in the camp. He managed to escape, and described the events in his book *A Year in Treblinka.* He is now in Israel.

Wladka—(Feygl Peltl-Miedzyrzecki) was born in Poland, and was seventeen years old when the Nazis occupied Warsaw. She was a member of the illegal Bundist youth organization and was assigned the dangerous task of serving as a courier on the Aryan side as an agent of the underground Bund. She came to America in 1946, is married and the mother of several children. She is now associated with the Jewish Labor Committee.

Samuel *Zygelbojm* was a leader of the Bund in Poland. As a member of the Warsaw *Judenrat,* he opposed the Nazi order for the formation of the ghetto. In 1940 he escaped from Warsaw, reached the United States and then went to London as the Bund representative in the Polish Government-in-Exile. He maintained contact with the Polish Jewish underground. He committed suicide on May 11, 1943 in London as a protest against the world's indifference to the slaughter of the Jews in Poland.

Acknowledgments

"The Death Train" by Elie Wiesel. Translated by Moshe Spiegel. From *The World Was Silent*. Central Farband Fun Poylishe Yidn in Argentina. Buenos Aires, 1956.
"Sabbath" by Marga Minco. Translated from Dutch by Roy Edwards in *Bitter Herbs*. Oxford University Press. London, 1960.
"Tiengen" by Maurice Meier. Translated from German by John W. Kurtz. From *Refuge*. W. W. Norton Co. New York, 1962.
"The Fraternal Grave of Four Jewish Settlements" by Abraham Eisen. Translated from Yiddish by Moshe Spiegel. *Foroys*. Vilna, 1947.
"City of Cracow" by Julian Gross. Translated from Yiddish by Moshe Spiegel. From *Documents of Crime and Martyrdom*. Jewish Historical Commission of Cracow. Cracow, 1945.
"City of Cracow" by Leon Salpeter. Ibid.
"Our Town Is Burning" by Mordecai Gebirtig. Translated from Yiddish by Joseph Leftwich. From *Golden Peacock*. Yoseloff, 1961.
"Notes from the Warsaw Ghetto" by Emmanuel Ringelbaum. Translated from the Yiddish and edited by Jacob Sloan. McGraw-Hill Book Co. New York, 1958.
"The Jewish Letter Carrier" by Perez Opoczinski. Translated from Yiddish by E. Chase. From *Reports from the Warsaw Ghetto*. Yiddish Bukh. Warsaw, 1945.
"Smugglers" by Levi Shalit. Translated from Yiddish by Adah Fogel. *From This Is How We Died*. Munich, 1949.
"The Ghetto Kingdom" by Isaiah Spiegel. Translated from Yiddish by Moshe Spiegel. From *The Ghetto Kingdom*. Dos Neie Lebn. Lodz, 1947.
"With My Martyred People" by Jacob Celemenski. Translated from Yiddish by Mirra Ginsberg. From *New Politics,* Vol. III, No. 14.
"Vilna—Story of a Ghetto" by Abraham Foxman. *Journal of Social Studies,* Vol. XX, No. 1, City College of New York, Fall-Winter 1962.
"A Cupboard in the Ghetto" by Rachmiel Bryks. Translated from Yiddish by S. Morris Engel. From *A Cat in the Ghetto*. Bloch Publishing Co. New York, 1959.

"Hell in the Streets" by Bernard Goldstein. Translated from Yiddish by Miriam Hoffman. *Five Years in the Warsaw Ghetto.* Undser Tsait. New York, 1947.

"Meierl" by Eliezer Jeruschalmi. Translated by Adah Fogel. *Das Judische Martyrerkind.* Oelsmenische Marienschwesternschaft, (Darmstadt-Eberstadt, 1961).

"Bodies of Children for the Animals in the Circus" by Regina Landau. Translated from Yiddish by Moshe Spiegel. From *Documents of Crime and Martyrdom.* Jewish Historical Commission of Cracow. Cracow, 1945.

"Fear of Fear" by Ilse Aichinger. Translated from German by Cornelia Schaeffer. From *In Herod's Children.* Atheneum Press. New York, 1963.

"Yanosz Korczak's Last Walk" by Hanna Mortkowicz-Olczakowa. From *The Massacre of European Jewry.* World Hashomer Hatzair, Kibbutz Merchavia. Israel, 1963.

Prose and Poetry by Three Children from Terezin. From *Children's Drawings and Poems* (Terezin 1942–44). Statni Zidovske Museum. Prague, 1959.

"Zonderkommando in Birkenau" by Shaye Gertner. Translated from Yiddish by Moshe Spiegel. From *Children's Martyrdom.* Central Farband Fun Poylische Yidn in Argentina. Buenos Aires, 1947.

"From One Camp to Another" by Reuben Rosenberg. Translated from Yiddish by Moshe Spiegel. Ibid.

"Winter in the Forest" by Feiga Kammer. Translated from Yiddish by Moshe Spiegel. Ibid.

From *The Diary of David Rubinovich.* Translated from Yiddish by Adah Fogel. Published in Warsaw.

"Letters from the Ghetto" by Nusja and Inja Shifman. Translated from Yiddish by Max Rosenfeld. From *My Whole Life Is Still Before Me.* Yad Vashem. Jerusalem, 1962.

"The Diary of a Young Girl" by Anne Frank. Translated from the Dutch by B. M. Mooyaart. From *The Diary of a Young Girl.* Doubleday and Co. New York, 1952.

"A Year in Treblinka Horror Camp" by Yankel Wiernik. Translated from Yiddish by Moshe Spiegel. From *A Year in Treblinka.* Undser Tsait. New York, 1944.

"The Story of Ten Days" by Primo Levi. Translated from Italian by Stuart Woolf. From *Survival in Auschwitz.* Collier Book, New York, 1961. Originally published as *If This Is Man.* Orion Press, New York. Copyright by Giulio Einyadi, editor (Italy).

"The Wache" by Sala Pawlowicz with Kevin Klose. From *I Will Survive.* W. W. Norton Co. New York, 1962.

"Stephen and Anne" by Arnost Lustig. Translated from Czech by George Theiner. From *Night and Hope.* E. P. Dutton and Co. New York, 1962.

"The Death Brigade" by Leon Wells. From *The Janowska Road.* MacMillan. New York, 1963.

From *The Terezin Requiem* by Josef Bor. Translated from Czech by Edith Pargeter. Alfred A. Knopf. New York, 1963.

"Execution in Plashow" by Jakob Stendig. Translated from Yiddish by Moshe Spiegel. From *Documents of Crime and Martyrdom*. Jewish Historical Commission of Cracow. Cracow, 1945.
"Scoundrels' Entertainments" by Adolph Wolfgang. Ibid.
"Maidanek" by Esther Garfinkel. Translated from Yiddish by Moshe Spiegel. Ibid.
"The Yellow Star" by S. B. Unsdorfer. Translated from Yiddish by Joseph Leftwich. From *The Golden Peacock*. Thomas Yoseloff. New York, 1961.
"In the Sick Hut" by Israel Kaplan. Translated from Yiddish by Miriam Hoffman. From *Paths and By-Paths*. I. L. Peretz Publishing House. Tel Aviv, 1964.
"Jewish Resistance to Nazism" by Philip Friedman. From *European Resistance Movements, 1939–45*. Oxford Pergamon Press. London, 1960.
"The Girl in Soldiers' Boots" by Shmerke Kaczerginski. Translated from Yiddish by Moshe Spiegel. From *Partisans Are Coming*. Munich, 1948.
"Dr. Yehezkel Atlas, Partisan Commander" by Samuel Bornstein. From *Extermination and Resistance*. Kibbutz Lohamei Haghetaoth. Haifa, 1958.
From *The Jewish Uprising in Warsaw* by Rachel Auerbach. Translated from Yiddish by Moshe Spiegel. Warsaw, 1943.
"In Fire and Blood" by Tovia Bozhikowski. Translated from Yiddish by Moshe Spiegel. From *Warsaw Ghetto Uprising*. Poale Zion. Munich, 1948.
"Hehalutz Resistance in Hungary" by Zvi Goldfarb. From *Extermination and Resistance*. Ghetto Fighters, Kibbutz Lohamei Haghetaoth. Haifa, 1958.
"The Treblinka Revolt" by Stanislaw Kohn. From *Story of the Battle of the Ghettos*. Edited by I. Cukievman and M. Bassok. Hakibbutz Hameuchad, Israel, 1954.
"Revolt" by Salomea Hannell. Translated from Yiddish by Moshe Spiegel. From *Documents of Crime and Martyrdom*. Jewish Historical Commission of Cracow. Cracow, 1945.
Appeal of the Jewish Fighting Organization. From newspapers.
"The Conscience of the World" by Samuel Zygelbojm. From newspapers, journals, etc.
A Manifesto of Jewish Resistance in Vilna. From newspapers, etc.
"The Last Wish of My Life Has Been Fulfilled" by Mordecai Anilewicz. From *Massacre of European Jewry*. World Hashomer Hatzair, English-Speaking Department, Kibbutz Merchavia. Israel, 1963.
"Jewish Cultural Activity in the Ghettos of Poland" by Emmanuel Ringelblum. Translated from Yiddish by Moshe Spiegel. From *Emmanuel Ringelblum* by Jacob Kenner. Jewish Labor Committee. New York, 1945.
"I Believe." From newspapers, etc.
"On the Agenda: Death." Record of a meeting held in February 1943 by the Executive Committee of the Hechalutz, organization of pioneers for Palestine, Bialystok Branch.

"Jewish Partisan Song" by Hirsh Glick. Translated from Yiddish by Aaron Kramer in *Folks-Shtimme*. Poland.

"Captain Jaquel's Story." From *Massacre of European Jewry*. World Hashomer Hatzair, English-Speaking Department. Kibbutz Merchavia. Israel, 1963.

"At the Railroad Tracks" by Sofia Nalkowska. Translated from Yiddish by Moshe Spiegel. Undser Tsait. New York.

"Polish Friends" by "Wladka" (Feygl Peltl-Miedzyrzecki). Translated from Yiddish by Moshe Spiegel. From *On Both Sides of the Ghetto Wall*. Educational Department, Workmen's Circle. New York, 1948.

"A Polish Woman Relates Her Story" by Carola Sapetowa. Translated from Yiddish by Moshe Spiegel. From *Children's Martyrdom*. Collected and edited by Noah Griss. Central Farband Fun Poylische Yidn in Argentina. Buenos Aires, 1947.

"To the Polish Jews" by Wladyslaw Broniewski. Translated from Polish by Ilona Ralf Sues. From *Folks-Shtimme*. Poland. April, 1963.

"Chambon-Sur-Lignon" by Donald Lowrie. From *The Hunted Children*. W. W. Norton Co. New York, 1963.

"Gallows in the Balut Market" by Rivka Kwiatkowski-Pinkhasik. Translated from Yiddish by Moshe Spiegel. From *Hands*. Haifa, 1957.

"Fugitives" by Benjamin Ellis. Translated from Yiddish by Moshe Spiegel. From *This Kind of World*. Stuttgart, 1948.

Jacob Glatstein, author of ten books of poetry, three novels, and five volumes of essays, is a columnist on *The Day-Jewish Journal* and is in charge of the Yiddish office in the Department of Public Relations of the American Jewish Congress and World Jewish Congress.

Samuel Margoshes, recently deceased, was editor of *The Jewish Day* for more than a quarter of a century. He wrote the "News and Views" column for *The Jewish Day*.

Israel Knox is the author of *The Aesthetic Theories of Kant, Hegel and Schopenhauer* and *Rabbi in America: The Story of Isaac Mayer Wise*. He is now Associate Professor of Philosophy at New York University.